AI for Organizational Excellence and Inclusive Growth

Rafael Ignacio Pérez-Uribe
https://orcid.org/0000-0001-9924-6657
Invesproject, Colombia

David Ocampo-Guzmán
https://orcid.org/0000-0002-6497-5646
Universidad EAN, Colombia

Maria Teresa Ramírez-Garzón
https://orcid.org/0000-0002-6319-3386
Invesproject, Colombia

Luz Janeth Lozano-Correa
Santo Tomas University, Colombia

IGI Global
Scientific Publishing
Publishing Tomorrow's Research Today

Vice President of Editorial	Melissa Wagner
Director of Acquisitions	Mikaela Felty
Director of Book Development	Jocelynn Hessler
Production Manager	Mike Brehm
Cover Design	Jose Rosado

Published in the United States of America by
IGI Global Scientific Publishing
701 East Chocolate Avenue
Hershey, PA, 17033, USA
Tel: 717-533-8845 | Fax: 717-533-7115
Website: https://www.igi-global.com E-mail: cust@igi-global.com

Library of Congress Cataloging-in-Publication Data

(CIP Data Pending)
ISBN13: 9798260004395
Isbn13Softcover: 9798260004401
EISBN13: 9798260004418
British Cataloguing in Publication Data
A Cataloguing in Publication record for this book is available from the British Library.

Table of Contents

Preface xii

Chapter 1
Digital Transformation of Internal Control Systems: The Role of Artificial Intelligence 1
Marta F. Ceia, University of Aveiro, Portugal
Rui P. Marques, University of Aveiro, Portugal
Helena Inácio, University of Aveiro, Portugal

Chapter 2
Management Model for Artifitial Intelligence (MMAI): The Concept 33
Rafael Ignacio Pérez-Uribe, Investproject, Colombia
Maria Teresa Ramírez-Garzón, Investproject, Colombia

Chapter 3
Efficiency and Sustainability in Co-Ownership: Utilizing Both the Balanced Scorecard and Artificial Intelligence 69
Edward Yecid Torres Nova, Universidad Nacional Abierta y a Distancia, Colombia
Andrea del Pilar Barrera Ortegón, Universidad Nacional Abierta y a Distancia, Colombia
William Camilo Martinez Sanabria, Universidad Nacional Abierta y a Distancia, Colombia
Neixon Fabian Rincón Ronderos, Universidad Nacional de Colombia, Colombia

Chapter 4
The Role of AI in Product Innovation: A Literature Review and Bibliometric Study 99
Ümmühan Nida Erol, Mersin University, Turkey
Seçil Özen, Mersin University, Turkey
Kalender Özcan Atilgan, Mersin University, Turkey

Chapter 5
AI in Supply Chain Optimization 133
Hamza Aboudiar, University "Abdelmalek Essaadi", Morocco
Ouail El Imrani, University "Abdelmalek Essaadi", Morocco

Chapter 6
Elevating Small Business Performance With Emerging Technologies and Artificial Intelligence in Africa 169
Timilehin Olasoji Olubiyi, Babcock University, Ilishan-Remo, Nigeria
Felicia Sokojinwon Abaniwo, Babcock University, Ilishan-Remo, Nigeria
Senyo Agbeblewu, Edith Cowan University, Austraiia
Kayode Samuel Adeyemi, Oduduwa University. Ipetumodu, Nigeria

Chapter 7
Effect of Artificial Intelligence Awareness on Job Performance: Mediating and Moderating Role of Gender.. 193
Oumeima Toumia, Higher Institute of Technological Studies of Kef, Tunisia & Research Laboratory LARIME, University of Tunis, Tunis, Tunisia
Farouk Zouari, University of Tunis El Manar, Tunisia
Rym Mefteh, IHEC Sousse, University of Sousse, Tunisia

Chapter 8
AI-Powered Destination Marketing: Personalization, Consumer Engagement, and Competitive Positioning.. 227
Parihar Suresh Dahake, Ramdeobaba University, Nagpur, India
Pragati Parihar Dahake, VMV Commerce, JMT Arts, and JJP Science College, Nagpur, India
Himanshu M. Shukla, Symbiosis Institute of Business Management, Symbiosis International University, Pune, India

Chapter 9
Competitor Orientation Effect on Augmenting Ethiopian SME Internal Technological Processes Through Customer Insight 265
Gada Gizachew Wakjira, Bule Hora University, Ethiopia
Shashi Kant, Lovely Professional University, India

Chapter 10
Digital Divide in Latin American Higher Education: Challenges and Obstacles in the Face of Artificial Intelligence.. 293
Yolanda Álvarez-Sánchez, University of La Salle, Colombia
Diana Carol Castro-Mazanett, University of La Salle, Colombia

Chapter 11
Ethical Standards in the Use of AI for Computer Science Students 317
Hanh Le, University of the Cumberlands, USA

Compilation of References 349

About the Contributors 415

Index 421

Detailed Table of Contents

Preface xii

Chapter 1
Digital Transformation of Internal Control Systems: The Role of Artificial Intelligence 1
Marta F. Ceia, University of Aveiro, Portugal
Rui P. Marques, University of Aveiro, Portugal
Helena Inácio, University of Aveiro, Portugal

This study investigates the integration of Artificial Intelligence (AI) into Internal Control Systems (ICS). The objective is to understand the role of AI within ICS: (1) identifying AI technologies that benefit ICS, (2) determining ICS procedures that AI can assist, (3) characterizing an AI-assisted ICS, and (4) assessing the challenges in implementing AI within ICS. The results reveal that machine learning for process automation and chatbots are the most well-known and used AI functionalities. Internal Control (IC) procedures are inherently linked, so all benefit from AI implementation. With or without AI, the fundamental characteristics of an ICS remain intact. Key challenges in AI implementation include cost, the need for training, resistance to change, ethical and legal considerations, and data and model suitability. The ICS benefits from AI implementation, directly contributing to improved governance and proactive risk prevention mechanisms, as well as providing time savings.

Chapter 2
Management Model for Artifitial Intelligence (MMAI): The Concept 33
Rafael Ignacio Pérez-Uribe, Investproject, Colombia
Maria Teresa Ramírez-Garzón, Investproject, Colombia

This chapter provides a Management Model for Artifitial Intelligence (MMAI) that, through its application and analysis, enables corporate decision-makers, academics, consultants, and others interested in the topic to seek the best alternatives for AI management, helping them streamline their organizations and achieve the highest standards of profitability, competitiveness, and sustainability. The MMAI is composed of nine key factors: 1) Clear objectives, 2) Ethics and regulation, 3) Data governance, 4) Transparency and explainability, 5) Performance and scalability, 6) Continuous training, 7) Risk management, 8) Integration and compatibility, and 9) Stakeholder engagement. Each factor, in turn, contains a series of variables that explain it. In total, there are twenty-seven (27) variables explained in detail in the theoretical framework of this chapter, which measure four levels ranging from 0 to 100%.

Chapter 3
Efficiency and Sustainability in Co-Ownership: Utilizing Both the Balanced Scorecard and Artificial Intelligence 69
Edward Yecid Torres Nova, Universidad Nacional Abierta y a Distancia, Colombia
Andrea del Pilar Barrera Ortegón, Universidad Nacional Abierta y a Distancia, Colombia
William Camilo Martinez Sanabria, Universidad Nacional Abierta y a Distancia, Colombia
Neixon Fabian Rincón Ronderos, Universidad Nacional de Colombia, Colombia

This study analyzes management performance in residential condominiums in Usaquén, Bogotá, comparing those using a Balanced Scorecard supported by artificial intelligence-A with those without AI. Using qualitative methods and data from 50 property managers through semi-structured interviews, results show that AI-enhanced BSCs improve financial liquidity, reduce delinquency, decrease social and operational incidents, and yield better management evaluations. AI enables real-time monitoring, enhances decision-making, and promotes sustainability by automating processes and anticipating potential issues. Findings suggest integrating AI into the BSC strengthens strategic alignment, transparency, and operational efficiency. Successful implementation requires digital literacy, ethical data use, and active resident engagement. The study recommends gradual digital transformation focusing on finance and maintenance. The AI-enabled BSC is a strategic tool for fostering sustainable, resilient, and efficient residential communities, highlighting opportunities for technology adoption in the sector.

Chapter 4
The Role of AI in Product Innovation: A Literature Review and Bibliometric Study 99
Ümmühan Nida Erol, Mersin University, Turkey
Seçil Özen, Mersin University, Turkey
Kalender Özcan Atilgan, Mersin University, Turkey

Artificial intelligence (AI) is positioned not only as a technological innovation but also as a key driving force of organizational transformation in today's digital economy. In this context, the aim of this study is to investigate the impact of AI on Product Innovation processes through a systematic literature review supported by bibliometric analysis. The study investigates existing academic publications to identify leading contributors, major research themes, and collaboration patterns within this interdisciplinary field. A total of 85 articles were analyzed using bibliometric techniques. Influential authors, institutions, and methodological trends were mapped using data derived from prominent academic databases. The analysis reveals the evolution of AI-related Product Innovation research, current gaps in the literature, and future research directions. This chapter provides both theoretical contributions and strategic insights for practitioners, offering a conceptual foundation for future studies at the intersection of AI and Product Innovation.

Chapter 5
AI in Supply Chain Optimization 133
Hamza Aboudiar, University "Abdelmalek Essaadi", Morocco
Ouail El Imrani, University "Abdelmalek Essaadi", Morocco

The integration of artificial intelligence (AI) in supply chain chains has led to a significant transformation, moving from a focus on individual businesses to a holistic view of supply chain operations. AI plays a crucial role in optimisation of the supply chain, improving competitiveness and operational efficiency. It offers instant transparency and improved product flow management through technologies like blockchain and IoT, enabling better operational performance and predictive optimization. However, integrating AI presents a technological and organizational challenge, requiring meticulous management of processes, data, and interdependent actors. AI-based supply chain optimization relies on advanced technologies to improve performance and respond quickly to market fluctuations. Despite challenges related to data quality, cybersecurity, and operational training, the benefits of AI, such as improved decision-making and operational efficiency, are indispensable. Businesses must invest in training and risk management strategies to maximize the benefits of this technology.

Chapter 6
Elevating Small Business Performance With Emerging Technologies and Artificial Intelligence in Africa 169
Timilehin Olasoji Olubiyi, Babcock University, Ilishan-Remo, Nigeria
Felicia Sokojinwon Abaniwo, Babcock University, Ilishan-Remo, Nigeria
Senyo Agbeblewu, Edith Cowan University, Austraiia
Kayode Samuel Adeyemi, Oduduwa University. Ipetumodu, Nigeria

A sustainable economy, particularly in the context of the fourth industrial revolution (4IR), necessitates a robust and globally competitive manufacturing sector. However, our understanding of how this emerging and rapidly changing technology impacts corporate performance, especially regarding turnover in small enterprises, may be lacking. This chapter examines the impact of developing technologies on the performance of small manufacturing enterprises, with a particular emphasis on Nigeria, the largest consumer market in Africa. Research indicated that developing technologies significantly influenced the business performance of SMEs in Nigeria. The research concludes that new technologies can improve the business performance of small manufacturing enterprises. Small businesses are advised to leverage AI to create disruptive innovation through innovative business models and processes, potentially transforming the manufacturing industry and global competitive landscape.

Chapter 7
Effect of Artificial Intelligence Awareness on Job Performance: Mediating and Moderating Role of Gender 193
Oumeima Toumia, Higher Institute of Technological Studies of Kef, Tunisia & Research Laboratory LARIME, University of Tunis, Tunis, Tunisia
Farouk Zouari, University of Tunis El Manar, Tunisia
Rym Mefteh, IHEC Sousse, University of Sousse, Tunisia

As artificial intelligence spreads, it is critical to comprehend how job performance may be impacted by this technology. However, to our knowledge, there is no research dealing with both the mediating and moderating role of gender in the association between artificial intelligence awareness and job performance. Therefore, we try to fill this gap. We distributed 204 online questionnaires to Tunisian employees in the service sector. We performed explanatory factor analysis, confirmatory factor analysis, structural equation modeling, and bootstrapping. Our results found that artificial intelligence has a negative impact on job performance. However, gender has neither a mediating nor moderating effect on the relationship between artificial intelligence awareness and job performance. This implies that artificial intelligence awareness may influence job performance in similar ways for both men and women.

Chapter 8
AI-Powered Destination Marketing: Personalization, Consumer Engagement, and Competitive Positioning 227
Parihar Suresh Dahake, Ramdeobaba University, Nagpur, India
Pragati Parihar Dahake, VMV Commerce, JMT Arts, and JJP Science College, Nagpur, India
Himanshu M. Shukla, Symbiosis Institute of Business Management, Symbiosis International University, Pune, India

The central aim of this research study is to highlight the opportunities and challenges surrounding the use of AI technology in the marketing and promotion of tourism destinations. Its promotion comprises a deliberate and well-conceived strategy for optimizing the benefits derived from tourism expenditure, aiming to generate economic returns while also fostering other social, cultural, or environmental values for the destination. This study focuses on AI-powered destination marketing with a special emphasis on personalization to enhance consumer engagement. Investigating the consumer viewpoint is a crucial aspect of this work, as it is essential to ensure that the design and implementation of AI-powered marketing strategies remain consumer-centric (Geisler,2018). With the advancement of technology, consumers can be individually addressed through marketing actions and tools based on in-depth knowledge about their preferences and behavior.

Chapter 9
Competitor Orientation Effect on Augmenting Ethiopian SME Internal Technological Processes Through Customer Insight 265
Gada Gizachew Wakjira, Bule Hora University, Ethiopia
Shashi Kant, Lovely Professional University, India

The purpose of this paper is to investigate how innovation future prospects pertaining to internal Artificial Intelligence sub structured technical capabilities in SMEs located in Ethiopia are influenced by orientation of competitor and insight of a customer. The outcomes manifest a modest positive association among innovation future prospects pertaining to internal Artificial Intelligence sub structured technical capabilities and orientation of competitor, with insight of a customer acting as a partial mediating factor. This manifests that corporates that actively monitor competitors and engage with customers are better positioned to innovate and augment their Artificial Intelligence sub structured technical capabilities. The implications of these outcomes manifest the necessity for SMEs to assimilate together competitor and customer analyses into their strategic frameworks. By fostering a proactive approach to get know market dynamics and customer wants, corporates can enhance their Artificial Intelligence sub structured technical capabilities innovation future prospects.

Chapter 10
Digital Divide in Latin American Higher Education: Challenges and Obstacles in the Face of Artificial Intelligence... 293
Yolanda Álvarez-Sánchez, University of La Salle, Colombia
Diana Carol Castro-Mazanett, University of La Salle, Colombia

In recent years, technological and digital advancements have profoundly transformed various fields of computer science, as well as human endeavors and diverse industries. Disruptive technologies have generated a significant impact on the social and productive spheres globally. Among these, cloud computing, cybe.rsecurity, and 5G technology stand out, with the growth of the Artificial Intelligence (AI) market being particularly relevant and the subject of this chapter. AI's pervasive influence on education has exacerbated the digital divide, which itself reflects existing societal inequalities—a persistent problem not only in education but also across various other societal domains. The interplay of several factors, including access to technology, existing infrastructure, educational training, and the level of technological literacy, alongside inequalities associated with geographical location and current socioeconomic conditions, plays a crucial role in this contex.

Chapter 11
Ethical Standards in the Use of AI for Computer Science Students 317
Hanh Le, University of the Cumberlands, USA

The rapid integration of artificial intelligence (AI) into education and professional practice has brought about transformative opportunities and pressing ethical challenges. This chapter examines the principles, guidelines, and responsibilities that students must understand and maintain when engaging with AI technologies. This book explores key topics such as academic integrity, data privacy, algorithmic bias, intellectual property, and the responsible use of generative AI tools like ChatGPT and GitHub Copilot. Through real-world case studies, theoretical frameworks, and practical scenarios, the chapter fosters critical thinking and ethical reasoning among computer science students. It also provides educators with strategies for promoting ethical awareness and decision-making in AI-assisted learning environments. By grounding technical education in strong ethical foundations, this book aims to prepare future programmers and engineers to contribute to a trustworthy and socially responsible AI landscape.

Compilation of References 349

About the Contributors 415

Index 421

Preface

INTRODUCTION

Small and medium-sized enterprises (SMEs and MSMEs) stand at a defining crossroads. The accelerating development of Artificial Intelligence (AI) is not merely introducing new tools; it is reshaping the very logic of competitiveness, productivity, innovation, and organizational learning. As editors of this volume, we conceived this reference book as a rigorous yet practical guide for understanding how AI can be strategically integrated into the management and transformation of SMEs.

The emergence of accessible AI technologies—accelerated in recent years by breakthroughs from organizations such as OpenAI—has fundamentally altered the technological landscape. What was once reserved for large corporations with extensive R&D budgets is now increasingly within reach of smaller firms. Yet accessibility alone does not guarantee impact. Strategic alignment, ethical governance, skill development, and organizational redesign are essential to convert AI potential into measurable value.

This book brings together diverse but interconnected perspectives to address that challenge.

We begin with the operational core: *AI-guided process automation and data analysis with AI*, exploring how intelligent systems can optimize workflows, reduce inefficiencies, and enhance evidence-based decision-making. These foundational capabilities directly influence *AI and competitiveness*, establishing a framework through which SMEs can leverage analytics, prediction, and automation as sources of differentiation.

Recognizing that competitiveness must translate into performance, several chapters examine *productivity in SMEs guided by AI*, including practical approaches to improving *customer experience*, strengthening *supply chain optimization*, and implementing robust *cybersecurity* systems in increasingly digital ecosystems.

However, technological adoption without responsibility is unsustainable. This volume addresses *ethical standards in the use of AI*, as well as the evolving *public policies and legal aspects for managing AI in SMEs*. As regulatory frameworks continue to evolve globally, SMEs must understand compliance not as a constraint but as a dimension of strategic maturity.

Equally critical is the human dimension. AI transformation demands *new skills and competencies for managing AI*, innovative approaches in *human resources management using AI*, and a reconfiguration of leadership mindsets. We explore how firms can cultivate *dynamic capabilities for innovation and AI*, ensuring adaptability in volatile environments. The discussion extends to *knowledge management systems for managing AI*, emphasizing that sustainable advantage depends on learning, knowledge transfer, and institutional memory.

Financial and market perspectives are also central. The book addresses *digital marketing as a strategy to improve competitiveness*, *strategies for financial innovation using AI in SMEs*, and the often-overlooked issues of *cost and accessibility of AI for MSMEs*. We examine *AI models for SMEs, models for AI management, and the level of acquisition and transfer of IT within companies*, recognizing that technological readiness varies widely across contexts.

Strategic posture and culture are recurring themes. Chapters on *strategies and negotiation culture in technology SMEs, building a vision of the future with AI, and transforming the paradigm of MSME management toward AI adoption* highlight that digital transformation is not purely technical—it is profoundly strategic and cultural.

Finally, the book grounds theory in reality through *application cases of AI in MSMEs*, demonstrating tangible outcomes, lessons learned, and replicable models. These cases illustrate that AI is not a distant or abstract concept; it is an operational and strategic instrument already redefining industries.

As editors, we do not present AI as a universal remedy. Rather, we frame it as a powerful enabler—one that requires thoughtful governance, interdisciplinary understanding, and responsible leadership. The transformation of SMEs through AI is neither automatic nor uniform. It depends on vision, preparedness, ethical commitment, and continuous learning.

We hope this reference work serves scholars, policymakers, practitioners, and entrepreneurs alike. More importantly, we hope it contributes to building SMEs that are not only more competitive and productive, but also more resilient, innovative, and socially responsible in the age of intelligent systems.

The future of SMEs will not be determined solely by the technologies they adopt, but by the strategic wisdom with which they integrate them.

CHAPTER OVERVIEWS

Chapter 1: Digital Transformation of Internal Control Systems: The Role of Artificial Intelligence

This study investigates the integration of Artificial Intelligence (AI) into Internal Control Systems (ICS). The objective is to understand the role of AI within ICS: (1) identifying AI technologies that benefit ICS, (2) determining ICS procedures that AI can assist, (3) characterizing an AI-assisted ICS, and (4) assessing the challenges in implementing AI within ICS. The results reveal that machine learning for process automation and chatbots are the most well-known and used AI functionalities. Internal Control (IC) procedures are inherently linked, so all benefit from AI implementation. With or without AI, the fundamental characteristics of an ICS remain intact. Key challenges in AI implementation include cost, the need for training, resistance to change, ethical and legal considerations, and data and model suitability. The ICS benefits from AI implementation, directly contributing to improved governance and proactive risk prevention mechanisms, as well as providing time savings.

Chapter 2: Management Model for Artifitial Intelligence (MMAI): The Concept

This chapter provides a Management Model for Artifitial Intelligence (MMAI) that, through its application and analysis, enables corporate decision-makers, academics, consultants, and others interested in the topic to seek the best alternatives for AI management, helping them streamline their organizations and achieve the highest standards of profitability, competitiveness, and sustainability. The MMAI is composed of nine key factors: 1) Clear objectives, 2) Ethics and regulation, 3) Data governance, 4) Transparency and explainability, 5) Performance and scalability, 6) Continuous training, 7) Risk management, 8) Integration and compatibility, and 9) Stakeholder engagement. Each factor, in turn, contains a series of variables that explain it. In total, there are twenty-seven (27) variables explained in detail in the theoretical framework of this chapter, which measure four levels ranging from 0 to 100%.

Chapter 3: Efficiency and Sustainability in Co-Ownership Utilizing Both the Balanced Scorecard and Artificial Intelligence

This study analyzes management performance in residential condominiums in Usaquén, Bogotá, comparing those using a Balanced Scorecard supported by artificial intelligence-A with those without AI. Using qualitative methods and data from 50 property managers through semi-structured interviews, results show that AI-enhanced BSCs improve financial liquidity, reduce delinquency, decrease social and operational incidents, and yield better management evaluations. AI enables real-time monitoring, enhances decision-making, and promotes sustainability by automating processes and anticipating potential issues. Findings suggest integrating AI into the BSC strengthens strategic alignment, transparency, and operational efficiency. Successful implementation requires digital literacy, ethical data use, and active resident engagement. The study recommends gradual digital transformation focusing on finance and maintenance. The AI-enabled BSC is a strategic tool for fostering sustainable, resilient, and efficient residential communities, highlighting opportunities for technology adoption in the sector.

Chapter 4: The Role of AI in Product Innovation: A Literature Review and Bibliometric Study

Artificial intelligence (AI) is positioned not only as a technological innovation but also as a key driving force of organizational transformation in today's digital economy. In this context, the aim of this study is to investigate the impact of AI on new product development (NPD) processes through a systematic literature review supported by bibliometric analysis. The study investigates existing academic publications to identify leading contributors, major research themes, and collaboration patterns within this interdisciplinary field. A total of 85 articles were analyzed using bibliometric techniques. Influential authors, institutions, and methodological trends were mapped using data derived from prominent academic databases. The analysis reveals the evolution of AI-related NPD research, current gaps in the literature, and future research directions. This chapter provides both theoretical contributions and strategic insights for practitioners, offering a conceptual foundation for future studies at the intersection of AI and NPD.

Chapter 5: AI In Supply Chain Optimization

The integration of artificial intelligence (AI) in supply chain chains has led to a significant transformation, moving from a focus on individual businesses to a holistic view of supply chain operations. AI plays a crucial role in optimisation of the supply chain, improving competitiveness and operational efficiency. It offers instant transparency and improved product flow management through technologies like blockchain and IoT, enabling better operational performance and predictive optimization. However, integrating AI presents a technological and organizational challenge, requiring meticulous management of processes, data, and interdependent actors. AI-based supply chain optimization relies on advanced technologies to improve performance and respond quickly to market fluctuations. Despite challenges related to data quality, cybersecurity, and operational training, the benefits of AI, such as improved decision-making and operational efficiency, are indispensable. Businesses must invest in training and risk management strategies to maximize the benefits of this technology.

Chapter 6: Elevating Small Business Performance With Emerging Technologies and Artificial Intelligence in Africa

A sustainable economy, particularly in the context of the fourth industrial revolution (4IR), necessitates a robust and globally competitive manufacturing sector. However, our understanding of how this emerging and rapidly changing technology impacts corporate performance, especially regarding turnover in small enterprises, may be lacking. This chapter examines the impact of developing technologies on the performance of small manufacturing enterprises, with a particular emphasis on Nigeria, the largest consumer market in Africa. Research indicated that developing technologies significantly influenced the business performance of SMEs in Nigeria. The research concludes that new technologies can improve the business performance of small manufacturing enterprises. Small businesses are advised to leverage AI to create disruptive innovation through innovative business models and processes, potentially transforming the manufacturing industry and global competitive landscape.

Chapter 7: Effect of Artificial Intelligence Awareness on Job Performance: Mediating and Moderating Role of Gender

As artificial intelligence spreads, it is critical to comprehend how job performance may be impacted by this technology. However, to our knowledge, there is no research dealing with both the mediating and moderating role of gender in the association between artificial intelligence awareness and job performance. Therefore, we try to fill this gap. We distributed 204 online questionnaires to Tunisian employees in the service sector. We performed explanatory factor analysis, confirmatory factor analysis, structural equation modeling, and bootstrapping. Our results found that artificial intelligence has a negative impact on job performance. However, gender has neither a mediating nor moderating effect on the relationship between artificial intelligence awareness and job performance. This implies that artificial intelligence awareness may influence job performance in similar ways for both men and women.

Chapter 8: AI-Powered Destination Marketing: Personalization, Consumer Engagement, and Competitive Positioning

The central aim of this research study is to highlight the opportunities and challenges surrounding the use of AI technology in the marketing and promotion of tourism destinations. Its promotion comprises a deliberate and well-conceived strategy for optimizing the benefits derived from tourism expenditure, aiming to generate economic returns while also fostering other social, cultural, or environmental values for the destination. This study focuses on AI-powered destination marketing with a special emphasis on personalization to enhance consumer engagement. Investigating the consumer viewpoint is a crucial aspect of this work, as it is essential to ensure that the design and implementation of AI-powered marketing strategies remain consumer-centric (Geisler,2018). With the advancement of technology, consumers can be individually addressed through marketing actions and tools based on in-depth knowledge about their preferences and behavior.

Chapter 9: Competitor Orientation Effect on Augmenting Ethiopia SME Internal Technological Process Through Customer Insight

The purpose of this paper is to investigate how innovation future prospects pertaining to internal Artificial Intelligence sub structured technical capabilities in SMEs located in Ethiopia are influenced by orientation of competitor and insight of a customer. The outcomes manifest a modest positive association among innovation future prospects pertaining to internal Artificial Intelligence sub structured technical capabilities and orientation of competitor, with insight of a customer acting as a partial mediating factor. This manifests that corporates that actively monitor competitors and engage with customers are better positioned to innovate and augment their Artificial Intelligence sub structured technical capabilities. The implications of these outcomes manifest the necessity for SMEs to assimilate together competitor and customer analyses into their strategic frameworks. By fostering a proactive approach to get know market dynamics and customer wants, corporates can enhance their Artificial Intelligence sub structured technical capabilities innovation future prospects.

Chapter 10: Digital Divide in Latin American Higher Education: Challenges and Obstacles in the Face of Artificial Intelligence

In recent years, technological and digital advancements have profoundly transformed various fields of computer science, as well as human endeavors and diverse industries. Disruptive technologies have generated a significant impact on the social and productive spheres globally. Among these, cloud computing, cybe.rsecurity, and 5G technology stand out, with the growth of the Artificial Intelligence (AI) market being particularly relevant and the subject of this chapter. AI's pervasive influence on education has exacerbated the digital divide, which itself reflects existing societal inequalities—a persistent problem not only in education but also across various other societal domains. The interplay of several factors, including access to technology, existing infrastructure, educational training, and the level of technological literacy, alongside inequalities associated with geographical location and current socioeconomic conditions, plays a crucial role in this contex.

Chapter 11: Ethical Standards in the Use of AI for Computer Science Students

The rapid integration of artificial intelligence (AI) into education and professional practice has brought about transformative opportunities and pressing ethical challenges. This chapter examines the principles, guidelines, and responsibilities that students must understand and maintain when engaging with AI technologies. This book explores key topics such as academic integrity, data privacy, algorithmic bias, intellectual property, and the responsible use of generative AI tools like ChatGPT and GitHub Copilot. Through real-world case studies, theoretical frameworks, and practical scenarios, the chapter fosters critical thinking and ethical reasoning among computer science students. It also provides educators with strategies for promoting ethical awareness and decision-making in AI-assisted learning environments. By grounding technical education in strong ethical foundations, this book aims to prepare future programmers and engineers to contribute to a trustworthy and socially responsible AI landscape.

CONCLUSION

As editors, we close this volume with a strengthened conviction: Artificial Intelligence is not a peripheral tool nor a passing trend, but a structural force reshaping how SMEs design strategy, allocate resources, manage risk, and create value. Across governance, innovation, supply chains, marketing, ethics, and education, the chapters collectively show that AI's impact is profound—but never automatic.

The empirical and regional studies demonstrate both promise and complexity. AI can enhance efficiency, foresight, and competitiveness, yet it may also generate skill gaps, organizational tension, or uneven outcomes when governance and strategic alignment are weak. Its benefits depend on leadership quality, digital literacy, cultural readiness, and ethical responsibility.

A consistent lesson emerges: AI delivers its greatest value when it deepens insight—into customers, processes, markets, and future scenarios. It is this augmentation of strategic intelligence, rather than automation alone, that distinguishes meaningful transformation from superficial digitization.

This book offers no single blueprint, but a set of models, evidence, and applications to guide informed action. Ultimately, the future of SMEs in the age of intelligent systems will be determined not by algorithms alone, but by the wisdom, integrity, and coherence with which they are integrated. If this volume supports that balanced and responsible integration, it has achieved its purpose.

Rafael Perez-Uribe
Invesproject, Colombia

David Ocampo-Guzman
Universidad EAN, Colombia

Maria Teresa Ramirez-Garzo
Invesproject, Colombia

Luz Janeth Lozano-Correa
Santo Tomas University, Colombia

Chapter 1

Digital Transformation of Internal Control Systems: The Role of Artificial Intelligence

Marta F. Ceia
http://orcid.org/0009-0001-7916-3747
University of Aveiro, Portugal

Rui P. Marques
http://orcid.org/0000-0001-8449-0526
University of Aveiro, Portugal

Helena Inácio
http://orcid.org/0000-0003-1281-2156
University of Aveiro, Portugal

ABSTRACT

This study investigates the integration of Artificial Intelligence (AI) into Internal Control Systems (ICS). The objective is to understand the role of AI within ICS: (1) identifying AI technologies that benefit ICS, (2) determining ICS procedures that AI can assist, (3) characterizing an AI-assisted ICS, and (4) assessing the challenges in implementing AI within ICS. The results reveal that machine learning for process automation and chatbots are the most well-known and used AI functionalities. Internal Control (IC) procedures are inherently linked, so all benefit from AI implementation. With or without AI, the fundamental characteristics of an ICS remain intact. Key challenges in AI implementation include cost, the need for training, resistance to change, ethical and legal considerations, and data and model suitability. The ICS benefits from AI implementation, directly contributing to improved governance and proactive risk prevention mechanisms, as well as providing time savings.

DOI: 10.4018/979-8-2600-0439-5.ch001

INTRODUCTION

In an era marked by economic globalization, accelerated technological change, the emergence of new business models, and growing regulatory complexity, organizations face an increasingly dynamic and uncertain environment. The vast amount of data produced daily, combined with the pervasive dependence on Information Technology (IT), has transformed the way entities operate, manage risks, and pursue strategic objectives. Within this context, the ICS has become a cornerstone of modern management, ensuring operational integrity, regulatory compliance, and the sustainable creation of value (PWC, 2019).

The implementation of innovative ideas and models to foster economic transformation and international competitiveness must be guided by robust and adaptive control systems (Liu, 2011). Regardless of organizational size or structure, an effective ICS serves as both a safeguard and a strategic enabler. It aligns operations with corporate objectives, protects assets, and ensures the reliability of financial and operational information (Masdi et al., 2022; Inácio, 2014). The relevance of ICS is evident across contexts, from the supervision of subsidiaries and state-owned enterprises to the prevention of fraud and enhancement of financial performance (Hu et al., 2021; Cheng, 2011; Abu Hamour et al., 2023; Donelson et al., 2017).

Parallel to this evolution, Information Technology has emerged as a catalyst for change, shaping virtually every aspect of business activity (Mandilas et al., 2022). Its integration with internal control mechanisms has driven research on tools for detecting control nonconformities (Doganata & Curbera, 2012), assessing control risks (Davis et al., 1997), and supporting internal auditing processes (Jans et al., 2011). Recent advances indicate that digital technologies not only enhance control efficiency but also enable continuous monitoring and adaptive governance structures (Fotoh & Lorentzon, 2023; Klius et al., 2020).

Among these technological innovations, AI stands out as a transformative force. AI systems are increasingly embedded in the design and execution of internal controls, offering unprecedented capabilities in automation, anomaly detection, and predictive analysis (Chen et al., 2022; Werner et al., 2021). Moreover, the integration of AI enables real-time automated data processing and enhances both internal communication and external disclosures (Zong & Guan, 2024). Studies have explored AI applications across diverse control functions – from procurement monitoring (Caruso et al., 2023) and financial reporting (Kokina & Blanchette, 2019) to auditing and continuous assurance services (Jans & Hosseinpour, 2019; Marques et al., 2015). Nonetheless, existing research remains fragmented, often limited to specific domains such as auditing or accounting, without providing a holistic understanding of AI's role within the overall architecture of internal control systems (Monteiro et al., 2023; Mehta et al., 2021).

Despite broad consensus on AI's transformative potential (Askary et al., 2018; Sun et al., 2025), several critical questions persist: Which AI technologies are most applicable to ICS? Which control procedures can be effectively supported by AI? Does the integration of AI strengthen or compromise the foundational principles of internal control? And what challenges arise in its implementation (Hulstijn, 2023; Guo, 2022)? Addressing these questions requires a deeper empirical investigation into the intersection between AI and ICS, an area where theoretical understanding and practical application have yet to fully converge.

The significance of this study thus lies in both its academic contribution – advancing knowledge on the digital transformation of control environments and its practical implications for organizations. As firms strive for greater efficiency, transparency, and resilience in an increasingly competitive and regulated world (Fotoh & Lorentzon, 2023; Abu Hamour et al., 2023), understanding how AI can be integrated into internal control systems, and under what conditions it can generate value, becomes not only relevant but essential for managers, auditors, and policymakers alike.

LITERATURE REVIEW

Internal Control System

In this study, the ICS is framed within a global and strategic approach (Henk, 2020), specifically based on the models developed by the Committee of Sponsoring Organizations of the Treadway Commission (COSO) (COSO, 2013) and the Control Objectives for Information and Related Technologies (COBIT) framework (ISACA, 2012). These are complementary models for the creation, management, and monitoring of ICS, widely accepted internationally, and when combined, they place the ICS within an IT environment - a minimum condition for the integration of AI.

In 1992, COSO released the "Internal Control – Integrated Framework," which was updated in 2013 and most recently in 2023. This framework aims to provide management with a flexible tool applicable to any type of entity, based on professional judgment, and designed to establish the requirements for an effective ICS. It supports risk identification and analysis and the development and management of appropriate responses, with a strong focus on anti-fraud measures. The COSO framework allows the ICS to be applied across all organizational areas and helps eliminate inefficient or redundant controls. COSO defines Internal Control as the process by which the board of directors, management, and other personnel provide reasonable assurance regarding the achievement of objectives related to the effectiveness and efficiency of operations, reliability of reporting, and compliance with applicable laws and regulations.

The COBIT framework, developed by Information Systems Audit and Control Association (ISACA) in 1996 and last updated in 2019, serves as a reference guide for the governance and management of IT across organizations. It consists of a set of best practices and recommendations, process-based, general, flexible, and universal, with the primary goal of helping organizations develop internal controls specifically in information technology.

Artificial Intelligence

There is consensus regarding the potential of AI in business and the economic value of investing in AI; however, a universally accepted definition of AI has yet to emerge (Collins et al., 2021). In Europe, the High-Level Expert Group on Artificial Intelligence (AI HLEG), through the document "A Definition of AI: Main Capabilities and Scientific Disciplines", proposed a working definition of AI (AI HLEG, 2018). According to the expert group, AI systems are software systems designed by humans to achieve specific goals. These systems perceive their environment by collecting data, interpreting this data, reasoning based on the knowledge or processing of the data, and deciding on the best actions to take to achieve their objectives.

The European Commission's Communication to the European Parliament "Artificial Intelligence for Europe" (Commission, 2018) also addresses the question, "What is Artificial Intelligence?" describing it as a collection of technologies that enable the performance of functions that would otherwise require human intelligence, with the goal of improving and automating decision-making processes.

For Kaplan & Haenlein (2019), AI refers to the ability of a system to collect and interpret data, learn from it, and adjust or apply the learning to perform tasks.

AI relies on large volumes of data from multiple sources, captured through technologies such as the Internet of Things (IoT), and processed by specific algorithms depending on the task at hand. Based on its ability to process and learn from data, two main subfields of AI can be identified: machine learning, where machines learn from data, and deep learning, where machines learn in a way like humans (Microsoft, 2024).

Although AI systems process information differently from human cognition, their interaction with human-like tasks can be observed in functions such as (IBM, 2024), Natural Language Processing (NLP), speech recognition, text analytics, virtual agents, robotics and biometrics.

Related Works

The related works aimed at understanding how the literature has addressed the integration of AI into internal control systems, has an exploratory and descriptive character and seeks to present the scientific contributions considered most relevant to contextualize the research topic.

Thc digital transformation of ICS has been progressively driven by the development and integration of emerging technologies such as AI, blockchain, big data, and robotic automation. Studies show that these technologies, whether used independently or jointly, serve as innovation engines for strengthening control mechanisms, risk detection, and organizational transparency. Klius et al. (2020) analyzed international approaches to ICS organization in the digital age, focusing on how leading companies integrate emerging technologies into their control and auditing processes. The use of AI is highlighted as one of the most promising technologies for automating data verification, detecting discrepancies, and enhancing real-time monitoring. The article also emphasizes that digital solutions can reduce auditing costs, improve transparency, and enhance the reliability of financial reports. Fan (2022) reflects on how AI can improve control mechanisms, early risk detection, and management efficiency. Based on the five-component IC model, the study identifies critical weaknesses in the control environment, risk assessment, control activities, communication, and internal monitoring. Fan (2022) highlights that technologies such as AI and big data can transform traditional IC by offering advanced monitoring capabilities, risk forecasting, and automation of auditing and financial reporting processes. Among the proposed solutions are the development of intelligent digital risk management platforms, training programs in data analysis and professional ethics, and the strengthening of corporate governance and disclosure. The study stresses the importance of managerial morality and effective supervision as complementary elements to the application of AI in fraud prevention. Zhu and Shen (2021) examined the relationship between the intensity of AI adoption and the quality of ICS and concluded that there is a significant positive association between AI application and ICS effectiveness, especially in anomaly detection, automated auditing, and the enhancement of financial information transparency. Chen et al. (2022) investigated the complexity of organizational IC in a big data context, proposing a hybrid decision model that integrates various AI-influenced techniques aimed at identifying critical IC factors, analyzing complex relationships among them, and proposing improvement strategies. Giudici, Centurelli, and Turchetta (2024) proposed an AI-driven risk measurement framework aimed at improving organizational resilience by anticipating threats and vulnerabilities. Recognizing that traditional risk assessment models, such as financial scoring systems, are limited in capturing real-time emerging risks, the authors developed a predictive model combining supervised machine learning techniques with Bayesian statistical methods applied to the banking sector. This approach focuses not only on predictive performance but also on the explainability of results, which is essential for its applicability in regulatory and IC contexts. The model was validated with banking data, demonstrating that AI can identify risk patterns with greater anticipation and granularity, supporting more robust mitigation decisions.

The technological potential of AI can directly support the execution of key procedures within ICS, bringing technology closer to organizational practices and serving as a bridge between technical potential and the practical implementation of IC. Wang et al. (2020) developed an intelligent audit and IC system based on blockchain and cloud storage technologies, aiming to modernize organizational auditing mechanisms and overcome the limitations of traditional systems. The proposed system employs AI to perform data classification tasks using Bayesian algorithms and to generate automatic audit reports based on pre-stored knowledge. The architecture also includes functions such as remote data analysis, cyber risk assessment, and real-time data management. The authors conclude that the integration of AI with blockchain and cloud computing allows for the construction of a more robust, transparent, and efficient ICS, promoting early risk detection, audit automation, and data-driven decision-making based on reliable and immutable information. Monteiro et al. (2023) investigated the relationship between the intensity of AI adoption, ICS effectiveness, and the quality of accounting information in Portuguese companies. The results show that intensive AI adoption is positively associated with the robustness of ICS and the quality of accounting information, highlighting AI as a critical factor in risk mitigation, reduction of human error, and improvement of organizational transparency. Mehta et al. (2021) conducted an empirical study to analyze the impact of IC measures on the perceived usefulness of forensic audits, considering the mediation of AI technologies. The study was motivated by the increasing complexity and volume of data in Indian financial institutions, were auditors face challenges in fraud detection. The research examined the relationships between variables such as internal controls, AI technologies, perceived benefits, and ease of use. The results indicated that the application of AI techniques has a positive and mediating effect on the perceived usefulness of forensic audits, whereas the direct influence of internal controls on perceived usefulness was statistically insignificant. AI was instrumental in facilitating the use of forensic audits and enhancing their perceived benefits, such as the ability to detect suspicious patterns and support decision-making based on large volumes of data. The study concludes that AI integration in forensic audits can mitigate the effects of human limitations in fraud detection, making IC mechanisms more robust, if auditors receive appropriate training and institutional awareness is raised. Chen, Wu, and Yan (2022) proposed a full-population data audit method supported by machine learning techniques to overcome the limitations of traditional sampling models. The study acknowledges that, given the volume and complexity of modern business data, conventional methods may overlook relevant fraud or anomalies. The proposed approach enables real-time and comprehensive analysis of financial transactions, identifying suspicious patterns using supervised learning algorithms. The results demonstrated significant gains in coverage, accuracy, and efficiency, making the model applicable to financial audit automation and enhancing the reliability of ICS. Mohd Noor and Mansor (2019) examined the adaptation of AI in whistleblowing practices by internal auditors in the Malaysian public sector, with the aim of assessing the impact of this practice on strengthening ICS and combating corruption. The authors analyzed auditors' perceptions regarding the effectiveness of whistleblowing systems and the role of AI in this process. They concluded that applying AI in management systems can significantly improve the detection of irregularities, accelerate institutional responses, and increase public trust in control mechanisms. The study also highlights that AI allows for the analysis of large volumes of data and the identification of patterns and suspicious relationships among individuals involved in fraudulent acts, reducing human error and increasing the accuracy of investigations. The authors advocate for AI integration into whistleblowing systems across all public agencies to reinforce integrity, transparency, and administrative accountability. Emmanuel, Wijaya, and Riantono (2023) developed a web-based system to modernize the accounting information system of a construction materials retailer in Indonesia. The research aimed to solve problems related to manual recording of sales and inventory, which generated errors, data inconsistencies, and opportunities for internal fraud. The proposed system incorporates AI technologies to improve decision-making, namely recommending promotions based on inventory turnover and profit margins, as well as monitoring store performance. The results showed that implementing accounting information system with AI can significantly improve inventory accuracy, reporting speed, and fraud prevention provided it is accompanied by strict IC measures, such as segregation of duties and access control. Caruso et al. (2023) addressed the problem of corruption in procurement processes in public health organizations and presented an innovative method based on the combination of business intelligence (BI) and AI. The method applies BI to automatically calculate Key Performance Indicators (KPIs) and visualize data, and AI, through neural networks, to analyze their evolution. The combined BI and AI solution was able to simplify calculations and assess large amounts of data and KPIs in a brief period, and with high accuracy. Relevant and reliable accounting information depends on a solid ICS and the ethical and integrity characteristics of management and employees. For this reason, Askary et al. (2018) propose a practical model for using AI to improve internal controls from different perspectives: efficiency, expertise, effectiveness, and innovation. AI is viewed as capable of detecting weaknesses, understanding problems, and acting to resolve them automatically, thus reducing the risk in accounting information.

More than supporting isolated functions, AI has the potential to transform the ICS into an integrated and adaptive system. Looi et al. (1989) developed an intelligent system called AUDITPRO, designed to simulate the auditors' reasoning process in identifying strengths and weaknesses in control procedures. The research was based on highly complex business environments, where documented processes, such as flowcharts, are analyzed by algorithms that replicate human judgment. The proposed architecture is based on a hierarchical tree of control objectives, sub-objectives, and procedures, allowing the system to establish relationships between components and assess their effectiveness. By applying this structure to a specific transactional cycle, the authors demonstrated that the system could make accurate and consistent diagnoses, even in demanding contexts. Its practical application showed gains in terms of efficiency, systematization, and rigor, with the potential to reduce subjectivity and common omissions in manual audits. This contribution represents an innovative perspective on the use of AI — still embryonic at the time — to strengthen ICS, anticipating trends now materialized in tools for algorithm-assisted auditing and automated reasoning. Zhang and Zhang (2021) proposed an intelligent model for evaluating ICS in the sales process of small and micro enterprises, based on fuzzy neural networks. The study was motivated by the realization that traditional ICS assessments are highly subjective and often conducted after failures occur, which compromises their preventive effectiveness. To overcome this limitation, the authors developed a hybrid approach combining fuzzy logic with artificial neural networks, allowing for automated and more objective evaluation of ICS weaknesses. The model was built upon the five fundamental elements of ICS: control environment, risk assessment, control activities, information and communication, and monitoring. The evaluation framework considered six critical points in the sales process: segregation of duties, traceability of information, document integrity, and the effectiveness of control measures. Experts assigned reference values to each control point for a sample of 30 companies, whose data was used to train and validate the fuzzy neural network. The system achieved an accurate rate of 96.7%, showing strong capacity to identify control deficiencies. The authors concluded that this type of approach enables risk anticipation, reduces supervision costs, and reinforces ICS reliability. However, they recommend adapting the model's implementation to the specific characteristics of each company, given the variability in data quality and disclosure across organizations. Guo (2022) proposed a method for evaluating financial IC in higher education institutions based on AI technology, aiming to overcome the limitations of traditional systems considering the increasing complexity and volume of financial operations. The study acknowledges that, despite the importance of financial management in universities, existing control methods face shortcomings, particularly in terms of risk detection and operational efficiency. The proposal involves building an IC evaluation chain that integrates AI technologies for real-time data collection, processing, and analysis, enabling the identification of anomalous data and precise performance assessment of control systems. The approach employs algorithms such as the Gini coefficient and selective ensemble learning models to detect anomalies in financial data, classifying control capacity levels according to performance scales. The solution also includes a budget management model designed to optimize resource allocation, improve oversight, and strengthen managerial accountability. Experimental results show that the proposed method achieves a more stable and effective error detection rate, even with large data volumes, when compared to previous approaches. The study concludes that AI offers a promising solution to enhance the reliability, accuracy, and adaptability of financial control systems in university contexts. Wang (2023) conducted a study focused on technological innovation in the financial management system of museums, emphasizing the impact of AI and the efficiency of internal controls. The research proposed a management system based on AI technology applied to the automation of financial processes, utilizing technologies such as Robotic Process Automation (RPA), image and voice recognition, big data, and cloud computing. The system was designed to optimize tasks such as document entry, auditing, general accounting, budgeting, and financial analysis. Regarding IC, the solution aims to identify process failures, improve the quality of financial information, and strengthen internal supervision mechanisms. The results demonstrate that the application of these technologies improved audit and control efficiency, increased information transparency, and reduced operational risks. Sun et al., (2025)investigated how the adoption of AI affects internal control systems (ICS) and how this influences the prevention of financial fraud. The results showed that the integration of AI technologies enables the automation of auditing tasks, improves anomaly detection, and strengthens supervisory mechanisms, thereby enhancing the monitoring of financial reporting processes and contributing both to the reinforcement of the ICS and to an effective strategy for reducing the incidence of financial fraud.

Despite the transformative potential of AI in ICS, several authors highlight critical limitations in its implementation. Zhu and Shen (2021) point to challenges related to technological integration, such as algorithmic opacity, a lack of qualified personnel in AI, and difficulties in adapting organizational infrastructures. Fan (2022) emphasizes the importance of ethics and specialized training. Xue (2020) analyzed the management of accounting records in Chinese public institutions in the context of increasing informatization, stressing the need to integrate technologies such as Internet+, big data, and cloud computing to strengthen governance and ICS. The study concludes that the success of informatization and ICS depends not only on technology but also on active leadership involvement and the development of an organizational culture committed to integrity and professional responsibility. This is reinforced by Guo (2022), who highlights both organizational and technical barriers, emphasizing the importance of enhancing managerial training and adopting a strategic vision of financial control supported by technology. Hulstijn (2023) introduces the debate on computational accountability in contexts where decision-making agents are non-human. The author develops a theoretical reflection on the concept of computational responsibility considering the growing adoption of AI systems in organizational processes subject to legal, ethical, and control norms. The study recognizes that AI systems are increasingly responsible for critical impact decisions — in areas such as auditing, financial management, or IC — yet they often escape traditional frameworks of legal and institutional accountability. Through a conceptual and normative approach, the author proposes a model of accountability for computational systems, based on principles of algorithmic explainability, auditability, traceability, and transparency. The research distinguishes between moral, legal, and functional responsibility and argues that IC mechanisms must be rethought when the decision-making agent is no longer human. The proposed model integrates elements from the philosophy of technology, computer science, and responsibility theory to propose a control framework oriented not only to AI performance but also to its ethical integration into organizational processes. The article argues that in an increasingly automated environment, IC must evolve to accommodate non-human entities, requiring new forms of monitoring, regulation, and accountability.

METHODOLOGY

The research design corresponds to the methodological structure that guides a given study to answer the research questions and, therefore, achieve the proposed objectives. This design involves the selection of methods, techniques, and procedures for data collection, processing, and analysis (Gonçalves et al., 2021; Vilelas, 2020).

In this study, the chosen methodology is of an exploratory nature. This approach is justified by the fact that the topic is still underexplored in scientific literature, yet historically, currently, and prospectively relevant, requiring further investigation for better understanding.

The general objective is to deepen the understanding of the integration of AI technology into ICS. The specific objectives are: (1) to identify AI technologies that could benefit ICS, (2) to identify ICS procedures that can be assisted by AI, (3) to characterize an AI-assisted ICS, and (4) to assess the challenges in implementing AI within ICS. To pursue these objectives, the following set of research questions was formulated:

QI1 – What AI technologies can be useful to ICS?
QI2 – Which ICS procedures can be assisted by AI?
QI3 – What are the main characteristics of an AI-assisted ICS?
QI4 – What are the main challenges in implementing AI in ICS?

Data Collection and Processing

For data collection and analysis, a qualitative approach was chosen using semi-structured interviews (Morgado, 2013) and subsequent content analysis (Vilelas, 2020).

The interview design was developed considering the research objectives and questions (Coutinho, 2011) and structured into two blocks of questions: the first aims to assess the interviewee's experience/knowledge regarding the topic, and the second addresses the core research areas. Interviewees were selected by convenience, following a non-probabilistic approach aligned with the study's objectives (Coutinho, 2011). This sampling technique is widely used in qualitative research when the goal is to obtain in-depth, specialized information on the phenomenon under analysis, without aiming to generalize the results to a broader population. Therefore, interviewees were chosen based on a predefined profile, considering their relevance and direct experience with the topic under study, ensuring that each participant had the necessary knowledge to provide meaningful and detailed data.

For this study, the universe of interviewees includes all companies operating in Portugal that develop and/or market AI-powered software and their potential clients - i.e., companies that purchase and/or use these solutions. The objective is to interview professionals from both groups, with decision-making power regarding AI implementation, to capture both perspectives: those who develop and those who use these tools. ICS is part of the fields of economics, accounting, auditing, and management; thus, it was deemed appropriate to select interviewees whose work is closely related - though not exclusively - to these areas. Two interviewee profiles were defined: P1 – developers/vendors and P2 – users/buyers.

The methodological choices described above justify a limited number of interviews for data collection. It was therefore established that at least three interviews should be conducted for each profile.

In this research, a total of 7 semi-structured interviews (E1, E2... E7) were conducted between July and October 2024, according to the availability of the interviewees. Each interview lasted an average of 40 minutes, ranging from 33 minutes (shortest) to 1 hour and 19 minutes (longest), totaling approximately 5 hours of interview data.

Each interview began with an introductory note presenting the core concepts of ICS and AI to ensure a shared understanding between the interviewer and interviewee. The questions were posed flexibly, adapting to the natural flow of conversation and the emergence of new topics, without strictly following the order of the interview script.

Content analysis was used to process the information provided by the interviewees, utilizing the Web Qualitative Data Analysis (WebQDA) tool in its Portuguese version.

WebQDA is an online qualitative data analysis software that allows for organizing, coding, and querying textual data, such as interview transcripts (Costa & Amado, 2018).

Initially, codes were created according to the objectives defined for each interview question, and during the reading and coding process, both three codes and free codes were created as new analytical categories emerged. This coding was developed by the researcher and validated by the academic advisors for coherence, relevance, and objectivity.

The coding process involved in-depth reading of all data sources and establishing concordance between excerpts and codes.

Given the objectives of this study, the following analytical elements were created in the "Query" area of WebQDA:

- The 50 most frequent words, with a minimum of four characters, excluding grammatical particles.
- Five text searches, and
- Five crosstab matrices as shown in Table 1.

Table 1. Crosstab matrices

Constructed Matrix	Questions in WebQDA
Technologies by profile	What AI technologies are mentioned by each interviewee profile?
Procedures by profile	What ICS procedures are mentioned by each interviewee profile?
Strengthened characteristics by profile	What ICS characteristics are identified as strengthened by each interviewee profile?
Compromised characteristics by profile	What ICS characteristics are identified as compromised by each interviewee profile?
Challenges by profile	What challenges are noted by each interviewee profile regarding AI use in ICS?

ANALYSIS AND DISCUSSION OF RESULTS

Analysis of Results

Regarding the analysis of results, given the qualitative approach adopted, the findings are presented in a descriptive and exploratory manner. Whenever deemed relevant, excerpts from the interviewees' responses are included in the text to illustrate their perspectives.

Preliminary Observations

The initial observation of the results focused on the analysis of the 50 most frequent words from the interviews. It was evident that the discourse developed primarily around AI, and not so much around IC. While this result is expected for AI, it is unexpected for IC, considering that both constitute the core pillars of the study's theme.

The discrepancy in frequency between the terms “intelligence,” “artificial,” “control,” and “internal” prompted a textual search for the expressions “artificial intelligence” and “internal control.” It was found that interviewees referred to AI 118 times, 100 times more than IC, which was mentioned only 18 times. All interviews began with a preliminary note presenting the concepts of AI and IC that underpin this research. In this context, only one interviewee explicitly acknowledged a lesser familiarity with the concept of IC compared to AI. The concept of AI elicited more observations, not only during this initial phase but throughout various stages of the interview. This discrepancy is justified, on one hand, by the fact that only 3 interviewees fell under the user/buyer profile, while 4 were from the developer/vendor profile—hence, more technologically oriented, and familiar with the topic. On the other hand, AI is currently a highly relevant and widely discussed issue that engages both developers/vendors and users/buyers, in contrast to the topic of IC.

The researcher perceived that the terms around “automation” it was of the most frequently mentioned by interviewees, so it was conducted a text search to include the maximum number of variations of the word – automatically, automation, automatic, automations to automate. It is confirmed that the term “automation”, when aggregated with its various lexical forms used with the same meaning and in the same context, is indeed expressive.

From the researcher’s perspective the terms “data” and “people,” are prominent suggesting that these are two key components in the context of implementing AI in ICS.

Data emerges as a crucial element in the scope of this study. To validate this perception, a text search was conducted for the term *“data”*. The term “data” was mentioned 63 times by the interviewees, with varying meanings and contexts. Given its recurrence and importance, it was deemed relevant to create a tree code under the category “Challenges of AI Implementation in ICS”, titled “Data”, and to associate the respective references accordingly.

Additionally, all interviewees made multiple references to people, amounting to a total of 83 mentions. The interviewees placed people at the center of the use and implementation of AI in ICS. Consequently, three codes were created under "Challenges of AI Implementation in ICS," in addition to the codes derived from the predefined research objectives, which already implicitly refer to people.

The alignment between the information provided by the sources and each code will be analyzed next, with the presentation of results of matrices created in WebQDA.

Artificial Intelligence Technologies That May Benefit Internal Control Systems

The analysis of the results obtained in the interviews conducted allows the identification of AI technologies that can be useful and integrated in ICS. Both developers and users were mentioned these technologies and reflect a growing interest in AI technologies, particularly those that allow the optimization of internal processes.

The developers mentioned machine learning solutions in the accounting field for the automatic classification of documents, in which "when classifying documents (...) I tell it that it is from that supplier, that type of document, that it goes to certain accounts, with those VAT rates (...) and then it learns, that is, it saves that information and the next time (...) it automatically classifies them based on what was done before" (E2P1). It is, therefore, about learning continuously and automatically and this is machine learning, or as one developer simplified it: "training the models" (E3P1), which need "to always be associated with a database (...) an algorithm" and "retrieve information that has been accumulated over time," use it to adapt and return responses to requests. An example: "we are collecting invoices, various types of invoices and invoice models to teach the model and say – all this is invoices and now look for the value" (E3P1).

One of the users shared that what he looks for with his team "is that all (...) identify a repetitive task to then try to automate it" (E1P2). A technology particularly relevant for users is process automation, for example, bank reconciliation "through robot systems" (E6P2), which allows checking the compliance between recorded transactions and the respective documents, ensuring the integrity and consistency of financial operations.

In the field of auditing, models are being developed and trained that, with AI, allow "the identification of risks based on the entity's framework, in the initial phase of audit planning" (E3P1), and at a later stage "already in the audit work, the automation phase, more in the phase of substantive tests, control tests" (E3P1) through the recognition and analysis of data from various sources (photographs, PDFs, etc.).

Additionally, among developers, AI has currently become data analysis, that is, the amount of available data allows "detecting patterns and with those patterns retrieving information and from there making an evolution" (E5P1). Clustering is an example of data analysis that groups information by identical characteristics, and another possibility is to look for anomalies or outliers and use these results to make decisions.

Another significant contribution of AI in supporting decision-making is the use of chatbots. Chatbots were indicated as useful tools to provide quick and accurate answers to users in which, for example, the user can consult the tool and "ask for information about issues within the company itself" (E5P1), obtain recommendations, "or a list of tasks and procedures that they should carry out to respond to that question" (E3P1). Chatbots can also help generate texts to "respond to emails (…) meeting preparation (…) provide a structure for a presentation" (E1P2). The most mentioned chatbot was ChatGPT from OpenAI, and its functionalities, namely the possibility of creating specialized chatbots, that is, "mini chatbots that retrieve information, for example, from a file in Google Drive (…) and thus, they will respond much more securely to the questions we ask in that specific chatbot, within OpenAI, within ChatGPT" (E1P2).

Other technologies like voice recognition and facial recognition were only listed, suggesting their application in access control.

Among users, there is no consensus regarding virtual assistants; for some, they are the ideal tool for customer service in a near future perspective "the virtual assistant is the next step" (E1P2), for others the nature of their activity requires proximity and human presence with clients and, therefore, virtual assistants are out of the question.

In response to the research question (Q1) about which AI technologies can be useful to ICS, machine learning for process automation and chatbots are the most well-known and used by the interviewees, whether in the automation of repetitive processes, in support of decision-making and risk identification, in the analysis and automatic collection of information, or in the integration of AI into audits. This set of evidence collected in the interviews indicates that AI has a high potential to transform and improve ICS, since the solutions presented ensure greater compliance, efficiency, and security in organizational operations.

ICS Procedures That can be Assisted by AI

The most prominent procedures are document flow and recording, and authorizations and approvals. It is important to note that there is consensus among all interviewees that each AI technology implemented in ICS affects more than one procedure, and that the procedure's function, and it is this whole that is intended to be optimized.

Both developers and users emphasized the ability of AI solutions to organize, classify, and fill in documents from different sources, exemplifying that "AI already extracts all the information from a PDF automatically, and can even generate the entry" (E7P1), and that "we take a photo of the document, which is read (…) and places all that information into a form" (E4P2). These procedures allow for more effective document management, ensuring that information is managed accurately, minimizing the risk of errors in classification and accounting registration, and reducing the need for manual intervention.

Some procedures were detailed, such as:

- An expense registration application, used by hundreds of employees operating in different countries, in which, through an image of the document, a set of information is automatically extracted and entered a form. This solution allows the person responsible to control and manage expenses, allows expense accounting, and enables the collection of a vast set of data used for statistical purposes, reporting, and training models.
- A browser-based ERP that imports a PDF file or image of a document and automatically extracts the information and fills out the purchase order, the order, the invoice— all those internal documents that are normally recorded in the ERP.
- An Optical Character Recognition (OCR) solution, in which there is no paper. The mail is all digitized, an internal reference is created, it is sent to the respective recipients, and all processing is done via digital document.
- A video system that automatically records, verifies, and validates an action, and in case of non-compliance triggers an alert process to verify the actual non-compliance, and if confirmed, initiates all necessary communications and document submissions for resolution.

All these procedures related to document flow and recording have a direct impact on all other procedures, as the information serves various stakeholders with different functions (segregation of duties) and responsibilities (authorizations and approvals), with different user profiles (access control), and digital processing allows reviews and reconciliations to be performed automatically.

A user exemplified that the automatic processing of purchases allows exceptions to be detected and responded to in a timely manner and that, therefore, "if there is any exception, higher-level approval will be required (…) otherwise, the process is automated" (E4P2). In practice, upon registering a receipt, if the previously established conditions are not met, the procedure only proceeds after that specific situation is reviewed and approved; only after (re)approval does the automatic registration process follow.

The detection of exceptions, outliers, and anomalies is facilitated as AI technologies allow for verification of the entire data set. During the interviews, the importance of automation in risk identification through real-time data analysis was emphasized, as it allows for quicker and more assertive responses in cases of irregularities and fraud. The simple auditing procedure to verify whether delivery notes have all been invoiced also allows checking access control and permissions, as mentioned by E6P2. Another procedure identified as extremely relevant is automatic bank reconciliation, which checks whether transactions align with accounting records.

Developers and users recognize great value in chatbots when it comes to consulting and searching for internal policies and procedures. Chatbots can provide immediate answers to questions related to audits, organizational policies, operational procedures, etc. One of the developer-profile interviewees highlighted a chatbot for auditing, in which, upon identifying a problem, one can "automatically get a response or a list of tasks and procedures" (E3P1) to resolve the issue.

Regarding chatbots, examples were presented of procedures in which, after reading a document, the tool returns comments and alerts deviations and trends. One tool includes a specialized chatbot used to analyze financial statements, capable of commenting on the information, analyzing and commenting on ratios, generating summaries, and answering questions in seconds, as presented by developer E7P1, stating that "clients see an example with concrete data from a company they know, they clearly see that what is there is correct, it doesn't even miss a comma."

In response to the research question (RQ2) on which ICS procedures can be assisted by AI, document flow and recording, and authorizations and approvals stand out, although ICS procedures are inseparable therefore all others, segregation of duties, reviews and reconciliations, access controls, are impacted.

The Main Characteristics of an AI-Assisted ICS

One of the first findings to highlight regarding the characteristics of an AI-assisted ICS is the fact that all interviewees agreed that the existence and maintenance of an organizational culture that values ICS does not depend on any technology, but rather on a way of being in companies and in business that should begin precisely at top management and extend throughout the organization, with no exceptions.

Secondly, it is also unanimous that there will be as many characteristics strengthened in an AI-assisted ICS as there are compromised ones, depending on the operator's intentions in using it, which may be constructive or destructive.

A specific note regarding segregation of duties. The interviewees identified segregation of duties as a characteristic that can be simultaneously strengthened and compromised. They explained that, on the one hand, AI tools, by enabling greater automation of processes and reducing the need for human intervention, decrease the occurrence of errors and the possibilities of collusion, thus reinforcing segregation of duties; on the other hand, a single person may end up controlling all phases of a process and even jeopardize other characteristics beyond segregation of duties, such as approval and authorization policies and procedures. E2P1 suggests that this concern could be mitigated if AI models are developed in a way that allows for the implementation of controls that specifically ensure that functions remain segregated, thus reducing the risks associated with human intervention.

Strengthened Characteristics

The reinforcement of risk identification and analysis processes was considered by both profiles of interviewees to be linked to the possibility of auditing the entirety of the data. That is, unlike traditional methods that rely on statistical sampling, AI allows for a comprehensive analysis of all available data, making it easier to identify risk areas and potential deviations. Both developers and users mentioned that the fact that technology enables the processing of large volumes of data, and in an automated way, helps identify patterns that would otherwise go unnoticed.

In terms of approval and authorization policies and procedures, the interviewees indicated that since AI facilitates the automation of processes, it makes operations more agile and avoids errors. Thus, in operations such as the receipt of goods, for example, alerts are only generated when there are deviations from the previously approved conditions. This automation of authorizations not only ensures compliance with organizational policies but also reduces processing time and potential manual errors, strengthening trust in ICS.

AI plays a crucial role in facilitating the automation of repetitive tasks and therefore contributes to improving internal and external communications. Regarding information, communication, and monitoring channels, the interviewees highlighted AI's ability to generate automatic responses to frequently asked questions, assist in the preparation of documents and reports, and thus enhance operational efficiency. Additionally, AI can be used for continuous monitoring of transactions and automatic verification of reports, strengthening the ability to detect and correct errors before they cause significant impact.

Finally, regarding independent checks, AI has brought a fundamental shift in the traditional audit approach, eliminating the need for sampling and enabling in-depth analysis of the entire dataset. Most interviewees mentioned the importance of auditing the total population of data. This transformation in auditing strengthens internal controls, allowing monitoring to be performed continuously and in real time, thereby significantly improving the ability to respond to anomalies and potential fraud.

In summary, the implementation of AI strengthens several key features in ICS, making them more efficient, accurate, and capable of handling large volumes of data in an automated manner.

Compromised Characteristics

Despite the benefits that AI brings to ICS, the interviews revealed that some characteristics may be compromised by its implementation.

The main concern expressed by the interviewees is the impact on trust and the need for human supervision of AI systems' operations. Specifically, one issue that worries developers is the users' tendency to "challenge" the system. According to E2P1, there are cases where users may deliberately test the limits of AI, challenging their ability to detect errors or anomalies. This tendency can compromise the effectiveness of the system, especially when users realize that the system has failed to identify an error. Examples like this may lead to a loss of confidence in the system's monitoring capabilities and reliability. This loss of trust may undermine the performance of the ICS, particularly if errors are not quickly identified and corrected.

Another identified risk concerns the over-automation of approval and authorization processes. Interviewee E2P1 pointed out that the reliance on algorithms to make decisions may lead to situations where the system begins to consider anomalous behaviors as normal if a certain pattern is frequently repeated. For instance, an AI system may begin to tolerate small irregularities, such as repeated records of activities occurring outside the expected time frame. The absence of continuous and critical supervision may result in the AI adapting to these human errors, thus compromising the approval mechanisms that are crucial for ensuring compliance.

Additionally, interviewee E1P2 indicated that, although AI is already taking over repetitive tasks, it is still necessary to closely supervise these operations. Without supervision, automation may allow errors to persist, compromising the security and effectiveness of internal processes themselves.

Therefore, if AI implementation is not enhanced and supervised, it may compromise key features of ICS and the overall reliability and integrity of the AI system.

Thus, in response to research question (QI3) - what the main characteristics of an AI-assisted ICS are - it is concluded that the implementation of AI does not alter the inherent characteristics of the ICS. What can in fact be assessed is that the operational changes resulting from AI implementation strengthen more than they compromise the characteristics of the ICS. Therefore, essential ICS characteristics such as risk identification and analysis processes, approval and authorization policies and procedures, segregation of duties, information, communication and monitoring mechanisms, and independent verifications, are reinforced with the implementation of AI.

However, it is important to emphasize that automation must be balanced with human supervision to effectively ensure the efficacy of internal controls.

The Main Challenges in Implementing AI in ICS

One of the main obstacles identified relates to the cost or value of the investment required to implement AI solutions. This factor is mentioned by both developers and users. Developers highlight that AI systems require a substantial financial investment, which can be a barrier for many organizations, especially those planning to make intensive use of this technology. One developer stated that "the financial cost (…) is not low if we are going to make extensive use" (E3P1), reflecting a common concern among AI solution providers. In turn, users also express reluctance to invest, as illustrated by one interviewee who classified investments in AI as substantial and significant.

Another major challenge is the training of people involved in the implementation and use of AI. The lack of proper training can limit the effectiveness of AI tools, and as such, it is essential to prepare people for technological changes. Both developers and users recognize the need for a significant investment in human resource training, with one interviewee emphasizing that "it is very important to train people" (E3P1) to ensure they understand and use the systems properly. Additionally, it was pointed out that the challenge is not only implementation, but also the adaptation of workers to the new tools. One interviewee stated that "the biggest challenge is preparing human resources, not so much for implementation, but for usage" (E6P2), underlining the need for continuous training, starting in schools, so that companies can later take full advantage of AI solutions.

Resistance to change from employees and organizations is another identified obstacle, a recurring factor when introducing innovative technologies. This resistance can manifest in several ways, from reluctance to adopt new working methods to fear that AI will replace workers. Interviewees pointed out that many employees are "used to doing tasks a certain way (…) it is not easy for many people used to certain routines and tasks to give them up" (E7P1). Moreover, uncertainty about AI's impact on jobs can generate insecurity, as one interviewee noted, observing that there is "some insecurity, perhaps some fear that the machine will replace them" (E1P2).

Furthermore, ethics, legislation, and regulation also pose crucial challenges for AI implementation, particularly in the European context. Developers and users expressed concerns about the excessive regulation of AI, which could hinder the development and implementation of innovative solutions. One interviewee emphasized that "the problem for us, here in Europe, is its excessive regulation" (E1P2), referring to the restrictions imposed by the European Union that may limit the potential of some AI technologies. The complexity of ethical and legal issues associated with using data to train AI algorithms was also mentioned, with one developer highlighting that "moral, ethical, legal issues (…) are difficult to scrutinize" (E5P1).

Another challenge raised is the parameterization of existing software and the creation and training of AI models. Implementing AI requires careful configuration and a clear definition of objectives and processes—requirements—so the system can be trained. One developer stated that "the problem starts right at the beginning, which is, in the definition, what it is supposed to be" (E2P1), emphasizing the importance of correct parameterization of existing software so that an AI solution can then function according to the organization's specific needs. The creation and training of models are activities that require time and dedicated human resources, as another developer explained: "these models need to be designed and trained" (E3P1), particularly by preparing or hiring specialized technical teams.

Lastly, data. The quality and quantity of data available for training AI systems are another fundamental challenge. AI depends on large volumes of high-quality data to learn and make effective decisions, but many companies struggle to collect and manage such data. Interviewee E5P1 highlighted that data quality is one of the major challenges, referring to the need to ensure that the data used is reliable and suitable for training algorithms. Furthermore, it was mentioned that for domain-specific AI systems, there may be a lack of data, which limits the potential of AI solutions in certain contexts, such as in healthcare.

In short, in response to the research question (QI4) about the main challenges in implementing AI in ICS, the following challenges are listed: high cost, the need for adequate training, resistance to change, ethical and legal issues, software parameterization, model creation and training, and data quality. These challenges, highlighted by both developers and users, demonstrate the complexity involved in integrating AI into organizational operations, requiring a careful approach and strategic planning to overcome these barriers and maximize both actual and potential benefits.

Discussion of Results

As regards AI technologies applicable to ICS, the analysis of the results shows that the adoption of technologies such as machine learning, RPA, big data, chatbots, and intelligent document recognition is significantly transforming ICS. Interviewees reported the use of trained models for automatic document classification and anomaly detection, highlighting the use of algorithms that continuously learn from accumulated data. These findings align with studies such as Klius et al. (2020), who emphasize the role of emerging technologies, and Wang (2023), who advocates the integration of AI with RPA and cloud to enhance financial automation. Zhu and Shen (2021) e Sun et al. (2025) confirm that the intensity of AI adoption improves ICS quality, while Fan (2022) views these technologies as drivers of transformation across the five components. Chen et al. (2022) and Giudici et al. (2024) also propose decision support models based on machine learning, demonstrating that AI can turn

ICS into a more adaptive, automated, and predictive system. The empirical data thus reinforces the idea that AI application is not merely an operational innovation but a structuring vector in the modernization of ICS.

Regarding ICS procedures that can be supported by AI, empirical results reveal that document and record flow procedures, as well as authorization and approval procedures, are the most impacted by AI implementation. Technologies such as OCR, automated verification systems, and predictive analytics were identified as key drivers of significant improvements in these areas. Automated document management minimizes human error, accelerates processes, and ensures compliance with internal policies. These findings are consistent with studies such as Wang et al. (2020), who integrated AI, blockchain, and cloud for smart audits, and Chen, Wu, and Yan (2022), who applied machine learning to audit 100% of data populations. Monteiro et al. (2023) and Mehta et al. (2021) reinforce the relevance of AI in auditing and financial reporting, while Mohd Noor and Mansor (2019) highlight its usefulness in whistleblowing management. The results show that AI not only transforms technical tasks, such as record-keeping and classification, but also critical decision-making and oversight procedures, consolidating its cross-cutting applicability within ICS.

The characterization of an AI-assisted ICS reveals a significant strengthening of structural attributes such as risk analysis, internal communication, monitoring, and independent verifications. Interviewees indicated that automation helps reduce errors, reinforce segregation of duties, and streamline approvals, although they acknowledged that misuse of technology could compromise those same features. This duality is addressed by authors such as Zhang & Zhang (2021), who proposed a fuzzy-neural model for ICS assessment in SMEs, and Guo (2022), who applied AI to university financial management, achieving gains in accuracy and risk detection. Looi et al. (1989) anticipated this paradigm with the AUDITPRO system, while Wang (2023) demonstrated improvements in internal controls in museums using AI, RPA, and big data. The research data confirm that AI, when applied responsibly, strengthens the core dimensions of ICS, but requires human oversight to prevent distortions and preserve institutional trust.

Finally, regarding challenges in implementing AI in ICS, despite the expected benefits, interviewees identified several challenges in adopting AI in ICS. The high implementation cost, the shortage of qualified professionals, and resistance to change stand out as significant barriers. The need for continuous training and the adaptation of staff to the new technological reality is a consensus, aligning with warnings from Zhu & Shen (2021) and Fan (2022), who emphasize the importance of technical training and ethics. Concerns about excessive regulation, especially in the European context, and difficulties in system parameterization and model training also emerge as obstacles. Hulstijn (2023) further adds the need for a new model of computational accountability for contexts in which decision-makers are no longer human. Xue (2020) and Guo (2022) reinforce that organizational culture and leadership involvement are critical success factors for digitization. Thus, the results show that the adoption of AI requires more than technology—it demands strategic planning, ethics, training, and cultural adaptation.

In summary, the intersection of empirical results with literature reinforces the validity of this study's findings. There is a strong convergence between the perceptions of interviewed professionals and academic contributions regarding the applicability, benefits, and challenges of AI in ICS. The discussion shows that AI, if well integrated, has the potential to profoundly transform ICS, provided it is accompanied by human oversight, continuous training, and a strategic approach to organizational change.

FUTURE RESEARCH DIRECTIONS

The findings of this study point to several avenues for future research on the integration of AI into ICS. The interviews revealed substantial advantages in the use of AI, both from the perspective of developers and users, particularly regarding efficiency gains and optimized time management. Although this was not the primary focus of the investigation, respondents repeatedly emphasized the concept of "AI time" - the reduction of routine tasks and the possibility of redirecting the time saved toward higher value-added activities. Therefore, future research should examine how human resources are reallocated and to which strategic or value-creating tasks are redirected following the adoption of AI in ICS.

Another relevant aspect concerns the confusion between traditional automation and AI. Most developers noted that many organizations have long used automated tools based on programmed algorithms that lack learning and adaptive capabilities. This conceptual overlap often leads to a misunderstanding of AI's actual potential and, consequently, to its underutilization. Hence, future studies should explore the practical and perceptual differences between AI and automation, clarifying conceptual boundaries and identifying the conditions required for a more effective and informed adoption of AI within ICS.

CONCLUSIONS

This research addressed the topic of integrating AI into ICS, aiming to identify the AI technologies useful to ICS, the internal control procedures that can be assisted by AI, to characterize an AI-assisted ICS, and to determine the main challenges in implementing AI in ICS, considering the perspectives of both developers and users of AI-based software.

The results suggest that machine learning for process automation and chatbots are the most well-known and used AI technologies for ICS among the interviewees - whether for automating repetitive processes, supporting decision-making and risk identification, performing automatic data analysis and collection, or integrating AI into audits. This set of evidence collected from the interviews indicates that AI holds high potential to transform and improve ICS, as the solutions presented ensure greater compliance, efficiency, and security in organizational operations.

Regarding the internal control procedures that can be assisted by AI, document, and record flow, as well as authorization and approval processes, stood out. However, because ICS procedures are interdependent, the implementation of AI also influences other areas - such as segregation of duties, reviews and reconciliations, and access controls.

The implementation of AI does not alter the fundamental characteristics of ICS. One of the core elements of an ICS is the organizational culture that values internal control, which, as concluded, should neither be affected by AI implementation nor by any other technology. It was observed that the operational changes resulting from AI implementation tend to strengthen, rather than compromise, the characteristics of ICS. Thus, fundamental ICS features - such as risk identification and analysis processes, approval and authorization policies and procedures, segregation of duties, information, communication and monitoring channels, and independent verifications - are potentially reinforced with the implementation of AI. However, excessive dependence on automated AI solutions may jeopardize aspects like approval and authorization policies and segregation of duties.

The main challenges identified in the implementation of AI in ICS include high cost, the need for adequate training of personnel, resistance to change, ethical and legal issues, software parameterization, model development and training, and data quality. These challenges, pointed out by both developers and users, highlight the complexity involved in integrating AI into organizational operations, requiring a careful approach and strategic planning to overcome these barriers and maximize both the actual and potential benefits.

This investigation aims to contribute to the literature on digital transformation in the economic sciences, particularly in accounting and auditing. It seeks to establish connections between traditional internal control practices and current AI technological tools that may benefit companies, education, and auditing work. For companies, the goal is to offer tools that help define and implement more efficient and effective ICS for decision-making. For education, the intent is to contribute to the modernization of educational systems. AI is changing the nature of work - new jobs will be created, others will disappear, and most will undergo transformation

- thus, it is essential to provide students with the qualifications needed to meet these changes. In auditing, this study aims to promote the shift toward more compliance-based approaches rather than substantive testing, optimizing audit resources.

REFERENCES

Abu Hamour, A. M., Massadeh, D. D. M., & Bshayreh, M. M. (2023). The impact of the COSO control components on the financial performance in the Jordanian banks and the moderating effect of board independence. *Journal of Sustainable Finance & Investment, 13*(1), 161–175. DOI: 10.1080/20430795.2021.1886553

Askary, S., Abu-Ghazaleh, N., & Tahat, Y. A. (2018, Oct 30-Nov 01). Artificial Intelligence and Reliability of Accounting Information. *Lecture Notes in Computer Science* [Challenges and opportunities in the digital era]. 17th International-Federation-of-Information-Processing (IFIP) WG 6.11 Conference on e-Business, e-Services, and e-Society (I3E), Gulf Univ Sci & Technol, Kuwait City, KUWAIT. https://doi.org/DOI: 10.1007/978-3-030-02131-3_28

Caruso, S., Bruccoleri, M., Pietrosi, A., & Scaccianoce, A. (2023). Artificial intelligence to counteract "KPI overload" in business process monitoring: The case of anti-corruption in public organizations. *Business Process Management Journal, 29*(4), 1227–1248. DOI: 10.1108/bpmj-11-2022-0578

Chen, F. H., Hsu, M. F., & Hu, K. H. (2022). Enterprise's internal control for knowledge discovery in a big data environment by an integrated hybrid model. *Information Technology Management, 23*(3), 213–231. DOI: 10.1007/s10799-021-00342-8

Chen, Y., Wu, Z., & Yan, H. (2022). A Full population auditing method based on machine learning. *Sustainability, 14*(24), 17008. DOI: 10.3390/su142417008

Cheng, M. E. (2011, August 8-10). Discussion of chief finance officer system perfection. *2011 2nd Artificial Intelligence, Management Science and Electronic Commerce (AIMSEC 2011),* Deng Feng, China. Deng Feng, China, 2011, pp. 312-315. https://doi.org/DOI: 10.1109/AIMSEC.2011.6010447

Collins, C., Dennehy, D., Conboy, K., & Mikalef, P. (2021). Artificial intelligence in information systems research: A systematic literature review and research agenda. *International Journal of Information Management, 60,* 102383. Advance online publication. DOI: 10.1016/j.ijinfomgt.2021.102383

Commission (2018). *Communication from the Commission to the European Parliament, the European Council, the Council, the European Economic and Social Committee and the Committee of the Regions - Artificial Intelligence for Europe.* https://eur-lex.europa.eu/legal-content/PT/TXT/PDF/?uri=CELEX:52018DC0237

COSO. (2013). *Internal Control - Integrated framework: Executive summary.* https://www.coso.org/_files/ugd/3059fc_1df7d5dd38074006bce8fdf621a942cf.pdf

Costa, A. P., & Amado, J. (2018). *Software-Supported Content Analysis* (2nd ed.). Ludomedia., https://ludomedia.org/publicacoes/e-book-analise-de-conteudo-suportada-por-software-2a-ed/

Coutinho, C. P. (2011). *Research Methodologies in Social Sciences and Humanities: theory and practice* (2nd ed.). Edições Almedina.

Davis, J. T., Massey, A. P., & Lovell, R. E. R. (1997). Supporting a complex audit judgment task: An expert network approach. *European Journal of Operational Research, 103*(2), 350–372. DOI: 10.1016/S0377-2217(97)00125-2

Doganata, Y., & Curbera, F. (2012). Designing an automated audit tool for the targeted risk exposure reduction. In Daniel, F., Barkaoui, K., & Dustdar, S. (Eds.), *Business Process Management Workshops. BPM 2011. Lecture Notes in Business Information Processing* (Vol. 100). Springer., DOI: 10.1007/978-3-642-28115-0_34

Donelson, D. C., Ege, M. S., & Mclnnis, J. M. (2017). Internal control weaknesses and financial reporting fraud. *Auditing: A Journal of Practice & Theory*, 36 (3)-45–69. https://doi.org/DOI: 10.2308/ajpt-51608

Emmanuel, A., Wijaya, M. I., & Riantono, I. E. (2023). Web-Based Accounting Information System Analysis and Design for Inventory and Sales in PT SIP based on Artificial Intelligence Technology. *In Proceedings of the 2023 9th International Conference on Industrial and Business Engineering (ICIBE '23)*. Association for Computing Machinery, New York, 312–318. https://doi.org/DOI: 10.1145/3629378.3629459

Fan, Y. (2022). Research on Internal Control of Yihua Company under Technology of Artificial Intelligence. *2022 2nd International Conference on Social Sciences and Intelligence Management (SSIM)*, Taichung, Taiwan, 2022, pp. 85-89. https://doi.org/DOI: 10.1109/SSIM55504.2022.10047950

Fotoh, L. E., & Lorentzon, J. I. (2023). Audit digitalization and its consequences on the audit expectation gap: A critical perspective. *Accounting Horizons, 37*(1), 43–69. DOI: 10.2308/horizons-2021-027

Giuduci, P., Centurelli, M., & Turchetta, S. (2024). Artificial Intelligence risk measurement. *Expert Systems with Applications, 235*. Advance online publication. DOI: 10.1016/j.eswa.2023.121220

Gonçalves, S. P., Gonçalves, J. P., & Marques, C. G. (2021). *Qualitative research manual: Design, analysis and applications*. Pactor.

Guo, S. (2022). Evaluation method of financial internal control in colleges and universities based on artificial intelligence technology. *Mobile Information Systems*. Advance online publication. DOI: 10.1155/2022/1556150

Henk, O. (2020). Internal control through the lens of institutional work: A systematic literature review [Article]. *Journal of Management Control, 31*(3), 239–273. DOI: 10.1007/s00187-020-00301-4

Hu, K. H., Chen, F. H., Hsu, M. F., & Tzeng, G. H. (2021). Identifying key factors for adopting artificial intelligence-enabled auditing techniques by joint utilization of fuzzy-rough set theory and MRDM technique. *Technological and Economic Development of Economy*, *27*(2), 459–492. DOI: 10.3846/tede.2020.13181

Hulstijn, J. (2023). Computational accountability. *In Proceedings of the Nineteenth International Conference on Artificial Intelligence and Law (ICAIL '23).* Association for Computing Machinery, New York, 121–130. https://doi.org/DOI: 10.1145/3594536.3595122

IBM. (2024). *Artificial intelligence.* https://www.ibm.com/topics/artificial-intelligence

Inácio, H. (2014). *Internal control - Theoretical framework and practical application.* Escolar Editora.

ISACA. (2012). Corporate model for governance and IT management of the organization: COBIT5 - Framework. In. Rolling Meadows.

Jans, M., Depaire, B., & Vanhoof, K. (2011). *Does process mining add to internal auditing? An experience report. Lecture Notes in Business Information Processing* (Vol. 81). Springer., DOI: 10.1007/978-3-642-21759-3_3

Jans, M., & Hosseinpour, M. (2019). How active learning and process mining can act as Continuous Auditing catalyst. *International Journal of Accounting Information Systems, 32*, 44–58. DOI: 10.1016/j.accinf.2018.11.002

Kaplan, A., & Haenlein, M. (2019). Siri, Siri, in my hand: Who's the fairest in the land? On the interpretations, illustrations, and implications of artificial intelligence. *Business Horizons*, *62*(1), 15–25. DOI: 10.1016/j.bushor.2018.08.004

Klius, Y., Ivchenko, Y., & Izhboldina, A. (2020). International approaches to organizing an internal control system at an enterprise in the digital era. *Economic Annals-Xxi*, *185*(9-10), 133–143. DOI: 10.21003/ea.V185-13

Kokina, J., & Blanchette, S. (2019). Early evidence of digital labor in accounting: Innovation with Robotic Process Automation. *International Journal of Accounting Information Systems*, *35*(13), 100431. Advance online publication. DOI: 10.1016/j.accinf.2019.100431

Liu, F. (2011, August 8-10). Cash flow management of modern enterprises under the guidance of the application of internal control. 2011 2nd Artificial Intelligence, Management Science and Electronic Commerce (AIMSEC 2011), Deng Feng, China, 2011, pp. 6176-6178. https://doi.org/DOI: 10.1109/AIMSEC.2011.6009650

Looi, C. K., Tan, S. L., Teow, P. C., & Chan, H. S. (1989). A knowledge-based approach for internal control evaluation. *In Proceedings of the 2nd international conference on Industrial and engineering applications of artificial intelligence and expert systems* - Volume 1 *(IEA/AIE '89)*. Association for Computing Machinery, New York, 254–261. https://doi.org/DOI: 10.1145/66617.66648

Mandilas, A. A., Kourtidis, D., Petasakis, I. E., & Valsamidis, S. I. (2022). Digital Disruption in the Accounting Profession. *International Journal of Knowledge-Based Organizations, 12*(11), 11–19. https://doi.org/https://doi.org/10.4018/ijkbo.305347

Marques, R. P., Santos, H., & Santos, C. (2015). Monitoring organizational transactions in enterprise information systems with continuous assurance requirements. *International Journal of Enterprise Information Systems, 11*(1), 13–32. DOI: 10.4018/ijeis.2015010102

Masdi, M. A. M. M., Hadanan, S. W., Zamain, N. S. A., Hasnan, A. H. A., Julaihi, M. H. S., Sani, B. N. Z., & Kamaluddin, A. M. (2022). Critical analysis on the necessity and techniques used in internal control in accounting operations. *2022 7th International Conference on Business and Industrial Research (ICBIR)*, Bangkok, Thailand, pp. 638-643. https://doi.org/DOI: 10.1109/ICBIR54589.2022.9786431

Mehta, C. K., Kaushik, V., & Bhargav, S. (2021). *A study of the impact of internal control measures on ease of use of forensic audit mediated by artificial intelligence techniques. 2021 Emerging Trends in Industry 4.0 (ETI4.0).* Raigarh., DOI: 10.1109/ETI4.051663.2021.9619447

Microsoft. (2024). Retrieved 05/06/2024 from https://azure.microsoft.com/pt-pt/resources/cloud-computing-dictionary/what-is-machine-learning-platform/

Monteiro, A., Cepêda, C., Da Silva, A. C. F., & Vale, J. (2023). The Relationship between AI Adoption Intensity and Internal Control System and Accounting Information Quality. *Systems, 11*(11), 536. DOI: 10.3390/systems11110536

Morgado, J. C. (2013). *The Case Study in Education Research (4.ª Ed).* De Facto Editors, Santo Tirso.

Noor, N. R. A. M., & Mansor, N. (2019). Exploring the adaptation of artificial intelligence in whistleblowing practice of the internal auditors in Malaysia. *Procedia Computer Science, 163*, 434–439. DOI: 10.1016/j.procs.2019.12.12

PWC. (2019). *Re-inventing Internal Controls in the Digital Age*. https://www.pwc.com/sg/en/publications/assets/reinventing-internal-controls-in-the-digital-age-201904.pdf

Sun, G., Ling, Z., Li, Y., & Xie, C. (2025). Artificial intelligence and financial fraud. *Pacific-Basin Finance Journal, 93*, 102830. DOI: 10.1016/J.PACFIN.2025.102830

Vilelas, J. (2020). *Research - The Process of Knowledge Construction* (3ª Edição ed.). Edições Sílabo, Lisboa.

Wang, K., Zipperle, M., Becherer, M., Gottwalt, F., & Zhang, Y. (2020). An ai-based automated continuous compliance awareness framework (CoCAF) for procurement auditing. *Big Data and Cognitive Computing, 4*(3), 1-14. *Article, 23*. Advance online publication. DOI: 10.3390/bdcc4030023

Wang, S. (2023). Research on the innovation system of computer artificial intelligence technology in museum financial management system. *2023 IEEE 3rd International Conference on Power, Electronics and Computer Applications (ICPECA)*, Shenyang, China, pp. 1483-1487. https://doi.org/DOI: 10.1109/ICPECA56706.2023.10075850

Wang, Y., Gou, Y., Guo, Y., & Wang, H. (2020). Construction of Audit Internal Control Intelligent System Based on Blockchain and Cloud Storage. *2020 4th International Conference on Trends in Electronics and Informatics (ICOEI) (48184)*, Tirunelveli, India, pp. 292-295. https://doi.org/DOI: 10.1109/ICOEI48184.2020.9143061

Werner, M., Wiese, M., & Maas, A. (2021). Embedding process mining into financial statement audits. *International Journal of Accounting Information Systems, 41*, 100514. Advance online publication. DOI: 10.1016/j.accinf.2021.100514

Xue, J. (2020). On the management of accounting files in public institutions based on informatization. *Journal of Physics: Conference Series, 1533*(2), 022055. DOI: 10.1088/1742-6596/1533/2/022055

Zhang, S., & Zhang, D. (2021). Internal control evaluation of small and micro enterprises' sales process based on fuzzy neural network. *2021 International Conference on Computer Network, Electronic and Automation (ICCNEA)*, Xi'an, China, pp. 177-180. https://doi.org/DOI: 10.1109/ICCNEA53019.2021.00047

Zhu, D., & Shen, S. (2021). Artificial intelligence and internal control: A perspective of Chinese enterprises. *2021 33rd Chinese Control and Decision Conference (CCDC)*, Kunming, China, 2021, pp. 4073-4076. https://doi.org/DOI: 10.1109/CCDC52312.2021.9601581

Zong, Z., & Guan, Y. (2024). AI-Driven intelligent data analytics and predictive analysis in Industry 4.0: Transforming knowledge, innovation, and efficiency. *Journal of the Knowledge Economy*. Advance online publication. DOI: 10.1007/S13132-024-02001-Z

KEY TERMS AND DEFINITIONS

Algorithms: Is a set of instructions that are given to a machine (computer) to perform a certain task.

Biometrics: Analyzing human emotional and physical traits, used for access control and identification.

Chatbot: A computer program that simulates human conversations to automatically answer questions and interact with users.

Deep Learning: Is a subarea of machine learning that allows AI models to learn in a similar way to humans, represented by neural networks in which information is encoded with the help of a structure of nodules, which aim to "simulate" the neurons of the human brain.

Machine Learning: Is a sub-area of AI that translates the ability of a computer to "learn" from data, supervised or not.

Natural Language Processing (NLP): Understanding, interpreting, and generating human language.

Robotics: Combining robots with AI to perform tasks more complex than those handled by traditional robots.

Speech Recognition: Converting spoken language into commands or transcribing it into written text.

Text Analytics: Computational analysis of text to make it interpretable by computer systems.

Virtual Agents: Computer-generated virtual individuals that interact with humans across different contexts (B2C, C2B, B2B).

Chapter 2
Management Model for Artifitial Intelligence (MMAI): The Concept

Rafael Ignacio Pérez-Uribe
http://orcid.org/0000-0001-9924-6657
Investproject, Colombia

Maria Teresa Ramírez-Garzón
http://orcid.org/0000-0002-6319-3386
Investproject, Colombia

ABSTRACT

This chapter provides a Management Model for Artifitial Intelligence (MMAI) that, through its application and analysis, enables corporate decision-makers, academics, consultants, and others interested in the topic to seek the best alternatives for AI management, helping them streamline their organizations and achieve the highest standards of profitability, competitiveness, and sustainability. The MMAI is composed of nine key factors: 1) Clear objectives, 2) Ethics and regulation, 3) Data governance, 4) Transparency and explainability, 5) Performance and scalability, 6) Continuous training, 7) Risk management, 8) Integration and compatibility, and 9) Stakeholder engagement. Each factor, in turn, contains a series of variables that explain it. In total, there are twenty-seven (27) variables explained in detail in the theoretical framework of this chapter, which measure four levels ranging from 0 to 100%.

DOI: 10.4018/979-8-2600-0439-5.ch002

INTRODUCTION

"The growing datafication of contemporary life in combination with AI involves the construction of a new reality that is being described as digital" (Salvador et al., 2020, p. 60). "In the world of digital business, one of the biggest challenges posed by the new situation is how to make the best use of the large amount of data, big data, to establish immediate reaction patterns, make predictions and improve the user experience." (Salvador et al., 2020, p. 68 y 69).

All of this has a direct impact on improving digital skills in AI management and the need to propose a model for managing this reality. To speak of MMAI (Management Model for Artificial Intelligence) is to merge a series of "*concepts*" that make dynamic the idea of giving the academic, business and government community a model that allows measuring the level or state of AI management focused on contributing to the sustainability of organizations, including MSMEs., whatever its origin of capital, economic sector and size.

In this sense, it is worth clarifying each of the concepts that make up this proposal:

Model: According to Perez-Uribe and colleagues (Perez-Uribe et al., 2023a), model means "simplification of reality that facilitates its understanding and study" and this concept "is used as a form of representation of some reality or series of realities, of some process or series of processes" (p. 220). According to Arthur Andersen's dictionary of economics and business (1999), model means the "simplification of reality that facilitates its understanding and study" (p. 413).

Management: This concept refers to administration, which is "a human activity through which people seek to obtain results (...) and is developed by executing the processes of planning, organizing, directing, coordinating and controlling" (Ramirez-Cardona and Ramirez-Salazar, 2016, p. 5).

Artificial Intelligence (AI): AI is made up of "large networks of devices that are connected to each other and share information automatically, without the need for direct human intervention" (Mathiver, 2018, p. 28) and according to Devang et al., (2019) quoted by Mathiver (2018, p. 28) it is "the simulation of human intelligence processes by means of machines that extends through capabilities such as voice recognition, decision making, semantic search and various machine learning techniques".

Sustainability: According to Perez-Uribe et al., (2023), "this word comes from the Latin -*Sustineri-,* which means that it can be sustained. Specifically in ecology and economy, that it can be maintained for a long period of time without depleting resources or causing serious damage to the environment. In this sense, entrepreneurs know the importance of sustaining over time by maximizing resources and, above all, taking special care of people and the environment" (p. 221).

"Sustainability and, consequently, the green economy essentially depend on the use or consumption of resources, as well as the capacity of the environment to absorb the waste that society generates. Sustainable development implies the use and consumption of resources, considering that the consumption of the resource does not exceed its regeneration capacity. They are the resources that are regenerated, therefore, the problem lies in the determination and estimation of the inventories of available and necessary resources, as well as the time required for their recovery" (Garzon Castrillon & Ibarra Mares, 2014, p. 54 and 55).

Taking these concepts into account, this chapter will describe the key factors and variables that comprise this model, the levels evaluated, the methodology that should be used to implement it, and the best practices proposed for excellent management of artificial intelligence in an organization.

BACKGROUND

AI Management Models

Some of the most relevant models (Rojas Patiño, 2024):

1. Supervised models: These are trained with labeled data to make accurate predictions. They are useful in applications such as email classification and fraud detection.
2. Deep neural networks: Inspired by the human brain, these networks enable complex pattern learning and are used in image recognition and natural language processing.
3. AI project management models: These are used to improve decision-making in project management by evaluating large volumes of data and optimizing resources.
4. Generative AI models: These use advanced algorithms to create new content, such as images, text, and music, based on learned patterns.
5. Recommender systems: These analyze user behavior to offer personalized suggestions, as in streaming and e-commerce platforms.

Management Model for Artificial Intelligence Structure (MMAI)

Unlike other models that work with AI, this model clearly focuses on the management of AI itself. The MMAI is made up of nine key factors and twenty-seven variables. The Key Factors (KF) are the main elements or basic pillars that allow the administration of an organization to develop an integral management of AI. There are nine KF: 1. Clear Objectives, 2. Ethics and Regulation, 3. Data Governance, 4. Transparency and Explainability, 5. Performance and Scalability, 6. Continuous Training, 7. Risk Management, 8. Integration and Compatibility, and 9. Participation of Stakeholders. In each KF, twenty-seven variables are analyzed (table 1).

Table 1. MMAI Key factors and variables

Key Factors	Variables
1. Clear Objectives: Clear definition of the objectives and purposes of using AI within the organization.	Specific and measurable goals
	Implementation deadlines
	Key Performance Indicators (KPIs)
2. Ethics and Regulation: Ensure that the model complies with relevant laws and regulations, in addition to considering ethical principles.	Compliance with privacy laws
	Ethical impact assessments
	Guidelines on the responsible use of AI
3. Data Governance: Implement policies for data management, ensuring its quality, integrity and security.	Data access and control policies
	Data quality and consistency
	Data protection and anonymization strategies
4. Transparency and Explainability: Guarantee that the algorithms and decisions made by AI are explainable and transparent to users and stakeholders.	Levels of transparency in AI models
	Documentation of processes and decisions
	Methods to explain algorithmic decisions to users and stakeholders
5. Performance and Scalibility: Ensure that the model can perform efficiently and scale according to the needs of the organization.	Response time and latency
	Processing capacity
	Adaptability to different data volumes
6. Continuous Training: Keep the model updated through constant training with new data.	Identifying and mitigating biases associated with AI
	Identification and mitigation of vulnerabilities associated with AI.
	Identification and mitigation of cyber-attacks associated with AI.
	Development of skills in relation to ethics for AI management
7. Risk Management: Identify and mitigate potential risks associated with the use of AI.	Identification of possible failures and vulnerabilities
	Risk mitigation strategies
	Contingency and recovery plans
8. Integration and Compatibility: Ensure that AI integrates well with the organization's existing systems and processes.	Compatibility with existing systems and platforms
	APIs (Application Programming Interfaces) and integration tools
	Interoperability testing
9. Participation of Stakeholders: Involve all interested parties in the design, implementation and maintenance of the model.	Identification and mapping of stakeholders
	Communication and feedback strategies
	Involvement in decision making and development

Source. Authors from Microsoft Copilot. (2025a).

Each of the key factors and their variables will be explained below.

Key Factors and Variables

Clear Objectives

It is necessary to establish specific, measurable goals with a timeframe for implementation, and key performance indicators, to monitor the results and take assertive decisions. AI management is based on jointly implementing best practices, with specific and measurable goals that are integrated into the organization's management process. This process gives priority to innovation and continuous improvement (Microsoft Copilot, 2025).

Considering the above, Garibo-Ignacio et al., (2023) states that having access to data and performing real-time analysis helps managers of organizations to have a more accurate and complete view of the company's status, making it easier to identify trends, early detect problems, and formulate strategies based on updated information. Technological data analysis tools such as AI and Big Data allow for proactive decision-making, thus generating a competitive advantage for organizations.

Business School Madrid (EAE, 2023), concludes that AI goes beyond the automation of daily tasks, AI has become an essential tool that offers different benefits to modern companies such as:

1) AI can use advanced algorithms to process and extract valuable information for the organization. These algorithms allow companies to identify patterns, trends, and hidden relationships in the data, leading to informed and strategic decisions. 2) Detailed customer profiles are created through AI data analysis, based on behavior, purchase histories, and consumption preferences. This information helps organizations to offer their customers tailor-made recommendations, specific content, and make exclusive bargains, making them more competitive in the market, thus improving customer satisfaction, which leads to boosting customer loyalty and retention. 3) By analyzing historical data in real time, AI identifies patterns in processes or systems that can indicate potential problems before they occur, allowing companies to take preventive measures, avoiding unplanned downtime and reducing operating costs. 4) AI enables supply chain optimization and provides advanced analysis and predictions. For example, it helps manage inventory in real time, plan more efficient shipping routes, and adapt quickly to changes in market demand. 5) By analyzing sales data, purchasing patterns, and consumer behavior, AI can accurately forecast future demand for products and services. Based on the results, AI can adjust production, inventory, and marketing strategies and quickly adapt to changing consumer and

market dynamics. 6) AI tailors product and service offers and recommendations individually, allowing for a better understanding of each customer. By personalizing, customer satisfaction is improved, and sales targets are increased. By creating more relevant and effective experiences for their customers thanks to the information provided by AI, companies will achieve greater market success and, consequently, a competitive advantage.

Otto (2011), in his research, emphasizes that data governance objectives, due to their morphology, are formal or functional in nature and are therefore measurable objectives that serve to evaluate the effectiveness of data governance. In his research, Otto (2011) proposes a set of formal objectives related to business objectives aimed at complying with legal and regulatory provisions. Based on his research, he suggests data governance objectives related to risk reduction, business objectives related to customer satisfaction, and objectives aimed at increasing operational efficiency. He also proposes that organizations should establish functional objectives related to the creation of data strategies that consider data management and data quality control.

Ethics and Regulation

In this factor, as part of the MMAI, the following variables are evaluated (Microsoft Copilot, 2025): Compliance with privacy laws, Ethical impact assessments and Guidelines on the responsible use of AI. It is necessary to study these variables because Companies working with AI must ensure they comply with relevant laws and regulations, in addition to considering ethical principles for its management and implementation.

Moran Espinosa (2021) states that AI is not just a tool; therefore, from an ethical perspective, it must be regulated by standards. In this sense, Microsoft Copilot (2025) suggests that organizations, from an ethical and regulatory perspective, must comply with privacy laws such as the GDPR (General Data Protection Regulation), have guidelines on the responsible use of AI, and assess the ethical impact within the organization.

Studies conducted by Villalba (2020) found that when incorporating artificial intelligence into processes, it is essential that this new technology be endowed with values and principles. Therefore, the developers of this technology must be aware of the moral and ethical implications that AI entails in the organization. Seeing the importance of the implications that people have in the development of AI, many companies are currently training their staff (responsible for training machines) in ethical practices that apply to the algorithms that govern AI.

In 2018, the European Parliament, concerned about ethics in the creation of new types of intelligence, developed a first draft of the "Ethics Guide" aimed at promoting the responsible use of artificial intelligence (European Commission, 2018). Villalba (2020) reports that this guide contains moral standards that technology creators must meet, including:

> *Ensuring that AI is human-centered; paying attention to vulnerable groups, such as minors or people with disabilities; respecting fundamental rights and applicable regulations; being technically robust and reliable; operating transparently and not restricting human freedom. (p. 684)*

It is emphasized that ethical responsibility in AI falls on those responsible for both its design and operation. Therefore, more specific design principles must be taken into account, given that the resulting information will affect certain decision-making processes with ethical implications and risks.

The Barcelona Declaration on the Responsible Use of Artificial Intelligence in Europe highlights six key principles: caution regarding intelligent robots due to current limitations in their "common sense" capacity; rigorously testing the reliability and safety of AI systems; ensuring transparency and accountability in decisions that impact users; clearly stating whether the user is interacting with a machine or a person, and if the former, detailing how to contact those responsible; restricting the autonomy of intelligent systems through clear rules; and, finally, precisely defining the role that humans should play (Pineda de Alcazar, 2020, quoting López, 2017).

As suggested above, it is important for organizations to consider privacy laws such as the GDPR. This European Union regulation aims to protect the privacy and personal data of European citizens. The GDPR defines clear and strict rules for the collection, storage, handling, and distribution of personal data, giving individuals greater control over their own information (European Union, 2016).

Data Governance

Data governance is related to implementing access and control policies for data management, ensuring its quality and consistency, and defining integrity and security strategies that enable data protection and anonymization (Microsoft Copilot, 2025).

Salvador Serna (2021), quoting various authors, defines data governance as the framework used to establish rights and responsibilities when making decisions regarding data management and use; that is, understanding the convergence of different areas that share data on processes, quality management, and security, among others. Data governance is associated with valuing data as an organizational asset to be managed; assigning decision-makers and associated tasks; and ensuring data quality and proper use through guidelines and standards (Salvador Serna, 2021, quoting Weber et al., 2009; Khatri and Brown, 2010; Begg and Caira, 2012; and Otto, 2011).

In summary, data governance is related to organizational processes that allow for the assignment of responsibilities and decisions, aligned with the organization's objectives, to drive desirable behavior in the treatment of data as an organizational asset (Salvador Serna 2021, quoting Otto, 2011, p. 24).

Likewise, Khatri & Brown (2010) assert that organizations' need to report a single version of the truth has led them to consider data as a business asset. In their research on data governance, they found a survey conducted in 2006 with 359 organizations in North America, which reported that one of the five key practices for adding business value to data assets is having a data governance program.

Khatri & Brown (2010) focused their study on providing a general framework for data governance. Considering that data governance involves determining who has the authority to make decisions and take responsibility for managing data assets within an organization, they propose five interrelated decision domains, as follows:

1. Data Principle: Provides the framework that guides all remaining decisions, including defining the role of data as a strategic resource and specifying expected behaviors in its use.
2. Data Quality: Establishes prerequisites for data use, including standards for accuracy, timeliness, completeness, and credibility of the data information provided.
3. Metadata: Determines the semantics or content of the data so that users can interpret it.
4. Data access: Defines the necessary conditions to access data, considering risk assessment and its alignment with compliance monitoring initiatives.
5. Data lifecycle: Establishes the guidelines for defining, generating, preserving, and deleting data.

Transparency and Explainability

Transparency and explainability aim to ensure that the algorithms and decisions made by AI are explainable and transparent to users and stakeholders (Microsoft Copilot, 2025).

Ruiz (2022) states that, although AI has become a strategic priority for any organization due to its significant advantages, the consequences its application can have and the risks and negative impact it can cause if not managed transparently must not be overlooked. Algorithms designed by programmers generate new algorithms with an increasingly greater degree of complexity, to the point where their understanding can be impossible. Therefore, the principle of transparency or explainability has become a primary requirement that must be complied with by organizations that integrate AI into their processes.

Ruiz (2020) also indicates that data processing is highly complex because it goes through several hands, making it difficult to track the different responsibilities in the process. Data can be biased since algorithms may be designed with a degree of impartiality, as they depend on the scientists or technicians who programmed them.

Following the same line, Cotino Hueso (2017) argues that the need for transparency and explainability implies a reasonable description of the decisions made by an algorithm. This does not mean revealing every detail about the system's internal mechanisms but rather ensuring accountability. This entails not hiding its traceability, that is, clearly showing the steps followed to achieve a result. To accomplish this, it is essential to understand how AI generates its recommendations, explaining the reasons and criteria that lead it to make a final decision. Therefore, scientific and ethical standards are fundamental in the handling of data with AI.

Although transparency is sometimes associated with revealing the secrets of business algorithms, this is not correct. The amount of information provided must be tailored to the impact the system may have on the rights and freedom of users. It is essential that users understand how the system is developed, trained, operated, and implemented, depending on the specific purpose of its application. Explainability refers to the ability of those involved and affected by the AI process to understand the results. Therefore, it is necessary to know which variables influence the final decision. It can be said, then, that explainability is closely related to transparency, because the results and subprocesses must be understandable and traceable for the different stakeholders involved in the process (Del Pozo et al., 2023).

Del Pozo et al., (2023) conclude that to achieve transparency and explainability, information must be disclosed in the following ways: 1) generate actions that allow stakeholders to understand the AI systems and their interaction with them. 2) allow stakeholders to understand the output of the AI system. 3) facilitate people affected by an AI system to question its results, providing clear and accessible information about the logic and factors that underpinned the prediction, recommendation, or decision.

Performance and Scalability

This factor consists of ensuring that the model can perform efficiently and scale according to the needs of the organization (Pampin Rodriguez, 2024). Three variables are evaluated in this factor (Vargas Diaz, 2022): response time and latency, processing capacity, and adaptability to different data volumes.

Response Time and Latency

Response time is the time it takes from the entry of a question or request until the AI system delivers a response (Romero Paredes, 2025).

Latency is the time it takes a system to process a request from the moment it is received until it is completed, and the response is delivered (Zambrano et al., 2024).

Scalability is the ability of a system to efficiently handle an increase in workload or demand without suffering a significant decrease in performance (Ruiz, 2023).

Processing Capacity

The ideal for AI systems is to operate with exceptional speed and accuracy, handling vast amounts of data and highly complex tasks flawlessly (Rouhiainen, 2018). Best practices involve the use of cutting-edge technologies, scalability, redundancy, and continuous monitoring to ensure consistently superior performance (Quinto et al., 2021).

Adaptability to Different Data Volumes

AI systems exhibit exceptional adaptability to any data volume, using advanced techniques such as horizontal scalability, distributed processing, and dynamic optimization to ensure optimal performance under all conditions (Domecq, 2023). These systems can instantly adapt to changes in data volume without manual intervention, while maintaining high efficiency and accuracy (Vadillo Bueno, 2020).

Continuous Training

Keeping the model up to date through constant training with new data on four variables (Microsoft Copilot, 2025): identifying and mitigating biases, vulnerabilities and cyberattacks associated with AI, and developing skills related to ethics for managing AI.

Bias Identification and Mitigation

For bias identification and mitigation, state-of-the-art tools and techniques must be used to detect and correct biases at all stages of the AI lifecycle (Sanchez-Vasquez & Toro-Valencia, 2021). There is ongoing work to develop a continuous commitment to improving and innovating the fairness and justice of AI systems, including regular external audits and collaboration with ethics experts to ensure that AI models are fair, transparent, and accountable (Cornelio et al., 2024).

Vulnerability Identification and Mitigation

Stating that security is a top priority, state-of-the-art tools and techniques must be used to identify and mitigate vulnerabilities at all stages of the AI lifecycle (Mejia et al., 2024). This includes the use of continuous security audits, penetration testing, and the implementation of advanced security controls, as well as maintaining a culture of constant commitment to improve security and adapting to new threats, ensuring that AI systems are resilient and trustworthy (Payanene, 2024; Garcia Berzosa, 2024).

Identifying and Mitigating Cyberattacks Associated With AI

Just as security is a top priority, cybersecurity is equally so. State-of-the-art tools and techniques must be used to identify and mitigate cyberattacks at all stages of the AI lifecycle (Zhang et al., 2022). Proactive measures such as threat intelligence, vulnerability analysis, and collaboration with cybersecurity experts must be implemented to ensure AI systems are highly resilient and can quickly adapt to new threats, ensuring consistent and robust protection (Shahriar et al., 2023; Abdullahi et al., 2022; Kaur et al., 2023).

Risk Management

Jimenez & Hernandez Cuadrado (2022) state that it is a reality that mainly large organizations have found it necessary to build powerful algorithms to simplify risk analysis using artificial intelligence (AI), which has made it possible to improve customer acquisition and loyalty processes, adjust the offers or prices of their services, their forecasts and, above all, to improve the predictive capacity of their risk management models and to avoid fraud (p.154). This statement allows risk management to be broken down into three variables, (Microsoft Copilot, 2025): Identification of possible failures and vulnerabilities, risk mitigation strategies, and formulation of contingency and recovery plans.

Identification of Potential Failures and Vulnerabilities

The use of cutting-edge tools and techniques, such as predictive analytics and machine learning, is essential for proactively identifying potential issues, in addition to conducting ongoing monitoring through regular, comprehensive audits (Lopez Sempere, 2022, p. 7; Eggers & Sample, 2020). This approach will enable organizations to develop a proactive approach to continuous improvement and adaptation to new threats and vulnerabilities, ensuring the resilience and reliability of AI systems (Mauri & Damiani, 2021; Pala, 2024; Fazelnia et al., 2024).

Risk Mitigation Strategies

Advanced risk management techniques, such as predictive analytics and artificial intelligence, must be used to proactively identify and mitigate risks (Aghware et al., 2025). The use of these techniques must be supported by a detailed contingency plan, so the organization is prepared to respond quickly to any incident (Yazmyradov & Lee, 2024). Companies must work permanently on maintaining a culture of risk management that is integrated at all levels of the organization and developing continuous improvement and adaptation to new threats as a work philosophy (Qureshi et al., 2024).

Formulation of Contingency and Recovery Plans

Contingency and recovery plans are comprehensive and proactive, utilizing advanced techniques such as system redundancy, real-time data replication, and recovery automation (Ambuli et al., 2025). Regular simulations and external audits are conducted to ensure maximum readiness, and the organization is fully prepared to handle any type of incident, minimizing the impact and ensuring a rapid recovery (Mitan, 2024; Peralta et al., 2025).

Integration and Compatibility

To ensure that AI integrates well with the organization's existing systems and processes, this model requires working on the following three variables (Microsoft Copilot, 2025a): Compatibility with existing systems and platforms, LPAs (Language Processing Applications), and integration tools and interoperability testing.

Compatibility With Existing Systems and Platforms

AI systems must be designed with a focus on full interoperability, implementing the latest technologies and best practices, ensuring optimal compatibility with existing systems and platforms (Noura et al., 2019; Vermesan et al., 2022). Integration of AI systems must be unified, ensuring that all the system can work seamlessly with a wide variety of platforms and technologies (Althati et al., 2024). For the above to work optimally, extensive testing must be performed to ensure compatibility, and adaptive solutions must be implemented to maintain compatibility over time (Baqar & Khanda, 2024).

LPAs (Language Processing Applications) and Integration Tools

It is very important to use open standards and cutting-edge protocols to ensure full compatibility and seamless integration with any system or platform, including state-of-the-art and highly efficient LPAs and integration tools (Yusupova & Ismailov, 2024; Hariri, 2023). Preferably, the integration tools used are sophisticated and allow for rapid and scalable implementation (Ilager et al., 2020). Testing and auditing should be performed on a regular basis to ensure that LPAs and tools maintain maximum quality and efficiency (Minkkinen et al., 2022; Li et al., 2024).

Integration Tools and Interoperability Testing

State-of-the-art tools and techniques are used to perform continuous, detailed, cutting-edge, and highly efficient interoperability testing at all stages of the AI lifecycle (Dini et al., 2024; Aminizadeh et al., 2024). Interoperability must be constantly monitored and optimized, ensuring a unified integration with any system and platform (Nookala et al., 2024; Zeid et al., 2019). Regular audits and continuous improvements are critical for system sustainability to maintain maximum quality and efficiency (Qudus, 2025; Chen & Yang, 2025).

Participation of Stakeholders

Involve all interested parties in the design, implementation and maintenance of the model. In this factor three variables are evaluated (Microsoft Copilot, 2025) in the MMAI: Identification and mapping of stakeholders, Communication and feedback strategies and Involvement in decision making and development.

Identification and Mapping of Stakeholders

Stakeholder identification and mapping is a comprehensive and ongoing process in AI management (Kallina & Singh, 2024). The use of advanced tools and techniques to ensure that all IA stakeholders are identified and their influence and priorities are understood, is essential (Wood et al., 2021; Martinez-Pelaez et al., 2023).

Communication and Feedback Strategies

Establishing constant, two-way communication with stakeholders and encouraging their active participation in all stages of AI development and management is important (Ishola et al., 2024), as well as ongoing transparency and collaboration with stakeholders as a priority, resulting in more informed and supported decisions (Deshpande & Sharp, 2022).

In this regard, it is important to emphasize the development of constant, two-way communication with stakeholders and encourage their active participation at all stages of AI development and management (Chukwurah et al., 2024).

Involvement in Decision Making and Development

One of the best management practices for comprehensive and proactive stakeholder engagement and development in decision-making is the use of advanced techniques and collaboration tools to ensure their inclusive and equitable participation throughout the AI process (Camacho et al., 2025). In this AI management process, feedback must be continuous and used to guide each stage of development and decision-making (Kaggwa et al., 2024). Furthermore, a culture of transparency, collaboration, and continuous improvement must be constantly promoted, ensuring that AI systems are developed and managed with responsibility and effectively (Radanliev, 2025).

MAIN FOCUS OF THE CHAPTER

The Levels of Analysis

In the MMAI, four levels of development are evaluated in the Key factors and its variables, as explained below (Meta AI, 2025):

Level 1 (Incipient) (0-25%):

AI is used in isolation and without a clear strategy. Decision-making is based on experience and intuition. There is no systematic monitoring or evaluation of AI performance. Lack of control and oversight. High risk of errors and bias. Difficult to scale and replicate.

Level 2 (Basic) (25,1-50%):

AI is being used more strategically, with clear objectives. AI performance monitoring and evaluation processes are being implemented. More advanced AI tools and techniques are beginning to be used. Significant investment in infrastructure and training is required. Changes in organizational culture may be required. There may still be moderate risks of errors and biases.

Level 3 (Advanced) (51,1%-75%):

AI is used comprehensively and strategically throughout the organization. Continuous improvement and performance optimization processes are implemented. Advanced AI techniques, such as deep learning and natural language processing, are used. A significant investment in technology and talent is required. Major changes to the organizational structure may be necessary. Risks of errors and biases may still exist, but these risks are controlled.

Level 4 (Best Practices) (75,1-100%):

AI is used to transform the organization and create an innovative business model. Continuous innovation and experimentation processes are implemented. Advanced AI techniques, such as machine learning and robotics, are used. A clear vision and leadership regarding AI are maintained. Significant changes in organizational culture and structure are continuously provided. Risks of errors and biases may still exist, but they are managed proactively and strategically.

Methodology

The methodology to be used in the MMAI arises from the authors' experience in the implementation of various management models in different types of companies from various economic sectors: Since 2003, the Modernization Management for Organizations Model (MMOM) (Perez-Uribe et al., 2021, pp. 83-84); since 2016, the Route for Innovation for Sustainability Enterprises model (RISE) (Perez-Uribe et al., 2023b, p. 382); since 2021, the Methodology Network of Trustfulness (MNT) (Perez-Uribe, et al., 2023c, p. 1) and since 2022, the Innovation Model for Organizational Sustainability (IMOS) (Perez-Uribe, et al., 2023c, p. 221).

For these models, the authors structured and formulated the factors and variables for each model in Excel, which can be used in a web-based format. Each factor and variable can be assessed for its maturity level. This can be done in person at organizations or online in virtual meetings to complete the instrument and collect the information.

In this sense, to evaluate the MMAI´s levels of each factor and variable, workers of any level who know the operation of each key factor in the organization must be selected. The following sections must be taken into account: 1) Identification of the organization; 2) Financial data; 3) evaluation of each key factor with its variables; 4) Results (figures formulated for the consolidation of key factors in radar and bars; figure formulated for the consolidated key factors in bars; figure formulated for the consolidation of key factors and variables in bars); 5) completion of the formats for the formulation of the plan to strengthen the management for AI (plan and schedule).

Company Identification

Those interested in this model must fill out the following form (Table 2) to identify the sector, size and specific data of the company: These data are the basis to carry out a study of the economic sector to which the company belongs, and to know the purpose of the company, as shown in the table.

The identification of the company must be completed by either the consultants or the CEO (Chief Executive Officer) with those directly responsible for each factor of the model. The data included in the form is confidential and is used for academic purposes, for specific research projects.

Table 2. Information and business profile

Management Model for Artificial Intelligence (MMAI)				
Information And Company Profile				
Version 1: February 14.2025				
Company Name:				
Recognized Trade Name:				
Creation Date:				
Tax Identification:				
CIIU Code:				
Main Activity (Core business):				
Family Business (Yes / No) (51% or more owned by one or several recognized families; and family members work in it)				
Legal Representative Name				
Contact Name:				
Contact Information (email and mobile phone number)				
Total Number of Plant Workers and Defined Contract				
Number of Workers by Areas (Please enter the name of the main areas of your organization)				
Address and City:				
Company Telephones, landline and mobile				
Web page				
Mark with an x the market coverage served				
	Local	Regional	National	International

continued on following page

Table 2. Continued

Management Model for Artificial Intelligence (MMAI)	
Description of the three representative lines of Products/Services:	
Name of the directly competing companies of the three representative lines of products or services	

Source. Own elaboration from Perez-Uribe et al., (2023a, p. 235)

Financial Profile

In this section, the consultants (in case a consultant applies), the CEO and the person in charge of finances of each organization, are requested to explore in the database of the Relevant Entity of each country or in the database of organizational data, financial statements and results for each year (write down the data in thousands or millions of local currency) that is requested in the model, according to table 3. The purpose of compiling this data is to evaluate each company's financial status and to be able to cross-reference this information with statistical analysis and the information provided by the MMAI variables.

Table 3. Example of financial profile

Name of Company:				
Tax Identification Number (depends on each country):				
Financial statements as of Dec. 31 (In thousands or millions of local currency. mark which one in red) (Last four years)	2021	2022	2023	2024
Initial Information (Enter the Requested Data in These Spaces)				
Total Assets	200,00	300,00	400,00	500,00
Equity	300,00	200,00	1.000,00	600,00
Operating Income	1.500,00	1.600,00	1.600,00	1.700,00
Gross Profit	60,00	70,00	80,00	90,00
Operational Profit	70,00	80,00	90,00	100,00
Earnings and Losses	5,00	10,00	20,00	30,00
Costs	500,00	600,00	700,00	800,00
Expenses	300,00	400,00	500,00	600,00
Ebitda	100,00	200,00	300,00	400,00

Source. Authors from Perez-Uribe et al., (2023a, pps. 235)

The financial indicators in the MMAI are formulated and result automatically (table 4) from the data that has been entered in the previous table (See table 4 and figure 1).

Table 4. Example of financial indicators

Financial Profile				
Indicators	**2021**	**2022**	**2023**	**2024**
Business Items and Indicators				
Return on Assets (ROA) (Operational profit/Total assets) *100	35,00	26,67	22,50	20,00
Return on Equity (ROE) (Profits and losses/Equity) *100	1,67	5,00	2,00	5,00
Net Margin (Profits and losses/Operational Income) *100	0,33	0,63	1,25	1,76
Gross Margin (Gross Profits/Operational Income) *100	4,00	4,38	5,00	5,29
Operating Margin (Operational profit/Operational Income) *100	4,67	5,00	5,63	5,88
Ebitda Margin (Ebitda/Operational Income) *100	6,67	12,50	18,75	23,53

Source. Authors from Perez-Uribe et al., (2023a, p. 237)

The results of the table above can be seen in the following figure:

Figure 1. Financial indicators (example)

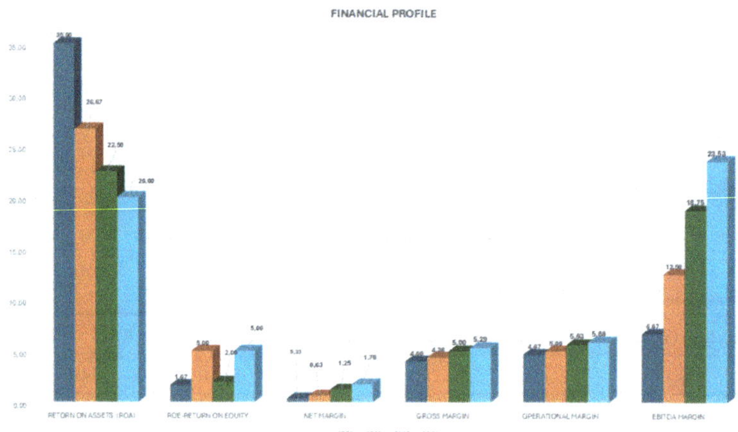

Source. Authors by Authors from Perez-Uribe et al., (2023a, p. 237)

Rating of the Levels of the Factors and Their Variables Proposed in the MMAI

After having filled out the identification data and financial data of the company, the nine key factors are evaluated according to their respective variables, which are those that indicate the characteristics of the level in which the organization is located.

This methodology is what gives added value to the model compared to others that exist in the reviewed literature.

Each factor in its variables is evaluated at the respective maturity levels with scores ranging from 1 to 4, by the individuals selected for this purpose, in matrices formulated in Excel or via the web, depending on the preference of each organization.

That is, they must choose level 1 or 2 or 3 or 4, the only condition is that the people in charge of the evaluation cannot choose two levels in the same row. It is convenient that there are more than two people who know how each factor and variable is being handled in the company. The group discussion on the level and the note that is given to the factors will result in a more objective evaluation (Perez-Uribe et al., 2023a, p. 237).

To contextualize the application of the model, the following table presents an example of the application of the levels in an organization in the "Clear Objectives" factor and its variables (Table 5):

Table 5. Application Example in Clear Objectives levels

1. Clear Objectives: Clear definition of the objectives and purposes of using AI within the organization.					**Rating**		
Variables	Level 1 (Incipient)	Level 2 (Basic)	Level 3 (Advanced)	Level 4 (Best Practices)	Level Variables		Key Factor
Specific and Measurable Goals	AI management is not well defined and lacks clear objectives. There are no performance indicators or established metrics to evaluate success.	AI management includes some specific goals, but performance metrics are not well defined or consistently implemented.	AI management has well-defined specific and measurable goals, with a focus on continuous improvement and performance optimization.	AI management is based on a set of best practices, with specific and measurable goals fully integrated into the management process. Innovation and continuous optimization are prioritized.	**3**	**75%**	
Implementation deadlines	Estimated time needed to reach implementation level: 0-6 months. The implementation of AI is inconsistent and unstructured. There is no dedicated team or specific resources assigned. Lack of clear objectives and performance metrics. Minimal understanding of the benefits and risks of AI.	Estimated time needed to reach implementation level: 6-12 months. An initial team has been created to work on the implementation of AI. There are some allocated resources, but they are limited. Basic objectives and initial metrics have been defined. There is a general understanding of the benefits and risks, but a clear strategy is missing.	Estimated time needed to reach implementation level: 12-18 months. AI is an integral part of daily operations. There are well-defined teams and resources allocated specifically for AI. Clear objectives and advanced performance metrics have been established. The AI strategy is aligned with the overall objectives of the organization. Risk management practices have begun to be implemented.	Estimated time needed to reach implementation level: 18-24 months. AI is fully integrated into all relevant areas of the organization. There is a team of AI experts with extensive and specialized resources. Objectives and performance metrics are detailed and well monitored. The AI strategy is robust and aligned with industry's best practices. Advanced risk management and contingency plans implemented. The organization stays up to date with technological advances and continually regulates its AI practices.	**4**	**100%**	**83,3%**
Key Performance Indicators (KPIs)	- Model accuracy: < 60% - Average implementation time: > 6 months - End user satisfaction: < 50% - Return on investment (ROI): < 5% - Adoption rate: < 30%	- Model accuracy: 60% - 75% - Average implementation time: 4 - 6 months - End user satisfaction: 50% - 70% - Return on Investment (ROI): 5% - 15% - Adoption rate: 30% - 50%	- Model accuracy: 75% - 90% - Average implementation time: 2 - 4 months - End user satisfaction: 70% - 85% - Return on investment (ROI): 15% - 30% - Adoption rate: 50% - 75%	- Model accuracy: > 90% Average implementation time: < 2 months - End user satisfaction: > 85% - Return on investment (ROI): > 30% - Adoption rate: > 75%	**3**	**75%**	

Source. Authors from Microsoft Copilot. (2025).

In this way, the nine key factors are filled out in their variables and the respective levels at which the organization is in AI management at the time the analysis is performed. When automatically finished, the model will give CEO some values where interested parties can observe an X-ray of how the organization is according to the MMAI.

Results

Once each one of the factors with their respective variables has been completed, the figures that are automatically presented can be observed. Continuing with the example of "Clear Objectives" factor, it can be observed (table 6 and Figure 2):

In the "Specific and measurable goals" variable, that the group or person who analyzed this variable rated it at 3 or 75%, presenting an advanced level of maturity.

That the "Implementation Deadlines" variable was rated 4, or 100%, showing best practices in management.

That the "Key Performance Indicators (KPIs)" variable was rated at 3 or 75% maturity, showing that it was at an advanced level of maturity in its management.

Table 6. Result of the evaluation of "Clear Objectives" factor

1. Objectives	**Ranking**		
Variables	Variables Levels		Key Factor
Specific and measurable goals	3	75%	**83,3%**
Implementation deadlines	4	**100%**	
Key Performance Indicators (KPIs)	3	75%	

Source. Authors

The following figure shows the diagram resulting from the previous table.

Figure 2. Results of variables levels in "Clear Objectives" factor

Source. Authors

Once the nine key factors have been completed in their respective variables of the MMAI, a figure 3 will be presented where the levels of each of the variables for each evaluated Factor are consolidated. In this way, it is possible to specifically show which are the factors that are found in levels 1, 2 and 3, in which several activities can be developed to take them to level 4 of world-class best practices.

In the example shown in figure 3, there is a factor (Risk Management) at 41.67%, at basic level 2, which means that activities should be developed as a priority to strengthen their respective variables to bring them to level 4 of best practices. Strengthening actions could also concentrate on the lowest variables of the factors that resulted in level 3 that would allow them to be brought to level 4 of best practices, which are: Continuous training (56.25%), integration and compatibility (58.33%) and performance and scalability (58.33%).

Figure 3. Consolidated Key Factors MMAI

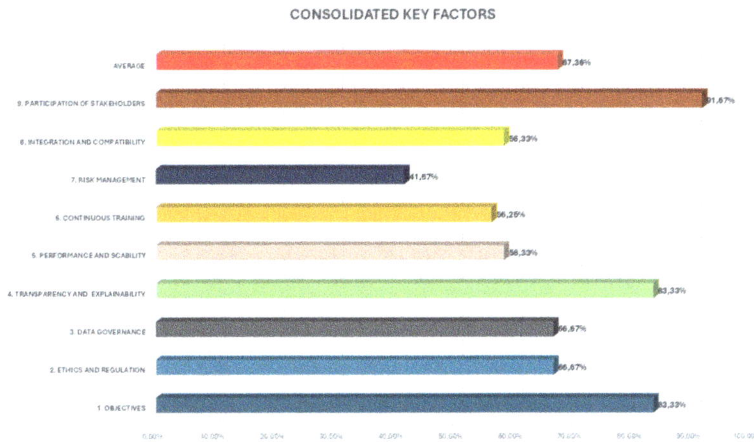

Source. Authors

Continuing with the previous example and having decided to prioritize the risk management factor, we begin to analyze which variables need to be addressed to define strengthening activities. In this case, the variables (Figure 4): Risk mitigation strategies with 25% (incipient level), Identification of possible failures and vulnerabilities (50%) (basic level), and Contingency and recovery plans (50%) (basic level).

Figure 4. Risk management variables

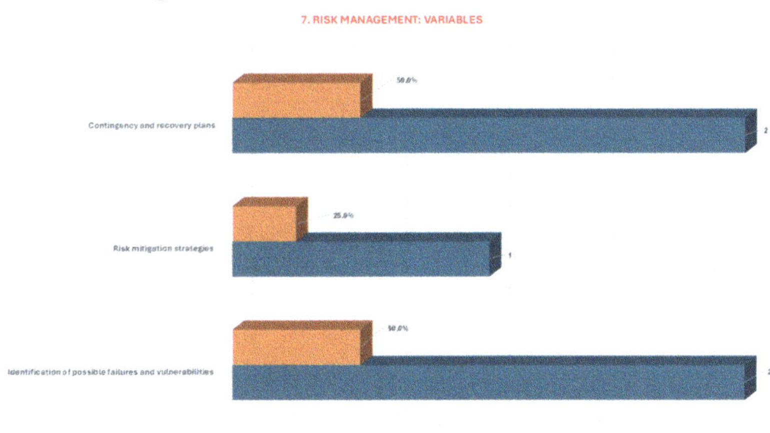

Source. Authors

Strengthening Plan for MMAI

Once the results of the application of the MMAI are evident, according to the priorities of each organization and the economic sector in which it operates, activities to strengthen management for AI must be formulated, considering the following criteria:

Table 7. Priorities for the formulation of activities to strengthen management of AI

Priorities
1 = To urgently start the plan to strengthen AI management in the variables below 25%
2= Develop activities to strengthen AI management in the variables between 25,1% and 50%
3= Validate AI management strengthening activities in the variables between 50,1% and 75%
4= Consolidate and maintain AI management activities for variables between 75,1% and 100%

Source. Authors from Perez-Uribe et al., (2023 a, p. 242)

As an example, returning to tables 5 and 6 on objectives, the following plan and schedule for strengthening management for AI can be seen (table 8 and figure 5):

Table 8. Example Format for structuring the plan of activities to strengthen management for AI

Strengthening plan for mmai management (mmai): mmai plan (short term-less than a year-). Example						
Key Factor	Variables activities	Priority	Resources (By Year)		Duration in Months	Responsible for the Evaluation of the Activity
			US $	Execution Responsible		
Clear Objectives	**Specific and measurable goals:** Development of AI management with specific and measurable goals, broad and specialized resources, prioritizing innovation and continuous optimization, through a team of AI experts fully integrated with the strategic direction of the company, with all relevant areas of the organization and aligned with the best practices in the industry.	**3**	$ -	**Chief Knowledge and Artificial Intelligence Officer**	**2**	**Management Committee**
	Key Performance Indicators (KPIs) Meet the following goals: Model accuracy: >90%; Average implementation time: < 2 months; End user satisfaction: > 85%; Return on investment (ROI): > 30%; Adoption rate: > 75%: Model accuracy: >90%; Average implementation time: < 2 months; End user satisfaction: > 85%; Return on investment (ROI): > 30%; Adoption rate: > 75%	**3**	$ -		**3**	
Budget Mmai One Year			**$ -**			

Source. Authors from Perez-Uribe et al., (2023 a, p. 244)

In the next figure the Gantt chart corresponding to Table 8 is presented.

Figure 5. Example Schedule format for formulating activities to strengthen management for AI

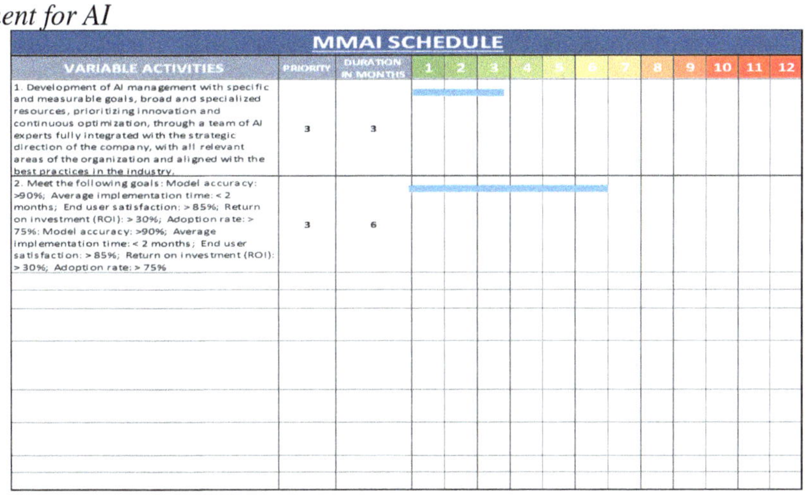

Source. Authors from Perez-Uribe et al., (2023 a, p. 245)

CONCLUSION AND RECOMMENDATIONS

Based on the experiences of applying some models developed by the authors in companies located in Colombia such as: MMOM (Parra-Moreno & Perez-Uribe, 2022; Perez-Uribe et al., 2021), and RISE Model (Perez-Uribe et al., 2023b) and IMOS (Perez-Uribe et al., 2023 a), databases have been built that have allowed inferences to be made between variables, thereby providing concepts on management in different types of organizations. This effort has made it possible to write various articles and book chapters that have served to enrich new research on the topics of modernization, innovation, sustainability and their relationship with management.

AI has strategic relevance due to the increasing digitalization that has boosted interest in artificial intelligence, recognizing it as a driver for improving decision-making and organizational performance. That is why the methodological proposal of MGIA with its 9 key factors and 27 variables, evaluated at four levels of maturity, will allow to objectively diagnose the use of AI in organizations.

This model is characterized by its practical and collaborative application since the evaluation can be carried out through meetings with managers and key teams, promoting honest and participatory analyses to assess the current state of AI management.

Data collection allows for statistical analysis and the discovery of managerial patterns, positioning this chapter as a comprehensive guide to applying MGIA in various contexts.

It would be very constructive for the academy and the organizations to extend the application of MMAI that will allow deepening in the Key factors and variables that are considered in it.

Academics, consultants and managers are recommended to be guided by the point of structure of the model described in this chapter, when it comes to carrying out activities to achieve the best practices of AI for world-class management and in general of course of the methodology explained in this writing (to request the AI management matrix in Excel send a message to ripudos@gmail.com or mariateresa_rg@yahoo.es).

FUTURE RESEARCH DIRECTIONS

To the extent that this model is applied by the academic, consultants and business community in accordance with the instructions given in this chapter and its results are sent to the authors' emails, a database with which statistical analyzes can be carried out in which data can be crossed and hypotheses inferred: Countries, size of organizations, sectors, financial results, key factors and variables.

Examples of these works have been carried out with the MMAI parent models (MMOM, RISE and IMOS) and have been published in several IGI books, as seen in the references.

REFERENCES

Abdullahi, M., Baashar, Y., Alhussian, H., Alwadain, A., Aziz, N., Capretz, L. F., & Abdulkadir, S. J. (2022). Detecting cybersecurity attacks on the internet of things using artificial intelligence methods: A systematic literature review. *Electronics (Basel)*, *11*(2), 198.

Aghware, F. O., Okoh, O. L., & Malasowe, B. O. (2025). *Security Implications and Risk Mitigation Strategies in the Implementation of Artificial Intelligence for Sustainable Development.* Covenant University Journal of Politics and International Affairs.

Althati, C., Tomar, M., & Shanmugam, L. (2024). Enhancing Data Integration and Management: The Role of AI and Machine Learning in Modern Data Platforms. *Journal of Artificial Intelligence General science (JAIGS) ISSN: 3006-4023, 2*(1), 220-232.

Ambuli, T. V., Vikram, G., Devendran, A., Logesh, S. K., Aancy, H. M., & Sudhakar, M. (2025). Strategic Integration of Smart Digital Business Continuity and Configuration Management. In *Essential Information Systems Service Management* (pp. 133–162). IGI Global.

Aminizadeh, S., Heidari, A., Dehghan, M., Toumaj, S., Rezaei, M., Navimipour, N. J., & Unal, M. (2024). Opportunities and challenges of artificial intelligence and distributed systems to improve the quality of healthcare service. *Artificial Intelligence in Medicine*, *149*, 102779. PMID: 38462281

Andersen, A. (1999). *Dictionary of economics and business, Model.* Editorial Espasa Siglo XXI.

Baqar, M., & Khanda, R. (2024). The Future of Software Testing: AI-Powered Test Case Generation and Validation. *arXiv preprint arXiv:2409.05808.*

Business School Madrid [EAE]. (2023, December 8). *AI Objectives.* https://www.eaemadrid.com/es/blog/objetivo-inteligencia-artificial

Camacho, M., Perramon, J., Puig-Bosch, X., Dang, V. N., Diaz, O., & Lekadir, K. (2025). Stakeholder engagement: the path to trustworthy AI in healthcare. In *Trustworthy AI in Medical Imaging* (pp. 471–493). Academic Press.

Chen, S., & Yang, J. (2025). Intelligent manufacturing, auditor selection and audit quality. *Management Decision*, *63*(3), 964–997.

Chukwurah, N., Ige, A. B., Idemudia, C., & Adebayo, V. I. (2024). Strategies for engaging stakeholders in data governance: Building effective communication and collaboration. *Open Access Res J Multidiscip Stud, 8*(1), 057-67.

Cornelio, O. M., Rodriguez, A. R., Alava, W. L. S., Mora, P. G. A., Mera, L. M. S., & Bravo, B. J. P. (2024). *Artificial Intelligence: Challenges for Education.* Editorial Internacional Alema.

Cotino Hueso, L. (2017). Big data and artificial intelligence: An approach to their legal treatment from the perspective of fundamental rights. *Dilemata*, (24), 131-150. https://dialnet.unirioja.es/servlet/articulo?codigo=6066829

Del Pozo, C., Nuno Gomes de Andrade, N., & Rojas Arroyo, D. (2023). *Prototype of public policies on transparency and explainability of artificial intelligence systems.* https://openloop. org/reports/2023/10/Prototipo-de-Politicas-Publicas-sobre-Transparencia-y-Explicabilidad-de-Sistemas-de-IA.pdf

Deshpande, A., & Sharp, H. (2022, July). Responsible AI systems: who are the stakeholders? In *Proceedings of the 2022 AAAI/ACM Conference on AI, Ethics, and Society* (pp. 227-236).

Dini, P., Diana, L., Elhanashi, A., & Saponara, S. (2024). Overview of AI-models and tools in embedded IIoT applications. *Electronics (Basel), 13*(12), 2322.

Domecq, H. M. (2023). *Artificial intelligence as an intelligence tool in the decision-making process at the operational level.* https://cefadigital.edu.ar/bitstream/1847939/2956/1/TFI%2027-2023%20DOMECQ.pdf

Eggers, S. L., & Sample, C. (2020). *Vulnerabilities in artificial intelligence and machine learning applications and data* (No. INL/RPT-22-66111-Rev000). Idaho National Lab.(INL), Idaho Falls, ID (United States).

European Commission. (2018). *Artificial intelligence for Europe.* https://ec.europa .eu/digital-single-market/en/news/communication-artificialintelligence-europe

European Union. (2016). *Regulation (EU) 2016/679 of the European Parliament and of the Council.*www.boe.es/doue/2016/119/L00001-00088.pdf

Fazelnia, M., Moshtari, S., & Mirakhorli, M. (2024). Establishing Minimum Elements for Effective Vulnerability Management in AI Software. *arXiv preprint arXiv:2411.11317.*

Garcia Berzosa, H. (2024). *Security and privacy: How to assess security in an AI-based system?*https://openaccess.uoc.edu/bitstream/10609/149664/1/hgarciaberTFM0124memoria.pdf

Garibo-Ignacio, G., Najera-Bautista, A., & Parra-Barrios, H. (2023). A theoretical look at business administration in the digital age: The administrative process and the artificial intelligence revolution. *Technological Innovations Journal*, *2*(4), 7–19. DOI: 10.35622/j.ti.2023.04.001

Garzon Castrillon, M. A., & Ibarra Mares, A. (2014). Review of Business Sustainability. *Journal of Advanced Leadership Studies,* 2014, Volume 1, Number 3. https://www.regent.edu/acad/global/publications/real/vol1no3/4-castrillon.pdf

Hariri, W. (2023). Unlocking the potential of ChatGPT: A comprehensive exploration of its applications, advantages, limitations, and future directions in natural language processing. *arXiv preprint arXiv:2304.02017.*

Ilager, S., Muralidhar, R., & Buyya, R. (2020, October). *Artificial intelligence (ai)-centric management of resources in modern distributed computing systems. In 2020 IEEE Cloud Summit*. IEEE.

Ishola, A. O., Odunaiya, O. G., & Soyombo, O. T. (2024). Stakeholder communication framework for successful implementation of community-based renewable energy projects. *International Journal of Frontiers in Science and Technology Research.* https://frontiersrj.com/journals/ijfstr/

Jimenez, I., & Hernandez Cuadrado, L. (2022). Credit risk management in the era of artificial intelligence. *Economía Industrial*, *423*, 153–164.

Kaggwa, S., Eleogu, T. F., Okonkwo, F., Farayola, O. A., Uwaoma, P. U., & Akinoso, A. (2024). AI in decision-making: Transforming business strategies. *International Journal of Research and Scientific Innovation*, *10*(12), 423–444.

Kallina, E., & Singh, J. (2024, October). Stakeholder Involvement for Responsible AI Development: A Process Framework. In *Proceedings of the 4th ACM Conference on Equity and Access in Algorithms, Mechanisms, and Optimization* (pp. 1-14).

Kaur, R., Gabrijelčič, D., & Klobučar, T. (2023). Artificial intelligence for cybersecurity: Literature review and future research directions. *Information Fusion*, *97*, 101804.

Khatri, V., & Brown, C. V. (2010). Designing data governance. *Communications of the ACM*, *53*(1), 148–152. DOI: 10.1145/1629175.1629210

Li, N., Kim, M., Dai, J., & Vasarhelyi, M. A. (2024). Using artificial intelligence in ESG assurance. *Journal of Emerging Technologies in Accounting*, *21*(2), 83–99.

Lopez Sempere, A. (2022). *Identification and detection of vulnerabilities.* (Doctoral dissertation, Universitat Politecnica de Valencia).

Martinez-Pelaez, R., Ochoa-Brust, A., Rivera, S., Felix, V. G., Ostos, R., Brito, H., & Mena, L. J. (2023). Role of digital transformation for achieving sustainability: Mediated role of stakeholders, key capabilities, and technology. *Sustainability, 15*(14), 11221.

Mathiver, V. (2018). *Artificial Intelligence for Developers: Concepts and Implementation in C.* Ediciones Eni.

Mauri, L., & Damiani, E. (2021). Stride-ai: An approach to identifying vulnerabilities of machine learning assets. In *2021 IEEE International conference on cyber security and resilience (CSR)* (pp. 147-154). July. IEEE.

Mejia, R. C., Nuñez, M. A., Villanueva, E., & Jaraba, I. (2024). Risk Management: A Business Approach. Revised, Updated, and Expanded Second Edition. Universidad Eafit.

Meta AI (2025). *Levels of Development of Artificial Intelligence Management.* Authors conversation with an AI assistant on March 1, 2025.

Microsoft Copilot (2025a). *Key factors and variables in AI management.* Authors conversation with an AI assistant on February 6, 2025.

Microsoft Copilot. (2025b). *Levels in clear objectives.* Authors conversation with an AI assistant on February 11, 2025.

Minkkinen, M., Laine, J., & Mäntymäki, M. (2022). Continuous auditing of artificial intelligence: A conceptualization and assessment of tools and frameworks. *Digital Society : Ethics, Socio-Legal and Governance of Digital Technology, 1*(3), 21.

Mitan, J. (2024). *Enhancing Audit Quality through Artificial Intelligence: An External Auditing Perspective.* Accounting Undergraduate Honors Theses. https://scholarworks.uark.edu/acctuht/58

Moran Espinosa, A., (2021). Criminal Liability of Artificial Intelligence (AI): The Next Frontier? *IUS. Revista del Instituto de Ciencias Jurídicas de Puebla A.C., 15*(48), 289-323. https://doi.org/DOI: 10.35487/rius.v15i48.2021.706

Nookala, G., Gade, K. R., Dulam, N., & Thumburu, S. K. R. (2024). Governance for Data Ecosystems: Managing Compliance, Privacy, and Interoperability. *MZ Journal of Artificial Intelligence, 1*(2).

Noura, M., Atiquzzaman, M., & Gaedke, M. (2019). Interoperability in internet of things: Taxonomies and open challenges. *Mobile Networks and Applications, 24*, 796–809.

Otto, B. (2011). A morphology of the organization of data governance. [Conference]. *European Conference on Information Systems (ECIS),* Helsinki, Finland. https://aisel.aisnet.org/ecis2011/272

Pala, S. K. (2024). Study to Develop AI Models for Early Detection of Network Vulnerabilities. *International Journal of Enhanced Research in Science, Technology & Engineering ISSN*, 2319-7463. Vol. 13 Issue 2, February.

Pampin Rodriguez, A. (2024). *Scalability and Efficiency in Artificial Intelligence through Green Federated Algorithms.* Final Degree Project, 2023/2024 Academic Year. Degree in Industrial Technology Engineering. Universidad Da Coruña. https://ruc.udc.es/dspace/bitstream/handle/2183/39572/PampinRodriguez_Abel_TFG_2024.pdf?sequence=2

Parra-Moreno, C. F., & Perez-Uribe, R. (2022). Modernization model for organizational management (MMOM) applied to a Public University (UP) in Colombia. Junio 7 de 2022. 14 p. DOI: DOI: 10.13140/RG.2.2.25620.78727

Payanene, L. Y. (2024). *Artificial Intelligence: A Risk or a Tool for the Practice of Law?* https://repository.ucc.edu.co/server/api/core/bitstreams/c5b5ca9b-4ad6-4bcc-a276-81914a34f7a8/content

Peralta, A., Olivas, J. A., Romero, F. P., & Navarro-Illana, P. (2025). Intelligent Incident Management Leveraging Artificial Intelligence, Knowledge Engineering, and Mathematical Models in Enterprise Operations. *Mathematics, 13*(7), 1055.

Perez-Uribe, R. Ramirez - Salazar, MDP., and Ramirez - Garzon, MT. (2023a). *Innovation Model for Organizational Sustainability (IMOS): The Concept.* Chapter 10. (Pps. 220-254). Pages: 35. DOI: DOI: 10.4018/978-1-6684-8223-0.ch010

Perez-Uribe, R., Lozano-Correa, LJ., Salcedo-Perez, C., and Moscoso-Duran, FF. (2023c). *Factors That Explain a Sustainable Organizational Culture in Medium-Sized Colombian Companies.* Copyright: © 2023 |Pages: 15. Pps. 1-15. DOI: .DOI: 10.4018/978-1-6684-6140-2.ch001

Perez-Uribe, R., Salcedo-Perez, C., and Ramírez-Salazar, MdP. (2021). *Organizational Components That Explain the Strategic Direction of SMEs for a New World Economic Order: The Case of Colombia.* Pps. 80-98. 19 pps. DOI: .DOI: 10.4018/978-1-7998-7689-2.ch005

Perez-Uribe, RI., Ocampo-Guzman, D., Moscoso-Duran, FF., Salcedo-Perez, C. & Munoz Maya, CM. (2023b). *Happiness at Work in Colombian Companies: A Perspective Under the Rise Model.* DOI: .DOI: 10.4018/978-1-6684-8822-5.ch019

Pineda de Alcazar, M. (2020). Dilemmas in communication sciences in the transition to encountering intelligent machines. *Quorum Académico, 17*(1), 39-51. https://www.redalyc.org/articulo.oa?id=199062926002

Qudus, L. (2025). Leveraging Artificial Intelligence to Enhance Process Control and Improve Efficiency in Manufacturing Industries. *International Journal of Computer Applications Technology and Research, 14*(02), 18–38.

Quinto, N. M. D., Villodas, A. J. C., Montero, C. P. C., Cueva, D. L. E., & Vera, S. A. N. (2021). Artificial Intelligence and Managerial Decision-Making. *Research Journal Added Value, 8*(1), 52–69.

Qureshi, N. I., Garg, A., Singh, P., & Retzlaff, N. (2024, April). AI and Corporate Risk Management: Identifying and Mitigating Technological and Ethical Risks. In *2024 International Conference on Knowledge Engineering and Communication Systems (ICKECS)* (Vol. 1, pp. 1-5). IEEE.

Radanliev, P. (2025). Cyber diplomacy: Defining the opportunities for cybersecurity and risks from Artificial Intelligence, IoT, Blockchains, and Quantum Computing. *Journal of Cyber Security Technology, 9*(1), 28–78.

Ramirez-Cardona, C., and Ramirez -Salazar, MdP (2016). *Fundamentals of Management. Fourth Edition.* Ecoe Ediciones. Bogotá, Colombia.

Rojas Patiño, E. (2024). *Application of artificial intelligence models to support decision-making within the framework of project management.* National Open and Distance University (UNAD). School of Basic Sciences, Technology, and Engineering (ECBTI). Master's Degree in Project Management.

Romero Paredes, L. E. (2025). *Execution of artificial intelligence algorithms in real-time systems* (master's thesis, Universitat Politècnica de Catalunya). https://upcommons.upc.edu/bitstream/handle/2117/425033/TFM_Memoria_Luis_Romero_Paredes.pdf?sequence=2,https://upcommons.upc.edu/bitstream/handle/2117/425033/TFM_Resumen_Luis_Romero_Paredes.pdf?sequence=3,https://upcommons.upc.edu/bitstream/handle/2117/425033/TFM_Anexos.zip?sequence=4

Rouhiainen, L. (2018). [*Things You Should Know Today About Our Future.* Editorial Planeta.]. *Artificial Intelligence,* •••, 101.

Ruiz, A. E. C. (2023). Digital Transformation for Scalability. *Systems Journal,* (169), 8–13.

Ruiz, F. J. B. (2022). The Transparency Paradox in AI: Opacity and Explainability. Attribution of Responsibility. *International Journal of Political Thought, 17,* 261–272.

Salvador, V. L., Mamaqi, X., & Bordes, F. J. V. (2020). Artificial Intelligence: Theoretical, educational, and communicative challenges of datafication. *Icono14, 18*(1), 58-88.

Salvador Serna, M., (2021). Artificial intelligence and data governance in public administrations: reflections and evidence for its development. *Public Policy Management and Analysis*, (26), 20-32. ttps://DOI: <ALIGNMENT.qj></ALIGNMENT>10.24965/gapp.i26.10855

Sanchez Vasquez, C., & Toro-Valencia, J. (2021). The Right to Human Control: A Legal Response to Artificial Intelligence. *Chilean Journal of Law and Technology, 10*(2), 211–228.

Shahriar, S., Allana, S., Hazratifard, S. M., & Dara, R. (2023). A survey of privacy risks and mitigation strategies in the artificial intelligence life cycle. *IEEE Access : Practical Innovations, Open Solutions, 11*, 61829–61854.

Vadillo Bueno, G. (2020). Futures of Artificial Intelligence. *Digital University Journal, 21*(1).

Vargas Diaz, J. H. (2022). *Interoperability, scalability, and security performance in communications of an electric power microgrid.* Doctoral dissertation, Universidad Nacional de Colombia. https://repositorio.unal.edu.co/bitstream/handle/unal/81778/71366200.2022.pdf?sequence=1

Vermesan, O., Bröring, A., Tragos, E., Serrano, M., Bacciu, D., Chessa, S., & Bahr, R. (2022). Internet of robotic things–converging sensing/actuating, hyperconnectivity, artificial intelligence and IoT platforms. In *Cognitive hyperconnected digital transformation* (pp. 97–155). River Publishers.

Villalba, J. F. (2020). Algor-ethics: Ethics in artificial intelligence. *Anales de la Facultad de Ciencias Juridicas y Sociales de la Universidad Nacional de La Plata*, (50), 679–698. DOI: 10.24215/25916386e062

Wood, D. J., Mitchell, R. K., Agle, B. R., & Bryan, L. M. (2021). Stakeholder identification and salience after 20 years: Progress, problems, and prospects. *Business & Society, 60*(1), 196–245.

Yazmyradov, S., & Lee, H. J. (2024). A Comprehensive Review of AI Security: Threats, Challenges, and Mitigation Strategies. *International Journal of Internet. Broadcasting and Communication, 16*(4), 375–384.

Yusupova, M., & Ismailov, T. (2024). Integration of Artificial Intelligence (AI) in ELT. *Nordic_Press, 3*(0003).

Zambrano, F. R., Delgado, P. F. V., Loor, M. J. Z., Zambrano, B. Y. V., & Zambrano, M. T. Z. (2024). Oreo Bot, a multifunctional AI assistant. Scientific Journal: *Biotech and Engineering, 4*(2).

Zeid, A., Sundaram, S., Moghaddam, M., Kamarthi, S., & Marion, T. (2019). Interoperability in smart manufacturing: Research challenges. *Machines (Basel), 7*(2), 21.

Zhang, Z., Al Hamadi, H., Damiani, E., Yeun, C. Y., & Taher, F. (2022). Explainable artificial intelligence applications in cyber security: State-of-the-art in research. *IEEE Access : Practical Innovations, Open Solutions, 10*, 93104–93139.

KEY TERMS AND DEFINITIONS

Artificial Intelligence (AI): Is a discipline that seeks to create algorithms and systems that can imitate human intelligence to perform complex tasks autonomously, such as perception, decision-making, or learning. It is also the ability of machines to use algorithms, learn from data, and use what they learn in decision-making, just as humans do.

IMOS: (Innovation Model for Organization Sustainability): It is made up of eight organizational components: Strategic direction, production and/or commercialization and/or transformation of goods and/or services, organizational culture, associativity, marketing, technology, legal matters, and financial indicators. In turn, each component analyzes four factors: social, environmental, Managerial and innovation. In each factor, a series of variables are presented (42), which allow four levels to be measured from one to four: one (emerging), two (survival), three (developing) and four (world class).

MMAI: (Management Model for Artificial Intelligence): Model that serves to evaluate the level of maturity in four levels of development of artificial intelligence management in an organization, based on nine key factors and twenty-eight variables.

MMOM: (Modernization Model for Organizations Management): It is a management model which allows SMEs to evaluate their management status in the light of four levels, the fourth level being the best management practices.

RISE: Route of Innovation and Sustainability for Enterprises, is a model that allows to measure the level of innovation and sustainability of organizations in the light of nine factors, four dimensions and thirty-six variables, on a scale from 0 to 100%.

Chapter 3
Efficiency and Sustainability in Co-Ownership:
Utilizing Both the Balanced Scorecard and Artificial Intelligence

Edward Yecid Torres Nova
http://orcid.org/0000-0001-5312-8639
Universidad Nacional Abierta y a Distancia, Colombia

Andrea del Pilar Barrera Ortegón
http://orcid.org/0000-0002-1286-2623
Universidad Nacional Abierta y a Distancia, Colombia

William Camilo Martinez Sanabria
Universidad Nacional Abierta y a Distancia, Colombia

Neixon Fabian Rincón Ronderos
http://orcid.org/0009-0005-1090-3451
Universidad Nacional de Colombia, Colombia

ABSTRACT

This study analyzes management performance in residential condominiums in Usaquén, Bogotá, comparing those using a Balanced Scorecard supported by artificial intelligence-A with those without AI. Using qualitative methods and data from 50 property managers through semi-structured interviews, results show that AI-enhanced BSCs improve financial liquidity, reduce delinquency, decrease social

DOI: 10.4018/979-8-2600-0439-5.ch003

and operational incidents, and yield better management evaluations. AI enables real-time monitoring, enhances decision-making, and promotes sustainability by automating processes and anticipating potential issues. Findings suggest integrating AI into the BSC strengthens strategic alignment, transparency, and operational efficiency. Successful implementation requires digital literacy, ethical data use, and active resident engagement. The study recommends gradual digital transformation focusing on finance and maintenance. The AI-enabled BSC is a strategic tool for fostering sustainable, resilient, and efficient residential communities, highlighting opportunities for technology adoption in the sector.

INTRODUCTION

The Balanced Scorecard (BSC) is a strategic management methodology that harmonizes widely used financial performance metrics over time, with measures from three additional perspectives, such as: customers, internal processes, learning and growth, perspectives or aspects of management that are articulated with each other to provide a comprehensive view of performance (Mio et al., 2022). In this sense, management objectives develop cause-and-effect relationships, where the performance results of some impact the performance of others.

Since its introduction by Kaplan & Norton in (1992), the Balanced Scorecard has been widely adopted as a strategic management tool by organizations across various sectors. Its implementation has evolved from a model focused primarily on financial metrics to a more comprehensive approach that links organizational strategy with operational execution, resulting in significant impacts on organizational culture and performance measurement (Madsen, 2025).

The implementation of a BSC has a positive impact on decision making processes, reducing time, and increasing accuracy. This is especially valuable in volatile environments, characterized by constant change and high levels of uncertainty; however, it must be kept in mind that the BSC must be accurately formulated because it is not infallible, and, although it is very successful when created and managed correctly, high failure rates have also been estimated (Tawse and Tabesh, 2023).

An increasing number of organizations are acknowledging the need to integrate sustainability criteria into their strategic planning to promote sustainable development. In this context, the Balanced Scorecard has proven effective due to its ability to adapt to different organizations and environments. According to Mio, et al. (2022), one of its advanced variants is the sustainable Balanced Scorecard, which broadens traditional perspectives by integrating economic, environmental, social, and ethical dimensions. Some studies highlight its usefulness as a management and control tool, capable of responding to the current demands of the market, industry, legislation, or society.

Precisely, the BSC, considered in accordance with the current context, should incorporate real-time data collection through artificial intelligence tools, allowing for the optimization of operations, efficiency, and sustainability. In line with this, Żółtowski (2022) stresses the importance of integrating AI and BSC and argues that AI can improve the measurement and analysis of performance indicators, which, in turn, facilitates the decision-making process and management control.

The objective of this study is to conduct a comparative analysis of the management of residential complexes in the Usaquén district of Bogotá (Colombi) that use scorecards. Those that employ artificial intelligence (AI) and those that do not are identified to compare the differences or similarities in key aspects of management, including financial, customer, internal processes, and learning and growth perspectives. Similarly, a rough analysis is performed to verify whether the use of artificial intelligence in dashboards contributes to reducing management incidents related to the perspectives.

BACKGROUND

Horizontal Property and Co-Ownership

For the purposes of this analysis, the term co-ownership is considered equivalent to horizontal property, encompassing within this category the gated communities examined in the study by Kostenwein (2021). Horizontal property refers to a legal framework and a specific management system applied to certain types of real estate developments or gated communities that share common elements and form an integrated unit. This framework is commonly observed in residential complexes, co-owned properties, or condominiums, and includes not only private units but also the associated land, shared areas, and other jointly owned assets among individual unit owners (United Nations, 2019).

In Colombia, Law 675 of 2001 governs the horizontal property regime, which applies to real estate divided into private units—such as apartments, houses, or commercial spaces—that share common areas. Under this regime, each owner has exclusive rights over their private unit and shared rights over the land and common areas (Congress of Colombia, 2001).

This topic is particularly relevant because gated communities have become a common feature in Latin American cities (Kostenwein, 2021). In recent decades, the global increase in residential developments enclosed by perimeter walls or fences has attracted attention from various academic disciplines. These developments, often referred to as condominiums, typically offer security services and possess more developed collective infrastructure compared to open residential areas (Roitman, 2016). In the case of Bogotá, it is noteworthy that more than two-thirds of buildings fall under the horizontal property regime established in Colombia (Bogotá Mayor's Office, 2019).

According to Colombian legislation and regulations, the main challenges in managing residential complexes under the horizontal property regime include administrative transparency, financial and economic management, maintenance of common areas and infrastructure, and physical security. Additionally, horizontal property leaders must foster respectful and collaborative environments and promote resilient organizations capable of adapting to changing external conditions (Schoemaker et al., 2018).

Management Objectives and Challenges in Condominiums

There are numerous articles and documents that address the issues to be managed by administrators of condominiums. Several widespread issues have been identified in condominiums such as imperfect bylaws, insufficient pet regulations and parking standards (Treffers and Lippert, 2019), unplanned operations, low resident or owner participation, low levels of emergency response, maintenance failures, limited funds for improvements, improper document management, and other shortcomings that adversely and systematically affect occupant satisfaction (Ren-Hsieh, 2009).

In Bogotá, more than 75.39% of buildings are residential, representing approximately 1.9 million properties under the Horizontal Property regime, regulated by Law 675 of 2001. These units face, on average, 473,346 problems related to coexistence, finances, maintenance, and administration (District Security Secretariat, 2023). These management challenges are further affected by the low participation of residents or owners, as some do not attend co-owner meetings or contribute to common area maintenance payments, displaying opportunistic or individualistic behavior.

Roitman (2016), in turn, points out that these housing units are equipped with security devices, which constitute the defining component of this type of residential development. Without these devices, a closed urbanization would not consider a gated community; therefore, they are an essential aspect of residential complex management. Considering the above, a challenge arises for residential units in Bogotá, which is to promote greater participation of owners and residents and better decision-making process within residential communities (Donoso & Elsinga, 2016).

To address these challenges and deal with difficulties, especially in terms of sustainability, homeowners' associations or assemblies must manage their day-to-day operations and sometimes take legal or political action, which requires significant material resources. Fortunately, associations have the possibility of charging fees to their members to finance these activities (Wang, 2014), a practice that is duly authorized by Law 675 of 2001 in Colombia. However, property administrators face significant challenges, such as late payment of maintenance fees, increased operating costs, and lack of trained and motivated staff, which often results in poor customer service delivery (Christopher Taylor, 2014).

Today, managers in this field assume a wide range of responsibilities that were not previously part of their traditional roles. These new responsibilities include the development and implementation of procedures focused on providing excellent customer service, which has become an essential added value in the management of residential units (Sanderson & Read, 2020). Residential satisfaction has become a key indicator for assessing the success of gated communities or condominiums, as it reflects residents' perception of the quality of life in their environment and entails inhabitants experiencing an accepted level of comfort or well-being in their environment (Tan, 2016).

Balanced Scorecard in Residential Units

According to Ghiglione (2020), the Balanced Scorecard, originally proposed by Norton and Kaplan (1992), is a management tool designed to diagnose situations and enable continuous monitoring through a methodology that organizes information and enhances its value for managerial decision-making. The Balanced Scorecard is understood as a clear framework for strategic management by linking strategic objectives with quantifiable indicators, thereby facilitating organizational alignment and effective communication of the strategy (Kumar et al., 2021). Its widespread adoption is attributed to its simplicity and usefulness as a foundation for implementing and monitoring corporate strategy. Utilizing this type of tool in the management of co-owned properties would provide a mechanism capable of anticipating potential issues inherent to the nature of horizontal property, thus enabling an administration that can promote the well-being of co-owners.

The Balanced Scorecard (BSC) emerged in 1992 as a strategic management tool that integrates financial and non-financial indicators to enhance managerial insight into organizational performance. The purpose of the BSC is to deliver a comprehensive and timely perspective on organizational performance, simplifying the design and execution of operational adjustments and strategic implementation. This model was very well accepted and adapted by all types of organizations until it became an indispensable management tool, reaching approximately 53% of applications by companies around the world in 2008 (Tawse & Tabesh, 2023)

To face challenges and promote sustainability in the management of residential complexes or condominiums, these units are advised to implement management tools, such as Norton and Kaplan's Balanced Scorecard (BSC) (1992). This model allows managers to translate the strategic vision into concrete processes and actions, review predefined metrics to evaluate organizational performance and then make informed decisions.

A properly established BSC helps organizations to reduce costs, generate more revenue and make better decisions, since it applies to a management system that includes financial and non-financial measures and, consequently, is more efficient than those that only use financial measures to evaluate performance. A study shows that the BSC facilitates the relationship between Artificial Intelligence (AI) and organizational performance, improving the measurement and analysis of performance indicators, which is why it is suggested to integrate AI systems or elements into the BSC to optimize operations and decision making (Mahboub and Ghanem, 2024). However, these BSCs must be adapted to the specific needs of each co-ownership (Bernal Palomo, 2020) and incorporate the collection and processing of information using artificial intelligence tools (Turing, 1936; McCarthy, 1956).

Indeed, a problem that arises in the management of organizations is focusing exclusively on financial figures, leaving aside key resources such as highly trained employees and agility in decision making, which are highly significant for the functioning of any organization. Therefore, it is essential to adapt or update the performance assessment architecture to include these elements, which are already incorporated into Balanced Scorecards, and to integrate artificial intelligence systems (Hsu & Lin, 2021).

However, the incorporation of the concept of sustainable development is significant due to the progressive demands and current social pressures. From this perspective, sustainability is understood as an approach that encompasses three dimensions: environmental, economic, and social, with the objective of promoting development that protects the environment and guarantees a dignified life. This orientation is applicable to all types of organizations, regardless of their size or nature, and includes, of course, specific contexts such as condominiums or residential units (Mina-Falsarella, et al. 2023). Therefore, the concept of sustainability must be incorporated to provide greater comprehensiveness and precision to the management tool to be implemented in the residential units. In other words, it is not enough to use only financial indicators, and it becomes necessary to include indicators of other dimensions or perspectives, due to the complex problems faced by the communities and the residential units themselves.

Management systems based on the Balanced Scorecard have been widely recognized for the numerous benefits they offer and for their adoption across diverse organizations worldwide. However, as these systems evolve, particularly through the integration of artificial intelligence (AI) components, new challenges have begun to emerge. Among the most significant risks are the collection and processing of sensitive data, such as images, access logs, and consumption patterns (Merabet et al., 2021), as well as increasing technological dependence, which may reduce community management autonomy and lead to failures in communication or security systems (Krishnakumar et al., 2023).

Furthermore, without ethical and responsible algorithmic governance, the legitimacy and public acceptance of these technologies may be seriously compromised. Additional concerns include potential limitations in the technological infrastructure required for effective implementation (Wolniak and Stecuła, 2024). In less developed countries, barriers may also arise from a limited culture of technology adoption. Moreover, there is often a lack or insufficient availability of technical, human, and financial resources, which hinders the effective implementation of AI-based solutions as complements to management systems. This represents a considerable challenge for the administrative bodies of residential complexes and homeowners' associations.

Artificial Intelligence and the Balanced Scorecard in Co-Ownership

Artificial intelligence is a field focused on the development of systems capable of collecting and processing large volumes of data. In this context, residential complex administrations seek to modernize by implementing these technologies to automate processes such as billing, maintenance, and security services. Real-time data analysis enables the optimization of resource use, enhances safety, and supports decision-making based on more accurate information, contributing to more sustainable management (Pedral Sampaio et al., 2022).

García, Mora & Ávila (2020) define artificial intelligence as the science and engineering that enables the creation of intelligent machines, particularly computer programs capable of understanding and replicating human intelligence by performing specific tasks guided by humans. In the management of residential complexes or horizontal property, artificial intelligence can serve as a management assistant that analyzes large volumes of data or information provided by the administration to measure and evaluate performance indicators.

Big data analytics is a recent technology with significant potential to improve services in smart cities. By incorporating digitization into everyday life, large amounts of data have been accumulated, which can be positively applied in various fields, which is why the analysis and effective management of this data are critical for success in business, service, and management sectors (Al Nuaimi, et. al., 2015). With the rapid evolution of information technology, global competition has intensified considerably. Many organizations predict that the future of supply chain management will undergo dramatic advances, ranging from planning, scheduling, and optimization, all technically driven by artificial intelligence (Helo & Hao, 2021).

Artificial intelligence systems feed on pre-established data and knowledge, which leads them to replicate existing realities. In this regard, Martínez (2024) indicates that no artificial intelligence system is completely neutral, since these data are generated by humans, either directly or through other systems. This lack of neutrality may result in biased representations and affect the results obtained. It is then paramount to consider these biases and seek to mitigate their impact in order to achieve more ethical and accepted results.

In addition to the above, in the management sphere, Divino (2024) concluded that artificial intelligence can be effectively incorporated into various areas of business management, including innovation, supply chain management, decision-making, human resource management, and strategic and product management.

Mahou & Ghanem (2024) concluded that artificial intelligence promotes organizational performance by integrating into various BSC perspectives; for example, in the financial area, it automates and optimizes processes such as cash flow management and budgeting, generating savings and better economic results. From the customer's perspective, it enhances the experience through personalized recommendations and tools such as chatbots, which provide ongoing support. In internal processes, it optimizes the supply chain and logistics, increasing operational efficiency and reducing costs.

According to the above, AI could be strengthened and used in the management of properties subject to the horizontal property regime in different aspects related to the automation of repetitive administrative processes, individualized attention to residents or owners through the use of automated chats, security and surveillance: through the use of cameras and security devices that send alerts in case of suspicious situations; alerts for maintenance of equipment, machinery and facilities, communications management and management of parking lots and other processes.

On the other hand, Mbau and Musiega (2022) define efficiency as the ability of an individual or group to achieve their goals. In management terms, efficiency focuses on improving processes to optimize outcomes. That is, an efficient organization is one that reaches its objectives while using fewer resources, or that achieves more goals without increasing resource consumption. In the context of horizontal property or residential complex administration, efficiency takes on strategic importance, as it enables the design of scenarios that optimize the execution of plans and the collection of financial resources needed for the maintenance of facilities, infrastructure, and administrative management.

Due to the lack of prior information about service quality, management committees often make decisions based on subjective judgments. This situation exposes residents to high levels of risk and potential physical or emotional harm when facing inefficient or inadequate services (Kuo et al., 2011). Therefore, data collection across various management areas should be conducted in real time, using automated methods that allow for instant processing.

Sustainability is a condition of a dynamic system in which the interaction between human and natural activities can continue indefinitely without degrading the natural environment (Morelli, 2011). Sustainability is based on three key dimensions: economic, social, and environmental. In this regard, corporate management should adopt a comprehensive approach that considers these three pillars to ensure more responsible and socially accepted actions. In the real estate sector, Hopkins et al. (2016) demonstrate that property managers use sustainability as a strategy to attract clients through practices ranging from recycling to comprehensive environmental audits.

In this context, artificial intelligence emerges as a strategic tool for sustainable management by enabling process automation, real-time data collection, and improved decision-making efficiency. However, for these technologies to have a significant impact, it is equally essential to clearly define the roles and responsibilities of the various stakeholders involved, such as resident owners and administrative personnel.

The Scope of AI Tools in Residential Management

The management of residential co-ownerships is experiencing a digital transformation, with an increasing adoption of Artificial Intelligence (AI) solutions. In this context, five major groups of AI tools with high optimization potential have been identified.

The first group is generative AI, which includes tools such as GPT-4, Claude 3, and Gemini. These tools are used for tasks such as summarizing meeting minutes, drafting informational circulars, and simulating maintenance scenarios for the complex. The main benefits are standardized documentation and easily identifying lessons learned. However, risks such as hallucinations that generate incorrect information and the need to protect data privacy must be considered (Di Vaio et al., 2024).

The second group is predictive analytics, with platforms such as Azure Auto Forecast, Prophet, and BigQuery ML. These tools are used to project utility consumption (Ahmad et al., 2022), control cash flow, and measure resident turnover rates. The great advantage of these tools is their ability to anticipate cost overruns and optimize budget reserves. However, they face limitations, such as possible model drift. This term refers to the degradation of a model's accuracy over time due to changes in real-world conditions. Additionally, these tools depend significantly on the quality of historical data series, which requires a long, clean, complete, and accurate data history.

The third group is natural language processing (NLP) and chatbots. These are powered by technologies such as Dialogflow or IBM Watson Assistant and are key to customer service. In condominiums, they allow requests, complaints, and claims to be managed 24 hours a day and automatically classified. While these systems can reduce the administrative burden and improve resident satisfaction (Prentice et al., 2020), they may have limited coverage and present language biases.

The fourth group is Robotic Process Automation (RPA). RPA uses tools such as UiPath and Power Automate to perform operational tasks, such as automatic invoice reconciliation and scheduled maintenance reminders. Implementing RPA reduces manual work and ensures complete traceability of processes (Oliveira et al., 2022). However, RPA can be fragile in the face of changes to program interfaces and in handling unexpected situations or exceptions.

The fifth group is computer vision, which uses technologies like YOLOv8 and AWS Rekognition to improve security and operational efficiency. These technologies are used for intrusion detection, controlling the capacity of common areas (Ullah et al., 2021), and automatically reading service meters. While they improve real-time security, challenges include managing false positives and meeting the high hardware requirements for operation. Each tool generates a large volume of data that, if not managed properly, can become informational noise. This underscores the necessity of a structured framework that can translate this data into actionable insights.

According to reports by Gartner (2025) and IFMA (2024), predictive analytics and chatbots have reached the late early adoption phase (TRL 6-7) in Latin America. Generative AI and computer vision are in the pilot stage (TRL 4–5). Colombia's local platforms, such as AdminProp and CondoAI, integrate GPT-4 modules that summarize minutes, demonstrating the technical feasibility of these solutions at a regional level.

Implementing these technologies provides tangible benefits that can be measured using a management framework. For instance, residential complexes that incorporate energy consumption prediction models can reduce their annual utility costs by 8-12%, which is a key performance indicator for the "Financial" perspective of a Balanced Scorecard (BSC). Similarly, robotic automation and computer vision algorithms can reduce the time staff spend on repetitive surveillance and recording tasks by up to 40%, impacting the Internal Processes perspective directly.

While generative models have advantages, such as identifying lessons learned, they also underscore the need to establish clear and robust data governance policies. These policies are essential to prevent leaks of sensitive information, and they are a cornerstone of the Learning and Growth Perspective, fostering a culture of secure and sustainable management within residential complexes.

MAIN FOCUS OF THE CHAPTER

Methodology

The objective of this case study is to develop a comparative analysis of management in residential complexes in the Usaquén neighborhood of Bogotá, Colombia, based on the application of scorecards, differentiating between those that incorporate artificial intelligence (AI) and those that use traditional tools. The purpose is to identify differences and similarities in the four key perspectives of the Balanced Scorecard model: financial, customers, internal processes, and learning and growth.

To achieve this objective, a descriptive qualitative approach was adopted, which is suitable for understanding social and organizational phenomena in depth without interfering with the natural conditions in which they develop. The sample consisted of 50 residential complexes, intentionally selected for their availability and for having documented and active management processes.

During August 2024, semi-structured interviews were conducted with co-property administrators using a virtual form, which allowed for systematic, efficient data collection that could be adapted to the availability of the participants. In addition, a documentary analysis was carried out of management plans, annual reports, financial statements, and performance evaluations for the year 2023. This procedure was complemented by direct observation of some operational processes in the housing complexes visited.

The sources of information used by administrators to support their responses included management reports, income statements, financial statements, and performance evaluations. According to Góngora (2016), management reports in the context of condominiums contain not only documentation of the work of the administrator and the board of directors, but also financial analysis, income and expenses, portfolio management, assembly decisions, maintenance carried out, and issues that affected residents during the period analyzed.

From a financial perspective, indicators such as the liquidity ratio (current assets/current liabilities) were analyzed, as well as the percentage of accounts receivable, determined by the vertical structure of assets. This information was taken directly from the financial statements of each complex.

From the customer perspective, the main issues reported in the management reports were identified, such as noise, inappropriate use of common areas, and pet ownership, all of which are critical elements in residential coexistence and reflect users' perceptions of management.

The internal processes perspective was addressed by analyzing the section on significant events in the management reports, where administrators describe the structural evolution of the properties, including maintenance, repairs, and improvements. Frequent problems such as cracks, leaks, and incidents in general facilities were also documented, which allowed us to identify common patterns in infrastructure management.

Finally, the learning and growth perspective was examined through performance evaluations carried out by co-owners, which measured the suitability and performance of the administrator and the board of directors. In addition, elements related to organizational risks and uncertainties were analyzed, such as contractor non-compliance and tax penalties, aspects that directly affect future projections and management sustainability.

This methodological design allowed for a comparative analysis between groups that have integrated artificial intelligence solutions into their control panels and those that still use traditional models, facilitating the identification of best practices, opportunities for improvement, and the impact of technology on condominium management.

Results

Table 1 below shows the results of the effects resulting from the dashboard-based management of the residential complexes in Usaquén, Bogotá. Residential complexes using artificial intelligence in their dashboards were identified, as well as those using management tools without artificial intelligence. In this way, contrasts emerged in key aspects resulting from the analysis of the content of the interviews conducted with the 50 administrators of the residential complexes.

Table 1 Comparative table of key aspects between the two approaches

Perspective	Key aspects	BSC WITHOUT AI Indicator	BSC WITH AI Indicator	Variation %
Financial In Horizontal Property: Economic	Liquidity (Current ratio)	0.56	1.97	+1.41
	Accounts receivable	32.7%	4.58%	-86%
Customers In Horizontal Property: Social	Noise	9.5 incidents/year	1.5 incidents/year	-85%
	Use of common areas	7.5 incidents/year	2 incidents/year	-67%
	Pet Ownership	12 incidents/year	3 incidents/year	-75%
Internal Processes In Horizontal Property: Operational	Facilities	12 incidents/year	3 incidents/year	-75%
	Cracks and fissures	12 incidents/year	3 incidents/year	-75%
	Leaks and dampness	8 incidents/year	2 incidents/year	-75%

continued on following page

Table 1 Continued

Perspective	Key aspects	BSC WITHOUT AI Indicator	BSC WITH AI Indicator	Variation %
Learning and Growth In Horizontal Property Administrative Management	Administrator's Competence (Performance Evaluation)	48%	87%	+39%
	Qualified personnel on management boards (Performance Evaluation)	35%	72%	+47%
	Contractor non-compliance	5 non-compliance events/year	3 non-compliance events/year	-60%
	Tax penalty payments	11 penalty payments/year	2 penalty payments/year	-82%

Source: Own elaboration

This analysis is based on data collected through interviews with 50 residential units located in the Usaquén sector of Bogotá, governed by the Colombian horizontal property regime. An initial analysis found that the co-owned properties were evenly split regarding the use of the BSC with artificial intelligence: 50% of the properties used it, while the remaining 50% had not yet incorporated artificial intelligence into their BSC. According to the same content analysis of these interviews, it was necessary to adapt the names of the BSC perspectives to the context of the co-owned properties under study. Accordingly, the financial perspective was adapted as the Economic Perspective; the Customer perspective became the Social Perspective; the Internal Processes perspective was renamed the Operational Perspective; and the Learning and Growth perspective was adapted as the Administrative Management Perspective.

Economic Perspective

The first results-oriented perspective is the Financial one. However, when adapted to the context of horizontal property, it may be referred to as the Economic Perspective, which examines the solvency of the co-owned properties. 100% of the group of 25 administrators who use the BSC with AI reported that their co-owned properties have sufficient liquidity and the necessary resources to sustain their horizontal property operations. This situation results from the absence of outstanding accounts receivable—in other words, residents in these properties are up to date with their administrative fee payments, which constitute the main source of income for residential co-owned properties. This is one of the most important aspects within the concept of sustainability, since in the absence of financial resources, various types of problems may arise, and the well-being of residents in the co-owned properties could not guarantee —one of the main objectives pursued by property administrations. Another relevant point worth highlighting is that these co-owned properties report current ratios above 1 in their financial statements, suggesting that their current assets are greater than their current liabilities.

In contrast, regarding the results from co-owned properties that use management tools other than the BSC with AI, 100% (25 horizontal properties) face liquidity problems in their Financial Perspective—an issue that negatively affects the sustainability of this type of organization. As mentioned earlier, the liquidity of a residential co-owned property relies on the revenue generated from administrative fees. However, in these types of properties, such resources are insufficient due to an average delinquency rate of 32.7% in the payment of these fees by residents.

In line with this, the inability of a co-owned property to secure sufficient resources for its maintenance results in poor financial efficiency indicators and forces the administration to concentrate its efforts on improving the collection of administrative fees to reduce outstanding accounts receivable. Moreover, the lack of financial resources is a factor that contributes to the persistence of other issues of an operational, administrative, social, and economic nature. It also leads to the constant turnover of administrators and other staff or companies providing cleaning, maintenance, or security services.

With these results, it could be said that the horizontal properties that use BSC with AI show better results in their current ratios, increasing this indicator by 1.41 compared to the co-owned properties that do not use BSC with AI. Another important aspect to mention in this perspective is that horizontal properties using BSC with AI show an 86% reduction in outstanding accounts receivable.

Social Perspective

The second perspective of analysis of the results is that of Clients, which in horizontal property could be called the Social Perspective and addresses all matters related to social coexistence in co-owned properties. On this issue, it was found that 68% of the respondents (17 administrators) in the group of administrators who use BSC with AI, state that during the year, the incidents that have more repetition are those related to responsible pet ownership, with an average of 3 incidents or complaints of this type. These incidents arise in co-owned properties due to pets being kept in the common areas of residential complexes in violation of certain regulations, which can lead to disagreements between neighbors.

Misuse of common areas is another key issue, with an average of two incidents per year, while cases of noise nuisance occur on average 1.5 times per year. The management of these coexistence problems is necessary to contribute to the efficiency and sustainability of the horizontal properties, since precarious management in this aspect can lead to lawsuits and indemnifications that, consequently, would negatively impact the economy of the co-owned property.

According to the Social Perspective data analysis, it was found that the 25 administrators of residential complexes without BSC with AI, corresponding to 100%, generally identified the same problems in complexes using BSC without AI. However, there was a significant difference in the frequency of these incidents. The use of BSC with AI suggests a significant decrease in the frequency of incidents compared to those complexes that use non-AI tools. For example, there was an 85% decrease in annual unwanted noise incidents, a 67% decrease in annual incidents of misuse of common areas, and a 75% decrease in pet-related incidents as shown in Table 1.

More effective management of coexistence in co-owned properties also involves improving communication channels and how messages are perceived by residents. To achieve this, it is worthwhile to design communication strategies with a neuromarketing approach that are empathetic, persuasive, and tailored to the emotions and habits of the residents (Barrera Ortegón & Tovar Muñiz , 2025). This would support administrators in implementing coexistence or organizational culture campaigns more effectively.

Operational Perspective

Within the results of this perspective, it is worth clarifying that, as such, residential co-owned properties do not have any type of profit motive. This perspective, as indicated above about co-owned properties, the administrators surveyed interpret it or liken it to the operational aspect thereof, which would include the subject of maintenance that all co-owned properties need for structural support and to mitigate the deterioration that a building may have due to its use and the passing of time.

It should be noted that the internal aspect of the co-owned properties should focus on the protection and care of the buildings for their sustainability and the owners' equity. Co-owned properties that do not prioritize preventive and corrective maintenance will, in the short term, be forced to allocate significant resources to structural repairs or upgrades. This situation undermines the efficient use of the financial resources collected within the property for the expenses required to ensure its sustainability.

In the Operational Perspective, there are three aspects or categories in which incidents occur: installations, fissures or cracks, and leaks or dampness. These properties showed a consistent 75% reduction in comparison to residential complexes that do not implement the BSC with AI. Residential complexes not using AI reported 12 incidents per year in each of the first two categories and 8 in the third, whereas those implementing AI registered 3, 3, and 2 incidents annually, respectively. This trend indicates that AI-supported BSC-based management could potentially reduce the frequency of operational incidents requiring intervention by the administrations of the co-owned properties under study.

Administrative Management Perspective

The Administrative Management Perspective focuses on analyzing the performance of property administrators and their support teams, including accountants, statutory auditors, administrative assistants, and others. Among the administrators who use the BSC with AI, 100% (25 administrators) reported that this perspective includes four key areas of analysis. The first of these is the administrator's competence, assessed through performance and result-oriented evaluations conducted during the annual results assembly. In that setting, 87% of the administrators (21.7) were considered competent to carry out the responsibilities defined for property administrators under Law 675 of 2001.

Another key area of analysis within this perspective is the competence of the individuals who make up the management boards, as these boards are responsible for making decisions that are crucial to the efficiency and sustainability of this type of organization. Based on the performance evaluations from the 25 residential complexes that use the BSC with AI, residents reported that 72% of the individuals serving on their management boards are competent and qualified to contribute to the efficiency and sustainability of their co-owned properties. At the same time, another of the key areas that can be pointed out in this perspective is the non-compliance of contractors in the execution and delivery of work and maintenance required by the co-owned properties for their sustainability in physical and structural terms. According to the respondents, this type of problem occurs on average 3 times per year. Finally, the last area of analysis presented by the administrators in this perspective is the payment of penalties for taxes and incorrectly filed returns, where 2 penalties were paid per year for this reason.

In the analysis of the results from this perspective but focusing on the co-owned properties that do not use the BSC with AI, 100% of the 25 administrators surveyed reported administrative issues related to the competence of the administrator. Residents of these residential complexes stated in their performance evaluations that only 48% (12 administrators) are deemed competent and capable of carrying out the responsibilities established by Law 675 of 2001. Likewise, under this evaluation framework, residents indicated that only 32% of the members serving on their management boards are considered competent to make critical decisions within those boards. Like the group of administrators who use BSC with AI, those who do not use it describe that they have had to pay penalties for not filing taxes or for having to rectify them, with a frequency of repetition of 11 times per year. In addition to the above, this perspective also reveals incidents related to contractor non-compliance, with an average of five cases reported per year.

The incidents described in the learning and growth perspective may be the result of the constant rotation of the residents that make up the management boards, who make decisions of vital importance for the sustainability of horizontal properties. Another point highlighted by the administrators surveyed is that, due to the lack of sufficient resources to hire qualified personnel, administrative functions are often carried out by residents who lack the experience and knowledge required to ensure proper management of the co-owned properties. This situation also limits the means available for their sustainability and affects the efficient use of resources and other key aspects.

Finally, within the comparison of the learning and growth perspective, it can be concluded that the horizontal properties that use BSC with AI show a 39% better result in the performance evaluations of their administrators, as well as a 47% better qualification of the competencies of the people who make up their management boards. Furthermore, regarding contractor non-compliance, the co-owned properties that implement the BSC with AI show a 60% reduction in such incidents, along with an 82% decrease in the payment of tax penalties.

Discussion

This section interprets the proposed framework, discusses its practical implications and limitations, and analyzes its resilience, thereby contextualizing its contribution to residential property management. The primary finding of this study is that integrating AI, the Balanced Scorecard, and sustainability into a cohesive management framework has more impact than any one of these used separately. Traditionally, property management has operated in silos: financial decisions were separate from maintenance operations, which were in turn disconnected from resident satisfaction initiatives.

The proposed framework dismantles silos. AI gathers objective, real-time data, translating it into Key Performance Indicators (KPIs) using a Balanced Scorecard. This combination ensures operational actions are aligned with the overarching strategic goal of long-term sustainability. The novelty lies in the explicit use of the BSC for sustainability goals, using AI-generated data as its fuel. It's an advance from simply using automation for strategy, moving towards value-driven governance.

Adopting this framework has transformative practical implications for property managers and co-ownership boards. It signifies a shift from a reactive administrative role to a proactive strategic one. For example, rather than relying on historical budget reports, managers can use the dashboard to make data-driven decisions. They can simulate the impact of installing solar panels and observe in real time how this investment affects the financial perspective through cost savings and the customer perspective through improved resident perception of sustainability.

Furthermore, the framework enhances transparency and communication. When a fee increase is necessary, management can present a clear case to residents, showing exactly how the funds will be used to meet specific sustainability and maintenance targets, based on predictive analytics from the AI and performance indicators from the BSC. This fosters trust and reduces friction. In essence, the framework empowers managers to anticipate problems before they escalate, justify decisions with objective evidence, and steer the community strategically towards greater efficiency and long-term value.

Resilience and Stress Scenario Analysis

An information system implemented in a critical residential environment must be efficient under normal conditions and robust and resilient in the face of disruptive events. In line with best practices for AI-based services (Niazi, Khan, & Abbas, 2020), analyzing the proposed framework's behavior under stress scenarios is essential. Although a physical implementation is beyond the scope of this study, this section outlines the system's designed responses to three potential critical events.

Scenario 1. General power outage. In the event of a main power supply interruption, the most critical AI components, such as access control and perimeter security cameras, would be kept operational by Uninterruptible Power Supply (UPS) systems. The system would enter low-power mode and prioritize security functions over administrative ones (e.g., report generation or non-urgent chatbot queries). This ensures the protection of residents and assets until the service is restored.

Scenario 2. Internet Network Failure. The system is designed with offline operational capabilities in order to address the potential vulnerability that comes with cloud dependency. Critical data, such as access logs from the computer vision system or urgent alerts, would be stored locally on an edge computing device. The data will automatically synchronize with the central platform once the internet connection is re-established. This will ensure that no critical information is lost and that data integrity for the Balanced Scorecard is maintained.

Scenario 3. Sudden Surge in Resident Requests During a community-wide emergency, such as a major water leak or fire alarm, a drastic increase in queries to the NLP chatbot is expected. The system is designed to manage this demand through cloud-based auto-scaling, which dynamically allocates more resources to maintain response times. Additionally, the NLP module identifies the nature of the emergency and triggers a predefined response protocol, broadcasting automated updates to all residents. This provides residents with timely information and reduces the administrative burden on staff during critical times.

This emphasis on resilience guarantees operational continuity and strengthens residents' confidence in the technology that has been implemented. This trust is an important intangible asset that contributes directly to the "customer" perspective within the balanced scorecard, thereby reinforcing the overall value of the integrated framework

SOLUTIONS AND RECOMMENDATIONS

It was observed that the Balanced Scorecard methodology, when complemented with artificial intelligence, facilitates the creation of strategic scenarios aimed at improving resource efficiency and the sustainability of co-owned properties in the Usaquén district, in the north of Bogotá, Colombia. For this study, 50 interviews were conducted with administrators of these residential units known as co-owned properties. It was identified that half of the sample, 25 administrators, or 50%, incorporate Balanced Scorecards with artificial intelligence elements in managing their co-owned properties, while the other half use different management tools that do not include artificial intelligence systems or components. This evidence confirms that artificial intelligence acts as a catalyst that enhances organizational performance when integrated into management models such as the Balanced Scorecard.

Balanced Scorecards enhanced with artificial intelligence, designed for horizontal property management, enable the processing and analysis of large volumes of operational, financial, and social data. This information is interpreted by the tool to facilitate decision-making and provide comprehensive control over property operations. This automation optimizes efficiency in co-ownership administration, reduces administrative burdens, and improves transparency toward residents, thereby building trust in management and contributing to the sustainability of the residential complex.

Based on the analysis of the interviews conducted, the results indicate that integrating AI into the Balanced Scorecards of the co-ownerships studied could have positive impacts on the management of these organizations. Specifically, the findings suggest that operational and financial optimization can be achieved, along with additional beneficial outcomes arising from the cause-and-effect relationships embedded within the Balanced Scorecard framework. Therefore, it is recommended to develop Balanced Scorecards incorporating AI elements or systems to support the sustainable management of residential units governed by the horizontal property regime.

According to the content of the interviews analyzed, the results demonstrate that incorporating AI into the BSCs of the co-owned properties under study could have positive impacts on the management of these organizations. The findings indicate that operational and financial optimization can be achieved, as well as other positive effects resulting from the cause-and-effect relationships inherent in the Balanced Scorecard framework. For this reason, it is recommended to develop Balanced Scorecards integrated with AI elements or systems for the sustainable management of residential units governed by the horizontal property regime.

The future of the Balanced Scorecard model is oriented toward the integration of more comprehensive, accurate, and real-time information, enabling intelligent systems for automated decision-making to optimize organizational processes. According to Kaplan and Norton (1996), the original authors of the BSC methodology, the evolution of this model must adapt to technological advancements and the increasing availability of data to achieve more efficient management. In this context, the incorporation of real-time big data not only enhances the accuracy of output information but also enables the anticipation of future scenarios and more proactive responses (Mayer-Schönberger & Cukier, 2013).

However, decisions that significantly affect individuals or groups require a rigorous and multidimensional data analysis approach. As Provost & Fawcett (2013) note, the interconnection of large datasets allows the identification of complex patterns and the anticipation of potential negative impacts, thus supporting more ethical and responsible decision-making.

In the field of residential management, this capacity for foresight is critical to protecting residents, property, and infrastructure by integrating advanced analytical tools with social and economic criteria Wang (2014). Therefore, the scorecard model of the future will not rely solely on automation, but rather on human intelligence augmented by massive data analytics that ensures a balance between efficiency and social well-being.

The advanced application of the Balanced Scorecard model supported by intelligent systems and big data analysis—represents a strategic tool for improving the management of residential complexes or horizontally governed properties. It enables more precise, objective, and timely decision-making based on updated and comprehensive information (Kaplan & Norton, 1996; Provost & Fawcett, 2013). This analytical capability helps anticipate negative impacts, optimize the administration of assets and infrastructure, and address the social needs of residents or owners (Mayer-Schönberger & Cukier, 2013). In doing so, administrations can promote more efficient, transparent, responsible, and collectively oriented governance—critical elements for managing the complexities of modern cities (Wang, 2013)

In addition to the challenges previously discussed, it is essential to promote broader and more effective participation from residents and property owners in the governance of residential complexes. The literature shows that when stakeholders perceive that their opinions influence decision-making and have access to transparent, accessible information, their engagement and participation increase significantly (Arnstein, 1969; Fung, 2006).

According to Morduchowicz (2023), artificial intelligence is about the ability of a system to collect and interpret large volumes of data and use it to achieve objectives that increase the probability of success in planning and management tasks. In this sense, the administration of residential complexes or co-owned properties should not remain distant from scientific and technological advances in management, but, on the contrary, AI will be progressively integrated until it becomes an indispensable tool for decision making, seeking to optimize efficiency and sustainability.

The relationship between the use of AI and improvements in management enables monitoring of the performance of administrators and boards, identifying competency gaps and proposing personalized improvement actions. This will allow co-ownerships to become more adaptive and develop organizational learning (Hsu & Lin, 2021). By responding quickly and proactively to the volatile, complex, and ambiguous scenarios observed today, they will be able to develop flexible organizational capabilities to manage uncertainty (Barrera-Ortegón et al., 2024).

Based on the above, it is proposed that co-ownerships begin processes of technological adoption and progressive digital transformation, starting with intelligent modules in key areas such as finance and maintenance. At this stage, industry associations or regulators should promote digital literacy programs for administrators, board members, and residents, fostering a culture of data and evidence-based management.

The incorporation of AI should be considered an operational necessity given the complexity required for managing horizontal property, transforming it into a strategic ally that minimizes risks and optimizes resources to build more sustainable, resilient, and cohesive communities.

FUTURE RESEARCH DIRECTIONS

Strategic Integration of the Balanced Scorecard (BSC) and Artificial Intelligence (AI) in Co-Ownership Governance.

Future research can focus on the convergence of BSC and AI frameworks. Combining traditional BSC perspectives (financial, customer, internal processes, learning/growth) with AI-based predictive analytics in the development of hybrid scorecards can improve dynamic and contextual performance assessment. Additionally, incorporating sustainability KPIs into the BSC via the Balanced Sustainability Scorecard (BSS) framework aligns operational objectives with environmental and social goals. AI tools could facilitate strategic scenario simulations to support the evaluation of trade-offs between long-term sustainability and cost management by boards of directors.

Operational Efficiency Through an AI-Enhanced BSC

From an operational perspective, AI can automate data collection and KPI tracking, reducing human error and enabling real-time decision-making. Natural language processing (NLP) can analyze meeting minutes and resident feedback to extract governance trends and sentiment insights. Reinforcement learning algorithms can optimize resource allocation decisions, such as maintenance budgets and energy consumption, based on historical data and performance parameters.

The Following Report Presents a Series of Sustainability Metrics That Have Been Adapted for Application in the Context of Colombian Condominiums

Given Colombia's unique environmental, regulatory, and social context, future studies should explore the development of local sustainability indicators relevant to Colombian condominiums. The incorporation of environmental, social, and governance (ESG) criteria into BSC frameworks can also facilitate alignment with national sustainability strategies and global goals. AI-based models have the potential to simulate eco-efficiency scenarios and assess the potential impact of green initiatives (e.g., solar energy, water recycling systems).

Stakeholder Engagement and Transparency are Enhanced by the Implementation of Artificial Intelligence

Research could examine the potential of AI-based platforms to support participatory decision-making among co-owners. Predictive analytics can assist in predicting residents' needs, enhancing service delivery, and optimizing communication. Furthermore, AI techniques such as stakeholder mapping and materiality analysis can be leveraged to identify and prioritize the most impactful sustainability actions for the community.

A Comparative Analysis and Benchmarking Will be Conducted

Comparative research can provide valuable insights by analyzing the distinct practices and contexts of co-ownership governance among various regions and countries. AI clustering algorithms can assist in identifying archetypes of performance among co-owned properties. Similarly, evaluating BSC implementations in Colombian SMEs could yield valuable insights for adapting performance management frameworks to the co-ownership sector.

Methodological Innovations

Future research could explore new methodological approaches, including the use of A0 architecture to represent independent social and environmental perspectives in SBSC applications. The development of AI-enhanced strategy maps has the Potential to improve the visualization and understanding of cause-and-effect relationships across the various dimensions of sustainability. Combining the life cycle approach with the BSC is an effective strategy to assess long-term sustainability of shared assets, such as energy infrastructure, elevators, and water systems.

These research areas offer opportunities for collaboration across different disciplines, with the aim of enhancing both the theoretical understanding of and the practical implementation of sustainable governance models in co-owned real estate.

CONCLUSION

The comparative analysis reveals that residential co-ownerships in Usaquén (Bogotá, Colombia) that integrate AI-assisted Balanced Scorecards achieve improved organizational performance, reflected in greater sustainability and efficiency. These co-ownerships report fewer incidents across economic, social, operational, and management dimensions, along with increased liquidity, reduced accounts receivable, lower frequency of social conflicts, and a significant decrease in technical failures. These results highlight the potential of artificial intelligence to optimize co-ownership management.

From the comparative analysis of the results, it can be qualitatively asserted that residential co-owned properties in the Usaquén district of Bogotá, Colombia, who employ Balanced Scorecards with artificial intelligence tend to achieve better organizational performance outcomes. Consequently, these co-owned properties could be more sustainable and efficient. It was observed that co-owned properties using artificial intelligence in their scorecards reported fewer incidents across issues related to the economic, social, operational, and administrative management perspectives.

Although theory does not claim that BSCs integrated with AI are the optimal tool for managing co-owned properties, they are regarded as more effective in supporting decision-making processes, as they enable the anticipation of potential issues through the visualization of various scenarios. The results indicate that co-owned properties implementing BSC with AI tend to exhibit greater economic solvency due to the presence of an alert system that encourages timely payment of administrative fees by private unit owners.

The BSC with AI undoubtedly retains the concept of using indicators to evaluate strategy but also incorporates additional features that make it distinct and more compelling. These enhancements have allowed it to evolve beyond the original definition presented by Kaplan and Norton (1992). The Balanced Scorecard can be defined as a set of indicators that provide the management of co-owned properties with a comprehensive view of the business, serving as a management tool that frames the strategy to be employed for this type of organization in order to make them more efficient and sustainable over time.

The integration of artificial intelligence into Balanced Scorecards (BSC) represents a key innovation for improving efficiency and sustainability in the management of residential co-ownerships. While the use of artificial intelligence alone does not guarantee optimal management, it strengthens strategic analysis, scenario review, decision-making processes, and transparency in administration. The use of this technology must always be accompanied by ethical data use policies, training for administrators, and a culture of continuous learning.

REFERENCES

Al Nuaimi, E., Al Neyadi, H., Mohamed, N., & Al-Jaroodi, J. (2015). Applications of big data to smart cities. *Journal of Internet Services and Applications*, *6*, 25. DOI: 10.1186/s13174-015-0041-5

Barrera-Ortegón, A. D. P., Medina-Ricaurte, G. F., & Jimenez-Hernandez, P. R. (2024). Organizational elements to confront turbulent and fragile VUCA to BANI scenarios. In Perez-Uribe, R., Ocampo-Guzman, D., Salcedo-Perez, C., & Carvajal-Contreras, A. (Eds.), *Organizational Management Sustainability in VUCA Contexts* (pp. 20–43). IGI Global., DOI: 10.4018/979-8-3693-0720-5.ch002

Barrera Ortegón, A. D. P., & Tovar Muñiz, M. S. (2025). Key neuromarketing factors in Alquería brand television commercials in Colombia. *European Public & Social Innovation Review*, *10*, 1–22. DOI: 10.31637/epsir-2025-1496

Bernal Palomo. (2020). *Balanced Scorecard Proposal for CHP Consulting SAS in Bogotá*. Universidad De La Salle.

Christopher Taylor, P. (2014). Management challenges and responses: Experiences of property managers operating in the small open economy of Jamaica. *Property Management*, *32*(1), 16–27. DOI: 10.1108/PM-11-2012-0040

Congress of Colombia. (2001). *Law 675 of 2001*. Bogotá, Colombia: Senate Secretary. Constitutional Court of the Republic of Colombia.

Divino, S. (2024). Governance and compliance recommendations for artificial intelligence in business management. *Nuevo Derecho*, *20*(35), 1–17. DOI: 10.25057/2500672X.1665

Donoso, R., & Elsinga, M. (2016). Management of low-income condominiums in Bogotá and Quito: The balance between property law and self-organisation. *International Journal of Housing Policy*, *18*(2), 312–334. DOI: 10.1080/14616718.2016.1248608

García, A., Mora, M., & Ávila, J. (2020). Artificial intelligence in education and administration. *Dominio de las Ciencias*, *6*(3). Advance online publication. DOI: 10.23857/dc.v6i3.1421

Ghiglione, F. (2020). *The balanced scorecard as a tool for efficiency in business management*. Universidad Nacional de La Plata., DOI: 10.24215/23143738e088

Góngora, F. (2016). *Management system for horizontal property in the city of Santiago de Cali*. Santiago de Cali: Universidad del Valle. https://bibliotecadigital.univalle.edu.co/server/api/core/bitstreams/6d350caa-7699-4594-b76b-7193a880e9c3/content

Helo, P., & Hao, Y. (2021). Artificial intelligence in operations management and supply chain management: An exploratory case study. *Production Planning and Control, 33*(16), 1573–1590. DOI: 10.1080/09537287.2021.188269

Hsieh, H. R. (2009). Issues and proposed improvements regarding condominium management in Taiwan. *Habitat International, 33*(1), 0–80. https://doi.org/DOI: 10.1016/j.habitatint.2008.05.002

Hsu, M.-F., & Lin, S.-J. (2021). A BSC-based network DEA model equipped with computational linguistics for performance assessment and improvement. *International Journal of Machine Learning and Cybernetics*. Advance online publication. DOI: 10.1007/s13042-021-01331-7

Kaplan, R. S., & Norton, D. P. (1992). *The Balanced Scorecard*. Barcelona. *Gestion*, •••, 2000.

Kostenwein, D. (2021). Between walls and fences: How different types of gated communities shape the streets around them. *Urban Studies (Edinburgh, Scotland)*. Advance online publication. DOI: 10.1177/0042098020984320

Krishnakumar, B., Gomathi, S., Sudharsan, V. S., Anbounadane, P. V., Solayappan, A., & Swamy, S. S. (2023, December). Smart building management with IoT and AI: Energy-efficient and cost-effective solutions. In *2023 10th IEEE Uttar Pradesh Section International Conference on Electrical, Electronics and Computer Engineering (UPCON)* (Vol. 10, pp. 1249–1254). IEEE.

Kumar, J., Prince, N., & Baker, H. K. (2021). Balanced scorecard: A systematic literature review and future research issues. *FIIB Business Review, 11*(2), 147–161. DOI: 10.1177/23197145211049625

Kuo, Y.-C., Chou, J.-S., & Sun, K.-S. (2011). How service quality influences resident satisfaction in condominium management. *Expert Systems with Applications, 38*(5), 5755–5763. DOI: 10.1016/j.eswa.2010.10.057

Mahboub, R., & Ghanem, M. G. (2024). The mediating role of knowledge management practices and balanced scorecard in the association between artificial intelligence and organization performance: Evidence from MENA region commercial banks. *Cogent Business & Management, 11*(1). Advance online publication. DOI: 10.1080/23311975.2024.2404484

Martínez, M. V. (2024). What we talk about when we talk about artificial intelligence. *UNESCO*. https://unesdoc.unesco.org/ark:/48223/pf0000391087

Mayer-Schönberger, V., & Cukier, K. (2013). *Big Data: A revolution that will transform how we live, work, and think*. Houghton Mifflin Harcourt.

Mbau, A., & Musiega, D. (2022). Analysing the efficiency of health systems. Oxford, UK: *Applied Health Economics and Health Policy*, University of Oxford. https://doi.org/DOI: 10.1007/s40258-022-00785-2

Merabet, G. H., Essaaidi, M., Haddou, M. B., Qolomany, B., Qadir, J., Anan, M. T., Al-Fuqaha, A. I., Abid, M. R., & Benhaddou, D. (2021). Intelligent building control systems for thermal comfort and energy-efficiency: A systematic review of artificial intelligence-assisted techniques. *Renewable & Sustainable Energy Reviews*. Advance online publication. DOI: 10.1016/j.rser.2021.110969

Mina-Falsarella, O., Silva de Oliveira, R., Angela-Branchi, B., & Ferreira-Mariosa, D. (2023). Sustainability in vertical residential condominiums: A study in the metropolitan region of Campinas. *Gestão & Regionalidade*, *39*, e20237634. DOI: 10.13037/gr.vol39.e20237634

Mio, C., Costantini, A., & Panfilo, S. (2022). Performance measurement tools for sustainable business: A systematic literature review on the sustainability balanced scorecard use. *Corporate Social Responsibility and Environmental Management*, *29*(2), 367–384. DOI: 10.1002/csr.2206

Morduchowicz, R. (2023). Artificial intelligence: Do we need a new education? *UNESCO*. https://unesdoc.unesco.org/ark:/48223/pf0000386262

Morelli, J. (2011). Environmental sustainability: A definition for environmental professionals. *Journal of Environmental Sustainability*, *1*(1), 2. Advance online publication. DOI: 10.14448/jes.01.0002

Pedral Sampaio, R., Aguiar Costa, A., & Flores-Colen, I. (2022). A systematic review of artificial intelligence applied to facility management in the building information modeling context and future research directions. *Buildings (Basel, Switzerland)*, *12*(11), 1939.

Provost, F., & Fawcett, T. (2013). *Data Science for Business: What you need to know about data mining and data-analytic thinking*. O'Reilly Media.

Roitman, S. (2016). Gated communities on a global scale. *Prospectiva. Journal of Social Work and Social Intervention*, (21), 13–22. DOI: 10.25100/prts.v0i21.918

Sanderson, D., & Read, D. (2020). Recognizing and realizing the value of customer-focused property management. *Property Management*, *38*(5), 749–764. DOI: 10.1108/pm-04-2020-0029

Tan, T. H. (2016). Residential satisfaction in gated communities: Case study of Desa Park City, Kuala Lumpur, Malaysia. *Property Management*, *34*(2), 84–99. DOI: 10.1108/PM-02-2015-0009

Tawse, A., & Tabesh, P. (2023). Thirty years with the balanced scorecard: What we have learned. *Business Horizons*, *66*(1), 123–132. DOI: 10.1016/j.bushor.2022.03.005

Treffers, S., & Lippert, R. (2019). Condominium self-governance? Issues, external interests, and the limits of statutory reform. *Housing Studies*, •••, 1–25. DOI: 10.1080/02673037.2019.1646217

Wang, F. (2013). Determinants of the effectiveness of Chinese homeowner associations in solving neighborhood issues. *Urban Affairs Review*, *50*(3), 311–339. DOI: 10.1177/1078087413501641

Wolniak, R., & Stecuła, K. (2024). Artificial intelligence in smart cities: Applications, barriers, and future directions—A review. *Smart Cities*, *7*(3), 1346–1389. DOI: 10.3390/smartcities7030057

Żółtowski, M. (2022). Artificial intelligence in management control systems: The role of AI in measuring and evaluating business performance. *Journal of Accounting and Management Control*, *28*(2), 98–112.

KEY TERMS AND DEFINITIONS

Artificial Intelligence: Technology that enables systems to learn, analyze information, and make decisions independently. In management contexts, AI facilitates tasks such as payment tracking, maintenance control, and real-time data analysis.

Balanced Scorecard (BSC): A management tool that presents key information about an organization in a variety of ways, including financial data, customer information, internal processes, and learning and development. The BSC helps make decisions, track objectives, and align actions with the overall strategy.

Balanced Scorecard Perspective: A framework for analyzing an organization's performance in categories such as financial, social, operational, and administrative. These perspectives provide a comprehensive view for making better decisions.

Data-driven decision making: is an analytical process that allows the best actions to be chosen using reliable information. An analytical process that allows one to choose the best course of action using reliable information. This approach helps avoid improvised decisions and enables clearer and more supported management decisions.

Digital Transformation in Community Management: It is the change that occurs when a community adopts digital technologies to improve its functioning. Examples include automating payments, digitizing documents, improving security, and facilitating resident participation

Efficiency: The ability to achieve expected results using as few resources as possible. In community contexts, efficiency means making good use of time, money, and effort to provide quality services without waste.

Horizontal property: A form of organization in which several people share the same buildings, such as apartments or houses, along with common areas, such as gardens, hallways, or lounges. This model is also called co-ownership or a gated community and involves shared rules for use, care, and administration. In Colombia, it is regulated by specific rules and requires collective management to ensure proper functioning and coexistence among residents.

Performance indicators: Numerical measures that show whether the objectives set by an organization or community are being met. They help identify achievements, problems, and areas for improvement in a clear, concrete way.

Sustainability: The ability to maintain a balance between the use of resources and people's well-being without affecting future generations. In a community, sustainability involves caring for the environment, using resources responsibly, and thinking long term.

Sustainable Co-ownership: A model of coexistence in which the shared resources of a residential complex are managed to balance economic, environmental, and social factors. This model promotes decisions that ensure the well-being of residents and the long-term care of the environment.

Chapter 4
The Role of AI in Product Innovation:
A Literature Review and Bibliometric Study

Ümmühan Nida Erol
http://orcid.org/0009-0007-2321-262X
Mersin University, Turkey

Seçil Özen
http://orcid.org/0000-0003-1657-3033
Mersin University, Turkey

Kalender Özcan Atilgan
http://orcid.org/0000-0003-1482-4505
Mersin University, Turkey

ABSTRACT

Artificial intelligence (AI) is positioned not only as a technological innovation but also as a key driving force of organizational transformation in today's digital economy. In this context, the aim of this study is to investigate the impact of AI on Product Innovation processes through a systematic literature review supported by bibliometric analysis. The study investigates existing academic publications to identify leading contributors, major research themes, and collaboration patterns within this interdisciplinary field. A total of 85 articles were analyzed using bibliometric techniques. Influential authors, institutions, and methodological trends were mapped using data derived from prominent academic databases. The analysis reveals the evolution of AI-related Product Innovation research, current gaps in the literature,

DOI: 10.4018/979-8-2600-0439-5.ch004

and future research directions. This chapter provides both theoretical contributions and strategic insights for practitioners, offering a conceptual foundation for future studies at the intersection of AI and Product Innovation.

INTRODUCTION

In recent years, AI has become a transformative force in various industries and has dramatically changed the way organizations pursue innovation (Ali et al., 2024; Haenlein & Kaplan, 2019). The incorporation of artificial intelligence into various industries has profoundly changed traditional innovation strategies (Mariani et al., 2023a). An important area affected by this change is product innovation, where AI not only accelerates development timelines, but also facilitates new forms of value creation. Product innovation encompasses the creation and improvement of products that meet evolving customer demands, benefit from technological progress, and offer a strategic advantage in the marketplace (Tehci, 2024).

Within its wide range of applications, the role of AI in product innovation is increasingly attracting academic and industrial attention by offering new ways to increase creativity, increase efficiency and strengthen competitive positioning (Mariani et al., 2023b; Zhu & Luo, 2023). AI significantly impacts contemporary innovation practices. It uses generative algorithms to improve product design and uses predictive analytics to facilitate faster decision making (Regenwetter et al., 2022).

The combination of AI and product innovation is generating growing interest in how AI can contribute to product development. However, despite the increase in the number of these studies, the existing literature has a dispersed structure, and there are no comprehensive assessments yet systematically revealing the intellectual structure and thematic evolution of this evolving field (Jabeur et al., 2024; Witkowski & Wodecki, 2025).

To fill this gap, this study combines a systematic literature review and bibliometric analysis to examine the role of AI in product innovation. By analyzing publication trends, leading authors, influential journals, and thematic clusters, it is aimed to provide researchers and practitioners with an overview of the current area of research and its future orientations. This two-pronged approach contributes to research and practice at the intersection of AI and product innovation, revealing areas that have not been adequately studied and emerging themes, in addition to synthesizing existing knowledge.

BACKGROUND

Emergence of Digital Technologies in Product Innovation

The economic and technology models that are developing in this "digital economy" have already had an impact on the old industries and given rise to whole new ones. The industry is changing and evolving in the direction of total digitization and intelligent production processes to guarantee high efficiency. The term "Fourth Industrial Revolution" (also known as Industry 4.0 and 4IR) describes this change and digitization of industrial processes is the main emphasis of this change (Petrillo et al., 2018; Sichoongwe, 2024).

The digital future is undergoing dynamic transformation due to technological trends. Information technology (IT) advancements are also pushing businesses to adopt new, creative business models and a variety of business adaptation procedures (Dwivedi et al., 2023; Tohănean et al., 2020).

The global proliferation of digital technologies is not only reshaping traditional manufacturing sectors but also revolutionizing services, healthcare, education, agriculture, and financial systems (Abiodun et al., 2023; do Nascimento et al., 2023; Gomber et al., 2018, Wolfert et al., 2017; Zahid et al., 2025). Emerging technologies such as the Internet of Things (IoT), AI, Machine Learning (ML), big data analytics, blockchain, and cloud computing are transforming how organizations collect, analyze, and act on data, thereby enabling more agile, intelligent, and customer-centric operations (Maroufkhani et al., 2020). In particular, AI-powered systems are enhancing predictive maintenance in manufacturing, personalizing consumer experiences in retail, and supporting decision-making in healthcare diagnostics (Lee et al., 2015). Moreover, digital platforms have facilitated the rise of the gig economy, reshaped labor markets, and introduced novel forms of employment and value creation (Kraus et al., 2021). However, this transformation is not without challenges. Issues related to data privacy, cybersecurity, digital literacy, and workforce displacement due to automation have become increasingly pressing (Brennen & Kreiss, 2016).

As the pace of digital transformation accelerates, it is imperative for policymakers, industry leaders, and academic researchers to collaboratively develop strategies that foster inclusive digital growth, ensure ethical technology deployment, and address the socio-economic disparities that may arise in a rapidly digitizing world (Buonocore et al., 2024). This has the potential to greatly improve business decision-making (Babina et al., 2024). From the perspective of businesses, AI has been briefly defined as "prediction technology that reduces the cost of predictions" (Agrawal et al., 2018). Whether AI technologies not only revolutionize the production of products and services but also enhance the innovation process itself will have a significant impact on the economy (Toner-Rodgers, 2024).

One of the digital technologies that helps companies develop and expand in the digital era is AI, which has an impact on how companies innovate and adapt to the shifting demands of their customers (Mariani et al., 2023b). According to one of the comprehensive definitions, AI is defined as "the system's ability to interpret data and leverage computers and machines to enhance humans' decision-making, problem-solving capabilities, and technology-driven innovativeness" (Bahoo et al., 2023). Especially in the era of Industry 4.0, apps backed by AI have started to be used in innovation management across numerous industrial sectors to evaluate vast volumes of information, make precise judgments, and instantly adjust product performance (Jiang et al., 2023; Gama & Magistretti, 2025).

Therefore, AI models and computerized information processing should represent information from a multidimensional perspective (Bertoni et al., 2020). The process of developing new products is being transformed and redesigned by AI technologies such as ML algorithms, the IoT, automation, and intelligence-driven robotics (Bahoo et al., 2023).

Implementation of Product Innovation

More than ever, marketing and innovation are seen as key elements of competitive advantage and drivers of economic progress (Aboelmaged et al., 2024; Lukas & Ferrell, 2000). Examining and improving knowledge of the unique forces behind innovation in emerging economies is becoming more and more important (Anand et al., 2021).

In today's volatile and globalized business environment, companies are compelled to differentiate themselves through innovative products that meet increasingly personalized and dynamic consumer demands (Calantone et al., 2006). Moreover, firms in emerging economies often face unique constraints (such as limited R&D resources, institutional voids, and infrastructure challenges), which make product innovation not just a strategic option but a necessity for survival and growth (Dobni & Sand, 2018; Wang & Wang, 2024). In this context, product innovation is closely linked with organizational learning, market orientation, and dynamic capabilities, which collectively enable firms to sense and respond to opportunities more effectively (Jansen et al., 2006; Teece et al., 1997).

In recent years, the integration of AI into product innovation processes has introduced unprecedented opportunities and complexities. AI enables data-driven insights, rapid prototyping, personalized design, and even predictive performance evaluation, all of which significantly accelerate the New Product Development (NPD) lifecycle (Chui et al., 2018; Davenport et al., 2020). Particularly in the early stages of innovation, such as trend analysis, idea generation, and concept testing, AI technologies like natural language processing, ML, and generative design are becoming integral tools for innovation managers and product teams (Zhang et al., 2022). However, while AI enhances innovation performance, it also raises important questions regarding creativity, human oversight, and ethical responsibility (Cooper, 2023; Mubarak et al., 2024). Since "product refers to an offering by a for-profit or a not-for-profit organization to potential customers for use or consumption to satisfy a need and a want", "product innovation is the creation of value by using relevant knowledge and resources to implement an idea for a new product that meets a currently unmet need, a currently met need better than products presently available in the market, or a currently met need differently compared to products presently available in the market, or improvements in an existing product" (Varadarajan, 2018, p.155).

Thus, product innovation requires a lot of information, and "stimulating knowledge creation, embodiment, and transfer to foster innovation" is one way to do this (Nonaka, 2009; Von Krogh et al., 2000). The marketing discipline is said to stand to benefit the most from AI, and it is anticipated that AI will impact marketing strategies in the future (Davenport et al., 2020). It is also noteworthy that AI has progressively started to play a significant role in product innovation stages, particularly in the area of product design, in recent years (Zhang et al., 2022). Also, it is commonly known that new-product development and innovation are critical to long-term company success (Knudsen et al., 2023). There is a need to better understand the potential of possible AI applications in NPD and product innovation, from idea generation to commercialization and planning the launch (Cooper, 2021). AI plays a new role in product innovation processes, according to existing research in the domains of marketing and computer science (Hong et al., 2023).

In the future, as AI becomes more prevalent in NPD and product innovation, firms will develop and launch new products much faster than traditional methods, but at the same time issues such as ethics, data security, and intellectual property will become bigger areas of debate (Cooper & McCausland, 2024; Haefner et al., 2021).

AI Usage in Product Innovation

AI has evolved beyond being a mere technological advancement; it now serves as a transformative force that redefines organizational workflows, decision-making dynamics, and, notably, the processes through which products are conceptualized, developed, and introduced to markets (Shrestha et al., 2021). Positioned at the convergence of computer science and data analytics, AI encompasses the development of systems designed to emulate human cognitive functions, such as learning, reasoning, and problem-solving, through advanced algorithmic architectures (Lake et al., 2017). Its foundational subfields, including ML, deep learning, natural language processing, and computer vision, have gained significant traction across diverse sectors ranging from healthcare and finance to education and manufacturing. This growth has been driven by exponential increases in computational power and widespread access to extensive data repositories (Bertolini et al., 2021; Chakraborty et al., 2024; Janiesch et al., 2021; Nazareth & Reddy, 2023; Ozbayoglu et al., 2020; Wang et al., 2018).

Rather than merely automating routine operations, AI systems facilitate the extraction of actionable insights from complex datasets, enabling more intelligent, rapid, and data-informed decision-making (Duan et al., 2019). Consequently, AI has become a cornerstone of digital transformation strategies and is widely recognized as a critical enabler of both economic competitiveness and social innovation at the global level (Nagy & Somosi, 2022; Rashid & Kausik, 2024).

By fostering the creation of novel business models, enhanced service offerings, and user-centric experiences, AI not only boosts operational efficiency but also catalyzes innovation capabilities that strengthen organizational adaptability and market positioning (Chen et al., 2023; Singh et al., 2024).

One of the most significant applications of AI can be observed in the realm of product innovation (Lake et al., 2017). Leveraging its capacities for data analysis, pattern detection, and iterative learning, AI empowers firms to more accurately anticipate customer needs, simulate and evaluate design alternatives, and accelerate time-to-market processes (Cooper, 2024; Füller & Tekic, 2022; Haleem et al., 2022; Janiesch et al., 2021; Yaiprasert & Hidayanto, 2023). AI plays a role throughout the entire product lifecycle, including ideation, prototyping, manufacturing, and commercialization. It functions not only as a productivity-enhancing tool but also as a co-creative partner that transforms traditional development paradigms (Lo et al., 2021; Naeem et al., 2024). It amplifies human creativity by enabling the realization of product concepts that might have previously been inconceivable (Manu, 2024). In this context, AI is not simply an auxiliary tool in the innovation process, but a strategic driver that shapes and accelerates the evolution of new products (Tekic & Füller, 2023; Truong & Papagiannidis, 2022). In highly dynamic and competitive market environments, where consumer preferences are in constant flux, organizations that integrate AI into their innovation frameworks are better positioned to achieve sustained growth and long-term differentiation (Bahoo et al., 2023; Gao et al., 2025).

Product innovation is the combination of creative ideas, advanced technologies, and strategic innovations to fill market gaps and meet customer expectations. AI is revolutionizing this process, expanding the boundaries of innovation by providing speed, accuracy, and predictive power at every stage, from idea generation to prototype testing (Fritsch & Meschede, 2001).

AI is transforming all areas of the business world, and while companies have embraced it for different purposes, the primary advantage they've gained is enhanced innovation (Enholm et al., 2022). Product innovation is crucial for companies looking to stay relevant and attract customers in the highly competitive marketplace of today

(Cooper & Edgett, 2010). AI has become an effective tool for driving innovation in a number of industries as technology advances (Lei et al., 2022).

AI is transforming product innovation by enabling businesses to more accurately predict market demands, anticipate trends and evaluate large amounts of customer data (Cooper, 2000).

Researchers can more efficiently prioritize possible improvements with AI-powered prediction models, which lowers the expenses and inefficiencies of trial-and-error experimentation. The productivity of research and the entire innovation process is greatly impacted by AI's capacity to improve forecasts and speed up innovation processes, even if it cannot completely replace human scientists (Cockburn et al., 2018; Saini et al., 2025).

For example, AI-enabled solutions can analyze comments from customers or social media comments to find trends and drive design improvements (Sreenivasan & Suresh, 2024; Güneş, 2023). In addition, AI algorithms can create design prototypes or model how a product can work in real situations, greatly reducing research and development time and costs (Tsang & Lee, 2022; Yu, 2025). Large companies like Amazon and Tesla have already set standards for other companies, using AI to improve the user experience and personalize products (Cooper, 2024; Davidson & Rajeswari, 2025).

AI is expected to play a crucial role in product creation in the future at all stages, from ideation and design to development and post-launch optimization (Hermann & Hermann, 2022). Significant advantages include cost savings, accelerated time to market, better product quality, and better alignment with changing customer demands when integrating AI into innovation processes (Martin & Zimmermann, 2024). Furthermore, AI-powered insights from big data analytics can help predict market trends more accurately and allow for real-time user feedback response (Saura et al., 2024). The use of AI in product development is not without its difficulties, nevertheless, despite its revolutionary promise. Data privacy concerns, algorithmic transparency, and ethical implications are still important challenges that businesses need to take proactive measures to resolve (Balasubramaniam et al., 2023; Xue & Pang 2022). Responsible AI governance, including regulatory compliance and ethical frameworks, is essential to ensure that technological advancement does not come at the expense of user trust or societal well-being (Brey & Dainow, 2024; Papagiannidis et al., 2025).

AI-Driven Methods on Product Innovation

In today's digital era, developing a data-driven culture has become a critical factor in organizational advancement. This transformation has been significantly shaped by the incorporation of AI into business analytics, allowing companies to enhance the speed and precision of their decision-making processes (Chaudhuri et al., 2024).

Businesses may make decisions more quickly and effectively using AI-supported innovation processes because of data analytics and ML methods. AI-driven innovation supports innovative problem-solving techniques, which makes it easier to find and apply new ideas (Ince et al., 2021; Vocke et al., 2019).

Innovation processes will become more automated, data-driven, and user experience-centered in the upcoming years as AI technologies continue to advance (Abdelfattah et al., 2024; Quan et al., 2023). In addition to efficiency, these developments are also expected to contribute to sustainability by supporting ecologically responsible production methods (Frank, 2021; Van Wynsberghe, 2021).

Throughout the whole product development lifecycle, from ideation to market launch, AI's integration into innovation is apparent (Cooper, 2024). At the ideation phase, AI-powered tools can mine data from customer reviews, social media, and market reports to identify unmet needs and emerging trends (Nasrabadi et al., 2024). Businesses may extract sentiment and feedback from large text databases using Natural Language Processing (NLP), which helps them innovate in a more focused and user-centered way (Jim et al., 2024). Decision-making is further improved by ML algorithms, which forecast consumer preferences by using demographic information and past purchasing behavior (GhorbanTanhaei et al., 2024). These models can simulate market reactions to hypothetical product features, allowing developers to fine-tune concepts before investing in full-scale production (Elalem et al., 2023).

AI is capable of suggesting the best material selections, design changes, or feature combinations, for example, that satisfy user expectations and budgetary restrictions (Al-Sarayreh et al., 2023). Such support enhances design accuracy and reduces trial-and-error iterations. Furthermore, generative AI has given product designers additional options (Furtado et al., 2024). Algorithms such as Generative Adversarial Networks (GANs) can mimic existing styles and optimize them according to predetermined criteria, thereby generating entirely new product designs (Narteni et al., 2025). These AI-generated prototypes accelerate the design process while fostering creative exploration beyond traditional methods. Compared to traditional approaches, industries such as consumer electronics, fashion and automotive use AI technologies to produce several prototypes in a very short time (Liao et al., 2024).

Finally, during the testing and launch phases, AI enhances efficiency through real-time monitoring, predictive analytics, and automated quality control systems (Füller et al., 2022). AI models can identify potential design flaws, predict demand fluctuations, and support dynamic pricing strategies so that the final product reaches the market with a higher chance of success (Elalem et al., 2023). This data-centric approach helps minimize product failure risk while optimizing launch timing.

In conclusion, AI-driven methods are fundamentally reshaping how companies approach product innovation, from ideation to market launch (Babina et al., 2024). By harnessing large-scale data and advanced algorithms, businesses are not only accelerating time-to-market and reducing development costs but also delivering products that are increasingly tailored to customer expectations (Tian et al., 2024). However, the integration of AI into innovation processes raises important ethical concerns surrounding data privacy, algorithmic transparency, and the evolving role of human creativity. While AI holds remarkable potential to augment and transform innovation, it should be viewed as a powerful enabler rather than a replacement for human insight (Kumar et al., 2025). The future of product innovation lies in a thoughtful synergy between human expertise and machine intelligence. Organizations that successfully navigate this balance will be best positioned to thrive in an increasingly innovation-driven and ethically-conscious economy (Sreenivasan & Suresh, 2024). Balancing human insight with machine intelligence will thus be key to unlocking the full potential of AI in product innovation (Roberts & Candi, 2024).

A Bibliometric Study on AI Usage in Product Innovation

The integration of AI into product innovation processes has become a growing area of academic interest in recent years. AI technologies have begun to redefine the boundaries of innovation by enabling firms to enhance efficiency, improve decision-making, and reduce time-to-market in product innovation. Cooper (2024) emphasizes that AI is revolutionizing product innovation by accelerating development timelines, optimizing resource allocation, and enabling more targeted customer insights.

As the intersection between AI and product innovation continues to evolve, it is essential to understand how this relationship has been explored within the academic literature. In a complementary work, Cooper and McCausland (2024) discuss how AI can be embedded into the traditional stage-gate process, leading to more agile and data-driven product development pipelines. Recent academic interest in the intersection of AI and product innovation has resulted in a diverse body of empirical studies. These contributions collectively demonstrate how AI technologies reshape innovation strategies and support firm growth through enhanced product development capabilities. Cooper (2023) highlights how the integration of AI into new product development represents a paradigm shift, redefining roles and decision mechanisms across the innovation lifecycle.

Although NPD and product innovation are closely related and often overlap, NPD generally refers to the broader process of bringing a new product to market, whereas product innovation may involve both the development of entirely new products and the improvement or redesign of existing ones (Wang & Chen 2020; Qin et al., 2024). Earlier foundational work by Cooper (2000) outlines the strategic importance of aligning technology and innovation efforts, laying the groundwork for AI-enabled innovation frameworks. AI has the potential to speed up product innovation, however, obstacles including data-related issues, a lack of AI knowledge, and a lack of a creative culture prevent its widespread implementation. Building on this, Cooper (2025) analyzes AI adoption among SMEs and reveals that organizational readiness, talent availability, and strategic vision are key enablers of successful implementation.

However, once these barriers are removed, AI may be incorporated into product development procedures to open up new avenues for creativity. A strategic approach built on ongoing learning and adaptation is necessary for the future of AI-driven innovation processes, but ethical concerns and obligations must also be taken into account (Cooper, 2025). In the study, Haefner et al. (2021) discusses how ML and AI systems can replace humans in innovation management and the key elements that should be considered in the transition to digital innovation organization. Cooper (2021), reflecting on the pandemic's impact, argues that turbulent times can catalyze innovation—particularly when AI is leveraged to enable remote ideation, rapid prototyping, and real-time feedback loops. Babina et al., (2024) have developed a new benchmark of AI investment using firm-level resume data and found that AI investments have increased sales, employment and market value in firms, especially through product innovation.

This aligns with Cooper and Edgett (2010), who emphasize the importance of having a robust innovation strategy to successfully incorporate emerging technologies such as AI into business models. Similarly, Chatterjee et al., (2024) emphasize the role of AI in improving innovation efficiency and outcomes. Expanding the technological perspective, Kim et al. (2022) present a practical implementation of AI-enabled innovation within a smart manufacturing context. Bai et al. (2022) explore how AI can be creatively integrated into innovation and entrepreneurship education, particularly among students at internet-based universities. Adigwe et al. (2024) quantitatively explore the transformative role of AI in enhancing organizational competitiveness, reshaping socioeconomic structures, and influencing national and global economic strategies.

Together, these studies highlight the multifaceted contributions of AI to product innovation, from strategic growth factors and enterprise capabilities to infrastructure-level applications in production. They also reflect a growing consensus that AI integration is no longer optional but rather essential for firms aiming to sustain innovation in rapidly changing markets. The current study contributes to the field of product innovation and AI by use of bibliometric analysis to examine the details of the studies conducted and laying out a comprehensive agenda for future research. For a comprehensive literature review, we searched the widely used Scopus scientific database. Since this database is known for indexing high-quality articles, we focused only on this database for our search. Scopus' broad scope, diverse subject areas, and ability to assess quality research make it a powerful and reliable resource in academic research (Dorta-González & Santana-Jiménez, 2018). This section starts with the description of the methodology adopted in the study.

MAIN FOCUS OF THE CHAPTER

Methodology

Bibliometric analysis is a popular and an effective method for exploring, summarizing, and synthesizing large volumes of literature. Scholars may (1) obtain a comprehensive picture, (2) pinpoint knowledge gaps, (3) generate new research ideas, and (4) place their planned contributions to the area with the use of bibliometric analysis. When the evaluation's scope is vast and the dataset is too big for manual review, bibliometric analysis is employed (Donthu et al., 2021). Bibliometric methods have been used for providing quantitative analysis of written publications such as citations and other scientific metrics, and research trends, institutions and countries, important authors of the field, and prominent publications (Ellegaard & Wallin, 2015; Ellegaard, 2018).

The only bibliographic databases that bibliometricians could use to create extensive bibliometric indicators were created for more than 50 years by the Institute for Scientific Information (ISI, which is now a part of Thomson Reuters). Prior to the establishment of Scopus by publisher Reed Elsevier in 2004, the primary sources of bibliometric data were ISI's citation indexes, which are now regrouped under the Web of Science (WoS) (Archambault et al., 2009).

It is known that the main sources of citation data are still WoS and Scopus. The majority of the journals indexed in WoS are included in Scopus, which also covers a far larger number of journals than WoS (Mongeon, & Paul-Hus, 2016). With time, Scopus has established itself as a trustworthy source of comprehensive bibliographic data, surpassing WoS in certain areas (Pranckutė, 2021). Thus, as in recent bibliometric studies related on AI and product innovation (eg., Aboelmaged et al., 2024; Dhamija & Bag, 2020; Gama & Magistretti, 2025) the Scopus database is selected due to its most comprehensive database and precise citation and indexing of scientific work. Furthermore, many pioneering bibliometric studies in the literature (e.g., Senthil et al., 2024) have presented reliable results based on Scopus-driven analyses.

This study identifies the necessary steps for conducting a literature review and to map scientific production, utilizing PRISMA, which is the accepted standard for presenting evidence in systematic reviews. Our preliminary search queries included the terms "product innovation" and "artificial intelligence". The scope of the study is limited to journal articles published in the English language; other types of publications such as books, conferences, letters, etc. are excluded from the analysis. This initial screening process generated a total of 94 studies. Subsequently, in the second step, the refinement was conducted based on subject areas as Business, Management and Accounting; Computer Science; Engineering; Social Sciences; Economics, Econometrics and Finance; Decision Sciences to achieve the incorporation of relevant study domains. After applying all relevant filters, 85 articles were retained for the final analysis.

Two bibliometric analysis methods were selected to find new trends and ways that people work together in the field: performance analysis and research field mapping based on network analyses. These studies are analyzed using different bibliometric analysis techniques such as keyword relationships, citation networks, and collaboration maps. During the analysis process, VOSviewer software has been used to visualize and interpret the data. The steps of the bibliometric study are shown in Figure 1.

Figure 1. Steps of the Bibliometric Analysis Process

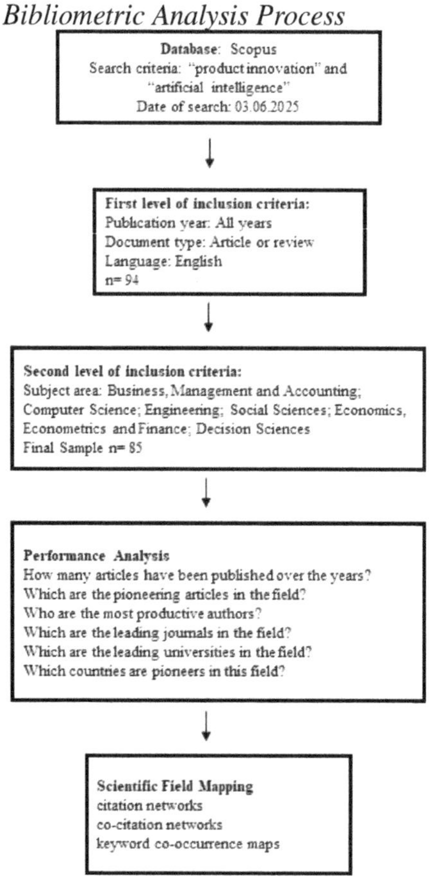

Source: Created by the authors.

Results of the Bibliometric Analysis

The bibliometric analysis started with the performance analysis of collected data. Scientific publications on AI Usage in Product Innovation began in 1987 and number of publications per year are presented in figure 2. As can be seen from figure 2, a steady increase in the number of publications can be observed since 2017. The highest number of publications was recorded in 2024, which indicates that interest on the topic has increased in recent years.

In figure 3, It is clearly seen that the country with the most publications is by far institutions in China, followed by the USA and Germany. This shows that the research area is particularly focused on China and is actively supported by the United States and European countries at the global level. The distribution of publications reveals that the subject attracts international academic interest and has a structure open to global collaborations.

Figure 2. Documents by year

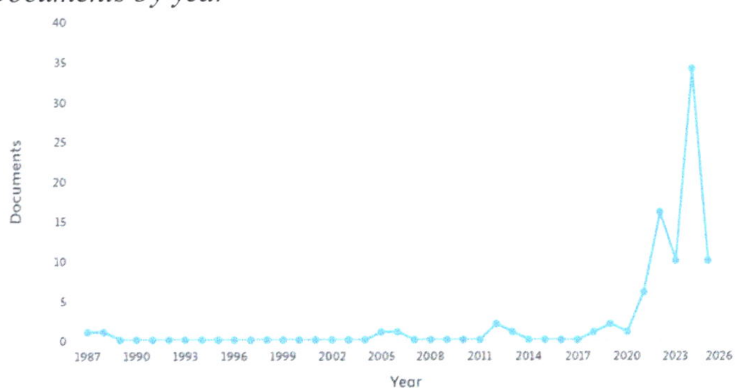

Source: Adapted from Scopus (Elsevier, 2025, data retrieved June 3, 2025).

According to the data obtained from the Scopus database, the authors with the most publications in the research field were analyzed graphically and presented in figure 4. Figure 4 shows the number of publications of the first 10 authors. The most productive author is Cooper, R.G., who heads the list with a total of 7 publications. All other authors (Bilgram, V., Brem, A.M., Chatterjee, S., Chaudhuri, R., Damioli, G., Hahn, A., He, A., Jin, S., Luh, D.B.) appear on the list with an equal number of publications, i.e. 2 each. This shows that Cooper, R.G., played a central and leading role in the development of the field.

Figure 3. Documents by country or territory

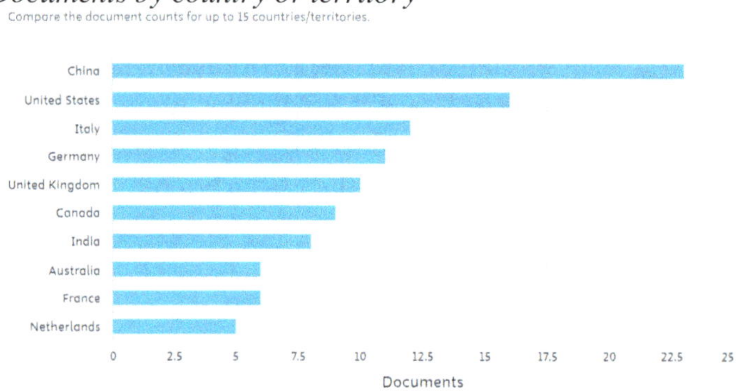

Source: Adapted from Scopus (Elsevier, 2025, data retrieved June 3, 2025).

Figure 5 represents the top 10 journals by publication count within the given dataset. IEEE Engineering Management Review and Technological Forecasting and Social Change stand out with the highest number of publications. These journals dominate the dataset, suggesting a strong focus on technology and management in the analyzed research. Other journals such as Annals of Operations Research and Journal of Business Research also show consistent representation. This analysis is valuable for identifying influential publication outlets in the field and can guide future literature reviews or journal targeting strategies.

Figure 4. Documents by author

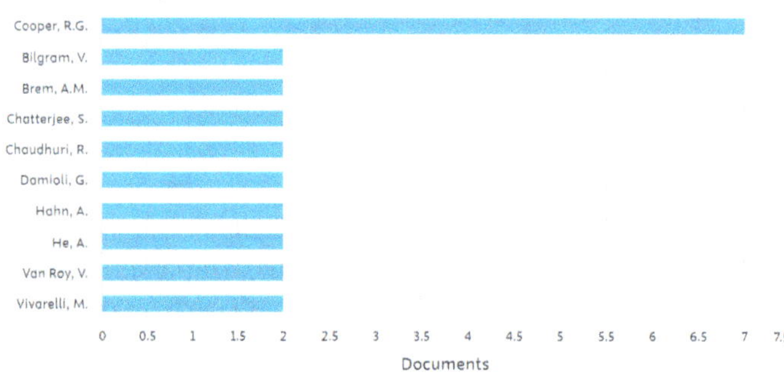

Source: Adapted from Scopus (Elsevier, 2025, data retrieved June 3, 2025).

In figure 6, contributions to the AI Usage in Product Innovation field of the universities are ranked according to the publications. McMaster University (Canada), DeGroote School of Business (Canada), Università Cattolica del Sacro Cuore (Italy), and United Nations University Maastricht (Netherlands) are the pioneering universities in this field.

Figure 5. Distribution of publications among top journals

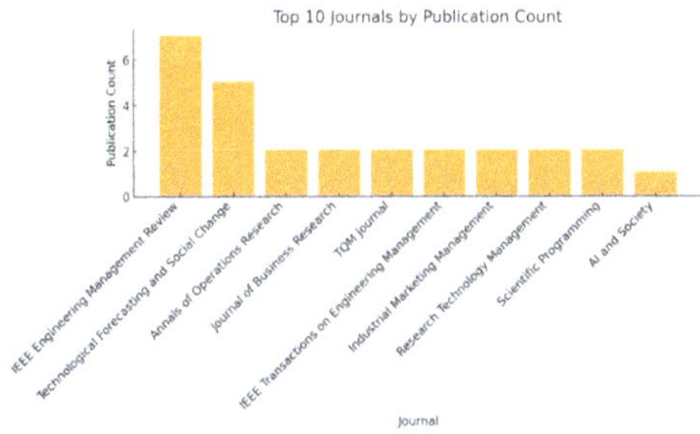

Source: Adapted from Scopus (Elsevier, 2025, data retrieved June 3, 2025).

Figure 6. Distribution of leading universities in the field

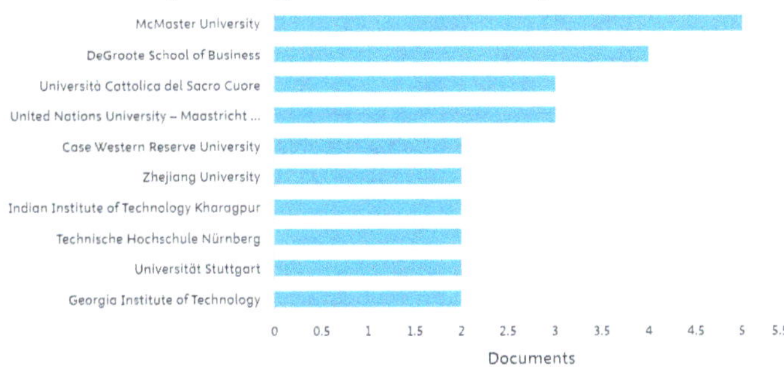

Source: Adapted from Scopus (Elsevier, 2025, data retrieved June 3, 2025).

Table 1 highlights the top 10 most cited articles in the dataset, which can be considered as pioneering works in their respective research areas. These articles have had a significant impact and are widely referenced in the field.

Table 1. Top 10 Pioneering Articles in the Field

Title	Year	Journal	# of citation
Artificial intelligence, firm growth, and product innovation	2024	Journal of Financial Economics	195
Artificial Intelligence-Based Sensors for Next Generation IoT Applications: A Review	2021	IEEE Sensors Journal	155
Types of innovation and artificial intelligence: A systematic quantitative literature review and research agenda	2023	Journal of Business Research	150

continued on following page

Table 1. Continued

Title	Year	Journal	# of citation
Artificial intelligence and industrial innovation: Evidence from German firm-level data	2022	Research Policy	149
Artificial intelligence and corporate innovation: A review and research agenda	2023	Technological Forecasting and Social Change	141
Does data-driven culture impact innovation and performance of a firm? An empirical examination	2024	Annals of Operations Research	137
Measuring GDP in the digital economy: Increasing dependence on uncaptured GDP	2018	Technological Forecasting and Social Change	131
Intelligent additive manufacturing and design state of the art and future perspectives	2022	Additive Manufacturing	95
Employee turnover: A neural network solution	2005	Computers and Operations Research	83
Adoption of robust business analytics for product innovation and organizational performance: the mediating role of organizational data-driven culture	2024	Annals of Operations Research	79

Source: Created by the authors based on bibliometric data retrieved from Scopus (June 3, 2025).

Scientific Field Mapping

The collected data were then subjected to scientific field mapping to analyze and visually represent the current and the evolving cognitive structure of the research field. Bibliometric analysis is frequently conducted alongside network visualization tools, including software like VOSviewer that offer a fully graphical user interface (Van Eck & Waltman, 2011).

This study utilized three primary visualizations: citation networks, which illustrate the intellectual connections formed when one publication cites another; co-authorship networks, which uncover collaborative ties among authors and their scholarly influence; and co-word (keyword co-occurrence) maps, which represent associations among keywords and emphasize key research themes (Donthu et al., 2021).

Citation Network Analysis

Citation network analysis is an effective technique that provides an objective and visual presentation of an area of study by providing crucial data to pinpoint knowledge gaps, patterns, and connections between scientific studies on any subject, aiding in the advancement of any area. Citation network analysis can be used to identify new relevant publications and to show the relationships between articles and authors both qualitatively and quantitatively by grouping them (Li et al., 2022; Martinez-Perez, et al., 2020).

In this study, firstly, a document-level network map was created as a citation network analysis, which analyzes the citation relationships between publications and shows which document has cited which document. Thus, the most cited articles and the studies that cite each other were revealed that can be seen from Figure 7. Afterwards, in order to examine international research collaborations and their impact areas, network analysis was conducted showing citation relationships according to the countries to which the authors are affiliated. When Figure 8 is examined, it is seen that the USA, Italy and Austria create a citation network among themselves, while China, Australia, India, France, the Netherlands and Russia create a citation network among themselves.

Figure 7. Network analysis by documents

Source: Created using VOSviewer software based on data retrieved from Scopus (June 3, 2025).

Figure 8 Network analysis by countries

Source: Created using VOSviewer software based on data retrieved from Scopus (June 3, 2025).

Co-Citation Networks

One kind of bibliometric network that is produced by examining the co-citation relationships among academic papers is called a co-citation network. When two or more articles are cited jointly by other publications, this is known as co-citation (Hernández & Dorta-González, 2020; Chen et al., 2024). The reference co-citation network with a minimum of five citations for a source is shown in Figure 9. In this study, the co-citation network is divided into five clusters with different colors: blue, yellow, green, red and purple. As can be from Figure 9, study of Cooper, R.G. (with 57 citations) has the largest node and is positioned in the middle, suggesting that it has played the most significant role in the evolution of the literature on AI usage in product innovation.

Figure 9. Co-Citation Networks

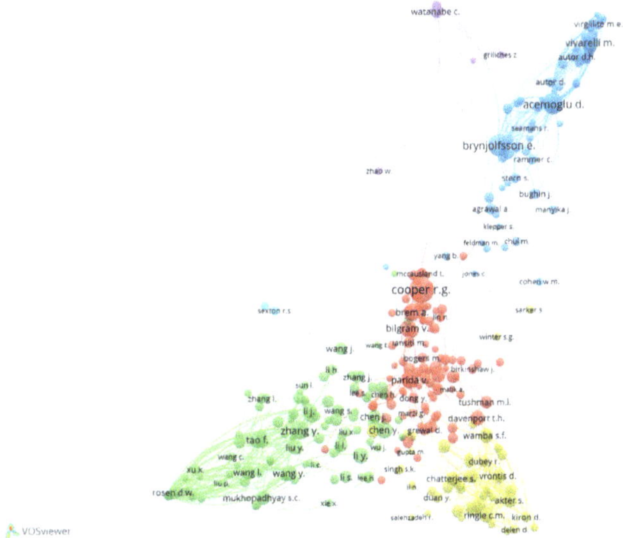

Source: Created using VOSviewer software based on data retrieved from Scopus (June 3, 2025).

Keyword Co-Occurrence Map

In addition to displaying the frequency of keyword occurrences, a co-occurrence map highlights the quantity and intensity of linkages between the keywords. Furthermore, the keywords were arranged into clusters that could be easily identified by their distinct colors, making it easier to spot related study trends (Cheng et al., 2020; Sinha & Dhillon, 2024). In this study, VOSviewer software was used to assess word co-occurrence. To guarantee that the most pertinent keywords for the topics were chosen, the minimum number of keywords was set at two in order to reduce noise in the co-occurrences map. Figure 10 illustrates the keyword co-occurrence network that identifies six clusters with different colors. Both "artificial intelligence" and "product innovation" as indicated by the most prominent nodes, have the highest occurrence and co-occurrence because they are part of the selection criteria for bibliometric data.

Figure 10. Keyword Co-Occurrence Map

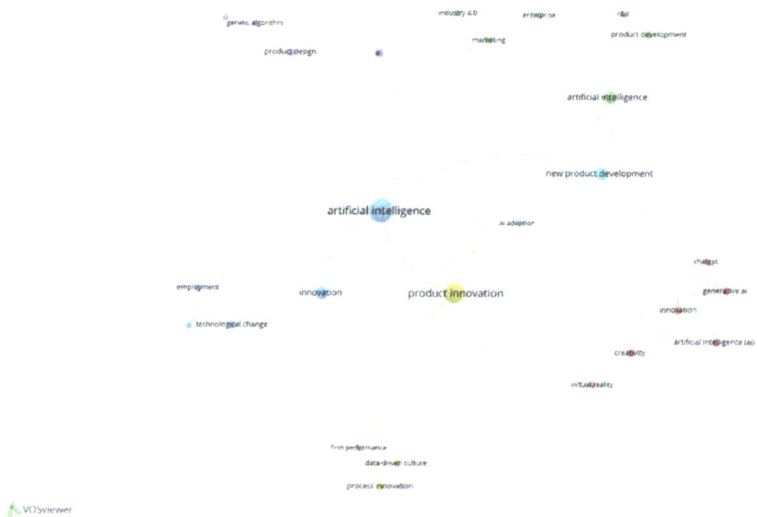

Source: Created using VOSviewer software based on data retrieved from Scopus (June 3, 2025).

FUTURE RESEARCH DIRECTIONS

In the future, this study could be repeated using different search parameters, multi-source databases, time periods, or bibliometric analytics. Additionally, the impact of AI on product development processes can be comparatively analyzed across various industries. The level of AI integration into product development may also be examined based on business type and digital maturity. In particular, an in-depth investigation into the influence of AI on new product development across different sectors could offer valuable contributions to the literature.

CONCLUSION

The current book chapter presents a bibliometric analysis of 85 papers on AI Usage in Product Innovation over the past 38 years. The authors, nations, top-cited articles, subject keywords, and research evolution have all been thoroughly examined in the review.

The most productive countries and trends in the field's research output are used to characterize the development patterns of AI usage in product innovation. Finding the leading contributions suggests potential researchers and universities for future studies. It is possible to say that there are publication opportunities for publications related to the Use of AI in Product Innovation. To assist scholars in identifying research gaps in AI Usage in Product Innovation, leading topic areas and emerging research areas are available.

When the history of studies in this field is examined, it can be said that the subject is still in the embryonic stage. Considering the interdisciplinary nature of this field, it seems that more research is needed by different researchers, especially in the fields of product and production management, marketing, and AI. The clustering of research into themes like AI-based product development, data-driven innovation, and AI in management practices points to the growing importance of interdisciplinary research in bridging the gap between technology and business management. This is consistent with the resource-based view, where firms leveraging AI technologies can create unique capabilities that lead to sustained innovation. Despite the fact that the current research's bibliometric analysis and mapping visualization of papers relevant to AI Usage in Product Innovation have yielded several fascinating results, while evaluating the results of current study, some limitations should be considered. These limitations may mostly arise from the structural features of the bibliometric analysis (such as filtering process) and the quality of the selected database.

Firstly, depending on the choice of keyword as the search strategy, it leads to missing publications that do not contain the selected keywords. Therefore, keyword selection should be taken into consideration when interpreting the findings of the study. The second limitation is that the data is downloaded only from Scopus database, maybe a search from a multi-source database would be more adequate. Thirdly, other different publication types other than articles, such as conference papers, were excluded during this study's filtering process.

Finally, publications were selected only from those in English; studies in other languages were not included in this research. As a result, these limitations mentioned continue to be problems that require more investigation. Even if this study's analysis may not have included all of the important publications on AI Usage in Product Innovation, it is reasonable to assume that the findings provide trustworthy insight into the field of expertise. In conclusion, while AI's integration into product innovation is still in its early stages, the field is ripe for further interdisciplinary research. Future studies should explore the intersections of AI with product and production management, marketing, and other sectors to fully understand its potential and challenges. The findings from this study offer a foundation for scholars to identify research gaps and emerging trends in AI-driven product innovation.

REFERENCES

Abdelfattah, F., Salah, M., Dahleez, K., Darwazeh, R., & Al Halbusi, H. (2024). The future of competitive advantage in Oman: Integrating green product innovation, AI, and intellectual capital in business strategies. *International Journal of Innovation Studies*, *8*(2), 154–171.

Abiodun, T., Rampersad, G., & Brinkworth, R. (2023). Driving industrial digital transformation. *Journal of Computer Information Systems*, *63*(6), 1345–1361.

Aboelmaged, M., Bani-Melhem, S., Al-Hawari, M. A., & Ali, I. (2024). Product innovation research over the past 60 years: A bibliometric analysis of intellectual structure and emergent trends. *Benchmarking*, *31*(6), 2034–2060.

Adigwe, C. S., Olaniyi, O. O., Olabanji, S. O., Okunleye, O. J., Mayeke, N. R., & Ajayi, S. A. (2024). Forecasting the future: The interplay of artificial intelligence, innovation, and competitiveness and its effect on the global economy. Innovation, and Competitiveness and its Effect on the Global Economy (February 26, 2024).

Agrawal, A., Gans, J., & Goldfarb, A. (2018). *Prediction machines: The simple economics of artificial intelligence*. Harvard Business Review Press.

Al-Sarayreh, M., Reis, M. G., Carr, A., & dos Reis, M. M. (2023). Inverse design and AI/Deep generative networks in food design: A comprehensive review. *Trends in Food Science & Technology*, *138*, 215–228.

Ali, M., Khan, T. I., & Khattak, M. N., & ŞENER, İ. (2024). Synergizing AI and business: Maximizing innovation, creativity, decision precision, and operational efficiency in high-tech enterprises. *Journal of Open Innovation*, *10*(3), 100352.

Anand, J., McDermott, G., Mudambi, R., & Narula, R. (2021). Innovation in and from emerging economies: New insights and lessons for international business research. *Journal of International Business Studies*, *52*, 545–559.

Archambault, É., Campbell, D., Gingras, Y., & Larivière, V. (2009). Comparing bibliometric statistics obtained from the Web of Science and Scopus. *Journal of the American Society for Information Science and Technology*, *60*(7), 1320–1326.

Babina, T., Fedyk, A., He, A., & Hodson, J. (2024). Artificial intelligence, firm growth, and product innovation. *Journal of Financial Economics*, *151*, 103745.

Bahoo, S., Cucculelli, M., & Qamar, D. (2023). Artificial intelligence and corporate innovation: A review and research agenda. *Technological Forecasting and Social Change*, *188*, 122264.

Bai, L., Sun, F., & Wang, W. (2022). [Retracted] Innovative Application of Artificial Intelligence in the Field of Innovation and Entrepreneurship of College Students in Internet Colleges and Universities. *Computational Intelligence and Neuroscience*, *2022*(1), 3538755. PMID: 35978911

Balasubramaniam, N., Kauppinen, M., Rannisto, A., Hiekkanen, K., & Kujala, S. (2023). Transparency and explainability of AI systems: From ethical guidelines to requirements. *Information and Software Technology*, *159*, 107197.

Bertolini, M., Mezzogori, D., Neroni, M., & Zammori, F. (2021). Machine Learning for industrial applications: A comprehensive literature review. *Expert Systems with Applications*, *175*, 114820.

Bertoni, A., Yi, X., Baron, C., Esteban, P., & Vingerhoeds, R. (2020). A framework for data-driven design in a product innovation process: Data analysis and visualisation for model-based decision making. *International Journal of Product Development*, *24*(1), 68–94.

Brennen, J. S., & Kreiss, D. (2016). Digitalization. The international encyclopedia of communication theory and philosophy, 1-11.

Brey, P., & Dainow, B. (2024). Ethics by design for artificial intelligence. *AI and Ethics*, *4*(4), 1265–1277.

Buonocore, F., Annosi, M. C., de Gennaro, D., & Riemma, F. (2024). Digital transformation and social change: Leadership strategies for responsible innovation. *Journal of Engineering and Technology Management*, *74*, 101843.

Calantone, R. J., Cavusgil, S. T., & Zhao, Y. (2006). Learning orientation, firm innovation capability, and firm performance. *Industrial Marketing Management*, *31*(6), 515–524.

Chakraborty, C., Bhattacharya, M., Pal, S., & Lee, S. S. (2024). From machine learning to deep learning: Advances of the recent data-driven paradigm shift in medicine and healthcare. *Current Research in Biotechnology*, *7*, 100164.

Chatterjee, S., Chaudhuri, R., & Vrontis, D. (2024). Does data-driven culture impact innovation and performance of a firm? An empirical examination. *Annals of Operations Research*, *333*(2), 601–626.

Chaudhuri, R., Chatterjee, S., Vrontis, D., & Thrassou, A. (2024). Adoption of robust business analytics for product innovation and organizational performance: The mediating role of organizational data-driven culture. *Annals of Operations Research*, *339*(3), 1757–1791.

Chen, Q., Wang, Y., Gong, Y., & Liu, S. (2023). Ripping off regular consumers? The antecedents and consequences of consumers' perceptions of e-commerce platforms' digital power abuse. *Journal of Business Research*, *166*, 114123.

Chen, X., Mao, J., & Li, G. (2024). A co-citation approach to the analysis on the interaction between scientific and technological knowledge. *Journal of Informetrics*, *18*(3), 101548.

Cheng, Q., Wang, J., Lu, W., Huang, Y., & Bu, Y. (2020). Keyword-citation-keyword network: A new perspective of discipline knowledge structure analysis. *Scientometrics*, *124*, 1923–1943.

Chui, M., Manyika, J., Miremadi, M., Henke, N., Chung, R., Nel, P., & Malhotra, S. (2018). Notes from the AI frontier: Insights from hundreds of use cases. *McKinsey Global Institute*, *2*(267), 1–31.

Cockburn, I. M., Henderson, R., & Stern, S. (2018). The impact of artificial intelligence on innovation (Vol. 24449). Cambridge, MA, USA: National bureau of economic research.

Cooper, R. G. (2000). Product innovation and technology strategy. *Research Technology Management*, *43*(1), 38–41.

Cooper, R. G. (2021). Accelerating innovation: Some lessons from the pandemic. *Journal of Product Innovation Management*, *38*(2), 221–232. PMID: 33821086

Cooper, R. G. (2023). The artificial intelligence revolution in new-product development. *IEEE Engineering Management Review*, *52*(1), 195–211.

Cooper, R. G. (2024). The AI transformation of product innovation. *Industrial Marketing Management*, *119*, 62–74.

Cooper, R. G. (2025). SMEs' use of AI for new product development: Adoption rates by application and readiness-to-adopt. *Industrial Marketing Management*, *126*, 159–167.

Cooper, R. G., & Edgett, S. J. (2010). Developing a product innovation and technology strategy for your business. *Research Technology Management*, *53*(3), 33–40.

Cooper, R. G., & McCausland, T. (2024). AI and new product development. *Research Technology Management*, *67*(1), 70–75.

Davenport, T., Guha, A., Grewal, D., & Bressgott, T. (2020). How artificial intelligence will change the future of marketing. *Journal of the Academy of Marketing Science*, *48*, 24–42.

Davidson, J. D., & Rajeswari, P. S. (2025). A case study on how Amazon uses personalization to win back Prime subscription lapsers. Journal of Information Technology Teaching Cases, 20438869251325244.

Dhamija, P., & Bag, S. (2020). Role of artificial intelligence in operations environment: A review and bibliometric analysis. *The TQM Journal*, *32*(4), 869–896.

do Nascimento, I. J. B., Abdulazeem, H. M., Vasanthan, L. T., Martinez, E. Z., Zucoloto, M. L., Østengaard, L., & Novillo-Ortiz, D. (2023). The global effect of digital health technologies on health workers' competencies and health workplace: An umbrella review of systematic reviews and lexical-based and sentence-based meta-analysis. *The Lancet. Digital Health*, *5*(8), e534–e544. PMID: 37507197

Dobni, C. B., & Sand, C. (2018). Strategy shift: Integrating strategy and the firm's capability to innovate. *Business Horizons*, *61*(5), 797–808.

Donthu, N., Kumar, S., Mukherjee, D., Pandey, N., & Lim, W. M. (2021). How to conduct a bibliometric analysis: An overview and guidelines. *Journal of Business Research*, *133*, 285–296.

Dorta-González, P., & Santana-Jiménez, Y. (2018). Prevalence and citation advantage of gold open access in the subject areas of the Scopus database. *Research Evaluation*, *27*(1), 1–15.

Duan, Y., Edwards, J. S., & Dwivedi, Y. K. (2019). Artificial intelligence for decision making in the era of Big Data–evolution, challenges and research agenda. *International Journal of Information Management*, *48*, 63–71.

Dwivedi, Y. K., Kshetri, N., Hughes, L., Slade, E. L., Jeyaraj, A., Kar, A. K., & Wright, R. (2023). Opinion Paper:"So what if ChatGPT wrote it?" Multidisciplinary perspectives on opportunities, challenges and implications of generative conversational AI for research, practice and policy. *International Journal of Information Management*, *71*, 102642.

Elalem, Y. K., Maier, S., & Seifert, R. W. (2023). A machine learning-based framework for forecasting sales of new products with short life cycles using deep neural networks. *International Journal of Forecasting*, *39*(4), 1874–1894.

Ellegaard, O. (2018). The application of bibliometric analysis: Disciplinary and user aspects. *Scientometrics*, *116*(1), 181–202.

Ellegaard, O., & Wallin, J. A. (2015). The bibliometric analysis of scholarly production: How great is the impact? *Scientometrics*, *105*, 1809–1831. PMID: 26594073

Enholm, I. M., Papagiannidis, E., Mikalef, P., & Krogstie, J. (2022). Artificial intelligence and business value: A literature review. *Information Systems Frontiers*, *24*(5), 1709–1734.

Frank, B. (2021). Artificial intelligence-enabled environmental sustainability of products: Marketing benefits and their variation by consumer, location, and product types. *Journal of Cleaner Production*, *285*, 125242.

Fritsch, M., & Meschede, M. (2001). Product innovation, process innovation, and size. *Review of Industrial Organization*, *19*, 335–350.

Füller, J., Hutter, K., Wahl, J., Bilgram, V., & Tekic, Z. (2022). How AI revolutionizes innovation management–Perceptions and implementation preferences of AI-based innovators. *Technological Forecasting and Social Change*, *178*, 121598.

Furtado, L. S., Soares, J. B., & Furtado, V. (2024). A task-oriented framework for generative AI in design. *Journal of Creativity*, *34*(2), 100086.

Gama, F., & Magistretti, S. (2025). Artificial intelligence in innovation management: A review of innovation capabilities and a taxonomy of AI applications. *Journal of Product Innovation Management*, *42*(1), 76–111.

Gao, Y., Liu, S., & Yang, L. (2025). Artificial intelligence and innovation capability: A dynamic capabilities perspective. *International Review of Economics & Finance*, *•••*, 103923.

GhorbanTanhaei, H., Boozary, P., Sheykhan, S., Rabiee, M., Rahmani, F., & Hosseini, I. (2024). Predictive analytics in customer behavior: Anticipating trends and preferences. *Results in Control and Optimization*, *17*, 100462.

Gomber, P., Kauffman, R. J., Parker, C., & Weber, B. W. (2018). On the fintech revolution: Interpreting the forces of innovation, disruption, and transformation in financial services. *Journal of Management Information Systems*, *35*(1), 220–265.

Güneş, S. (2023). Extracting design knowledge from online product reviews to support design creativity. *International Journal of Design Creativity and Innovation*, *11*(4), 273–293.

Haefner, N., Wincent, J., Parida, V., & Gassmann, O. (2021). Artificial intelligence and innovation management: A review, framework, and research agenda . *Technological Forecasting and Social Change*, *162*, 120392.

Haenlein, M., & Kaplan, A. (2019). A brief history of artificial intelligence: On the past, present, and future of artificial intelligence. *California Management Review*, *61*(4), 5–14.

Haleem, A., Javaid, M., Qadri, M. A., Singh, R. P., & Suman, R. (2022). Artificial intelligence (AI) applications for marketing: A literature-based study. *International Journal of Intelligent Networks, 3*, 119–132.

Hermann, E., & Hermann, G. (2022). Artificial intelligence in research and development for sustainability: The centrality of explicability and research data management. *AI and Ethics*, *2*(1), 29–33.

Hernández, J. M., & Dorta-González, P. (2020). Interdisciplinarity metric based on the co-citation network. *Mathematics*, *8*(4), 544.

Hong, M. K., Hakimi, S., Chen, Y. Y., Toyoda, H., Wu, C., & Klenk, M. (2023). Generative AI for product design: Getting the right design and the design right. arXiv preprint arXiv:2306.01217.

İnce, H., İmamoğlu, S. E., & İmamoğlu, S. Z. (2021). Yapay Zeka Uygulamalarının Karar Verme Üzerine Etkileri: Kavramsal Bir Çalişma. *International Review of Economics and Management*, *9*(1), 50–63.

Jabeur, S. B., Stef, N., & Arfi, W. B. (2024). Artificial intelligence for innovation: a bibliometric analysis and structural variation approach. International Journal of Innovation Management, 28(05n06), 2450020.

Janiesch, C., Zschech, P., & Heinrich, K. (2021). Machine learning and deep learning. *Electronic Markets*, *31*(3), 685–695.

Jansen, J. J., Van Den Bosch, F. A., & Volberda, H. W. (2006). Exploratory innovation, exploitative innovation, and performance: Effects of organizational antecedents and environmental moderators. *Management Science*, *52*(11), 1661–1674.

Jiang, X., Jiang, X., Sun, W., & Fan, W. (2023). How do manufacturing firms manage artificial intelligence to drive iterative product innovation? *IEEE Transactions on Engineering Management.*

Jim, J. R., Talukder, M. A. R., Malakar, P., Kabir, M. M., Nur, K., & Mridha, M. F. (2024). Recent advancements and challenges of NLP-based sentiment analysis: A state-of-the-art review. Natural Language Processing Journal, 100059.

Kim, J., Seo, D., Moon, J., Kim, J., Kim, H., & Jeong, J. (2022). Design and implementation of an HCPS-based PCB smart factory system for next-generation intelligent manufacturing. *Applied Sciences (Basel, Switzerland)*, *12*(15), 7645.

Knudsen, M. P., Von Zedtwitz, M., Griffin, A., & Barczak, G. (2023). Best practices in new product development and innovation: Results from PDMA's 2021 global survey. *Journal of Product Innovation Management*, *40*(3), 257–275.

Kraus, S., Palmer, C., Kailer, N., Kallinger, F. L., & Spitzer, J. (2021). Digital entrepreneurship: A research agenda on new business models for the twenty-first century. *International Journal of Entrepreneurial Behaviour & Research, 25*(2), 353–375.

Kumar, M., Beninger, S., Reppel, A., Stanton, J., Vlaminck, D., & Watson, F. (2025). Your synthetic teammate: Enriching new product development with generative AI. *Business Horizons.*

Lake, B. M., Ullman, T. D., Tenenbaum, J. B., & Gershman, S. J. (2017). Building machines that learn and think like people. *Behavioral and Brain Sciences, 40*, e253. PMID: 27881212

Lee, J., Bagheri, B., & Kao, H. A. (2015). A cyber-physical systems architecture for industry 4.0-based manufacturing systems. *Manufacturing Letters, 3*, 18–23.

Lei, Y., Vyas, S., Gupta, S., & Shabaz, M. (2022). AI based study on product development and process design. *International Journal of System Assurance Engineering and Management*, •••, 1–7.

Li, Z., Wang, Y., & Deng, Z. (2022). Research on Evolution Characteristics and Factors of Nordic Green Patent Citation Network. *Sustainability, 14*(13), 7743.

Liao, W., Lu, X., Fei, Y., Gu, Y., & Huang, Y. (2024). Generative AI design for building structures. *Automation in Construction, 157*, 105187.

Lo, C. K., Chen, C. H., & Zhong, R. Y. (2021). A review of digital twin in product design and development. *Advanced Engineering Informatics, 48*, 101297.

Lukas, B. A., & Ferrell, O. C. (2000). The effect of market orientation on product innovation. *Journal of the Academy of Marketing Science, 28*(2), 239–247.

Manu, A. (2024). *Transcending imagination: Artificial intelligence and the future of creativity* (1st ed.). Chapman and Hall/CRC., DOI: 10.1201/9781003450139

Mariani, M. M., Machado, I., Magrelli, V., & Dwivedi, Y. K. (2023a). Artificial intelligence in innovation research: A systematic review, conceptual framework, and future research directions. *Technovation, 122*, 102623.

Mariani, M. M., Machado, I., & Nambisan, S. (2023b). Types of innovation and artificial intelligence: A systematic quantitative literature review and research agenda. *Journal of Business Research, 155*, 113364.

Maroufkhani, P., Wan Ismail, W. K., & Ghobakhloo, M. (2020). Big data analytics adoption model for small and medium enterprises. *Journal of Science and Technology Policy Management, 11*(4), 483–513.

Martin, K. D., & Zimmermann, J. (2024). Artificial intelligence and its implications for data privacy. *Current Opinion in Psychology*, •••, 101829. PMID: 38954851

Martinez-Perez, C., Alvarez-Peregrina, C., Villa-Collar, C., & Sánchez-Tena, M. Á. (2020). Current state and future trends: A citation network analysis of the academic performance field. *International Journal of Environmental Research and Public Health*, *17*(15), 5352. PMID: 32722277

Mongeon, P., & Paul-Hus, A. (2016). The journal coverage of Web of Science and Scopus: A comparative analysis. *Scientometrics*, *106*, 213–228.

Mubarak, M. F., Biggadike, C., Ahumada-Tello, E., & Evans, R. (2024). AI in New Product Development: Opportunities, Applications, and Managerial Implications. *IEEE Engineering Management Review*.

Naeem, R., Kohtamäki, M., & Parida, V. (2024). Artificial intelligence enabled product–service innovation: Past achievements and future directions. *Review of Managerial Science*, •••, 44–1.

Nagy, S., & Somosi, M. V. (2022). The relationship between social innovation and digital economy and society. arXiv preprint arXiv:2212.13840.

Narteni, S., Orani, V., Ferrari, E., Verda, D., Cambiaso, E., & Mongelli, M. (2025). Explainable evaluation of generative adversarial networks for wearables data augmentation. *Engineering Applications of Artificial Intelligence*, *145*, 110133.

Nasrabadi, M. A., Beauregard, Y., & Ekhlassi, A. (2024). The implication of user-generated content in new product development process: A systematic literature review and future research agenda. *Technological Forecasting and Social Change*, *206*, 123551.

Nazareth, N., & Reddy, Y. V. R. (2023). Financial applications of machine learning: A literature review. *Expert Systems with Applications*, *219*, 119640.

Nonaka, I. (2009). The knowledge-creating company. In *The economic impact of knowledge* (pp. 175–187). Routledge.

Ozbayoglu, A. M., Gudelek, M. U., & Sezer, O. B. (2020). Deep learning for financial applications: A survey. *Applied Soft Computing*, *93*, 106384.

Papagiannidis, E., Mikalef, P., & Conboy, K. (2025). Responsible artificial intelligence governance: A review and research framework. *The Journal of Strategic Information Systems*, *34*(2), 101885.

Petrillo, A., De Felice, F., Cioffi, R., & Zomparelli, F. (2018). *Fourth industrial revolution: Current practices, challenges, and opportunities*. IntechOpen.

Pranckutė, R. (2021). Web of Science (WoS) and Scopus: The titans of bibliographic information in today's academic world. *Publications*, *9*(1), 12.

Qin, J., Zheng, P., & Wang, X. (2024). Product redesign and innovation based on online reviews: A multistage combined search method. *INFORMS Journal on Computing*, *36*(3), 742–765.

Quan, H., Li, S., Zeng, C., Wei, H., & Hu, J. (2023). Big data and AI-driven product design: A survey. *Applied Sciences (Basel, Switzerland)*, *13*(16), 9433.

Rashid, A. B., & Kausik, A. K. (2024). AI revolutionizing industries worldwide: A comprehensive overview of its diverse applications. Hybrid Advances, 100277.

Regenwetter, L., Nobari, A. H., & Ahmed, F. (2022). Deep generative models in engineering design: A review. *Journal of Mechanical Design*, *144*(7), 071704.

Roberts, D. L., & Candi, M. (2024). Artificial intelligence and innovation management: Charting the evolving landscape. *Technovation*, *136*, 103081.

Saini, J. P. S., Thakur, A., & Yadav, D. (2025). AI driven Innovations in Pharmaceuticals: Optimizing Drug Discovery and Industry Operations. RSC Pharmaceutics.

Saura, J. R., Škare, V., & Dosen, D. O. (2024). Is AI-based digital marketing ethical? Assessing a new data privacy paradox. *Journal of Innovation & Knowledge*, *9*(4), 100597.

Senthil, R., Anand, T., Somala, C. S., & Saravanan, K. M. (2024). Bibliometric analysis of artificial intelligence in healthcare research: Trends and future directions. *Future Healthcare Journal*, *11*(3), 100182. PMID: 39310219

Shrestha, Y. R., Krishna, V., & von Krogh, G. (2021). Augmenting organizational decision-making with deep learning algorithms: Principles, promises, and challenges. *Journal of Business Research*, *123*, 588–603.

Sichoongwe, K. (2024). Adoption behaviour of digital technologies by firms: Evidence from South Africa's manufacturing sector. *Global Business Review*, *25*(2, suppl), S244–S264.

Singh, N., Chaudhary, V., Singh, N., Soni, N., & Kapoor, A. (2024). Transforming Business with Generative AI: Research, Innovation, Market Deployment and Future Shifts in Business Models. arXiv preprint arXiv:2411.14437.

Sinha, N., & Dhillon, J. S. (2024). Bibliometric analysis of management practices in US corn (1990–2020). *Agrosystems, Geosciences & Environment*, *7*(2), e20536.

Sreenivasan, A., & Suresh, M. (2024). Design thinking and artificial intelligence: A systematic literature review exploring synergies. International Journal of Innovation Studies.

Teece, D. J., Pisano, G., & Shuen, A. (1997). Dynamic capabilities and strategic management. *Strategic Management Journal*, *18*(7), 509–533.

Tehci, A. (2024). Artificial intelligence and product innovation. In Artificial intelligence in material science: Advances (p. 160). Taylor & Francis.

Tekic, Z., & Füller, J. (2023). Managing innovation in the era of AI. *Technology in Society*, *73*, 102254.

Tian, T., Zichen, H., & Tang, Y. (2024). Enhancing Organizational Performance: Harnessing AI and NLP for User Feedback Analysis in Product Development. arXiv preprint arXiv:2405.04692.

Tohãnean, D., Buzatu, A. I., Baba, C. A., & Georgescu, B. (2020). Business model innovation through the use of digital technologies: Managing risks and creating sustainability. *Amfiteatru Economic*, *22*(55), 758–774.

Toner-Rodgers, A. (2024). Artificial intelligence, scientific discovery, and product innovation. arXiv preprint arXiv:2412.17866.

Truong, Y., & Papagiannidis, S. (2022). Artificial intelligence as an enabler for innovation: A review and future research agenda. *Technological Forecasting and Social Change*, *183*, 121852.

Tsang, Y. P., & Lee, C. K. M. (2022). Artificial intelligence in industrial design: A semi-automated literature survey. *Engineering Applications of Artificial Intelligence*, *112*, 104884.

Van Eck, N. J., & Waltman, L. (2011). Text mining and visualization using VOSviewer. arXiv preprint arXiv:1109.2058.

Van Wynsberghe, A. (2021). Sustainable AI: AI for sustainability and the sustainability of AI. *AI and Ethics*, *1*(3), 213–218.

Varadarajan, R. (2018). Innovation, innovation strategy, and strategic innovation. In *Innovation and strategy* (pp. 143–166). Emerald Publishing Limited.

Vocke, C., Constantinescu, C., & Popescu, D. (2019). Application potentials of artificial intelligence for the design of innovation processes. *Procedia CIRP*, *84*, 810–813.

Von Krogh, G., Ichijo, K., & Nonaka, I. (2000). *Enabling knowledge creation: How to unlock the mystery of tacit knowledge and release the power of innovation*. Oxford university press.

Wang, F., & Chen, K. (2020). Do product imitation and innovation require different patterns of organizational innovation? Evidence from Chinese firms. *Journal of Business Research*, *106*, 60–74.

Wang, J., Ma, Y., Zhang, L., Gao, R. X., & Wu, D. (2018). Deep learning for smart manufacturing: Methods and applications. *Journal of Manufacturing Systems*, *48*, 144–156.

Wang, K., & Wang, T. (2024). Competition from informal firms and new-to-market product innovation: A competitive rivalry framework. *Journal of Product Innovation Management*, *41*(4), 816–842.

Witkowski, A., & Wodecki, A. (2025). Where does AI play a major role in the new product development and product management process?. Management Review Quarterly, 1-38.

Wolfert, S., Ge, L., Verdouw, C., & Bogaardt, M. J. (2017). Big data in smart farming–a review. *Agricultural Systems*, *153*, 69–80.

Xue, L., & Pang, Z. (2022). Ethical governance of artificial intelligence: An integrated analytical framework. *Journal of Digital Economy*, *1*(1), 44–52.

Yaiprasert, C., & Hidayanto, A. N. (2023). AI-driven ensemble three machine learning to enhance digital marketing strategies in the food delivery business. *Intelligent Systems with Applications*, *18*, 200235.

Yu, W. F. (2025). AI as a co-creator and a design material: Transforming the design process. *Design Studies*, *97*, 101303.

Zahid, A., Leclaire, P., Hammadi, L., Roberta, C. A., & El Ballouti, A. (2025). Exploring the potential of industry 4.0 in manufacturing and supply chain systems: Insights and emerging trends from bibliometric analysis. Supply Chain Analytics, 100108.

Zhang, H., Bai, X., & Ma, Z. (2022). Consumer reactions to AI design: Exploring consumer willingness to pay for AI-designed products. *Psychology and Marketing*, *39*(11), 2171–2183.

Zhu, Q., & Luo, J. (2023). Generative transformers for design concept generation. *Journal of Computing and Information Science in Engineering*, *23*(4), 041003.

KEY TERMS AND DEFINITIONS

AI-Driven Innovation: The process of leveraging artificial intelligence technologies to accelerate the generation, development, and implementation of novel ideas, enhancing both product and process innovation.

AI-Driven Product Development: A methodology where artificial intelligence is employed to guide or optimize various stages of new product development—from idea screening to design and market fit analysis.

Artificial Intelligence (AI): A discipline within computer science is dedicated to developing systems that can perform functions traditionally associated with human intelligence, including learning, reasoning, and solving complex problems.

Bibliometric Analysis: A research technique that quantitatively evaluates academic publications and citation data to explore patterns, influence, and the evolution of scholarly fields.

New Product Development (NPD): The comprehensive journey from initial idea generation to the market launch of a new product, encompassing concept development, design, and commercialization.

Product Innovation: The enhancement or creation of product attributes, functionalities, or user experiences aimed at fulfilling market demands and distinguishing offerings from competitors.

VOSviewer: A specialized software application used to construct and visualize bibliometric networks based on co-authorship, co-citation, or keyword co-occurrence relationships among academic entities.

Chapter 5
AI in Supply Chain Optimization

Hamza Aboudiar
http://orcid.org/0009-0006-3970-8286
University "Abdelmalek Essaadi", Morocco

Ouail El Imrani
http://orcid.org/0000-0003-0080-0975
University "Abdelmalek Essaadi", Morocco

ABSTRACT

The integration of artificial intelligence (AI) in supply chain chains has led to a significant transformation, moving from a focus on individual businesses to a holistic view of supply chain operations. AI plays a crucial role in optimisation of the supply chain, improving competitiveness and operational efficiency. It offers instant transparency and improved product flow management through technologies like blockchain and IoT, enabling better operational performance and predictive optimization. However, integrating AI presents a technological and organizational challenge, requiring meticulous management of processes, data, and interdependent actors. AI-based supply chain optimization relies on advanced technologies to improve performance and respond quickly to market fluctuations. Despite challenges related to data quality, cybersecurity, and operational training, the benefits of AI, such as improved decision-making and operational efficiency, are indispensable. Businesses must invest in training and risk management strategies to maximize the benefits of this technology.

DOI: 10.4018/979-8-2600-0439-5.ch005

INTRODUCTION

The integration of AI into supply chains has revolutionized modern economics, shifting focus from individual firms to holistic operations (Meng, 2015). This transformation emphasizes strategic restructuring of production chains, supplier diversification, and distribution channel expansion. To meet global competition and rising consumer demands, firms must adopt competitive strategies enabled by technology-driven information exchange, ensuring seamless coordination. Supply chain optimization has become crucial to address growing quality standards, regulatory compliance, and shortened delivery timelines.

Research on AI's role in the supply chain highlights its importance as a catalyst for development and business-to-business cooperation. AI has transformed the supply chain, enabling increased resilience, predictive, and efficient optimization. It provides transparency across the entire supply chain, facilitating improved product flow management and rapid reaction to contingencies. However, AI integration presents both challenges and opportunities for organizations. It involves a heterogeneous set of processes, data, and interdependent actors with various objectives.

This chapter explores the multiple facets of integrating AI into supply chains, analysing the historical evolution of logistics and defining supply chains. It examines different types of supply chains and key functions such as procurement, production, storage, distribution, and sales. Additionally, it assesses the impact of emerging technologies like AI, IoT, Big Data, and blockchain on supply chain management and optimization, while exploring related challenges and future trends.

BACKGROUND

What Does the Term "Supply Chain" Mean?

Although researchers struggle to establish an official classification in the field of supply chain management, Croom et al. (2000) note that all the definitions found in the literature focus on the external environment of an organization, with the boundaries of the organization traditionally defined in terms of a legal entity. However, this does not offer an accurate understanding of what constitutes a supply chain. Furthermore, Croom et al. (2000) point out the lack of consensus on a universal definition, which is due in part to the way the concept of the supply chain has been developed in recent decades as well as the fact that it can be viewed from several different perspectives and angles.

The supply chain (SC) is often perceived as a simple matter of logistics. Yet, the supply chain is broader and strategic. It encompasses not only logistics, but also the management of processes, partners and resources across the entire supply chain. It benefits from a long-term vision supported by strategic choices encompassing the perspectives of the global networks to be set up (Daehy et al 2019).

Countless definitions since its introduction into the literature in 1982, through a paper by Keith and Webber (Gibson et al., 2005) have been proposed for the supply chain. They all agree on the purpose of a supply chain. A review of the supply chain literature suggests that there is no universal definition (Christopher, 1992; La Londe and Masters, 1994; Ganeshan et al., 1998; Rota-Franz, 1998; Lummus & Vokurka, 1999; Tayur & al., 1999; Stadlter and Kilger, 2000; Mentzer & al., 2001; Génin, 2003).

The supply chain is defined as « the flow of goods from the very first process encountered in the production of a product right through to the final sale to the end consumer » (Bruce et al., 2004).

Petrovic-Lazerevic et al. (2007), define it as a set that encompasses vertical chains, networks, collaborations, logistics, value creation, e-commerce and the application of information technology. This definition reflects the inherent complexity of the supply chain.

SUPPLY CHAIN FLOWS

The effective management of a supply chain relies on mastering three interdependent types of flows: material flows, information flows, and financial flows. These three categories form the backbone of logistics operations, and their harmonious integration is crucial for optimizing overall performance (Christopher, 2016).

Figure 1. the flows of the supply chain

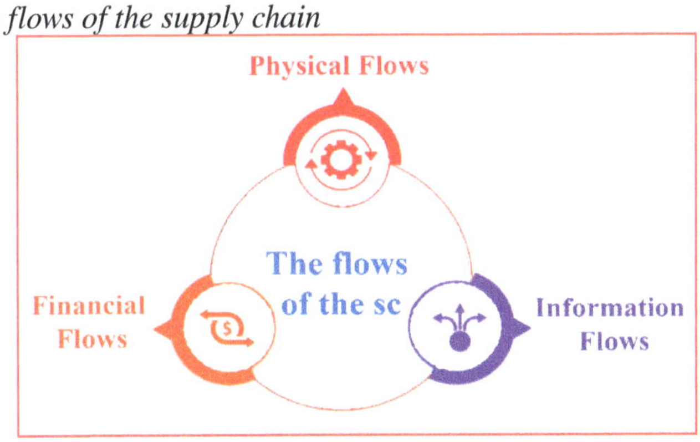

Source: author's elaboration

Physical Flows

Material flows represent the physical movement of goods through the supply chain, from raw material procurement to the distribution of finished products to consumers. These flows encompass all transportation, storage, and handling activities of products. Managing material flows requires precise coordination between the various links in the chain to ensure smooth circulation of goods, minimize waiting times, and optimize logistics costs. The efficiency of these flows is often considered a key indicator of the operational performance of a supply chain (Chopra & Meindl, 2016).

Information Flows

The information flow refers to all transfers or exchanges of data between the various stakeholders in the supply chain. This mainly concerns commercial information, including orders placed between customers and suppliers. An order typically includes the product code, the number of units ordered, the desired delivery date, and the price possibly agreed upon during the transaction. This list can be supplemented by other elements: the choice of desired options for the product, the regularity of deliveries, if necessary, etc. However, companies also share more technical data: physical characteristics of the product, production ranges, manufacturing and potentially transportation capacities, information on inventory level management. These are increasingly requested by customers who wish to know the progress of the manufacturing of their product. More generally, the principle of traceability translates into increased oversight by the customer over the supplier (Dupuy et al., 2004). The information flow is becoming increasingly rapid thanks to advances in ICT. The development of information flows within the supply chain finds its limits in the need for confidentiality between actors. Furthermore, the problem of the quality of the data transmitted persists, and there is a risk that decisions may be based on erroneous or simply outdated data.

Financial Flows

Financial flows represent the monetary movements associated with commercial transactions and logistics operations. These flows include payments to suppliers, sales revenues, transportation and storage costs, as well as investments in logistics infrastructure. Effective management of financial flows is crucial for ensuring the economic viability of the supply chain, optimizing costs, and maximizing profitability. Successful management of these flows requires close coordination with material and information flows to achieve optimal synchronization of operations (Christopher, 2016).

TYPES OF SUPPLY CHAINS

Supply chains can be categorized into several distinct types based on their structure, operational characteristics, and strategic objectives. Understanding these different types is crucial for designing and managing effective supply chain systems that align with business requirements and market demands.

1. Global Supply Chains

Global supply chains extend across multiple countries and involve complex networks of international suppliers, manufacturers, and distributors. These chains are characterized by their geographical dispersion and the need to manage cross-border logistics, including customs regulations, currency fluctuations, and international trade laws. Global supply chains are essential for companies seeking to leverage cost advantages, access new markets, and benefit from global sourcing opportunities (Chopra & Meindl, 2016). Figure 2 illustrates a typical example of such a supply chain.

Figure 2. Global Supply Chain

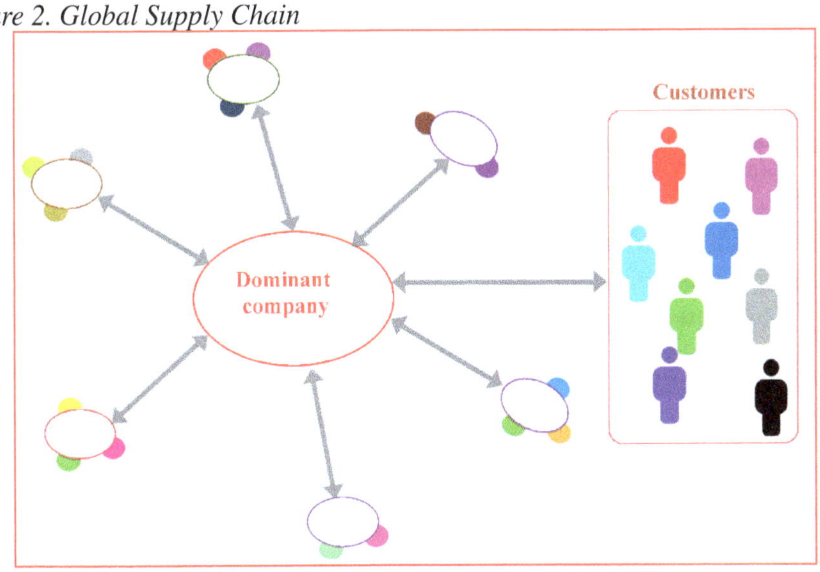

Source: author's elaboration

2. Internal Supply Chains

Internal supply chains operate within a single organization, often across multiple sites or departments. These chains focus on the internal flow of materials, information, and financial resources to support the organization's operations. Internal supply chains are typically easier to manage due to the centralized control and unified objectives, but they still require effective coordination and integration to ensure operational efficiency (Christopher, 2016). (Figure 3).

Figure 3. Internal logistics chain

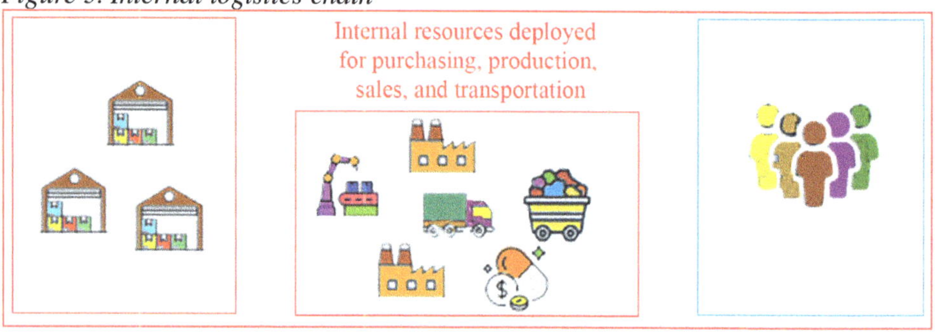

Source: author's elaboration

3. Extended Supply Chains

Extended supply chains involve collaboration between multiple independent companies, with one dominant firm acting as the central coordinator. This type of supply chain is often referred to as an "extended enterprise" and includes customers, suppliers, and subcontractors working together to design, develop, produce, and deliver products. The dominant firm, often called the "lead firm" or "orchestrator," plays a crucial role in coordinating activities and ensuring alignment among all partners (Lambert & Cooper, 2000). Figure 4 illustrates a typical diagram of an extended enterprise.

Figure 4. Dominant Company

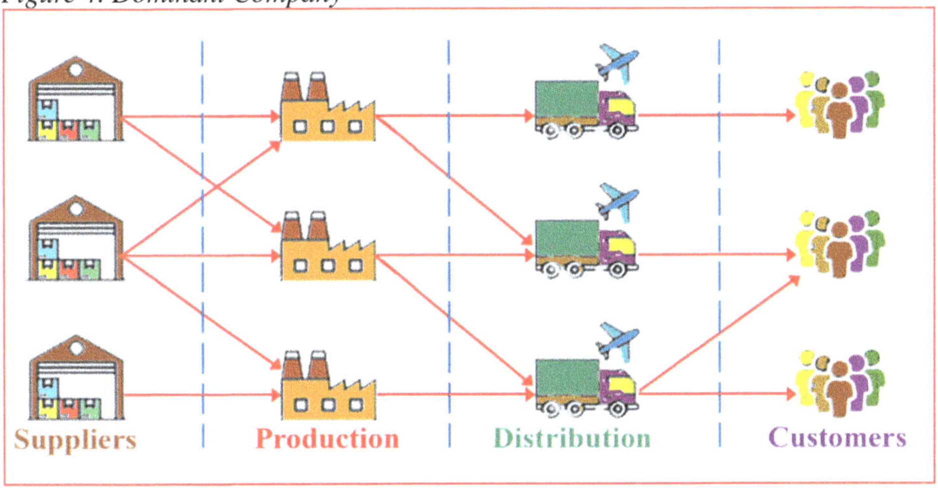

Source: author's elaboration

4. Agile Supply Chains

Agile supply chains are designed to respond quickly to changes in demand and market conditions. These chains emphasize flexibility, responsiveness, and adaptability, enabling companies to meet customer needs efficiently and effectively. Agile supply chains are particularly suitable for industries with high levels of uncertainty and volatility, such as fashion and electronics (Christopher & Towill, 2001).

5. Lean Supply Chains

Lean supply chains focus on eliminating waste and improving efficiency throughout the supply chain. These chains emphasize continuous improvement, just-in-time (JIT) production, and the reduction of non-value-added activities. Lean supply chains are particularly effective in industries with stable demand and predictable production processes, such as automotive and consumer goods manufacturing (Womack & Jones, 2003).

6. Green Supply Chains

Green supply chains incorporate environmental sustainability into supply chain management practices. These chains focus on reducing the environmental impact of supply chain activities, including sourcing, production, transportation, and disposal.

Green supply chains aim to minimize waste, reduce emissions, and promote the use of sustainable materials and processes (Srivastava, 2007).

SUPPLY CHAIN OPTIMIZATION

What is Supply Chain Optimization?

Supply chain optimization is a strategic process aimed at improving the efficiency, responsiveness, and overall profitability of a logistics network. It involves systematically analyzing, designing, and managing material, information, and financial flows throughout the entire supply chain, from suppliers to end customers (Simchi-Levi et al., 2008). Primarily, supply chain optimization aims to maximize profits while reducing costs. To achieve this, producers use key performance indicators (KPIs).

Supply chain optimization represents a dynamic and iterative process requiring regular evaluations and continuous adjustments to adapt to market developments and changing customer expectations (Chopra & Meindl, 2016). This systematic approach aims to continuously improve operational efficiency while maintaining optimal service levels.

Supply chain optimization plays a central role in the competitiveness and sustainability of modern businesses. It not only enables companies to achieve an almost optimal level of efficiency, but also to proactively respond to evolving customer expectations (Christopher, 2016). Indeed, companies that neglect continuous improvement in their supply chains expose themselves to a range of strategic, operational, and financial risks. Among these risks are slow response times to external disruptions such as supplier delays or geopolitical crises, inefficient production cycles, delays in delivering finished products, and inadequate customer service quality. Furthermore, poor visibility over stock levels often leads to increased waste, higher management costs, and inaccurate demand forecasting.

In contrast, companies that adopt modern supply chain optimization practices benefit from significant advantages. These include reduced operational costs through improved planning and increased automation, enhanced profitability, lower risks of stock out or excess inventory, and a notable improvement in the quality of products and services offered. The integration of digital tools such as artificial intelligence, predictive analytics, and blockchain also enables greater traceability and more informed, real-time decision-making (Ivanov and Sokolov, 2013).

Supply Chain Optimization Goals

In their pursuit of operational excellence, modern enterprises are developing comprehensive supply chain optimization strategies that integrate cost efficiency, quality improvement, operational agility, risk management, collaboration, sustainability, and technological innovation (Christopher, 2016). This holistic approach combines cost optimization through transport rationalization and process automation (van der Vorst & Beulens, 2002) with quality enhancement via IoT and AI technologies for real-time monitoring (Kagermann et al., 2013). Operational agility is achieved through digital twins and prescriptive analytics (Ivanov & Sokolov, 2013), supported by proactive risk management systems (Tang, 2006) and collaborative platforms (Christopher & Peck, 2004). Sustainability is integrated through eco-friendly partner selection and transportation optimization (Seuring & Müller, 2008), while inventory management benefits from predictive techniques and blockchain traceability (Saberi et al., 2019). This framework is sustained by continuous innovation through emerging technology adoption and ongoing employee training, creating adaptive supply chain ecosystems.

Supply Chain Optimization Techniques

The strategic optimization of modern supply chains follows a systematic three-phase methodology for continuous performance improvement (Christopher, 2016). The initial strategic design phase determines optimal facility locations through geo-economic analysis and spatial optimization algorithms (van der Vorst & Beulens, 2002). The subsequent operational planning phase develops dynamic production plans integrating inventory costs, demand variations, and transportation uncertainties using advanced ERP systems (Ivanov & Sokolov, 2013). The final execution phase coordinates logistics activities through integrated management systems and route optimization to ensure efficient delivery while minimizing costs (Saberi et al., 2019; Tang, 2006).

Inventory Optimization

Inventory optimization, considered the essential foundation of contemporary logistics excellence, represents a crucial challenge for modern organizations seeking to balance economic performance with customer satisfaction (Christopher, 2016). This systemic approach revolves around three complementary methodologies, with the Just-in-Time (JIT) method as its central element. Originating from Japanese industrial engineering principles and perfected by the Toyota Production System, this revolutionary flow management approach relies on precise synchronization between supplies and production needs (Mondén, 2011). This sophisticated system enables both significant reductions in storage costs and notable quality improvements through advanced mechanisms for early detection of non-conformities (Schonberger, 1982). As illustrated in Table 1, this approach utilizes a set of cutting-edge analytical tools. However, this methodology presents certain intrinsic vulnerabilities that warrant attention. On one hand, it creates increased sensitivity to external disruptions, requiring particularly robust resilience mechanisms (Tang, 2006). On the other hand, it can lead to higher logistics costs, particularly due to the need for more frequent and smaller-scale transportation (Schonberger, 1982). These operational challenges must be carefully evaluated and mitigated through appropriate risk management strategies to ensure the long-term viability of this inventory optimization approach.

Table 1. Methods and algorithms for the Just-in-Time method

Methods	Descriptions
Material Requirements Planning (MRP)	Method using algorithms to determine material requirements
Manufacturing Resource Planning Algorithms (MRP II)	Extension of MRP integrating production resource planning
Exponential Smoothing Methods	Forecasting techniques using algorithms to adjust production levels
Queue Management Algorithms	Production flow optimization tools
Simulation Techniques	Process modeling and analysis methods

Source: author's elaboration

The strategic management of safety stocks, as presented in Table 2, represents a fundamental approach in modern logistics, combining several complementary methodologies to optimize the balance between product availability and cost control (Silver et al., 1998). This approach integrates advanced statistical models such as stochastic processes and Markov chains for precise demand estimation (Nahmias, 2009), Monte Carlo simulations for risk assessment (Law & Kelton, 2000), and sophisticated optimization algorithms to determine optimal stock levels (Tempelmeier, 2011). Complemented by ABC analysis based on the Pareto principle (Fogarty et al., 1991), it enables strategic classification of items into three categories (A, B, C) according to their added value (Partovi & Anandarajan, 2002). However, this method has limitations related to its conceptual rigidity and dependence on historical data, which may reduce its effectiveness in volatile environments (Chopra & Meindl, 2016). These limitations highlight the need to adopt a hybrid approach for more resilient logistics management.

Table 2. Methods for Safety Stock Management

Methods	Descriptions
Safety Stock Model	Formula based on demand and delivery times
Economic Order Quantity (EOQ) Model	Storage and ordering cost optimization model
Monte Carlo Simulation	Demand variation assessment technique
Optimization Algorithms	Linear and nonlinear programming methods

Source: author's elaboration

Demand Forecasting

Demand forecasting constitutes a key element of modern supply chain management, enabling companies to optimize their operations while anticipating future customer needs (Chopra & Meindl, 2016). This strategic discipline, based on advanced statistical models and predictive analysis techniques, plays a crucial role at multiple levels: optimization of production, storage, and distribution processes (Christopher, 2016), optimal inventory management (Silver et al., 1998), and strategic decision-making for investments and innovations (Mentzer & Moon, 2005). However, this complex approach faces several major challenges: the uncertainty of contemporary markets characterized by unpredictable economic fluctuations and volatile trends (Snyder et al., 2016), the quality of historical data essential for accurate forecasts (Hugos, 2018), and the increasing complexity of models requiring specialized skills (Shapiro, 2001). To meet these challenges, companies use various complementary methods: time series models for seasonal trends (Box & Jenkins, 1970), multidimensional regression models (Montgomery et al., 2012), and exponential smoothing methods for short-term forecasting (Gardner, 2006), whose rigorous application can significantly improve operational efficiency and reduce logistics costs (Makridakis et al., 1998).

Optimizing Stock Levels

Optimizing stock levels is crucial for balancing storage costs with product availability in supply chain management, employing strategies such as mathematical models like the Economic Order Quantity (EOQ) model to determine optimal inventory levels by considering order costs, warehousing expenses, and demand (Vidal, 2002). Effective inventory optimization also requires supplier collaboration to enhance supply chain transparency and reduce lead times through real-time information sharing and automated replenishment systems, while leveraging technologies like inventory management systems (IMS) and traceability solutions (RFID/barcodes) to improve inventory accuracy (Lee et al., 2018). Additionally,

AI and machine learning applications analyze inventory data to optimize replenishment decisions, while risk management strategies address potential supply chain disruptions through supplier diversification and safety stock establishment (Khan & Kumar, 2020). Continuous performance monitoring using metrics such as inventory turnover rates and service levels enables ongoing strategy refinement (Smith et al., 2019), ultimately allowing businesses to reduce operational costs while improving customer demand responsiveness.

Technology & Automation

The use of technology and automation can improve the efficiency and accuracy of inventory management. Supply chain management (SCM) systems use software to manage and optimize supply chain processes. The Internet of Things (IoT) uses sensors and connected devices to monitor and control processes in real-time. Artificial intelligence (AI) and machine learning use algorithms to analyze data and make optimized decisions. According to Lee et al. (2018), the adoption of these technologies can improve supply chain visibility and responsiveness.

While technology and automation offer many benefits, they also raise significant challenges and considerations. The collection and analysis of large amounts of customer data raises crucial privacy and security questions, requiring companies to strictly comply with regulations to protect sensitive information. In addition, integrating new technologies into existing infrastructures can be complex and expensive, requiring careful planning to ensure optimal compatibility and interoperability between systems. Finally, the effective deployment of advanced technologies requires specialized skills in data science and analytics, prompting companies to invest in training their staff or recruiting qualified experts in order to maximize the benefits of these technological innovations.

Risk Management

Risk management is essential for maintaining stability and continuity in operations, particularly within personalized customer experiences and supply chain automation. It involves identifying and mitigating potential risks through techniques such as risk identification, business continuity planning, and diversification of supply sources. Research by Tang (2006) highlights that proactive risk management can significantly reduce disruptions and enhance supply chain resilience. However, risk management faces several challenges, including the accurate identification of risks, which requires a thorough understanding of business processes and technologies. Operational risks, such as technology failures and human errors, are difficult to anticipate due to the complexity and interdependence of automated systems. Additionally, security risks, particularly those related to cybersecurity and data protection, demand constant vigilance and regular updates to security protocols to address evolving threats. Risk assessment is challenging as it involves determining the likelihood of risks and estimating their potential impact on operations and customer experience, necessitating sophisticated analytical tools and deep expertise. Risk matrices, although useful, can sometimes oversimplify complex situations, leading to incomplete assessments. Mitigating risks requires developing effective contingency plans and backup solutions, which demand substantial resources and careful planning, alongside continually updated training and awareness programs. Effective risk management also requires cross-departmental collaboration and transparent communication with all stakeholders, including customers, which can be challenging in organizations with established departmental silos. Clear and consistent communication about risk management measures is crucial for maintaining trust. In summary, effective risk management, while essential for protecting operations and customers, necessitates a proactive approach, adequate resources, and an organizational culture that values transparency and collaboration (Tang, 2006; Smith & Jones, 2019; Lee et al., 2020).

THE REGULATORY FRAMEWORK, LEGAL RESPONSIBILITIES AND ETHICS RELATED TO AI IN SUPPLY CHAIN OPTIMIZATION

The integration of artificial intelligence (AI) into supply chain optimization raises several legal, ethical, and regulatory questions.

Regulatory Framework

The regulatory framework for artificial intelligence (AI) in the supply chain is evolving, with several jurisdictions developing specific regulations to govern its use. This framework must strike a delicate balance between preventing abuses, such as algorithmic bias and privacy violations, and promoting responsible innovation. While some legal professionals remain cautious, early adoption of these regulations would allow organizations to better adapt to the evolving legal landscape. The optimal strategy appears to be a combination of rapid implementation and gradual adjustments based on practical experience, complemented by the identification of priority use cases, rigorous data governance, and appropriate team training. Globally, regulatory approaches diverge: the European Union has adopted differentiated risk-based regulation with its June 2024 AI law, the United States is navigating between state legislation and federal approaches, while Japan prioritizes flexibility to spur innovation, highlighting the need for international cooperation to harmonize regulations. The European AI regulation, which classifies recruitment-related AI systems as high-risk, illustrates the desire to balance innovation with the protection of fundamental rights. With these technologies evolving rapidly, legislators must adopt an agile approach to maintain this delicate balance. Companies, meanwhile, must stay abreast of regulatory developments and ensure their AI systems comply with new laws and regulations, which may involve regular audits of AI systems, training employees on new regulations, and working with legal experts to ensure compliance with all legal obligations.

Legal Responsibilities

The use of AI in supply chain management involves a series of legal responsibilities that must be clearly defined and understood by all stakeholders. One key concern is liability in the event of AI failure or error. For example, if an AI system recommends a decision that results in a costly stockout or surplus, who is liable? Current legal frameworks may not be adequately equipped to address these issues, as they were designed before the advent of advanced AI technologies (European Commission, 2020).

Contracts between AI technology providers and user companies must be carefully drafted to include specific liability clauses. These contracts should specify expectations, performance limits, and remedies for breaches of contractual obligations. Additionally, companies must ensure that their AI systems comply with data protection laws, such as the General Data Protection Regulation (GDPR) in the European Union, which imposes strict obligations on the processing of personal data (Voigt & Von dem Bussche, 2017).

Ethical Considerations

The ethics of AI in the supply chain is a complex area that requires careful attention. One of the main ethical challenges is the transparency of AI algorithms. AI systems are often perceived as "black boxes" due to their complexity and lack of transparency. This can make it difficult to understand the decisions made by AI, which can lead to distrust among stakeholders (Burrell, 2016).

Another ethical challenge is fairness. AI algorithms can unintentionally perpetuate or amplify existing biases in the data they are trained on. For example, if an AI system is trained on historical data that reflects discriminatory practices, it may continue to make biased decisions. Companies must therefore ensure that their AI systems are trained on representative and fair data (Mehrabi et al., 2021).

FINANCING STRATEGIES FOR AI ADOPTION IN SUPPLY CHAIN OPTIMIZATION

Adopting artificial intelligence (AI) in supply chain optimization represents a major strategic investment for companies seeking to improve their efficiency and competitiveness. However, financing such initiatives can be a significant challenge.

Internal Financing

One of the most direct strategies for financing AI adoption is the use of internal funds. Companies can allocate a portion of their annual budget to technological innovation projects, including AI. This approach allows for great flexibility and complete control over financial resources. However, it can also limit the company's ability to invest in other critical areas, especially if the initial costs of AI are high (Davenport et al., 2020).

To maximize the effectiveness of this strategy, companies must conduct a detailed cost-benefit analysis to ensure that AI investments will generate a sufficient return on investment (ROI). This involves defining key performance indicators (KPIs) and implementing monitoring mechanisms to assess the progress and results of AI projects (Brynjolfsson & McAfee, 2017).

Adopting AI to optimize the supply chain isn't just for large companies. SMEs, like StyleThread, an online clothing retailer, are innovating in this area. StyleThread allocated 10% of its budget to an AI pilot project to optimize inventory management. Using an AI system that analyzes sales trends and predicts demand, the company reduced overstocks and stockouts, improving customer satisfaction and lowering inventory costs. This led to a 15% increase in revenue and a 20% reduction in inventory costs within one year. StyleThread plans to increase its AI budget to expand this technology to other aspects of its supply chain.

Public-Private Partnerships

Public-private partnerships (PPPs) are another effective strategy for financing AI adoption. These partnerships allow companies to collaborate with government institutions and research organizations to share the costs and risks associated with AI projects. Governments can offer grants, low-interest loans, and tax incentives to encourage technological innovation (OECD, 2019).

PPPs can also facilitate access to additional resources, such as public data and research infrastructure, which can be crucial for the development and implementation of AI solutions. Moreover, these partnerships can help create an innovation-friendly ecosystem by encouraging collaboration between the public and private sectors (European Commission, 2020).

MediSupply's example demonstrates how this type of financing can be implemented. By partnering with a Canadian government public health agency, this SME developed an AI system to optimize medical supply inventory management. With partial funding and access to data on consumer trends, MediSupply used AI to analyse this data and anticipate future needs. This minimized stockouts and ensured consistent availability of essential supplies. As a result, the company reduced its inventory costs by 20% and improved the availability of medical supplies by 30%, thereby strengthening the public health system's resilience to health crises.

Financing by Venture Capital and External Investors

Using external investors, such as venture capitalists and investment funds, is another common strategy for financing AI adoption. Venture capitalists are often willing to take high risks in exchange for potentially high returns. They can provide not only funding but also valuable expertise and networks of contacts (Gompers & Lerner, 2001).

To attract external investors, companies must present a solid business plan and demonstrate the growth and profitability potential of their AI projects. This may involve conducting extensive market research, developing working prototypes, and demonstrating compelling proofs of concept (Kerr et al., 2014).

For example, SwiftLogix, a logistics and transportation company, raised $2 million from a venture capital fund specializing in logistics technologies, attracted by the potential of AI in supply chain management. With this funding, the company developed an AI system to optimize delivery routes in real time, taking into account traffic, weather, and logistics emergencies. This reduced delivery times and improved overall efficiency. As a result, SwiftLogix reduced its operational costs by 25% and increased its delivery capacity by 30%, attracting new customers through faster and more reliable delivery services.

Crowdfunding and Participatory Financing

Crowdfunding is an increasingly popular financing strategy for technological innovation projects. This approach allows companies to raise funds from a wide audience via online platforms. Crowdfunding can be particularly useful for start-ups and small businesses that may not have access to traditional funding sources (Mollick, 2014).

To successfully run a crowdfunding campaign, companies must create a clear and compelling value proposition and use effective marketing strategies to reach their target audience. They must also offer attractive incentives to backers, such as exclusive products, discounts, or unique experiences (Allison et al., 2017).

FarmFresh, an agribusiness company, launched a crowdfunding campaign to finance an AI project to optimize its fresh produce supply chain. In exchange for contributions, the company offered produce baskets and farm tours. With the funds raised, FarmFresh developed an AI system to predict demand and optimize deliveries, thereby reducing food waste and improving produce freshness. The campaign raised $200,000, far exceeding the initial goal, and helped the company reduce post-harvest losses by 30% while improving customer satisfaction.

MAIN FOCUS OF THE CHAPTER

Artificial Intelligence In Supply Chain Management

The integration of artificial intelligence (AI) into the supply chain represents a major evolution for companies seeking to refine their processes, reduce costs, and enhance overall efficiency. With its advanced capabilities in data analysis, machine learning, and autonomous decision-making, AI offers unprecedented opportunities to modernize and optimize logistics operations (Christopher, 2016). It not only enables the automation of repetitive tasks but also provides predictive and prescriptive insights that transform the management of logistics flows (Ivanov & Sokolov, 2013). AI can be applied across various areas such as inventory management, demand forecasting, delivery route optimization, and predictive maintenance. By using sophisticated machine learning algorithms, companies can anticipate market variations, identify potential bottlenecks, and make informed real-time decisions, while improving coordination among different actors in the supply chain (Saberi et al., 2019). Thus, the integration of AI is not merely a technological trend, but a strategic imperative for maintaining enhanced competitiveness in an ever-evolving environment.

The Evolution of Artificial Intelligence in Supply Chain Management

For several decades, artificial intelligence (AI) has profoundly transformed supply chain management and logistics processes. As early as the 1950s, the first rule-based systems laid the foundation for what would become a major technological evolution, leading today to advanced machine learning algorithms capable of handling complex and multivariate optimizations (Christopher, 2016). This progression illustrates how AI has enabled increased automation, improved risk anticipation, and faster, more informed decision-making in logistics operations (Ivanov & Sokolov, 2013). A visual synthesis of this evolution is often presented in the form of a summary figure highlighting the key stages in the development of AI applied to the supply chain.

Figure 5. the evolution of AI in supply chain management

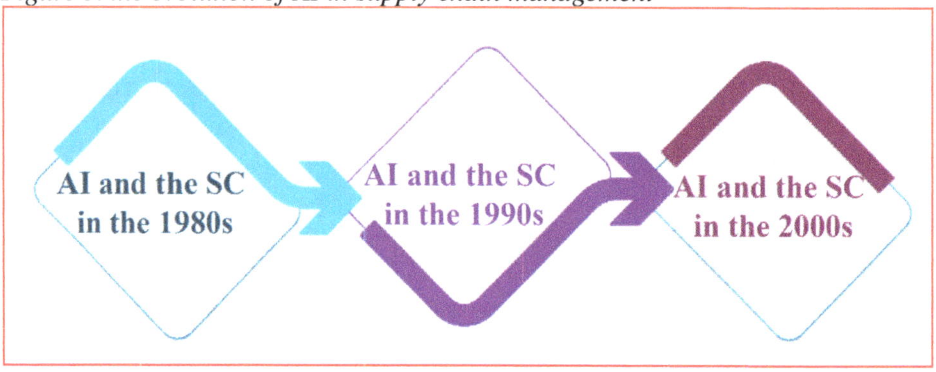

Source: author's elaboration

1. AI and SC in the 1980s

The initial applications of Artificial Intelligence (AI) in supply chain management focused on inventory management and demand forecasting. As early as the 1980s, companies began to utilize expert systems to formalize human knowledge in areas such as warehouse layout and the logistical organization of transport operations (Christopher, 2016). These tools enabled the structuring of decisions based on rules defined by experts, marking a key step in the automation and optimization of logistics processes (Ivanov and Sokolov, 2013).

2. AI and CS During the 1990s

The 1990s saw a significant expansion in supply chain analytical capabilities, largely thanks to the emergence of data mining and neural networks. Pioneer companies like Walmart leveraged these technologies to scrutinize crucial transactional data and refine their demand forecasts (Christopher, 2016). This decade also witnessed the introduction of the first automated planning and scheduling systems in the manufacturing industry, illustrating a major leap forward in optimizing logistics processes (Ivanov and Sokolov, 2013).

3. AI and CS During the 2000s

The 2000s saw significant advancements in machine learning algorithms and optimization techniques. These methods enabled companies to adopt dynamic pricing, develop complex supply networks, and optimize real-time logistics. The emergence of cloud computing and Big Data technologies in the 2010s further accelerated the integration of AI into supply chains (Christopher, 2016). Currently, artificial intelligence is deployed across the entire supply chain, from procurement to last-mile distribution. Machine learning algorithms can now predict demand with unparalleled accuracy, while reinforcement learning techniques optimize sophisticated logistics networks in real time (Ivanov and Sokolov, 2013).

The Benefits of Using Artificial Intelligence in Supply Chain Management

Integrating Artificial Intelligence (AI) into the supply chain offers a multitude of benefits, enabling companies to optimize decisions, reduce costs, increase operational efficiency, and enhance sustainability, all while remaining competitive in the face of complex challenges in ever-evolving markets. AI is revolutionizing decision-making by providing up-to-date, data-driven insights, fostering a proactive approach. By analyzing vast volumes of data—including historical data, market trends, and external factors like weather or economic variations—AI generates predictive intelligence and proposes actions. This improves decision-making in two key ways: by supporting informed, data-driven choices with greater speed and accuracy than humans, and by automating repetitive tasks. This frees up employees' time, allowing them to focus on higher-value activities requiring creativity and critical analysis.

Furthermore, AI ensures a quick response to fluctuations by detecting problems in real-time and anticipating demand, which helps modulate inventory and minimize the risks of shortages or excess stock. It also contributes to cost reduction and operational efficiency through the automation and optimization of critical supply chain processes, maintaining optimal inventory levels, and optimizing production and logistics schedules. Finally, AI strengthens sustainability by promoting more efficient resource use, reducing waste and emissions, and helping companies comply with global sustainability initiatives, thereby improving their brand image and attracting environmentally conscious customers (Christopher, 2016; Ivanov & Sokolov, 2013).

Main Applications of AI in Supply Chain Optimization

Artificial intelligence (AI) has emerged as a revolutionary tool in the supply chain management industry, offering innovative approaches to optimize operations and increase overall efficiency. The main applications of artificial intelligence in the supply chain are presented below.

Autonomous Planning and Execution

Automating supply chain planning and execution aims to minimize human intervention, thereby increasing accuracy and efficiency through advanced algorithms and mathematical methods. These approaches enable a rapid response to demand fluctuations and real-time market conditions, while optimizing costs and risks. According to Simchi-Levi et al. (2008), this automation can significantly enhance supply chain responsiveness and flexibility. For successful implementation, tight integration of Supply Chain Management (SCM) systems and information technology is essential. Companies must also adopt Total Quality Management (TQM) practices and, as Liker (2004) emphasizes, cultivate a culture of continuous improvement and close collaboration with suppliers. Despite numerous benefits, challenges such as algorithm complexity and reliance on accurate data persist. To overcome these, adopting risk management strategies, like diversifying supply sources and business continuity planning, is crucial; Tang (2006) has shown that such proactive risk management can reduce disruptions and strengthen supply chain resilience.

Intelligent Warehouse Automation

Intelligent warehouse automation has become a critical pillar in the modernization of supply chains. Intelligent warehouse automation uses technologies such as artificial intelligence (AI), the Internet of Things (IoT), robotics, computer vision, and automated management systems to optimize storage and distribution processes. According to Gu et al. (2010), warehouse automation can improve operational efficiency and reduce human error. These technologies can monitor inventory levels, locations, and conditions in real time, reduce operational costs, improve inventory accuracy, and speed up delivery times. This ensures that companies always have an accurate view of their inventory and develop flexible, customer-driven supply chains, strengthening their competitive position for long-term success.

AI-driven systems use IoT sensors to track the movement and status of inventory in real-time, detecting when items are added or removed, where they are located in the warehouse, as well as environmental conditions affecting perishables. Additionally, the integration of AI with computer vision allows products to be automatically scanned and recognized, reducing the need for manual inventories, while AI-equipped cameras identify and count items, alerting managers to discrepancies or low inventory levels. In addition, AI improves demand forecasting by analyzing large amounts of data from various sources, such as sales history and market trends, allowing for more accurate forecasts through machine learning algorithms. These models analyze historical sales data to predict future demand, adapting and improving their accuracy over time. In addition, AI optimizes replenishment processes by determining the ideal times and quantities to minimize excess inventory and reduce stock-outs, while enabling just-in-time inventory management, reducing storage costs and the risk of overstocking. Finally, by improving inventory levels and reducing the need for excess inventory, AI helps businesses save on storage and retention costs, while minimizing stock-outs, which improves customer satisfaction and retention, as well as overall business performance.

Implementing intelligent warehouse automation requires tight integration of warehouse management systems (WMS) and information technology. Companies must adopt Total Quality Management (TQM) practices to ensure the quality of products and processes. According to Liker (2004), the successful implementation of intelligent automation requires a culture of continuous improvement and close collaboration with suppliers and logistics partners.

While intelligent warehouse automation offers many benefits, it also presents challenges, such as the complexity of algorithms and reliance on accurate data. To overcome these challenges, businesses can adopt risk management strategies, such as diversifying supply sources and business continuity planning. Tang (2006) has shown that proactive risk management can reduce disruptions and improve supply chain resilience.

To implement intelligent warehouse automation, several algorithms and methods are used to optimize inventory management processes and logistics operations:

Supply Chain Visibility and Risk Management

Supply chain visibility allows businesses to monitor and track goods flows, inventory levels, and logistics processes in real-time. This transparency improves coordination between the different links in the supply chain and allows for a rapid response to changes in demand and market conditions. According to Simchi-Levi et al. (2008), increased visibility can improve supply chain responsiveness and flexibility. Risk management, on the other hand, aims to identify, assess, and mitigate potential risks in the supply chain. This includes risks related to suppliers, logistics processes, fluctuations in demand and external disruptions. Tang (2006) has shown that proactive risk management can reduce disruptions and improve supply chain resilience.

While there are many benefits to supply chain visibility and risk management, these processes also pose challenges, such as algorithmic complexity and the need for accurate data. In order to address these challenges, companies have the opportunity to put in place risk management strategies, such as diversifying their sources of supply and developing a business continuity plan. According to Tang (2006), proactive risk management can minimize disruptions while strengthening supply chain resilience.

Predictive Analysis

Predictive analytics is a fundamental approach that combines meticulous data examination, statistical modeling, machine learning algorithms, and artificial intelligence to anticipate future outcomes based on vast historical datasets. This method not only forecasts upcoming trends and events but also suggests concrete actions for substantial operational improvements. Its key steps, including data collection and preparation, statistical modeling, the development of machine learning algorithms, as well as model validation and deployment, ensure the production of precise and actionable information. Predictive analytics offers numerous benefits, such as converting unstructured data into valuable insights, optimizing decision-making, reducing risks through proactive problem identification, improving operational performance, and personalizing customer interactions for enhanced experience and optimized revenue via refined pricing and marketing strategies (Davenport & Harris, 2007).

However, despite its advantages, challenges remain, notably ensuring data quality, the need for specialized skills in model management, integration with legacy systems, managing scalability issues, and considering ethical aspects to prevent bias. To overcome these obstacles, businesses can implement risk management strategies, such as diversifying supply sources and business continuity planning, as proactive risk management is essential for reducing disruptions and strengthening supply chain resilience (Christopher, 2016; Ivanov & Sokolov, 2013; Tang, 2006).

Customer Personalized Experience

Implementing Artificial Intelligence (AI) in supply chains enables a sophisticated personalization of the customer experience through various complementary approaches. At the heart of this transformation lies data-driven customization, where AI systems analyze customer information from multiple sources to generate tailored product recommendations that align with individual preferences, thereby enhancing both sales performance and customer satisfaction (Davenport & Harris, 2007). This personalization extends to customer service through AI-powered chatbots and virtual assistants that provide continuous, 24/7 support, efficiently resolving inquiries to build brand loyalty (Christopher, 2016).

Moreover, AI facilitates the creation of unique shopping experiences by suggesting products based on purchase histories and search patterns, while optimizing delivery routes and offering flexible shipping options (Ivanov & Sokolov, 2013).

However, this AI-driven personalization presents significant challenges, particularly regarding data privacy and security, requiring strict compliance with regulations to protect sensitive customer information. Integrating these solutions into existing infrastructures also poses technical complexities that necessitate careful planning to ensure system compatibility. Furthermore, the effective deployment of these technologies demands specialized skills in data science and analytics, prompting organizations to invest in staff training programs (Tang, 2006). To achieve this sophisticated personalization, companies employ various methods, including comprehensive customer data collection, audience segmentation, omnichannel strategy adoption, and interaction customization based on individual customer journeys, all while implementing Voice of Customer (VoC) analysis and CRM solutions to create a cohesive customer experience ecosystem (Payne & Frow, 2017).

CHALLENGES AND CONSIDERATIONS FOR USING AI IN SUPPLY CHAINS

Integrating Artificial Intelligence (AI) into supply chains, while offering substantial benefits for optimization, presents significant challenges that organizations must diligently address. Data quality emerges as a primary obstacle, as inaccurate or incomplete information in complex supply chain environments can lead to flawed analyses and incorrect forecasts, necessitating robust data governance protocols (Davenport & Harris, 2007). Cybersecurity concerns constitute another critical challenge; the increasing integration of AI systems creates vulnerabilities that could expose sensitive information or disrupt essential operations, demanding strengthened digital security measures (Christopher, 2016).

Workforce adaptation is a third paramount consideration, where AI-driven automation may necessitate substantial retraining efforts to develop new competencies, while resistance to change could impede adoption. Companies must therefore cultivate an innovation-oriented culture and clearly communicate the advantages of AI integration to facilitate this transition and maximize synergies between human and artificial intelligence capabilities (Liker, 2004). Finally, implementing these advanced technologies entails significant initial investments for recruiting specialized talent, upgrading infrastructure, and maintaining systems. However, the long-term benefits typically justify these expenditures by delivering enhanced operational efficiency and competitive advantages that outweigh the financial and operational challenges of adoption (Ivanov & Sokolov, 2013; Tang, 2006).

Table 3. Challenges related to the use of AI in supply chains and mitigation strategies

Challenges	Description	Mitigation Strategies
Data Quality	Inaccurate data leading to flawed analyses	Implement strict data governance protocols
Cybersecurity	Vulnerabilities in AI systems	Strengthening digital security measures
Workforce Adaptation	Need for retraining and upskilling	Cultivate innovation culture and clear communication
Implementation Costs	Significant initial investments	Focus on long-term benefits and competitive advantages

Source: author's elaboration

FUTURE TRENDS AND INNOVATIONS OF AI IN THE SUPPLY CHAIN

The future of supply chain management will be profoundly transformed by the integration of Artificial Intelligence (AI), promising a revolution in logistics operations (Christopher, 2016). Among the emerging trends, autonomous supply chains stand out as a revolutionary paradigm, offering end-to-end process management with minimal human intervention, from product design to final delivery. These systems, characterized by their predictive capabilities, intelligence, scalability, and complete process digitization, will enable unprecedented operational efficiency and product traceability (Ivanov & Sokolov, 2013).

The convergence between blockchain technology and AI represents another major advancement, combining the immutability and transparency of blockchain with AI's analytical capabilities to create more secure, efficient, and collaborative supply networks (Queiroz et al., 2020). Quantum computing emerges as a third transformative technology, offering exceptional computing power to solve complex optimization problems in areas like route planning and inventory management (Wittek, 2014). Additionally, the evolution of predictive analytics, fueled by the integration of advanced technologies like AI and IoT, will enable more accurate demand forecasting and proactive risk management (Davenport & Harris, 2007). Finally, generative AI, leveraging deep learning to create innovative solutions, will drive process optimization, demand forecasting, and product innovation, while supporting sustainability initiatives through resource optimization and waste reduction. Collectively, these technological advancements promise to create more resilient, efficient, and intelligent supply chains capable of adapting to market fluctuations and meeting evolving customer demands.

Table 4. The future trends and innovations of AI in the supply chain

Future Trends	Description
Autonomous Supply Chains	AI-based systems managing end-to-end processes with minimal human intervention
Blockchain-AI Convergence	Combination of blockchain's immutability with AI's analytical capabilities
Quantum Computing	Exceptional computing power for solving complex optimization problems
Predictive Analytics	Advanced technologies for accurate demand forecasting and risk management
Generative AI	Deep learning for process optimization, innovation and sustainability initiatives

Source: author's elaboration

RECOMMENDATIONS

To maximize the opportunities offered by artificial intelligence (AI) while mitigating associated risks, companies should implement the following actions:

1. Establish Standardized Frameworks

a. Collaborate with ISO to develop AI-specific standards for logistics within 12 months, particularly targeting ISO 42001 (AI) and ISO 28000 (logistics) standards
b. Implement a quarterly feedback system with key performance indicators (KPIs) such as:
   i. Standardized framework adoption rate (>80% within 18 months).
   ii. Number of processes optimized through standards.
   iii. Reduction in performance gaps between departments.

2. Strengthen Internal Skills

a. Develop an internal certification program with 3 levels:
   i. Level 1: AI Fundamentals (6 months).
   ii. Level 2: Logistics Applications (12 months).
   iii. Level 3: Advanced Expertise (18 months).
b. Create a continuous learning platform with:
   i. Monthly interactive modules.
   ii. Quarterly practical simulations.

    iii. Digital badge system to motivate employees.
c. Objective: 90% of employees trained at Level 1 within 24 months

3. Manage Operational Risks

a. Implement a risk analysis solution such as:
    i. IBM OpenPages for risk management.
    ii. ServiceNow for incident management.
b. Establish business continuity plans including:
    i. Cloud-based backup solutions.
    ii. Quarterly disaster recovery tests.
    iii. Semi-annual crisis simulation scenarios.
c. Objective: 30% reduction in unplanned downtime.

4. Secure Data and Systems

a. Implement a layered security architecture including:
    i. AES-256 encryption for sensitive data.
    ii. Mandatory multi-factor authentication (MFA).
    iii. Role-based access control (RBAC) system.
b. Conduct quarterly security audits using:
    i. Analysis tools like Nessus or Qualys.
    ii. NIST CSF framework for evaluation.
    iii. Annual penetration tests by independent third parties.
c. Objective: 50% reduction in major security incidents.

5. Ensure Data Quality

a. Implement a 3-step validation process:
    i. Automatic data cleansing (using tools like Talend).
    ii. Manual validation by experts.
    iii. Cross-verification with external sources.
b. Implement strict access controls:
    i. Data classification by sensitivity level.
    ii. Access based on the principle of least privilege.
    iii. Comprehensive logging of all access.
c. Objective: 40% reduction in critical data errors.

6. Invest in Specialized Talent

a. Create a targeted recruitment program for:
    i. Data Scientists specializing in logistics.
    ii. Process automation engineers.
    iii. Industrial cybersecurity experts.
b. Implement a continuous training program with:
    i. Partnerships with platforms like Coursera or Udacity.
    ii. Access to recognized certifications (AWS, Microsoft, etc.).
    iii. Annual budget of €5,000 per employee for professional development.
c. Objective: 25% increase in critical technical skills.

7. Implement Smart Automation

a. Deploy automation solutions such as:
    i. RPA (Robotic Process Automation) for repetitive tasks.
    ii. Autonomous systems for warehouse management.
    iii. Optimization algorithms for delivery routing.
b. Use predictive analytics tools like:
    i. SAS Advanced Analytics.
    ii. IBM Watson Studio.
    iii. Google Cloud AI Platform.
c. Objective: 20% reduction in operational costs

8. Promote Collaboration

a. Implement a collaborative platform such as:
    i. Microsoft Teams with AI tool integration.
    ii. Centralized knowledge management system/
b. Create interdisciplinary teams with:
    i. Representatives from each department.
    ii. Common goals aligned with company strategy.
    iii. Bi-weekly coordination meetings.
c. Objective: 35% improvement in customer satisfaction

CONCLUSION

The integration of artificial intelligence (AI) into supply chains is a significant innovation and a radical disruption in contemporary logistics management. This integration, which leverages cutting-edge technologies such as artificial intelligence, the Internet of Things (IoT), blockchain and quantum computing, opens up new opportunities to improve operations, improve efficiency and strengthen the resilience of supply chains. Artificial intelligence, in particular, is central to this transformation by facilitating intelligent automation, accurate predictive analytics, and fast, informed decision-making.

Artificial intelligence has radically changed supply chains by bringing capabilities for data analysis and processing that were previously out of reach. With the help of artificial intelligence, companies are now able to predict market developments, optimize their inventories and perfect their logistics planning with greater accuracy. Machine learning techniques and artificial intelligence models have the ability to spot complex patterns in data, providing more accurate and scalable demand predictions. This offers companies the opportunity to respond more quickly to market changes and to better meet customer requirements.

The integration of AI with other emerging technologies, such as IoT and blockchain, strengthens its potential and unlocks new opportunities for improving supply chains. For example, IoT offers real-time information on inventory status and transportation conditions, enhancing visibility and tracking of products throughout the procurement process. Blockchain, on the other hand, offers a secure and decentralized platform for data sharing, building transparency and trust between different players in the supply chain.

Despite the many benefits of AI, integrating it into supply chains also presents significant challenges. Data relevance, for example, is critical to AI's success, and incorrect or incomplete information can lead to inaccurate predictions and inefficient choices. In addition, cybersecurity and data protection issues are becoming increasingly crucial, requiring the implementation of robust measures to guarantee the security of systems and information. Workers' education and training are also crucial to maximizing the potential of AI, and companies need to dedicate resources to training and upskilling their staff.

In the future, artificial intelligence will remain a key player in the transformation of supply chains, thanks to advancements such as autonomous supply chains, blockchain-AI fusion, and quantum computing. These technologies aim to improve the intelligence, autonomy and resilience of supply chains in the face of disruptions. For example, autonomous supply chains could automate a multitude of procedures, thereby reducing the need for human intervention and increasing the efficiency and accuracy of operations. And the convergence between blockchain and AI could bring more transparency and security while facilitating collaboration and coordination among the various stakeholders in the supply chain.

REFERENCES

Allison, T. H., Davis, B. C., Short, J. C., & Webb, J. W. (2017). Crowdfunding in a Prosocial Microlending Environment: Examining the Role of Intrinsic and Extrinsic Cues. *Entrepreneurship Theory and Practice*, *41*(2), 237–260.

Box, G. E. P., & Jenkins, G. M. (1970). *Time Series Analysis: Forecasting and Control*. Holden-Day.

Bruce, M., Daly, L., & Towers, N. (2004). Lean or agile: A solution for supply chain management in the textiles and clothing industry? *International Journal of Operations & Production Management*, *24*(2), 151–170.

Brynjolfsson, E., & McAfee, A. (2017). *Machine, Platform, Crowd: Harnessing Our Digital Future*. W. W. Norton & Company.

Burrell, J. (2016). How the machine 'thinks': Understanding opacity in machine learning algorithms. *Big Data & Society*, *3*(1), 2053951715622512.

Chopra, S., & Meindl, P. (2016). *Supply Chain Management: Strategy, Planning, and Operation* (6th ed.). Pearson.

Christopher, M. (2016). *Logistics & Supply Chain Management* (5th ed.). Pearson.

Christopher, M., & Peck, H. (2004). Building the resilient supply chain. *International Journal of Logistics Management*, *15*(2), 1–13.

Christopher, M., & Towill, D. (2001). An integrated model for the design of agile supply chains. *International Journal of Physical Distribution & Logistics Management*, *31*(4), 235–246.

Christopher, M. L. (1992). *Logistics and Supply Chain Management*. Pitman Publishing.

Croom, S., Romano, P., & Giannakis, M. (2000). Supply chain management: An analytical framework for critical literature review. *European Journal of Purchasing & Supply Management*, *6*(1), 67–83.

Daehy, Y., Krishnan, K., Alsaadi, A., & Alghamdi, S. (2019). Effective cost minimization strategy and an optimization model of a reliable global supply chain system. *Uncertain Supply Chain Management*, *7*(3), 381–398.

Davenport, T. H., Guha, A., Grewal, D., & Bressgott, T. (2020). How Artificial Intelligence Will Change the Future of Marketing. *Journal of the Academy of Marketing Science*, *48*(1), 24–42.

Davenport, T. H., & Harris, J. G. (2007). *Competing on Analytics: The New Science of Winning*. Harvard Business School Press.

European Commission. (2020). "White Paper on Artificial Intelligence - A European approach to excellence and trust."

Fogarty, D. W., Blackstone, J. H., & Hoffman, T. R. (1991). *Production and Inventory Management* (2nd ed.). South-Western.

Ganeshan, R., Jack, E., Magazine, M. J., & Stephens, P. (1998). A taxonomic review of supply chain management research. In *Quantitative models for supply chain management* (pp. 841–880). Kluwer Academic Publishers.

Gardner, E. S. (2006). Exponential Smoothing: The State of the Art. *Journal of Forecasting*, *4*(1), 1–28.

Génin, P. (2003). *Robust tactical planning with the use of an A.P.S., proposal of a management mode by reference plane* [Doctoral thesis, Ecole des Mines de Paris].

Gibson, R. B., Hassan, S., Holtz, S., Tansey, J., & Whitelaw, G. (2005). *Sustainability Assessment: Criteria and Processes*. Earthscan.

Gompers, P., & Lerner, J. (2001). *The Venture Capital Cycle*. MIT Press.

Hugos, M. H. (2018). *Essentials of Supply Chain Management* (4th ed.). Wiley.

Ivanov, D., & Sokolov, B. (2013). Control of risks in dual-period supply chain scheduling. *International Journal of Production Research, 51*(7), 2100–2116.

Kagermann, H., Wahlster, W., & Helbig, J. (2013). *Recommendations for implementing the strategic initiative INDUSTRIE 4.0: Final report of the Industrie 4.0 Working Group*. Acatech.

Kerr, W. R., Lerner, J., & Schoar, A. (2014). The Consequences of Entrepreneurial Finance: Evidence from Angel Financings. *Review of Financial Studies*, *27*(1), 20–55.

Khan, M., & Kumar, V. (2020). Risk Management in Supply Chains: Strategies and Solutions. *Journal of Risk Research, 23*(7), 897–912.

La Londe, B. J., & Masters, J. M. (1994). Emerging Logistics Strategies: Blue-print for the next century. *International Journal of Physical Distribution & Logistics Management*, *24*(7), 35–47.

Lambert, D. M., & Cooper, M. C. (2000). Issues in supply chain management. *Industrial Marketing Management*, *29*(1), 65–83.

Law, A. M., & Kelton, W. D. (2000). *Simulation Modeling and Analysis* (3rd ed.). McGraw-Hill.

Lee, H. L., So, K. C., & Tang, C. S. (2018). The Evolution of Inventory Management Models: From EOQ to AI. *International Journal of Production Economics, 205*, 123–135.

Lee, H. L., So, K. C., & Tang, C. S. (2020). Risk Mitigation and Cybersecurity in Supply Chains. *International Journal of Production Economics, 225*, 123–135.

Lee, J., Davari, H., Singh, J., & Pandhare, V. (2018). Industrial Artificial Intelligence for industry 4.0-based manufacturing systems. *Manufacturing Letters, 18*, 20–23.

Liker, J. K. (2004). *The Toyota Way: 14 Management Principles from the World's Greatest Manufacturer*. McGraw-Hill.

Lummus, R. R., & Vokurka, R. J. (1999). Defining supply chain management: A historical perspective and practical guidelines. *Industrial Management & Data Systems, 99*(1), 11–17.

Makridakis, S., Wheelwright, S. C., & Hyndman, R. J. (1998). *Forecasting: Methods and Applications* (3rd ed.). Wiley.

Mehrabi, N., Morstatter, F., Saxena, N., Lerman, K., & Galstyan, A. (2021). A survey on bias and fairness in machine learning. *ACM Computing Surveys, 54*(6), 1–35.

Meng, C. (2015). *Advances in logistics and supply chain management*. Springer.

Mentzer, J. T., Dewitt, W., Keebler, J. S., Min, S., Nix, N. W., Smith, C. D., & Zacharia, Z. G. (2001). Defining the supply chain Management. *Journal of Business Logistics, 22*(2).

Mentzer, J. T., & Moon, M. A. (2005). *Sales forecasting management: A demand management approach* (2nd ed.). Thomson South-Western.

Mollick, E. (2014). The Dynamics of Crowdfunding: An Exploratory Study. *Journal of Business Venturing, 29*(1), 1–16.

Mondén, T. (2011). Implementing Lean Principles in Supply Chains. Springer.

Montgomery, D. C., Jennings, C. L., & Kulahci, M. (2012). *Introduction to Time Series Analysis and Forecasting* (2nd ed.). Wiley.

Nahmias, S. (2009). *Production and Operations Analysis* (6th ed.). McGraw-Hill.

OECD. (2019). *Artificial Intelligence in Society*. OECD Publishing.

Partovi, F. Y., & Anandarajan, M. (2002). Supply chain performance measurement. *International Journal of Production Research, 40*(1), 1–20.

Payne, A., & Frow, P. (2017). *Strategic Customer Management: Integrating Relationship Marketing and CRM.* Cambridge University Press.

Petrovic-Lazarevic, S.. (2007). Supply Chain Improvement Initiatives in the Australian Textiles, Clothing, Footwear and Leather Industry: A Field Study. *International Journal of Logistics Systems and Management, 3*(1), 1–19.

Queiroz, M. M., Telles, R., & Lima, R. (2020). Blockchain and supply chain management: A systematic review of the literature. *Supply Chain Management, 25*(5), 619–631.

Rota-Franz, K. (1998). *Temporal coordination of centres managing resources autonomously. Application to integrated supply chains in aeronautics* [PhD thesis, École Nationale Supérieure de l'Aéronautique et de l'Espace]. ENSAE.

Saberi, S., Kouhizadeh, M., Sarkis, J., & Shen, L. (2019). Blockchain technology and its relationships to sustainable supply chain management. *International Journal of Production Research, 57*(7), 2117–2135.

Schonberger, R. J. (1982). *Japanese Manufacturing Techniques: Nine Hidden Lessons in Simplicity.* Free Press.

Seuring, S., & Müller, M. (2008). From a literature review to a conceptual framework for sustainable supply chain management. *Journal of Cleaner Production, 16*(15), 1699–1710.

Shapiro, J. F. (2001). *Modeling the Supply Chain.* Duxbury Press.

Silver, E. A., Pyke, D. F., & Peterson, R. (1998). *Inventory Management and Production Planning and Scheduling* (3rd ed.). Wiley.

Simchi-Levi, D., Kaminsky, P., & Simchi-Levi, E. (2008). *Designing and managing the supply chain: Concepts, strategies, and case studies* (3rd ed.). McGraw-Hill.

Smith, T., & Jones, P. (2019). Performance Metrics in Inventory Management: A Review. *Journal of Operations Management, 65*(4), 345–367.

Snyder, R. D., Shen, Z.-J. M., & Henly, E. (2016). *Fundamentals of Supply Chain Theory* (2nd ed.). Wiley.

Srivastava, P. (2007). Green supply-chain management: A literature review and framework for future research. *International Journal of Production Research, 45*(18-19), 4355–4394.

Tang, C. S. (2006). Perspectives in supply chain risk management. *International Journal of Production Economics, 103*(2), 451–488.

Tayur, S., Ganeshan, R., & Magazine, M. (1999). *Quantitative models for supply chain management*. Kluwer Academic Publishers.

Tempelmeier, H. (2011). *Inventory Management in Supply Chains*. Niemeyer.

Van der Vorst, J. G. A. J., & Beulens, A. J. M. (2002). Identifying sources of cost inefficiency in food supply chains. *International Journal of Physical Distribution & Logistics Management, 32*(9), 729–747.

Vidal, C. J. (2002). Collaborative Supply Chain Practices: A Comprehensive Study. *The Journal of Supply Chain Management, 38*(3), 4–12.

Voigt, P., & Von dem Bussche, A. (2017). *The EU General Data Protection Regulation (GDPR): A Commentary*. Springer.

Wittek, P. (2014). *Quantum Machine Learning: What Quantum Computing Means to Data Mining*. Academic Press.

Womack, J. P., & Jones, D. T. (2003). *Lean Thinking: Banish Waste and Create Wealth in Your Corporation* (2e éd.). Free Press.

KEY TERMS AND DEFINITIONS

Artificial Intelligence (AI): is a branch of computer science that develops machines capable of performing tasks requiring human intelligence, such as reasoning and learning. Using rules, statistics, or neural networks, AI finds various applications, from virtual assistants to autonomous cars.

Autonomous Supply Chains: Autonomous supply chains symbolize a revolutionary perspective for businesses. AI-based systems would be capable of managing end-to-end processes with minimal human intervention, ranging from product design to sending and shipping products to the final consumer, including forecasting needs, inventory management, and transportation optimization.

Informatique Quantique: Quantum computing leverages the principles of quantum mechanics to perform calculations. By using qubits capable of superposition, it allows for the simultaneous processing of multiple states, thus offering parallel processing capabilities far superior to those of classical computers. This paves the way for major advancements in cryptography, optimization, and the simulation of quantum systems.

Internet des Objects (IOT): The Internet of Things (IoT) is a network of physical objects with sensors and software that collects and exchanges data via the internet, improving integration between the physical world and computer systems.

Inventory Optimization: Supply inventory optimization involves maintaining an optimal balance between product availability to meet demand and minimizing storage-related costs, using strategies and technologies to improve efficiency and reduce excess shortages.

Predictive Analytics: It represents a crucial approach that encompasses the thorough examination of data, statistical modeling, machine learning algorithms, artificial intelligence, as well as various sophisticated methods to forecast future outcomes.

Supply Chain Management (SCM): is a set of processes that plan, execute, and control production and delivery operations, including managing initial materials, product transformation, and distribution to the final customer.

Supply Chain Optimization: It includes all the measures taken by a company to enhance the efficiency and profitability of its supply chain.

Supply Chain: It encompasses the planning and management of all flows (material, information, and financial) from the supplier to the end customer, including the producer and distributor.

Chapter 6
Elevating Small Business Performance With Emerging Technologies and Artificial Intelligence in Africa

Timilehin Olasoji Olubiyi
http://orcid.org/0000-0003-0690-7722
Babcock University, Ilishan-Remo, Nigeria

Felicia Sokojinwon Abaniwo
Babcock University, Ilishan-Remo, Nigeria

Senyo Agbeblewu
http://orcid.org/0000-0003-1510-2934
Edith Cowan University, Austraiia

Kayode Samuel Adeyemi
Oduduwa University. Ipetumodu, Nigeria

ABSTRACT

A sustainable economy, particularly in the context of the fourth industrial revolution (4IR), necessitates a robust and globally competitive manufacturing sector. However, our understanding of how this emerging and rapidly changing technology impacts corporate performance, especially regarding turnover in small enterprises, may be lacking. This chapter examines the impact of developing technologies on the performance of small manufacturing enterprises, with a particular emphasis on

DOI: 10.4018/979-8-2600-0439-5.ch006

Nigeria, the largest consumer market in Africa. Research indicated that developing technologies significantly influenced the business performance of SMEs in Nigeria. The research concludes that new technologies can improve the business performance of small manufacturing enterprises. Small businesses are advised to leverage AI to create disruptive innovation through innovative business models and processes, potentially transforming the manufacturing industry and global competitive landscape.

INTRODUCTION

A sustainable economy, particularly during the fourth industrial revolution (4IR), necessitates a robust and globally competitive manufacturing sector. The strategies for survival of manufacturing SMEs in the new normal and beyond, amid intense global competition driven by the Fourth Industrial Revolution (4IR), necessitate the effective adoption of advanced technologies. Concurrently, the automation of numerous white-collar jobs, prompted by 4IR technologies and Covid-19 survival measures, has resulted in a dual disruption within the labor market; the precise effects of the 4IR paradigm on employment remain unpredictable at this time. Small and medium-sized enterprises (SMEs) have emerged as the most dynamic category of companies inside the European Union (EU) and are the foundation of the European economy (Dabic et al., 2016), since they account for 99% of all business entities in the EU (Uwem et al., 2021; Müller, 2019). Emerging innovations and technologies were initially analyzed and are now projected to significantly influence future smart factory development in terms of technological advancements, as well as the introduction of creative goods and business models. These principles allow manufacturing firms to lower expenses, augment flexibility and productivity, elevate quality, and accelerate business operations (Brunelli et al., 2017; Junaid, 2020).

In the United States in 2020, over 3 billion workers worldwide were to be overseen by robotic supervisors, and 59% of US manufacturers had implemented various forms of robotics technology and cloud computing advancements that facilitated sustained innovative leadership (World Economic Forum, 2015). Experts forecasted that 10% of warehouse personnel will be supplanted by autonomous robots by 2021, and by 2025, manufacturers anticipated an average efficiency increase of 12% from Industry 4.0 implementations. Certain manufacturing SMEs in many economies are progressively embracing Internet and web-based technologies for social enterprises and the development of innovative business models (Omotosho, 2020; Shaltoni, 2017). Despite these advancements enhancing the current situation, the entrenched problems in Emerging and Developing Economies (EMDEs) persist in obstructing the adoption and application of technology (Makiwa & Steyn, 2018; Omotosho,

2020; Suyambu et al., 2020). The use of technology by SMEs in EMDEs lags far behind that of wealthy nations (Makiwa & Steyn, 2018).

Small and medium manufacturing firms have underperformed and failed to fulfil their anticipated role in Nigeria's economic growth and development. In recent years, some manufacturing enterprises have ceased operations, while those remaining face a multitude of issues that have resulted in diminished consumer demand for products both in Nigeria and internationally. Identified issues encompass a deficiency in research, a lack of innovation, and insufficient adoption of modern technology, which are significant factors contributing to the demise of certain enterprises and the poor performance of existing manufacturing SMEs (Olubiyi, 2023b; Haruna et al., 2015). The incapacity of SMEs to implement advanced technologies in EMDEs, including virtual reality and cloud computing for remote operations, alongside the non-digitization of business activities, has adversely affected firms in these nations, including Nigeria, amid the ongoing COVID-19 pandemic and subsequent lockdown measures to mitigate the spread of SARS-CoV-2 (Attaran & Woods, 2019; Akpan & Shanker, 2019). This contrasts with SMEs in developed nations, where firms promptly adapted technologies and transitioned public and private sector enterprises to virtual platforms to sustain economic activity (Akpan et al., 2020; Papadopoulos et al., 2020). Agboola et al. (2019) discovered that manufacturing goods and services is prohibitively costly due to numerous problems in the Nigerian business climate, including unreliable power supply, poor road conditions, outdated infrastructure, and economic instability. Consequently, no single firm may encounter these issues inside the Nigerian business landscape that would be inclined to invest significantly in cutting-edge technological software and gear to combat scammers and hackers. Research indicates that 90% of organizations cease operations by their third anniversary due to unfavorable environmental reasons; however, some companies experience stagnation throughout the survival phase, potentially attributable to inadequate performance. Various studies on the efficacy of internal and external corporate settings have been undertaken, although the findings have produced inconclusive and contradictory outcomes. Research has not advanced the understanding of the relationship between the internal and external business environments and agribusiness performance (Ayodele et al., 2019). Despite the government's efforts to initiate and maintain rapid industrialization in Nigeria, achieving the necessary level of industrialization to effect significant changes in the economic structure and provide substantial benefits to the populace has proven to be a formidable challenge. For more than thirty years, Nigeria's economic metrics reflecting industrialization levels have been unsatisfactory. Nigeria's industrial sector is marked by significant import dependence for industrial inputs, reduced capacity utilization, elevated production costs, minimal value addition, declining output growth, limited job creation, and insufficient intersectoral linkages (The World Bank, 2022). As a result, research has not yet addressed the gap regarding the impact of developing technological components on the business performance of manufacturing SMEs in Nigeria. The objective of this research is to explore the role of emerging technologies, with a specific focus on Artificial Intelligence (AI), in elevating the performance of small businesses in Africa. As the continent grapples with challenges such as limited access to capital, inadequate infrastructure, and evolving market demands, the integration of AI and other digital innovations offers transformative potential. This study aims to identify how AI can be leveraged to enhance operational efficiency, customer engagement, and decision-making processes within small enterprises. Additionally, the research seeks to understand how AI can contribute to overcoming traditional barriers faced by African small businesses, such as scalability issues, market access, and resource constraints. By analyzing case studies, industry data, and expert insights, the study will provide a comprehensive understanding of the practical applications of AI in various sectors, including agriculture, retail, and manufacturing, within the African context. The research will also examine the adoption barriers, such as technological readiness, digital literacy, and affordability, and offer recommendations to foster a supportive environment for AI integration into small business operations across Africa. Ultimately, the goal is to provide actionable insights for entrepreneurs, policymakers, and stakeholders to maximize the potential of AI, ensuring that small businesses in Africa can thrive in a rapidly evolving digital economy.

> $\mathbf{H}_{01:}$ Emerging technology components have no significant effect on business performance in selected manufacturing SMEs in Nigeria

BACKGROUND

The Concept of Emerging Technology

The term "emerging technology" (DT) was coined by Joseph Bower and Clayton Christensen in 1995. It also pertains to the selection and deployment of technologies or contemporary innovations that substantially transform corporate operations. Singh and Hanafi (2019) asserted that disruptive technology (DT) originates from a niche market, then becoming dominant and destabilizing the market equilibrium, often displacing established leading enterprises. An emerging technology supplants an old technology, disrupting the sector, or a revolutionary product engenders an entirely new industry (Salau, 2019). It may be considerably less expensive while yet delivering the requisite functionalities (Vaidya, 2022). Ultimately, emerging technology encompasses a succession of advancements stemming from numerous significant and minor discoveries, positioning it as a dominant force over established technologies in the marketplace (Smith, 2022). The acquisition of knowledge through diffusion and the spread of knowledge through learning is a fundamental catalyst for the advancement and acceptance of developing technologies in volatile marketplaces (Clayton & Christensen, 2016). Technological investment is defined as the commitment made by organisations out of their resources to acquire information technology facilities and capabilities which will help in improving their productivity, service delivery and profitability (Aminu, 2019). Technology investments predominantly favor bigger firms given the total resource commitment required (Cho & Linderman, 2020). Although the diffusion rate of information technology in small and medium-sized enterprises has gained much popularity over the past decade because of the age of globalization and competition (Coffie et al., 2021) information systems diffusion amongst SMEs still lags behind bigger firms (Stoneman & Karshenas, 2018).Technology awareness refers to the skill of an individual to be aware and mindful of new and popular technology that has been gaining widespread acceptance across concerned industries or markets (Rahimah et al., 2018). Thus, awareness is an antecedent for the attitude formation stage of innovation diffusion. They further opined that innovation diffusion theory (IDT) (Rogers, 1995) used it as the initial stage of an innovation diffusion process model. Awareness in IDT is developed from the perspective of positive technologies. More companies are building on existing information systems, along with new technologies such as social media to get to know their customers better (Weill & Woerner, 2015).

The technological response in today's swiftly evolving business landscape necessitates that businesses swiftly adapt and respond. A response is a reaction to a question, experience, or stimulus, manifesting in various ways such as an answer, emotional reaction, or reply. Nonetheless, despite the widespread nature of this proposal, numerous organizations fail to effectively address disruption (Khanagha et al., 2018), prompting enquiries into the validity, feasibility, or limitations of this internal fit perspective. Organizations cannot investigate all possible disruption strategies or their potential prospects uniformly; therefore, they must develop a prioritized investment strategy for addressing digital disruption that aligns with their business needs (Plummer et al., 2017). Technology adaptation pertains to comprehending consumers' behaviors in relation to the acceptance and effective utilization of technology (Kee & Rubel, 2021). Various companies have adapted through digital technologies; however, the transition to digitalization poses significant challenges for small and medium enterprises (SMEs) in creative industries that produce non-essential physical products during the pandemic (Seetharaman, 2020). Technology adaptation specifically pertains to comprehending users' behaviors in relation to the acceptance and effective utilization of technology (Rubel et al., 2016). Appropriate technology adaptation signifies a certain alignment between the behaviors required by the environment and those exhibited by the individual, enabling the individual to attain valued objectives through its effective use (Kee & Rubel, 2021). Technology transfer (TT) denotes the process of disseminating outcomes derived from scientific and technological research to the marketplace and broader society, together with the requisite skills and methodologies, hence constituting an integral component of the technological innovation process. Surpassing technology transfer necessitates a pragmatic and systematic approach to the provision of agricultural extension services, moving beyond the existing linear model of technology dissemination. The technology transfer process is directed by the policies and principles of each organization. The United Nations Conference on Trade and Development (UNCTAD, 2018) defines it as any modalities of technical exchange that enhance the technological capabilities of the user or recipient. The procurement of technology may be executed by the government, entrepreneurs, external agents (such as technology brokers), or a combination of these three entities. It facilitates the establishment of new enterprises, employment opportunities, and economic expansion (OECD, 2020). Researchers are pivotal in technology transfer and serve as a crucial resource for transitioning technology from the laboratory to the marketplace (Simelyte et al., 2021).

Business Turnover

Business turnover refers to the aggregate sales generated by a company within a specified timeframe. It is occasionally termed 'gross revenue' or 'income'. This differs from profit, which is an indicator of earnings. It is a crucial indicator of a business's performance. Adkins (2021) defines turnover as the aggregate sales generated by a business throughout a specific timeframe. It is occasionally termed 'gross revenue' or 'income'. This differs from profit, which is an indicator of earnings. It is a crucial metric of your business performance. The firm's turnover is the predominant metric of growth, addressing taxes issues, while the staff count serves as an alternative growth measure, focusing on employment difficulties (Investopedia, 2022).

Emerging Technology Components and Business Turnover

Odiboh et al. (2017) concluded in their analysis that the internet is a remarkable innovation in human history. It has engendered significant transformation in the execution of business transactions worldwide. Nonetheless, the surge in criminal activities and victimization within the computer-generated corporate environment has significantly exacerbated the loss of business capital and investments. The dissociative anonymity and identity flexibility of offenders of these offences persistently present significant obstacles to investigation and conviction. Similarly, the findings of Igwe et al. (2020) indicated that of all contemporary e-business technologies, internet technology was the most embraced by SMEs. This has led to innovation in the operational methods of small enterprises over the past five years. The findings of Ramdansyah and Taufik (2017) indicated that SME performance has a favorable and significant impact on the adoption of e-commerce. The adaptation of digital media in the UAE and Middle East is evaluated as inferior compared to other global regions. Despite the widespread presence of smartphones, laptops, and computers among consumers, who actively utilize Facebook and other social media platforms, small and medium-sized enterprises (SMEs) in the region lack trained personnel and expertise and remain unmotivated to incorporate digital media into their business operations (Abed et al., 2015; Wellalage & Locke, 2016; Nelson, 2016; Samuel & Sarprasatha, 2016). Moreover, technological instruments such as e-commerce, proprietary websites, cloud computing, mobile commerce, and microblogging platforms (social media) have been demonstrated to substantially influence the performance of business organizations (Olubiyi, 2024b; Haller & Lyons, 2015; Hagsten, 2016; Khairuddin & Olowosuyi, 2020). The innovation idea was first articulated by Schumpeter in 1934 (as referenced in Obunike & Udu, 2018). Schumpeter was an economist who introduced the phrase "creative destruction" to characterize the effects of innovation resulting from the competition among enterprises within a specific marketplace, which serves as the foundation of the research. The approach is based on three principal assumptions: opportunities are subjective; opportunities are not merely recognized but produced; and entrepreneurs endure uncertainty.

Opportunities arise from a sequence of decisions aimed at capitalizing on a possible prospect. They are generated by economic agents; they do not exist autonomously. Their existence possesses the capacity for wealth production. The theory posits uncertainty rather than risk. In uncertain conditions, the characteristics of an industry are either ascertainable or subject to unpredictable changes. Schumpeter's theory of creative destruction posits that technical innovation fosters the emergence of new, innovative enterprises while leading to the decline of firms reliant on outdated technologies. However, not all disrupted companies perish; instead, some endure and thrive by employing strategic entrepreneurship (Thomas & Douglas, 2021). It presupposes the dismantling or destruction of entrenched systems and practices to liberate resources and energy for innovation. This paves the way for innovative technology, novel goods, advanced production methods, and enhanced distribution mechanisms. Established enterprises must swiftly acclimatize to a novel environment or face failure. The theory is highly relevant for investigating the elements of emerging technology and their impact on business performance, since it offers a framework for studying the adoption of new technologies by individuals and organizations.

Figure 1. Research Conceptual Model

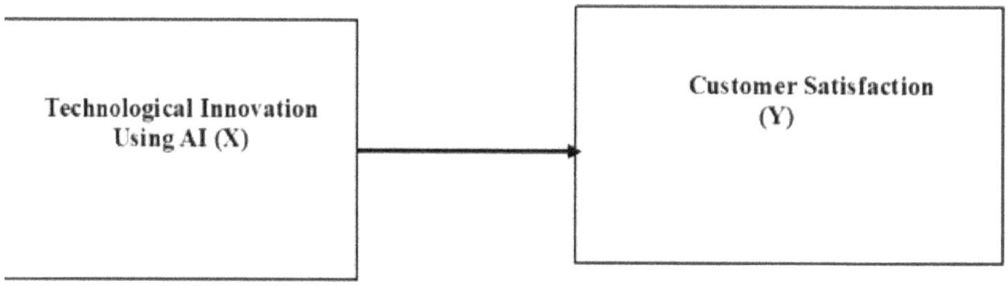

Source: Authors' model, (2025).

According to Day (2018), the study's findings revealed that technology is extensively utilized by small enterprises nationwide. A case study of Facebook showed that small enterprises utilize social media for expansion, recruitment, and commerce. Asunka (2016) determined that ICT has facilitated the expansion of SMEs by reducing communication and transaction costs, while improving relationships with customers and suppliers. Despite a high knowledge of the advantages of ICT among SME owners in the Bawku Municipality, its adoption and utilization remain low. The elevated expenses associated with hardware and software infrastructure, the absence of support systems, and the deficiency of experience constitute significant obstacles to the adoption of ICT among SMEs. The adaptation of technology can be improved through an organization's High-Impact Work Practices (HIWP) by means of information dissemination, active involvement, and training initiatives. The study by Kee and Rubel (2021) indicated that technological adaptation is likely to stem from practices that foster support and trust within an organization. Organizations that implement HIWP to bolster support and confidence may see increased efficiency in achieving technological adaption. Similarly, Olomu et al. (2016) observed that product, process, and marketing innovations significantly influence the performance of SMEs.

Ramdansyah and Taufik (2017) concluded that top management support, organizational readiness, and perceived benefits significantly positively influence the adoption of e-commerce. Wan et al. (2015) contended that established enterprises frequently presume that these technologies cater solely to a certain demand and market, and that the majority of their clients may not appreciate their use. Technology-oriented SMEs that adopt new technologies or upgrade current ones will recognize that these innovations favorably impact overall business operations and lead to improved firm performance. Digital media adaptation in the UAE and Middle East is evaluated as inferior compared to other global regions. Despite the widespread presence of smartphones, laptops, and computers among consumers, who actively engage with Facebook and other social media platforms, small and medium-sized enterprises (SMEs) in the region lack trained personnel and expertise and remain unmotivated to incorporate digital media into their business operations (Wellalage & Locke, 2016; Nelson, 2016; Samuel & Sarprasatha, 2016). Technological technologies, including e-commerce, corporate websites, cloud computing, mobile commerce, and microblogging platforms (social media), have been demonstrated to greatly influence the performance of commercial organizations (Olubiyi et al., 2024; Hagsten, 2016; Khairuddin & Olowosuyi, 2020).

MAIN FOCUS OF THE CHAPTER

The main focus of this research is to investigate how emerging technologies, particularly Artificial Intelligence (AI), can be utilized to enhance the performance of small businesses in Africa. With the rapid digital transformation occurring globally, small businesses in Africa have the potential to harness AI to overcome traditional challenges such as limited access to finance, market competition, and operational inefficiencies (Papadopoulos et al., 2020). This study will explore the various applications of AI, including automation, data analytics, customer personalization, and predictive modeling, to improve decision-making, optimize business processes, and enhance customer experiences. The research will also examine the barriers to AI adoption, such as lack of digital infrastructure, insufficient technical skills, and high implementation costs, while identifying strategies to overcome these obstacles. Furthermore, the study will focus on specific sectors, including agriculture, retail, and manufacturing, to highlight sector-specific benefits and challenges. Ultimately, the goal is to provide small business owners, policymakers, and industry stakeholders with practical insights into how AI and emerging technologies can drive growth, innovation, and sustainability in Africa's small business sector, contributing to the broader economic development of the continent.

Methodology

The research utilized a survey design. The overall population comprised 385 owner-managers of manufacturing SMEs in Nigeria. This paper utilized the methodological framework established by Ukabi, Uba, Ewum, and Olubiyi (2023), Olowoporoku, and Olubiyi, (2023); Olubiyi, et. al (2019) as well as Olubiyi (2024a) and Olubiyi, Adeoye, Jubril, Adeyemi, and Eyanuku (2023). The research using Cochran's (1977) formula to ascertain a sample size of 436. A straightforward random sample method with proportional allocation was employed to pick the participants. A standardized and validated closed-ended questionnaire was employed for data collection. The questionnaire items were sourced from the past literature to collect data on the factors under investigation in the study. The Cronbach's alpha reliability coefficients for the constructs varied between 0.726 and 0.900. The response rate was 99 percent.

Table 1. Sources of the Adapted Questionnaire

Main Variables	Specific Main Variables	Sources of Instrument
Independent Variable: Emerging Technology	Technology Investment	Karhade and Dong (2020).
	Technology Awareness	Sharma et al., (2020).
	Technology Response	Prevost et al., (2018)
	Technology Adaptation	Kumar and Ayedee (2021).
	Technology Transfer	Handoko et al., (2019).
	Technology Accessibility	Horton (2021).
Dependent Variable	Business Performance	Nicodemus et al., (2020)

Source: Researchers' Literature Review, (2025).

Model Specification

The two main variables in the study were Emerging technology (Independent variable) and business performance of selected manufacturing SMEs (Dependent variable) business performance measured by business turnover. Emerging technology has the following dimensions: Technology investment (TI), Technology awareness (TA), Technology response (TR), Technology adaptation (TAD), Technology transfer (TT) and Technology accessibility (TAC) and business performance (BT).

Y = f (X)

Y = Dependent Variable (BT)

X = Independent Variable (DT)

Y = BT

$X = (x_1, x_2, x_{3,} x_4, x_5, x_6)$

Where:

X = Emerging technology (DT)

x_1 = Technology investment (TI)

x_2 = Technology awareness (TA)

x_3 = Technology response (TR)

x_4= Technology adaptation (TAD)

x_5 = Technology transfer (TT)

x_6 = Technology accessibility (TAC)

The model formulated for the hypotheses is written as:

$BT= {}_0+ {}_1TI+ {}_2TA+ {}_3TR+ {}_4TAD+ {}_5TT {}_{+} {}_6TAC {}_{+}\varepsilon$---------- Regression eqn.

Table 2. Multiple Regression of the effect of emerging technology dimensions on business performance in Nigeria.

N	Model	B	Sig.	T	ANOVA (Sig.)	R	Adjusted R^2	F (6, 378)
385	(Constant)	1.158	0.010	2.573	0.000[b]	0.916[a]	0.837	330.349
	Technology Investment	0.343	0.000	7.490				
	Technology Awareness	0.244	0.000	5.633				
	Technology Response	-0.001	0.984	-0.020				
	Technology Adaptation	0.113	0.021	2.319				
	Technology Transfer	0.082	0.133	1.507				
	Technology Accessibility	0.169	0.002	3.175				
	• Predictors: (Constant), Technology Accessibility, Technology Investment, Technology Awareness, Technology Adaptation, Technology Response, Technology Transfer							
	Dependent Variable: Business Performance							

Source: Researchers' Findings, (2025).

Interpretation

Table 2 showed the multiple regression analysis results for the dimensions of emerging technology on business performance in selected manufacturing SMEs in Nigeria. The results showed that for the emerging technology component on business performance in Nigeria. The results revealed that technology investment ($\beta = 0.343$, $t=7.490$, $p<0.05$), technology awareness ($\beta = 0.244$, $t = 5.633$, $p<0.05$), technology adaptation ($\beta = 0.113$, $t=2.319$, $p<0.05$), technology transfer ($\beta = 0.082$, $t=1.507$, $p<0.05$) and technology accessibility (($\beta = 0.169$, $t= 3.175$ $p<0.05$) have a positive and significant effect on business performance however, technology response ($\beta =$ - 0.001, $t = -0.020$, $p>0.05$) had a negative and insignificant effect. This implies that all the components of emerging technology that are positive and significant are important factors in the manufacturing SMEs' firms which in turn yielded an increase in business performance of the manufacturing SME firms.

The R value of 0.916 supported this result and it indicated that emerging technology components had a very strong positive relationship with business performance of selected manufacturing SMEs in Nigeria. The coefficient of multiple determination $AdjR^2 = 0.837$ revealed that about 83.7% variation that occurred on the business performance in selected manufacturing SMEs firms can be accounted for by the components of emerging technology while the remaining 16.3% changes that occurred was accounted for by other variables not captured in the model. The predictive and prescriptive multiple regression models are thus expressed:

$P = 1.158 + 0.343TI + 0.244TA - 0.001TR + 0.113TAD + 0.082TT + 0.169TAC + U_i$ --- Eqn(i) (Predictive Model)

$P = 1.158 + 0.343TI + 0.244TA + 0.113TAD + 0.082TT + 0.169TAC + U_i$ --- Eqn(ii) (Prescriptive Model)

Where:
BT = Business performance
TI = Technology Investment
TA = Technology awareness
TR = Technology response
TAD = Technology adaptation
TT = Technology transfer
TAC = Technology accessibility

The regression model indicated that if new technology is held constant at zero, business performance would be 1.158, which is favorable. The prediction model indicated that all factors were positive and significant, with the exception of technological reaction, which had a negative and insignificant influence. The management of the manufacturing enterprises required them to priorities certain variables, which is why they were incorporated into the prescriptive model. The outcomes of the multiple regression analysis presented in the prescriptive model demonstrated that enhancements of one unit in technology investment, technology awareness, technology adaptation, technology transfer, and technology accessibility would correspondingly elevate business performance by 0.343, 0.244, 0.113, 0.082, and 0.169, respectively. This suggests that enhanced investment in technology, heightened technology awareness, improved technology adaptation, effective technology transfer, and greater technology accessibility would result in improved company performance among selected manufacturing SMEs in Nigeria. The F-statistic (df = 6, 378) = 330.349 at p = 0.000 ($p<0.05$) demonstrated that the overall model significantly predicted the impact of emerging technology on business performance. This suggests that components of emerging technology, particularly technology investment, technology awareness, technology accessibility, technology adaptation, and technology transfer, are critical determinants of the business performance of selected manufacturing firms in Lagos and Ogun States, Nigeria. The findings indicated that manufacturing companies ought to priorities the development of technology disruption components, particularly focusing on technology investment, awareness, accessibility, adaptation, and transfer to enhance business performance.

Consequently, the null hypothesis (H01), which posited that new technology components exert no substantial influence on the business performance of selected manufacturing SMEs in Nigeria, was rejected.

SOLUTIONS AND RECOMMENDATIONS

The hypothesis test demonstrated that new technological components significantly impacted the business performance of the selected manufacturing SMEs in Nigeria. The empirical findings of this study concur with those of Suleiman (2016), who demonstrated that even a modest firm could achieve competitiveness and surpass its competitors by fostering a culture that effectively leveraged the opportunities presented by ICTs, including the internet, electronic commerce, e-business, communication technologies, and knowledge-based innovation management. Moreover, it was discovered that ICT facilitated enterprises in swiftly identifying additional clients, outsourcing optimal suppliers, and, most critically, connecting with appropriate business partners globally. Wan et al. (2015) contended that established firms frequently perceive technologies as serving only specific needs and markets, and that the majority of their customers may not appreciate their utility. Conversely, technology-oriented SMEs that adopt new technologies or enhance existing ones will discover that these innovations positively influence overall business operations and contribute favorably to firm performance. Additionally, Dharalief et al. (2019) empirically validated the critical role of institutional factors, identifying the source of technological knowledge as a significant and positive determinant in the adoption of IT.

Shanmugam et al. (2019) concluded in their study on IT adoption models and SME performance that organizational awareness is a critical factor in enhancing SME performance through information technology adoption. Conversely, Martin et al. (2017) asserted that not all companies and countries within current value chains equally harness the value generated by these technologies. The study by Adebosin et al. (2019) revealed that emerging innovation did not significantly impact the performance of family businesses, concluding that it had no effect. Conversely, the research by Gathogo and Ragui (2014) indicated that respondents were largely dissatisfied with the technological level utilized by their firms, which adversely affected their business performance.

FUTURE RESEARCH DIRECTIONS

Future research regarding the influence of emerging technologies on business performance in manufacturing SMEs in Nigeria and throughout Africa should investigate several key and critical domains. An analysis of the long-term sustainability impacts of technological adoption on SMEs, specifically on operational efficiency, environmental sustainability, and company resilience, would provide significant insights. Comparative analyses across many sectors, including agriculture, services, and retail, would elucidate sector-specific barriers in technology adoption and yield customized recommendations. Furthermore, research may examine the impact of digital transformation, including AI and IoT, on fostering innovation in African SMEs, emphasizing the contribution of these technologies to creativity and competitiveness. Evaluating the influence of technological infrastructure and the skills gap on the adoption of new technologies is essential, as both represent considerable obstacles for numerous SMEs in Nigeria and Africa. Future research may investigate the influence of developing manufacturing technologies on customer satisfaction, focusing on product quality, service, and delivery times. Moreover, studying the influence of government policies, financial resources, and support systems on technology adoption by SMEs in Africa may yield insights on the efficacy of initiatives designed to promote digital transformation. Ultimately, an investigation of the impact of emerging technologies on post-pandemic recovery in African SMEs would provide significant insights into resilience and adaptability, especially within the framework of a swiftly evolving global business landscape. By focusing on these domains, subsequent research can yield thorough insights into the potential of emerging technologies to transform company performance, innovation, and sustainability for SMEs throughout Nigeria and Africa.

CONCLUSION

In conclusion, the integration of Artificial Intelligence (AI) into manufacturing small businesses in Africa presents a transformative opportunity for growth and sustainability. As the continent continues to navigate complex challenges such as limited access to capital, infrastructure gaps, and market barriers, AI offers solutions that can address these issues and help elevate small businesses to new heights. From enhancing operational efficiency through automation to improving decision-making with data analytics, AI has the potential to revolutionize how small businesses in Africa operate and compete in an increasingly digital global economy. This research highlights the critical role that emerging technologies, especially AI, can play in driving innovation within small businesses across various sectors. In agriculture, for example, AI can optimize crop yields and improve supply chain management, while in retail, it can enhance customer experience through personal recommendations and targeted marketing. In manufacturing, AI can streamline production processes and minimize costs, providing small businesses with the tools to scale efficiently. These sector-specific applications demonstrate the adaptability of AI and its potential to foster sectoral growth and job creation, contributing to economic development in Africa. However, the successful adoption of AI by small businesses in Africa is not without its challenges. Issues such as limited technological infrastructure, low levels of digital literacy, and the high initial costs of AI implementation remain significant barriers.

For AI to truly transform small businesses across the continent, it is essential to address these challenges through investments in infrastructure, skills development, and affordable AI solutions tailored to the needs of small enterprises. Furthermore, fostering a conducive environment for AI adoption requires collaboration between governments, educational institutions, and private sector stakeholders. Policymakers must create frameworks that encourage innovation, support digital literacy programs, and facilitate access to funding and technical expertise. Localizing AI solutions to suit Africa's unique context, including languages, business practices, and market conditions, is equally important to ensure the successful integration of AI into small businesses.

In light of these considerations, this research provides valuable insights for African entrepreneurs, policymakers, and other stakeholders, offering strategies to harness the power of AI for improving small business performance. By embracing AI and emerging technologies, African small businesses can not only overcome current challenges but also position themselves for long-term success in the global digital economy. Ultimately, AI can be a catalyst for inclusive economic growth, enabling small businesses to innovate, create jobs, and contribute meaningfully to the socio-economic development of Africa. The research indicated that the use of emerging technologies enhanced company performance for specific manufacturing SMEs in Nigeria. By adopting rising technological elements, these companies enhanced their performance. These improvements undoubtedly led to improved efficiency and output, hence augmenting revenue and enhancing corporate success. Emerging technology in the contemporary economy transcends mere innovation. Disruptions are permanent and will surpass and enhance current performance and company outcomes. In the forthcoming years, disconcerting upheavals will dramatically alter the landscape. Transformation necessitates experimentation when the creative attitude is cultivated. In contrast to large organizations, proprietors of midsized companies can implement developing technologies. The advent of Robotic Process Automation has enabled the automation of repetitive processes. The primary aim of RPA is to replace the efficiency and dependability of virtual automation technologies for monotonous, repetitive, and error-prone manual tasks.

REFERENCES

Adebosin, G. W., Toriola, A. K., Oyewole, S. A., & Saula, D. T. (2019). Disruptive innovation and performance of family business in Ogun state. *3rd Covenant University International Conference on Entrepreneurship (CU–ICE), March 20–22, 351–371.*

Adkins, T. (2021). Optimal use of financial leverage in a corporate capital structure: Corporate finance accounting. (Rev. by Drury. A) Investopedia, Dotdash Meredith, California. https://www.investopedia.com/articles/investing/111813/optimal-use-financial-leverage-corporate-capital-structure.asp

Agboola, M. G., Akinbode, M., Segun-Adeniran, C., Dibia, P. I., Oloruntoba, A., Dinyain, T., Fabunmi, T. J., Funsho, T., Akinde, O. A., & Betek, C. M. (2019). Technology usage and employee behavior: Controversies, complications, and implications in the Nigerian business environment. *IOP Conference Series. Earth and Environmental Science, 331*(2), 1–6.

Akpan, I. J., & Shanker, M. (2019). A comparative evaluation of the effectiveness of virtual reality, 3D visualization and 2D visual interactive simulation: An exploratory meta-analysis. *Simulation, 95*(2), 145–170.

Akpan, I. J., Soopramanien, D., & Kwak, D. H. A. (2020). Cutting-edge technologies for small business and innovation in the era of COVID-19 global health pandemic. *Journal of Small Business and Entrepreneurship*, •••, 1–11.

Akpan, I. J., Udoh, E. A. P., & Adebisi, B. (2020). Small business awareness and adoption of state-of-the-art technologies in emerging and developing markets and lessons from the COVID – 19 pandemic. *Journal of Small Business and Entrepreneurship, 10*, 1–18.

Aminu, R. (2019). *Information technology investment.* Academia.edu https:// www.academia.edu

Attaran, M., & Woods, J. (2019). Cloud computing technology: Improving small business performance using the internet. *Journal of Small Business and Entrepreneurship, 31*(6), 495–519.

Ayodele, J. O., Idachaba, O. I., & Sule, J. G. (2019). Innovation as a mediating of relationship between internal and external environment in agribusiness. *Marketing and Management of Innovations, 1*, 1–16.

Brunelli, J., Lukic, V., Milon, T., & Tandardine, M. (2017). *Five lessons from the frontlines of industry 4.0.* BCG Boston Consulting Group.

Cho, Y. S., & Linderman, K. (2020). Resource-based product and process innovation model: Theory development and empirical validation. *Sustainability*, *12*(3), 913.

Clayton, M., & Christensen, C. M. (2016). *The innovators' dilemma: When new technologies cause great firms to fail*. Harvard Business School press.

Cochran, W. G. (1977). *Sampling techniques* (3rd ed.). John Wiley & Sons.

Coffie, C. P. K., Hongjiang, Z., Mensah, I. A., Kiconco, R., & Simon, A. E. O. (2021). Determinants of FinTech payment services diffusion by SMEs in sub-Saharan Africa: Evidence from Ghana. *Information Technology for Development*, *27*(3), 539–560.

Dabic, M., Svarc, J., & Becic, E. (2016). In Haar, J., & Ernst, R. (Eds.), *"Innovation in Central Europe" in Innovation in emerging markets* (pp. 102–120). Palgrave Macmillan.

Day, T. (2018). Examining the impact of technology on small business: How small businesses use social media and digital platforms to grow, sell, and hire. *U.S. Chamber Technology Engagement Center, C_TEC*, 1 – 18.

Dharalief, M. Z., Bedhiaf, S., & Dhehibi, B., Oueslati – Zlaoui, M., Jebali, O., & Ben – Youssef, S. (2019). Factors affecting innovative technologies adoption by livestock holders in arid area of Tunisia. *New Mediterranean*, *18*(4), 3–18.

Gathogo, G., & Ragui, M. (2014). Effects of capital and technology on the performance of SMEs in the manufacturing sector in Kenya - Case of selected firms in Thika Municipality. *European Journal of Business and Management*, *6*(7), 308–311.

Hagsten, E. (2016). Broadband connected employees and labour productivity: A comparative analysis of 14 European countries based on distributed micro data access. *Economics of Innovation and new Technology*, 1 – 7.

Haller, S., & Lyons, S. (2015). Broadband adoption and firm productivity: Evidence from Irish manufacturing firms. *Telecommunications Policy*, *39*(1), 1–13.

Handoko, F., Vitasari, P., Hidayat, S., & Tjahjadi, M. E. (2019). Technology transfer program for SMEs in Indonesia. In *Journal of Physics: Conference Series* 1375 (1), IOP Publishing

Haruna, M. S., Gakure, R., & Orwa, G. (2015). Effect of advanced manufacturing technology (Amt) on the product output of manufacturing small and medium scale enterprises in Nigeria. *International Academic Journal of Innovation. Leadership and Entrepreneurship*, *1*(5), 1–18.

Horton, S. (2021). Empathy cannot sustain action in technology accessibility. *Frontiers of Computer Science*, *3*, 31.

Igwe, S. R., Ebenuwa, A., & Idenedo, O. W. (2020). Technology adoption and sales performance of manufacturing small and medium enterprises in Port –Harcourt. *Journal of Marketing Development*, *5*(1), 44–59.

Investopedia (2022). Investopedia. https://www.investopedia.

Joseph, L. B., & Clayton, M. C. (1995). Disruptive technologies: Catching the Wave. *Harvard Business Review*, *73*(1), 43–53.

Junaid, M. (2020). Wireless network sensors applications and challenges in a real – life environment. *IEEM – SEM*, *8*(7), 111 – 117.

Karhade, P., & Dong, J. Q. (2020). Information technology investment and commercialized innovation performance: Dynamic adjustment costs and curvilinear impacts. *Management Information Systems Quarterly*, •••, 1–40.

Kee, D. M. H., & Rubel, M. R. B. (2021). Technology adaptation is on its way: The role of high involvement work practice. *International Journal of Business Innovation & Research*, *25*(1), 35–50.

Khairuddin, S. M. H. S., & Olowosuyi, O. S. (2020). Digital adoption of SME in Nigeria: The relationship with business performance. *Journal of Management and Muamalah*, *10*(2), 21–33.

Khanagha, S., Zadeh, M. T. R., Mihalache, O., & Volberda, H. (2018). Embracing bewilderment: Responding to technological disruption in heterogenous market environments. *Journal of Management Studies*, *55*(7), 1079–1121.

Kumar, A., & Ayedee, D. (2021). Technology adoption: A solution for SMEs to overcome problems during COVID-19. *Forthcoming. Academy of Marketing Studies Journal*, *25*(1).

Makiwa, P., & Steyn, R. (2018). An investigation of the government-related factors that inhibit small to medium enterprises adoption and effective use of information and communication technology in developing countries: The case of Zimbabwe". *International Development Informatics Association Conference,* Springer, Cham, 3 – 16.

Martin, C., Leurent, H., & Kearney, A. T. (2017). Technology and innovation for the future of production: Accelerating Value Creation. *Report of World Economic Forum,* 3 – 36.

Nicodemus, T., Mowaiye, B., & Fasola, I. O. (2020). When technology transfer enables sales growth. *Global Journal of Management and Business Research*, *20*(9), 45–53.

Odiboh, O., Ben-Enukora, C., Oresanya, T., Yartey, D., & Aiyelabola, A. (2017). Awareness on digital security and e-business in Nigeria. *Proceedings of SOCIOINT 2017- 4th International Conference on Education, Social Sciences and Humanities, 1402 - 1408; Dubai, UAE.* dr odiboh dubai. (covenantuniversity.edu.ng)

OECD. (2020). Social economy and the Covid – 19 crisis: Current and future roles. https://www.oecd.org/coronavirus/policy-responses/social-economy-and-the-covid -19-crisis-current-and-future-roles-f904b89f/

Olomu, M. O., Irefin, I. A., & Olomu, O. E. (2016). ICT adoption in emerging contemporary marketing practices: the case of the Nigerian paints industry. Ecoforum Journal, 5(3).

Olowoporoku, A. A., & Olubiyi, T. O. (2023). Evaluating Service Quality and Business Outcomes Post-Pandemic: Perspective from Hotels in Emerging Market. *Sawala: Jurnal Administrasi Negara, 11*(2), 182–201.

Olubiyi, T. O. (2023b). *Leveraging competitive strategies on business outcomes post-covid-19 pandemic: Empirical investigation from Africa. Journal of Management and Business: Research and Practice.* University of Presov in Prešov, Slovakia Faculty of Management & Business., DOI: 10.54933/jmbrp-2023-15-2-1

Olubiyi, T. O. (2024a). Improving Customer Experience Through Differentiation Capability: The Rise of Competition among Africa's Consumer Goods Companies. *PaperASIA, 40*(5b), 230–240. DOI: 10.59953/paperasia.v40i5b.233

Olubiyi, T. O. (2024b). An investigation of the role of airline safety management and its impact on passenger satisfaction: A study of commercial airline businesses in Nigeria. *Journal of the Management Sciences, 60*(4). https://journals.unizik.edu .ng/jfms/article/view/3396

Olubiyi, T. O., Adeoye, O. O., Jubril, B., Adeyemi, O. S., & Eyanuku, J. P. (2023). Measuring Inequality in Sub-Saharan Africa Post-Pandemic: Correlation Results for Workplace Inequalities and Implication for Sustainable Development Goal ten. *International Journal of Professional Business Review, 8*(4), e01405. DOI: 10.26668/ businessreview/2023.v8i4.1405

Olubiyi, T. O., Egwakhe, A. J., & Egwuonwu, T. K. (2019). Managerial Roles and Competitive Advantage: SMEs, perspective from Lagos state. *International Journal of Small Business and Entrepreneurship Research, 7*(3), 1–14.

Olubiyi, T. O., Omoyele, O. S., Ilodigwe, S. C., Adeoye, O. O., Makinde, G. O., & Ravinder, R. (2024). The Linkage between Knowledge Management Practices and Sustainable Business Growth: Empirical Evidence from Nigeria. *Revista De Gestão Social E Ambiental, 18*(5), e05432. https://doi.org/DOI: 10.24857/rgsa.v18n5-022

Omotosho, B. J. (2020). Small scale craft workers and the use of social media platform for business performance in Southwest Nigeria. *Journal of Small Business and Entrepreneurship*, •••, 1–6.

Papadopoulos, T. K., Baltas, N., & Balta, M. E. (2020). The use of digital technologies by small and medium enterprises during COVID-19: Implications for theory and practice. *International Journal of Information Management*, •••, 1–4. PMID: 32836646

Prevost, M., Johnston Prof, K. A., & Tanner, M. C. (2018). Awareness and preparedness of IT managers to digital disruption: A South African exploratory case study. *The African Journal of Information Systems*, *10*(4), 2.

Rahimah, K., NorAziat, A. H., & Adnan, H. B. (2018). Organisational support for cloud computing implementation success in education system: Scale development and validity in Delphi. *IACSIT International Journal of Engineering and Technology*, *7*, 512–516.

Rogers, E. M. (1995). Diffusion of Innovations. 4th Edition, the Free Press, New York.

Rubel, M. R. B., Kee, D. M. H., Rimi, N. N., & Yusuf, Y. M. (2016). 'Adapting technology: Effect of high – involvement human resource management and organisational trust'. *Behaviour & Information Technology*, *36*(3), 1–13.

Salau, A. (2019). *Disruptive technologies: Redefining the business and its functional models*. Automata Associates Ltd.

Samuel, B. S., & Sarprasatha, J. (2016). Entrepreneurship in social – media services in Oman – A socio – economic scanning of the Sultanate. *Canadian Centre of Science and Education*, *12*(4), 138–148.

Schumpeter, J. (1934). *The theory of economic development*. Harvard University Press.

Seetharaman, P. (2020). Business models shifts: Impact of Covid-19. *International Journal of Information Management*, *54*, 1–5. PMID: 32834338

Shaltoni, A. M. (2017). From websites to social media: Exploring the adoption of internet marketing in emerging industrial markets. *Journal of Business and Industrial Marketing*, *32*(7), 1009–1019.

Sharma, B. P., Jain, H., & Prasad, M. (2020). Block chain technology: Awareness among MSME Business Owners and its Implementers. *Innovation in Global Business and Technology: Trends, Goals and Strategies*, 215.

Simelyte, A., Tvaronaviciene, M., Holmen, R. B., Burinkskas, A., & Razminene, K. (2021). Knowledge and technology transfer as driving force for social innovations. *Polish Journal of Management Studies*, *23*(2), 512–536.

Singh, D. S. M., & Hanafi, N. B. (2019). Disruptive technology and SMEs performance in Malaysia. *International Journal of Academic Research in Business & Social Sciences*, *9*(12), 136–148.

Stoneman, P., & Karshenas, M. (2018). The diffusion of new technology: Extensions to theory and evidence. In New Technologies and the Firm, 177–200.

Suleiman, O. (2016). Assessment of information and communication technology on the performance of selected small and medium scale enterprises in Ilorin metropolis, Nigeria. *International Journal of Capacity Building in Education and Management*, *3*(1), 1–12.

Suyambu, G.T.M., Anand, & Janakirani, M. (2020). Block chain – A most disruptive technology on the spotlight of world engineering education paradigm. *Procedia Computer Science*, *172*, 152–158.

The World Bank (2022). *Nigeria development update.*

Ukabi, O. B., Uba, U. J., Ewum, C. O., & Olubiyi, T. O. (2023). Measuring Entrepreneurial Skills and Sustainability in Small Business Enterprises Post-Pandemic: Empirical Study from Cross River State, Nigeria. International Journal of Business. *Management and Economics*, *4*(2), 132–149.

United Nations Conference on Trade and Development (UNCTAD) (2018). Trade and development report: Power, platforms and the free trade delusion. United Nations, New York and Geneva. https:// unctad.org

Uwem, E. I., Oyedele, O. O., & Olubiyi, O. T. (2021). Workplace green behavior for sustainable competitive advantage. In human resource management practices for

Vaidya, D. (2022). *Disruptive technology – what is it, types, examples, pros and cons*.

Wellalage, N. H., & Locke, S. (2016). Informality and credit constraints: Evidence from Sub-Saharan African MSEs. *Applied Economics*, *48*(29), 2756–2770.

KEY TERMS AND DEFINITIONS

Artificial Intelligence (AI): The simulation of human intelligence processes by machines, particularly computer systems, to perform tasks such as learning, reasoning, and problem-solving.

Business Automation: The use of technology and AI to perform repetitive tasks, reducing the need for human intervention and increasing operational efficiency.

Digital Transformation: The integration of digital technologies into all areas of a business, fundamentally changing how businesses operate and deliver value to customers.

Entrepreneurial Ecosystem: The network of individuals, organizations, and resources that support the growth and development of entrepreneurs, fostering innovation and business sustainability.

FinTech: Financial technology that uses digital innovation to enhance and streamline financial services, including banking, insurance, and investment, often leveraging AI to improve efficiency and customer experience.

Machine Learning: A subset of AI that allows computers to learn from data, identify patterns, and make decisions with minimal human intervention.

Small and Medium Enterprises (SMEs): Businesses whose personnel numbers fall below certain limits, playing a key role in the economy by driving innovation, job creation, and contributing to economic development.

Sustainability: The ability of a business to operate in a way that balances economic, social, and environmental factors, ensuring long-term viability without depleting resources or causing harm to future generations.

Technology Adoption: The process by which businesses incorporate new technologies, such as AI, into their operations, enhancing productivity, efficiency, and innovation.

Venture Capital: Funding provided to early-stage, high-potential startups, typically involving equity investment, aimed at scaling innovative businesses with the potential for rapid growth.

Chapter 7
Effect of Artificial Intelligence Awareness on Job Performance: Mediating and Moderating Role of Gender

Oumeima Toumia
http://orcid.org/0000-0002-7377-6366
Higher Institute of Technological Studies of Kef, Tunisia & Research Laboratory LARIME, University of Tunis, Tunis, Tunisia

Farouk Zouari
http://orcid.org/0000-0002-3108-6447
University of Tunis El Manar, Tunisia

Rym Mefteh
IHEC Sousse, University of Sousse, Tunisia

ABSTRACT

As artificial intelligence spreads, it is critical to comprehend how job performance may be impacted by this technology. However, to our knowledge, there is no research dealing with both the mediating and moderating role of gender in the association between artificial intelligence awareness and job performance. Therefore, we try to fill this gap. We distributed 204 online questionnaires to Tunisian employees in the service sector. We performed explanatory factor analysis, confirmatory factor analysis, structural equation modeling, and bootstrapping. Our results found that artificial intelligence has a negative impact on job performance. However, gender

DOI: 10.4018/979-8-2600-0439-5.ch007

has neither a mediating nor moderating effect on the relationship between artificial intelligence awareness and job performance. This implies that artificial intelligence awareness may influence job performance in similar ways for both men and women.

INTRODUCTION

Artificial intelligence (AI) is one of the most cutting-edge inventions in the world (Samala et al., 2020). The concept of AI was first put forth at the Dartmouth Conference in 1956 (Benko & Lányi, 2009; Toumia & Zouari, 2024a). On the one hand, Shi (2019) states that AI is a subfield of computer science that studies AI and the methods of creating intelligent computers or intelligent systems to replicate, extend, and actualize intelligent behavior. However, AI has not advanced quickly because of the limitations of computer data processing (Xu et al., 2023).

On the other hand, other contributions have ascertained that AI goes beyond computer science and touches on issues related to various service industries such as health, security, education, music, art, retail distribution, customer service, and banks (Ahmad et al., 2023; Chen et al., 2023; Cheng, 2022; Kang et al., 2023; Kayid, 2020; Mahroof, 2019; Noreen et al., 2023; Yang, 2020; Zhang et al., 2022). For instance, chatbots significantly impact satisfaction and the quality of communication (i.e., answering queries, providing translation services, and addressing problems) (Baabdullah et al., 2022; Yetgin & Toumia, 2023).

Employee awareness of AI technologies is becoming an increasingly prominent topic in discussions about the future of the workplace and job performance in general. Workers may hold positive or negative preconceptions about the impact of AI technologies on their jobs, which is described as employee awareness (Hughes et al., 2019). As firms increasingly invest in AI innovations to boost productivity, the differentiated responses from workers with varying levels of awareness impact the effectiveness of AI technology implementation within firms. Workers with positive AI awareness may proactively adopt these technologies and redistribute contract roles towards data analysis and collection, thus increasing overall productivity for both firms and workers. In contrast, workers with negative awareness may resist technology adoption and renegotiate contracts for easier jobs, thus leaving firms with lower profitability and hampering workers' economic gains. Worker awareness of AI becomes a double-edged sword for firms, which can positively or negatively influence the partnership regarding firms' investment and workers' welfare. This poses a significant challenge for organizations, especially within the dynamic service sector.

Indeed, despite equal opportunities being offered in the workplace, gender stereotyping still exists and impacts career progression (Tabassum & Nayak, 2021).

The impacts of gender stereotyping include stereotype threat, disparate treatment, prejudice, tokenism, instability, weaknesses, and risk averseness (Tabassum & Nayak, 2021). Although, currently, there are few studies on how gender affects the relationship between job performance and AI awareness, some studies have shown no effect (Mackey et al., 2019; Shirom et al., 2008; Sinangil & Ones, 2003; Ufuophu-Biri and Iwu, 2014), while others have discovered that gender can have a significant effect on job performance (Abusalma, 2021; Banjo & Olufemi, 2014; Younus et al., 2022). However, to our knowledge, there is no consideration of the decades of research that has been done on the role of gender as both a mediator and a moderator in the relationship between AI and job performance, particularly within the service sector. Toumia and Zouari (2024c) examined gender solely as a moderator and experience as a mediator across three distinct sectors (primary, secondary, and tertiary), without isolating the unique dynamics of the service industry. This chapter is therefore necessary to address two related issues: (1) understanding how AI impacts job performance and (2) investigating the academic gap concerning gender's multi-faceted role. To bridge this knowledge gap in the literature, our chapter aims to examine the effect of AI awareness on job performance in the service sector, explicitly analysing gender as both a mediating and moderating variable. The remainder of this chapter is organized as follows: We begin with a review of the literature. More precisely, the literature review is divided into four sections: (1) AI and job performance, (2) Gender and job performance, (3) Mediator role of gender in the relationship between AI awareness and job performance, and (4) Moderator role of gender in the relationship between AI awareness and job performance. We then describe the methodology employed in our study. Subsequently, we present and discuss the main findings. Finally, we provide a conclusion and a set of implications and limitations for future research.

BACKGROUND

Artificial Intelligence and Job Performance

Many firms have implemented AI to prevent direct contact between service personnel and clients (Pelau et al., 2021). However, the resultant impact of AI on job performance remains a subject of considerable debate, yielding varied outcomes ranging from positive, negative, or absent effects on job performance (Lu et al., 2020; Toumia & Zouari, 2024b, 2024c; Zouari & Toumia, 2024). On the one hand, there is broad recognition of AI's potential benefits. AI may reduce routine work, automate tasks, increase productivity and efficiency, monitor how employees behave at work, automate performance evaluations, increase the quality of feedback, suggest work-related improvements, achieve greater job performance, create value for firms, and ensure job satisfaction (Lu et al., 2020; Tong et al., 2021). These assertions are supported by empirical evidence. Younus et al. (2022) demonstrated that AI has a statistically significant effect on job performance in small and medium enterprises (SMEs) in China. In the same context, Abusalma (2021) aimed to shed light on how AI affects job performance in the banking sector. They concluded the significant effect of AI on job performance through only two AI dimensions (genetic algorithms and intelligence agents). Fan et al. (2023) added that the use of AI technologies helps employees feel psychologically empowered and enhances their work efficiency. In the same vein, Vrontis et al. (2022) conducted a systematic review of 13.136 studies to identify the key benefits and drawbacks of intelligent automation, such as AI and robotics, for human resource management (HRM). They discovered 45 articles exploring intelligent automation (i.e., artificial intelligence, robotics, and other cutting-edge technologies) in HRM. According to their findings, intelligent automation technologies represent a novel way of managing personnel and improving business performance. In the same context, Abusalma (2021) aimed to shed light on how AI affects job performance in the banking sector. They concluded the significant effect of AI on job performance through two AI dimensions (genetic algorithms and intelligence agents) only. On the other hand, there are some challenges with the implementation of AI. More explicitly, AI can lead to loss of autonomy, job insecurity, and a number of negative psychological outcomes (Lu et al., 2020). For instance, according to Chen and Xu (2018), 76.76% of China's working population will be replaced by AI in the next 20 years. In the same vein, Presbitero and Teng-Calleja (2023) added that employees' beliefs about AI replacing them at work affect how they explore career options because of job uncertainty and psychological discomfort. Malik et al. (2021) acknowledged that AI increases job performance by increasing flexibility and autonomy at work. However, it also has significant negative effects, including information security, data privacy, growing employment risk, and insecurity among employees. These discussions enable us to develop the following hypothesis:

H1: Artificial intelligence awareness negatively influences job performance

Gender and Job Performance

Researchers have debated whether gender has a substantial impact on job performance for many years. Younus et al. (2022) surveyed 220 managers in China's small and medium-sized enterprises and concluded that job performance is statistically influenced by gender. Some studies (Kotur & Anbazhagan, 2014; Sdiri, 2023; Stoet et al., 2013) have argued that workers who were female outperformed those who were male. More specifically, women are considered superior to men in specific areas like multitasking and innovation (Sdiri, 2023; Stoet et al., 2013). Additionally, women are more risk-taking, cooperative, and dedicated than men (Ali & Davies, 2003). Nevertheless, in other contributions, men have better performance than women (Allison et al., 2023; Eagly and Karau, 2002; Landy, 2008; Nekhili et al., 2018; Ng et al., 2016; Stroh et al., 1996; Wood, 1987). This may be attributed to factors such as (1) task content and settings favoring men, organizational and business environment (Nekhili et al., 2018; Wood, 1987); (2) men are perceived as being more mechanical and scientific (Eagly and Karau, 2002); (3) women felt disloyalty toward their employer, suffered job discontent, and perceived a lack of career opportunities (Stroh et al., 1996); and (4) women make worse contributions and are less dedicated to the organization than men (Fairlie & Robb, 2009; Landy, 2008; Ng et al., 2016).Therefore, we develop the following hypothesis:

H2: Gender has an impact on job performance

Indeed, there have been attempts to investigate the impact of gender stereotypes and biases on AI adoption and perception. Nouraldeen (2023) argued that men are more likely than women to adopt AI. More explicitly, women are more anxious about technology than men are (Brosnan and Davidson, 1996; Gilbert et al., 2003). Moreover, how people view AI recommendations is influenced by gender stereotypes (Ahn et al., 2022). Ahn et al. (2022) found a significant impact of gender stereotypes while assessing AI recommendations. More specifically, they found that when a male AI advised utilitarian (as opposed to hedonistic) goods, participants had higher favorable sentiments toward the AI suggestions. However, when a female (as opposed to a male) AI agent recommended a hedonistic product, it was regarded more favorably. In this vein, Steinberg and Hohenberger (2023) reported that people would rather use a human evaluator than an AI one, but only in certain situations-and only if the human evaluator is a woman. However, Belanche et al. (2019) highlighted that AI has equal benefits for men and women. In addition to its influence on adoption, gender has a direct effect on the development of AI systems. Gender bias in data-algorithmic processes may have significant effects on women and society at large (Castaneda et al., 2022). More precisely, Castaneda et al. (2022) affirmed that the effects of biased algorithms can be extensive, ranging from limited job possibilities to financial loans. For example, Kelly-Lyth (2021) affirmed that hiring algorithms may have discriminatory consequences for women, members of ethnic minorities, individuals with disabilities, and other groups that are legally protected. Indeed, facial recognition algorithms that have been trained on data that mostly consists of male faces may find trouble identifying female faces correctly. Nadeem et al. (2021) also highlighted that AI systems are frequently biased towards gender. For instance, AI hiring tools are frequently biased in favor of women. Thus, to ensure fair decision-making, it is important to reconsider the organizational managerial procedures for AI-enabled decision systems (Nadeem et al., 2021). As a result, we propose the following hypothesis:

H3: Gender has an impact on artificial intelligence adoption

Mediator Role of Gender on the Relationship Between Artificial Intelligence Awareness and Job Performance

The association between job performance and awareness of AI can be significantly mediated by gender. By enabling individualized learning, automating processes, offering insights and suggestions, and increasing stress and job insecurity, AI has the potential to influence job performance (Abusalma, 2021; Malik et al., 2021; Presbitero & Teng-Calleja, 2023). For example, while Wilson and Daugherty (2018) ascertained that AI enables workers to become more creative and make better decisions, Presbitero and Teng-Calleja (2023) affirmed that AI may increase job insecurity and stress. Meanwhile, gender differences may have a significant impact on how people perceive and use AI, which could affect job performance (Abusalma, 2021; Armutat et al., 2024; Hoque et Awang, 2019; Ofosu-Ampong, 2023). Gender differences influence perceptions of artificial intelligence-based tools (Ofosu-Ampong, 2023). Ofosu-Ampong (2023) showed a discernible gender difference in the total degree of perceived innovation characteristics. More precisely, men had a more favorable opinion of AI-based tools in learning than women. He also explained that African women are 25% less likely than men to use the internet. In the same vein, Armutat et al. (2024) argued that men have more trust in AI technologies (i.e., they have a more positive opinion of their applications). Therefore, it is essential to comprehend the advantages and disadvantages of AI decisions and overcome multiple obstacles, for instance, discrimination, gender inequality, and gender stereotypes. As a result, gender can act as a mediator in the relationship between job performance and AI perception. More explicitly, women are more threatened than men by AI (Bozkurt & Gursoy, 2023). Brussevich et al. (2018) explained that women often work in repetitive and low-skilled tasks that have more risks of being replaced by AI. They stated that automation will lead to 180 million female jobs worldwide. Thus, women will be more reluctant to develop these technologies, and this behaviour will have a negative impact on their performance. Therefore, we propose this hypothesis:

H4: Gender mediates the relationship between artificial intelligence awareness and job performance

Moderator Role of Gender on the Relationship Between Artificial Intelligence Awareness and Job Performance

Gender can also act as a moderator in the relationship between AI awareness and job performance. This means that gender influences how AI awareness affects job performance. Research has shown that gender may have different influences on the performance of employees at work (Abusalma, 2021). While Hoque and Awang (2019) found that men had better performance than women, Kiefer et al. (2022) added that the performance of women surpassed men in some situations. They highlighted that women compete with men in some sectors, such as retail trade, education, health care, and other services. This implies that people's perceptions and use of AI tools in the workplace may be influenced by their gender. For instance, males may use AI-driven insights more easily to improve their job performance since they frequently show a greater level of trust (Araujo et al., 2020; Armutat et al., 2024; Mays et al., 2022; Omrani et al., 2022) and interest in AI technologies (Rosser, 2009). As a result, men might use AI-driven insights to improve their performance more easily. On the other hand, women, who might be more concerned about AI-related job displacement (Bozkurt & Gursoy, 2023), might be more cautious, which could have a distinct effect on their performance. This cautious approach may be explained by the fact that women have fewer technological resources and lower skill levels (Dominguez Castillo et al., 2018). Considering these gender-related factors, we develop this hypothesis:

> H5: Gender moderates the relationship between artificial intelligence awareness and job performance

Figure 1 shows the conceptual model of our study.

Figure 1. Mediation and moderation model of gender, artificial intelligence and Job performance

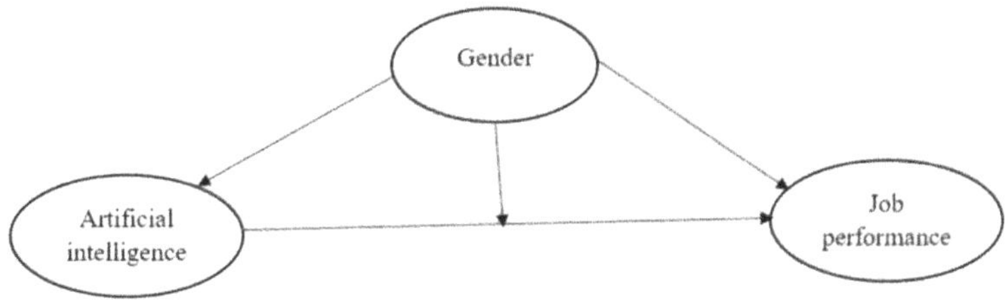

Source: own research

MAIN FOCUS OF THE CHAPTER

Materials and Methods

We collected information in 2023 using online self-administered surveys to assess our research methods. We used a random sampling method by targeting companies and professional networking sites within the service sector. More specifically, we distributed surveys through company mailing lists. To ensure clarity and effectiveness, we conducted a pilot test of the survey with a small group of potential respondents before starting the main data collection. We then interviewed 204 Tunisian employees in the service sector (29.9% from banking and insurance, 27% from education, 19.1% from hospitality, and 24% from real estate activities). We decided to target the service sector because AI is becoming a more integral aspect of value creation processes in the service industry and is no longer limited to the industrial sector (Decker et al., 2017).

According to many contributions (Boomsma, 1982; Hair et al., 2017; Jiang et al., 2023), our sample size is adequate. For instance, Monte Carlo research on maximum likelihood confirmatory factor analysis was carried out by Boomsma (1982). For sample sizes of 25, 50, 100, 200, or 400, Boomsma (1982) changed the factor correlation, factor loading pattern, and number of indicators per factor. He concluded that for sample sizes greater than 100, the bias in the parameter estimates and standard error estimations is insignificant.

There are three sections in the questionnaire. The first section includes demographic data. Items to gauge AI awareness are included in Section 2. Items to gauge job performance are included in Section three. A five-point Likert scale was used to measure the variables in our study (see Brougham and Haar, 2018; Çalışkan & Köroğlu, 2022). The scale anchors were: 1 = strongly disagree, 2 = disagree, 3 = neutral, 4 = agree, and 5 = strongly agree. Four items were taken from the study of Brougham and Haar (2018) to measure AI awareness. An eleven-item scale developed by Çalışkan and Köroğlu (2022) was used to measure job performance. For data processing, IBM SPSS.26 and IBM SPSS AMOS.24 were used. The summary of descriptive statistics is shown in Table 1.

Table 1. Sample characteristics

Characteristics		Frequency	Percentage
Gender	Male	112	54.9
	Female	92	45.1
Age	<30	49	24
	31-40	82	40.2
	41-50	54	26.5
	51-60	15	7.4
	>60	4	2
Current situation	Single	80	39.2
	Married	113	55.4
	Divorced	8	3.9
	Widow	3	1.5
Region of origin	Urban	165	80.9
	Rural	39	19.1
Education	Higher degree: Bachelor	120	58.8
	Higher degree: Master's degree	60	29.4
	Higher degree: Doctorate	24	11.8
Experience	Less than 1 year	18	8.8
	1-3 years	21	10.3
	3-5 years	35	17.2
	5-10 years	70	34.3
	More than 10 years	60	29.4

Source: own research

The respondents were 54.9% male and 45.1% female. The majority of them were married couples (55.4%) and lived in urban areas (80.9%). Respondents in their 30s were the largest group (40.2%), followed by 26.5% in their 40s, 24% in their 20s, 7.4% in their 50s, and 2% in their 60s or older. Regarding educational qualifications, 58.8% held a bachelor's degree, 29.4% held a master's degree, and 11.8% held a Ph.D. degree. With regard to job tenure, employees with experience ranging between 5 and 10 years constitute the biggest group (34.3%), followed by those with more than 10 years (29.4%), and the remaining percentage is for those with less than 5 years of experience. Consequently, we think that the respondents fairly represent the broader population.

RESULTS AND DISCUSSIONS

Table 2 presents the descriptive statistics, including the means and standard deviations for all items. As reported in Table 2, the mean scores of all items ranges from 2.976 to 4.162 on a likely 5-point scale. Therefore, there is a positive and moderately high response from the participants about AI and job performance. Indeed, the score distribution is consistent because the standard deviation for each item is smaller than 1.5 (Dehisat and Awang, 2020). As a result, for every item, the responses are largely the same throughout individuals. Using Cronbach's alpha, which assesses internal consistency, the reliability of the questionnaire was evaluated (Cronbach, 1951; Taber, 2018). Unequivocally, we found that all values of Cronbach's alpha coefficients exceeded the recommended value of 0.7 (see Hair et al., 2013). More concretely, $\alpha_{\text{overall}} = 0.806$, $\alpha_{\text{AI-awareness}} = 0.943$, and $\alpha_{\text{Job performance}} = 0.913$ (see Table 2). Therefore, as determined by Cronbach's alpha criterion, the data's validity is good and readily available. To further evaluate the reliability of our constructs, we calculated composite reliability (CR), which is equivalent to Cronbach's alpha (Cheung et al., 2024). According to Hair et al. (2010), good reliability is indicated by CR values of 0.7 or higher. Our analysis revealed excellent reliability for both constructs, with CR(AI) = 0.957 and CR(JP) = 0.938, exceeding the suggested threshold. Indeed, we computed the average variance extracted (AVE), which allows us to represent the average amount of variance explained by a construct in its indicators in relation to the total variance of its indicators (Cheung et al., 2024; Fornell & Larcker, 1981). In addition, the AVE must not fall below 0.5 (Cheung et al., 2024; Fornell & Larcker, 1981; Yu et al., 2022). In our case, we found that the values of AVE for both constructs exhibited an acceptable level of convergent validity (i.e., AVE (AI awareness) = 0.846 and AVE (Job performance) = 0.672). We may conclude that the AI awareness construct explains 84.6% of the variance in its indicators, while the job performance construct explains 67.2%.

Table 2. Measurement items

Items	**Mean**	**SD**
AI awareness: Cronbach's Alpha = 0.943		
I think my job could be replaced by AI	3.324	1.344
I am personally worried that what I do now in my job will be able to be replaced by AI	3.152	1.418
I am personally worried about my future in my organization due to AI replacing employees	2.976	1.395
I am personally worried about my future in my industry due to AI replacing employees	3.005	1.416
Job performance: **Cronbach's Alpha** = 0.913		
I have the competencies that my job requires (JP1)	4.083	0.693

continued on following page

Table 2. Continued

Items	Mean	SD
I work effectively/efficiently (JP2)	4.113	0.682
I understand and carry out work-related procedures (JP3)	4.030	0.749
I work in a planned and organized manner to conclude the task defined to me in full and on time (JP4)	4.162	0.817
I am eager to acquire new skills related to my job (JP5)	3.951	0.976
I take extra care and take extra responsibilities while doing my duty (JP6)	3.995	0.874
I contribute to the creation of a positive working environment in my institution (JP7)	3.642	1.121
If I encounter a situation that prevents the task from being done, I try to fix it (JP8)	3.941	0.880
I help and encourage my friends to complete their work (JP9)	3.588	1.231
Even if there are criticisms inside or outside the institution, I defend my institution (JP10)	3.544	1.192
I am proud to be a part of this institution (JP11)	3.956	0.890

Source: own research

To identify the constructs and validate our conceptual research framework, we carried out explanatory factor analysis (EFA). More precisely, EFA is often carried out to serve as the foundation for defining the confirmatory factor analysis (CFA) model (Tanwar & Prasad, 2016). Barlett's test of sphericity (Bartlett, 1954) was found to be significant (see Table 3). As shown, the p-value was less than 5%. This means that the variables are correlated and appropriate for factor analysis. This confirms that the correlation matrix is not an identity matrix (Beavers et al., 2013; Field, 2024).

Table 3. KMO and Bartlett's Test

Kaiser-Meyer-Olkin Measure of Sampling Adequacy (overall)		0.842
Bartlett's Test of Sphericity (overall)	Approx. Chi-Square	2494.930
	df	105
	Sig.	0.000
Kaiser-Meyer-Olkin Measure of Sampling Adequacy (AI awareness)		0.808
Bartlett's Test of Sphericity (AI awareness)	Approx. Chi-Square	827.522
	df	6
	Sig.	0.000
Kaiser-Meyer-Olkin Measure of Sampling Adequacy (Job performance)		0.862
Bartlett's Test of Sphericity (Job performance)	Approx. Chi-Square	1630.715
	df	55
	Sig.	0.000

Source: own research

The Kaiser-Meyer-Olkin (KMO) values ranged between 0.7 and 0.8 (i.e., $KMO_{overall} = 0.842$, $KMO_{AI\ awareness} = 0.808$, $KMO_{Job\ performance} = 0.862$), indicating that the sample is adequate (Kaiser 1974). More specifically, KMO values between 0.7 and 0.9 are generally indicated as good suitability (Hutcheson & Sofroniou, 1999). We employed principal component analysis (PCA) as the inference method for the EFA. According to Field (2024), taking into account the communalities was the primary criterion for cleaning up the results after running the PCA. As reported in Table 4, the values of the communalities were all greater than 0.4 (Costello & Osborne, 2005; Field, 2024; Guadagnoli & Velicer, 1988); therefore, the values are stable.

Table 4. Communalities

Items	**Initial**	**Extraction**
AI awareness		
AI1	1.000	0.807
AI2	1.000	0.857
AI3	1.000	0.888
AI4	1.000	0.870
Job performance		
JP1	1.000	0.734
JP2	1.000	0.782
JP3	1.000	0.707
JP4	1.000	0.655
JP5	1.000	0.548
JP6	1.000	0.549
JP7	1.000	0.719
JP8	1.000	0.551
JP9	1.000	0.876
JP10	1.000	0.822
JP11	1.000	0.741

Extraction Method: Principal Component Analysis
Source: own research

In order to determine how many factors to preserve, we used the Kaiser-Guttman criterion method (Child, 2006). According to this criterion, only components that have eigenvalues higher than 1.0 should be chosen (Child, 2006; Mandongwe & Jaravaza, 2020). As shown in Table 5, the first three principal components accounted for 42.097% (eigenvalue = 6.315), 21.944% (eigenvalue = 3.292), and 9.979% (eigenvalue = 1.497) of the variance, respectively. As a result, a total of three extracted factors were kept because they explained 74.020% of the variance. More precisely, the components were valid if they were greater than the recommended value of 50% (Hair et al., 2010; Yusof et al., 2017).

Table 5. Total Variance Explained

	Initial Eigenvalues			Extraction Sums of Squared Loadings		
Component	**Total**	**% of Variance**	**Cumulative %**	**Total**	**% of Variance**	**Cumulative %**
1	6.315	42.097	42.097	6.315	42.097	42.097
2	3.292	21.944	64.041	3.292	21.944	64.041
3	1.497	9.979	74.020	1.497	9.979	74.020
4	0.725	4.836	78.855			
5	0.576	3.839	82.694			
6	0.491	3.276	85.970			
7	0.427	2.846	88.816			
8	0.344	2.293	91.109			
9	0.325	2.164	93.273			
10	0.303	2.023	95.296			
11	0.244	1.628	96.924			
12	0.166	1.104	98.028			
13	0.138	0.919	98.947			
14	0.084	0.562	99.509			
15	0.074	0.491	100.000			

Extraction Method: Principal Component Analysis
Source: own research

Additionally, we computed the varimax rotated matrix, which is the most popular type of orthogonal rotation for converting vectors related to factor or principal component analysis into a simple structure (Jackson, 2005). The varimax-rotated three-factor matrix is presented in Table 6.

Table 6. Rotated Component Matrix

Items	**Components**		
	1	**2**	**3**
AI1	-0.034	0.891	-0.098
AI2	-0.012	0.921	-0.087
AI3	-0.038	0.939	-0.068

continued on following page

Table 6. Continued

Items	Components		
	1	2	3
AI4	-0.069	0.928	-0.065
JP1	0.836	-0.085	0.167
JP2	0.857	-0.132	0.171
JP3	0.830	-0.013	0.138
JP4	0.773	0.009	0.238
JP5	0.690	0.007	0.270
JP6	0.539	0.044	0.506
JP7	0.138	-0.129	0.826
JP8	0.540	-0.050	0.506
JP9	0.238	-0.101	0.900
JP10	0.274	-0.126	0.855
JP11	0.555	-0.037	0.656

Extraction Method: Principal Component Analysis
Rotation Method: Varimax with Kaiser Normalization
Source: own research

The loadings of all factors are positive. Indeed, as shown by the literature, the decision to keep or to exclude items depends on two conditions: (1) we have to remove items with factor loadings lower than 0.6 (Awang, 2018; Awang et al., 2023; Ghazali and Fauzi, 2025), and (2) each component must contain a minimum of three items (Hair et al., 2010). Therefore, in our case, we only exclude J6 and J8.

In order for a distribution to be deemed univariate normal, Kline (1998) states that the absolute values of skewness and kurtosis must be less than three and ten, respectively. Our findings satisfy these requirements. Indeed, we used the Mardia test (see Mardia, 1970, 1974) to check the multivariate normality of the variables. According to Bollen (1989), all dimensions have multinormality if the value of Mardia is less than p (p+2), where p is the number of observed variables. The Mardia value in the research is 20.318, which is less than 9 (9+2) and suggests a multivariate normality distribution. Therefore, we may use the maximum likelihood estimator, although the distribution is not multinormal (see Kuo et al., 2014).

The maximum-likelihood estimator is used to run the model in confirmatory factor analysis. In fact, CFA allows testing hypotheses about the structure of a data set (Toumia & Zouari, 2024c).

To assess the measurement and structural model's fitness, Hair et al. (2010) have suggested utilizing at least three fit indices (parsimonious fit, incremental fit, and absolute fit). Table 7 includes selected fit statistics from the CFA output. As reported in Table 7, the model fit shows good fit across various indices.

Parsimonious fit: The chi-square divided by degrees of freedom is 3.586, which falls within the acceptable range (≤ 5.00), indicating a reasonable parsimony of the model. The Parsimony Normed Fit Index is 0.607, which is also considered acceptable (> 0.05).
Incremental fit: The model shows excellent incremental fit with a Comparative Fit Index of 0.959 (≥ 0.95). The Tucker-Lewis Index of 0.936 (≥ 0.9), Incremental Fit Index of 0.960, and Normed Fit Index of 0.945 (≥ 0.8) all indicate very good fit. While the Adjusted Goodness of Fit Index (AGFI) is 0.855 (≥ 0.8), indicating acceptable fit.
Absolute fit: An acceptable fit is shown by the Goodness of Fit Index of 0.928 (≥ 0.9). The Root Mean Squared Error of Approximation, on the other hand, is 0.1 (≤ 0.1), which is regarded as borderline.

Table 7. The goodness of fit indices

Category	Index	Reported values	Level	Comments
Parsimonious fit	Chi-square divided by degree of freedom (*x^2/df*)	3.586	≤ 5.00 (Marsh and Hocevar, 1985) 1.00 - 5.00 (Kline, 2023)	Reasonable fit
	Parsimony Normed Fixed Index (*PNFI*)	0.607	>0.05 (Bentler & Bonnet, 1980; Wu, 2009)	Acceptable fit
Incremental fit	Comparative Fit Index (*CFI*)	0.959	≥ 0.95 (West et al., 2012)	Excellent fit
	Tucker-Lewis Index (*TLI*)	0.936	≥ 0.9 (Bagozzi & Yi, 1988; Tucker, & Lewis, 1973)	Very good fit
	Incremental Fit Index (*IFI*)	0.960	≥ 0.9 (Bollen, 1990)	Very good fit
	Normed Fit Index (*NFI*)	0.945	≥ 0.8 (Bentler & Bonnet, 1980)	Very good fit
	Adjusted Goodness of Fit Index (*AGFI*)	0.855	≥ 0.8 (Chau & Hu, 2001; Jöreskog & Sörbom, 1993; MacCallum & Hong, 1997)	Acceptable fit

continued on following page

Table 7. Continued

Category	Index	Reported values	Level	Comments
Absolute fit	The goodness of Fitness Index (*GFI*)	0.928	≥ 0.9 (Hu & Bentler, 1998)	Acceptable fit
	Root Mean Squared Error of Approximation (*RMSEA*)	0.1	≤ 0.1 (MacCallum et al., 1996)	The value of RMSEA is considered borderline

Source: own research

Additionally, the correlations between variables were estimated using a structural equation model (SEM). Achieving unidimensionality required the elimination of items with factor loadings of less than 0.6 (Hair et al., 2010). Consequently, we removed items that are less than the recommended threshold. Then, we reran the model. The loading factor varied between 0.77 and 0.96, as can be seen in Figure 2. Thus, the factors are reliable.

Figure 2. Structural Equation Modeling

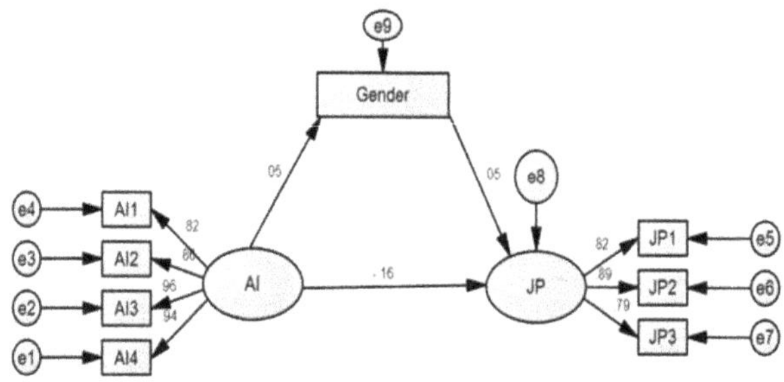

Source: own research

Using the maximum likelihood estimator, we ran a bootstrap with 5000 samples (see Efron & Tishirani, 1994; Preacher & Hayes, 2008). For each parameter estimates, bias-corrected confidence intervals were provided at the 95% level. This statistical technique permits the extraction of several simulated samples from a dataset (Toumia & Zouari, 2024b). The results of the structural path analysis are reported in Table 8.

Table 8. Structural path analysis results (direct and indirect hypotheses)

Description of path	Bootstrapping	P-value
Direct effect		
Gender → AI	0.052	0.468
Gender → JP	0.049	0.507
AI → JP	-0.163	0.032
Indirect effect		
AI → Gender →JP	0.003	0.371

Source: own research

We found that AI has a negative and significant effect on job performance (bootstrapping = -0.163; p = 0.032 < 0.05) (H1 is supported). It has previously been reported that AI may negatively impact job performance (Chen & Xu, 2018; Lu et al., 2020; Malik et al., 2021; Pandya and Wang, 2024; Xie et al., 2020). For instance, AI may cause job displacement, increased workload deskilling, job insecurity, technostress, and ethical concerns (Pandya and Wang, 2024). Pandya and Wang (2024) affirmed that excessive reliance on AI may hinder career progression. However, we found the absence of a mediating effect of gender on the relationship between AI and job performance (bootstrapping = 0.003; p = 0.371 > 0.05) (H3 is not supported). In fact, contrary to our expectations, we found no significant effect of gender on job performance (bootstrapping = 0.049; p = 0.507 > 0.05) (H2 is not supported). This finding is in line with other studies demonstrating the lack of a gender-performance relationship (Mackey et al., 2019; Sinangil & Ones, 2003; Shirom et al., 2008; Ufuophu-Biri & Iwu, 2014). More precisely, according to social construction theory, gender itself is a social construct, and there is no difference in a way that makes one gender superior managers (Mutongi, 2020). For instance, Ufuophu-Biri and Iwu (2014) used a sample of 600 employees in six broadcasting stations in Delta State, Nigeria, to analyze the link between job motivation, job performance, and gender. They found no correlation between gender and either job performance or job motivation. Gender is not the most crucial aspect of job performance but rather an individual's talents, abilities, and motivations. Although a person's gender may affect their preferences and interests, it does not affect their capacity for work. In the same vein, Mackey et al. (2019) contradicted the Critical Mass Theory and Tokenism Hypothesis, which suggested that being female has a negative impact on performance in a male-dominated environment. They ascertained the absence of evidence in favor of the gender token effect on subjective task performance, organizational citizenship behaviors, and objective task performance. This implies that although gender may not have a direct effect on their job performance, organizational strategies may have a significant impact. For example,

Asare Obeng et al. (2025) argued that workforce diversity has a positive and significant impact on employee performance. Indeed, gender has no direct effect on AI (bootstrapping = 0.052, p = 0.468 > 0.05). In fact, there is no gender assigned to the AI itself. It is merely a tool that may be applied in many ways by users of all genders. Finally, our findings do not support Hypothesis 3 regarding the mediation path of gender underlying the relationship between AI and job performance. Now that we have examined gender's mediating role in the relationship between job performance and AI awareness, we can focus on gender's potential moderating effect (see Table 9). The sample was split into two groups: males and females. Next, we compared two regression models: one that didn't have an interaction term between gender and AI awareness (i.e., constrained model), and one that did (i.e., unconstrained model).

Table 9. Assuming model Unconstrained to be correct

Model	DF	CMIN	P-value	NFI Delta-2	RFI Rho-1
Structural weights	1	0.273	0.601	0.044	0.044

Source: own research

According to Table 9, the two models (constrained and unconstrained) are not significantly different (P-value = 0.601 > 5%). Therefore, we may conclude that there is an absence of significant differences between males and females. The relationship between AI awareness and job performance is the same between males and females. So, gender does not moderate the relationship between AI awareness and job performance (H4 is not supported). Our finding is in line with the contribution of Toumia and Zouari (2024c). In their analysis of the effects of AI on work performance, they explicitly analyzed experience as a mediator and gender as a moderator in three different sectors (primary, secondary, and tertiary). They offered the convincing explanation that AI is gender-neutral by design. According to what they said: « *Since artificial intelligence is not designed to discriminate based on gender, gender has no effect on the relationship between AI and job performance. AI is a technology that can help people of all genders perform better in the workplace (i.e., AI can make workers of both genders more effective and productive* » (Toumia and Zouari, 2024c, p.123). Another explanation is the fact that in the industrialized world, numerous nations, both large and small, have been attempting to establish inclusive and diverse workplaces. This could make the effects of AI technologies more equal (Vohra et al., 2015).

SOLUTIONS AND RECOMMENDATIONS

Given that AI has attracted increasing interest from academics and practitioners alike, our study makes several theoretical and practical contributions. Our research advances the literature on the factors that influence job performance. More precisely, we offer insightful information about how AI is transforming the workplace and how employees may adapt to these changes. As discussed above, AI has a negative influence on job performance (Chen & Xu, 2018; Lu et al., 2020; Malik et al., 2021; Xie et al., 2020). Therefore, managers have to attenuate the anxiety of employees toward AI. Employers must be more proactive in talking to their employees about the goals, advantages, and scope of AI applications to prevent them from quitting their occupations due to a sense of threat (Presbitero & Teng-Calleja, 2023; Tong et al., 2021). In fact, employees need to feel that AI is there to help them, not to take their place. Employees will resist AI if it is perceived as a danger, which will negate any gains it might have. For instance, an AI training program is being used by MetLife, a leading insurance provider, to monitor service staff members' interactions with clients and provide feedback to staff members on how to improve their performance (Roose, 2019). Furthermore, managers have to create a positive work environment and focus their attention on human qualities rather than AI capabilities. More specifically, creativity, problem-solving, and empathy cannot be imitated by AI. Therefore, a crucial practical implication is that companies should proactively rethink job roles and workflows in order to best integrate AI capabilities with human strengths. In the same vein, Scholze and Hecker (2024) reported the necessity to further strengthen organizational culture to fully realize the potential of digitalization inside enterprises. They identified five practical implications for organizations: (1) digital technology optimization; (2) digital health protection; (3) digital health protection; (4) digital communication and collaboration; and (5) employee feedback and participation in digitalization. Indeed, Sofia et al. (2023) stated that managers should prioritize employee upskilling and reskilling due to the adoption of AI. They described three strategies, which are: determining the skills needed, supporting employees, and offering training and development opportunities. Moreover, according to our study, companies do not need to worry about gender bias when they build and implement AI systems. In fact, it is imperative for practitioners and managers to employ and retain a diverse staff due to social and legal considerations (Roth et al., 2003). This has the potential to hasten the adoption of AI and realize its advantages for all workers, male or female. To do so, managers have to understand and pay attention to the factors of gender stereotyping, such as individual factors, cognitive factors, family factors, socio-cultural factors, and organizational factors (Tabassum & Nayak, 2021). Furthermore, the government should also think about offering incentives to companies so they can improve their digital capabilities. These incentives can be classified as either non-financial (i.e., government resources, regulatory exemptions, sponsorship initiatives, education and training programs, etc.) or financial (grants, loans, tax benefits, awards, etc.) (Toumia et al., 2023). Finally, managers need to set up explicit ethical rules and governance structures for how AI is used. This is particularly crucial for guaranteeing the privacy of employee data, equity, and openness in all decision-making.

FUTURE RESEARCH DIRECTIONS

However, our research has some limitations. First, our study was limited to Tunisian employees in the service sector. Therefore, it may not be generalizable to other contexts. More precisely, cultural factors specific to Tunisia, such as technology adoption in Tunisia, may influence Tunisian employees' artificial intelligence awareness. Moreover, our study focuses on the Tunisian service sector. As a result, it is possible to conduct a similar investigation in other countries with different economic backgrounds or other sectors (i.e., primary and secondary sectors). In addition, a mediator (i.e., gender) was identified. Future studies could also empirically investigate how individual, organizational, and environmental factors affect employee attitudes and behaviours, such as AI resistance or use. For instance, Pedrami and Vaezi (2025) used a qualitative meta-synthesis approach to analyse studies published between 2015 and 2023. They found that AI adoption is influenced by five themes which are: organizational and strategic factors, technological and operational factors, human-centric factors, challenges and opportunities and environmental and economic factors. Indeed, a longitudinal research design or an experimental approach could be used to validate the causal inferences between these two variables. Finally, as AI awareness is an individual-level construct, this may decrease the awareness level of the organization and ultimately the company's performance. As an important organization-level variable, company AI awareness should also be considered to clarify how it impacts company performance, either in research or in action.

CONCLUSION

The debate about artificial intelligence's beneficial and detrimental effects on job performance is still in its early stages. A positive view of AI can lead to enthusiasm for learning and using new tools that enhance one's career. Conversely, negative perceptions may arise from concerns about job loss or loss of control. Many studies have demonstrated that many factors may mediate or moderate the relationship between these two concepts. Through a survey of 204 employees, our results showed a negative relationship between AI and job performance, suggesting that AI is viewed as a threat that might result in many employees losing their jobs or earning less money than they had anticipated. Indeed, our research suggests that the relationship between AI and job performance is not mediated or moderated by gender.

ACKNOWLEDGMENT

The author(s) received no financial support for the research, authorship, and/or publication of this article.

REFERENCES

Abusalma, A. (2021). The effect of implementing artificial intelligence on job performance in commercial banks of Jordan. *Management Science Letters, 11*(7), 2061–2070. DOI: 10.5267/j.msl.2021.3.003

Ahmad, N., Murugesan, S., & Kshetri, N. (2023). Generative Artificial Intelligence and the Education Sector. *Computer, 56*(6), 72–76. DOI: 10.1109/MC.2023.3263576

Ahn, J., Kim, J., & Sung, Y. (2022). The effect of gender stereotypes on artificial intelligence recommendations. *Journal of Business Research, 141*(C), 50–59. DOI: 10.1016/j.jbusres.2021.12.007

Ali, H., & Davies, D. R. (2003). The effects of age, sex and tenure on the job performance of rubber tappers. *Journal of Occupational and Organizational Psychology, 76*(3), 381–391. DOI: 10.1348/096317903769647238

Allison, L., Liu, Y., Murtinu, S., & Wei, Z. (2023). Gender and firm performance around the world: The roles of finance, technology and labor. *Journal of Business Research, 154*, 113322. DOI: 10.1016/j.jbusres.2022.113322

Araujo, T., Helberger, N., Kruikemeier, S., & De Vreese, C. H. (2020). In AI we trust? Perceptions about automated decision-making by artificial intelligence. *AI & Society, 35*(3), 611–623. DOI: 10.1007/s00146-019-00931-w

Armutat, S., Wattenberg, M., & Mauritz, N. (2024, April). Artificial Intelligence–Gender-Specific Differences in Perception, Understanding, and Training Interest. In *International Conference on Gender Research* (Vol. 7, No. 1, pp. 36-43). https://doi.org/DOI: 10.34190/icgr.7.1.2163

Asare Obeng, H., Gyamfi, B. A., Arhinful, R., & Mensah, L. (2025). Unlocking Performance Potential: Workforce Diversity Management and Gender Diversity as Drivers of Employee Performance in Ghana's Public Healthcare Sector. *Societies (Basel, Switzerland), 15*(5), 132. DOI: 10.3390/soc15050132

Awang, P. (2018). Pendekatan Mudah SEM. *Structural Equation Modeling*.

Awang, Z., Afthanorhan, W. M. A. A., Lim, S. H., & Zainudin, N. F. S. (2023). SEM Made Simple 2.0 A Gentle Approach of Structural Equation Modelling. *Gong Badak: Penerbit Unisza.*

Baabdullah, A. M., Alalwan, A. A., Algharabat, R. S., Metri, B., & Rana, N. P. (2022). Virtual agents and flow experience: An empirical examination of AI-powered chatbots. *Technological Forecasting and Social Change, 181*, 121772. DOI: 10.1016/j.techfore.2022.121772

Bagozzi, R. P., & Yi, Y. (1988). On the Evaluation of Structural Equation Models. *Journal of the Academy of Marketing Science, 16*(1), 74–94. DOI: 10.1007/BF02723327

Banjo, H., & Olufemi, O. (2014). Demographic Variables and Job Performance: Any Link? (A Case of Insurance Salesmen). *Acta Universitatis Danubius. Economica, 10*(4), 19–30.

Bartlett, M. S. (1954). A note on the multiplying factors for various χ 2 approximations. *Journal of the Royal Statistical Society. Series B. Methodological*, •••, 296–298.

Beavers, A. S., Lounsbury, J. W., Richards, J. K., Huck, S. W., Skolits, G. J., & Esquivel, S. L. (2013). Practical considerations for using exploratory factor analysis in educational research. *Practical Assessment, Research & Evaluation, 18*(6), 1–13.

Belanche, D., Casaló, L. V., & Flavián, C. (2019). Artificial Intelligence in FinTech: Understanding robo-advisors adoption among customers. *Industrial Management & Data Systems, 119*(7), 1411–1430. DOI: 10.1108/IMDS-08-2018-0368

Benko, A., & Lányi, C. S. (2009). History of artificial intelligence. In *Encyclopedia of Information Science and Technology* (2nd ed., pp. 1759–1762). IGI Global., DOI: 10.4018/978-1-60566-026-4

Bentler, P. M., & Bonett, D. G. (1980). Significance tests and goodness of fit in the analysis of covariance structures. *Psychological Bulletin, 88*(3), 588–606. DOI: 10.1037/0033-2909.88.3.588

Bollen, K. A. (1989). *Structural equations with latent variables* (Vol. 210). John Wiley & Sons.

Bollen, K. A. (1990). Overall Fit in Covariance Structure Models: Two Types of Sample Size Effects. *Psychological Bulletin, 107*(2), 256–259. DOI: 10.1037/0033-2909.107.2.256

Boomsma, A. (1982). The robustness of LISREL against small sample sizes in factor analysis models. *Systems under indirect observation: Causality, structure, prediction*, 149-173.

Bozkurt, V., & Gursoy, D. (2023). The Artificial Intelligence Paradox: Opportunity or Threat for Humanity? *International Journal of Human-Computer Interaction*, •••, 1–14. DOI: 10.1080/10447318.2023.2297114

Brosnan, M. J., & Davidson, M. J. (1996). Psychological gender issues in computing. *Gender, Work and Organization*, *3*(1), 13–25. DOI: 10.1111/j.1468-0432.1996.tb00045.x

Brougham, D., & Haar, J. (2018). Smart technology, artificial intelligence, robotics, and algorithms (STARA): Employees' perceptions of our future workplace. *Journal of Management & Organization*, *24*(2), 239–257. DOI: 10.1017/jmo.2016.55

Brussevich, M., Dabla-Norris, M. E., Kamunge, C., Karnane, P., Khalid, S., & Kochhar, M. K. (2018). *Gender, technology, and the future of work*. International Monetary Fund.

Çalışkan, A., & Köroğlu, E. Ö. (2022). Job performance, Task performance, Contextual performance: Development and validation of a new scale. *Uluslararası İktisadi ve İdari Bilimler Dergisi*, *8*(2), 180–201. DOI: 10.29131/uiibd.1201880

Castaneda, J., Jover, A., Calvet, L., Yanes, S., Juan, A. A., & Sainz, M. (2022). Dealing with gender bias issues in data-algorithmic processes: A social-statistical perspective. *Algorithms*, *15*(9), 303. DOI: 10.3390/a15090303

Chau, P. Y., & Hu, P. J. H. (2001). Information technology acceptance by individual professionals: A model comparison approach. *Decision Sciences*, *32*(4), 699–719. DOI: 10.1111/j.1540-5915.2001.tb00978.x

Chen, Y., Hu, Y., Zhou, S., & Yang, S. (2023). Investigating the determinants of performance of artificial intelligence adoption in hospitality industry during COVID-19. *International Journal of Contemporary Hospitality Management*, *35*(8), 2868–2889. DOI: 10.1108/IJCHM-04-2022-0433

Chen, Y., & Xu, D. (2018). The impact of artificial intelligence on employment. *Composition Studies*, *2*, 135–160. DOI: 10.2139/ssrn.3116753

Cheng, M. (2022, April). The Creativity of Artificial Intelligence in Art. In *Proceedings* (Vol. 81, No. 1, p. 110). MDPI. https://doi.org/DOI: 10.3390/proceedings2022081110

Cheung, G. W., Cooper-Thomas, H. D., Lau, R. S., & Wang, L. C. (2024). Reporting reliability, convergent and discriminant validity with structural equation modeling: A review and best-practice recommendations. *Asia Pacific Journal of Management*, *41*(2), 745–783. DOI: 10.1007/s10490-023-09871-y

Child, D. (2006). *The essentials of factor analysis*. A&C Black.

Costello, A. B., & Osborne, J. W. (2005). Best practices in exploratory factor analysis: Four recommendations for getting the most from your analysis. *Practical Assessment, Research & Evaluation*, *10*(7), 1–9. DOI: 10.7275/jyj1-4868

Cronbach, L. J. (1951). Coefficient alpha and the internal structure of tests. *Psychometrika*, *16*(3), 297–334. DOI: 10.1007/bf02310555

Decker, M., Fischer, M., & Ott, I. (2017). Service Robotics and Human Labor: A first technology assessment of substitution and cooperation. *Robotics and Autonomous Systems*, *87*, 348–354. DOI: 10.1016/j.robot.2016.09.017

Dehisat, M. M., & Awang, Z. (2020). Exploring items and developing instrument for measuring organizational performance among small medium enterprises in Jordan. *International Review of Management and Marketing*, *10*(6), 51–57. DOI: 10.32479/irmm.10531

Dominguez Castillo, J. G., Cisneros Cohernour, E. J., & Barberà, E. (2018). Factors influencing technology use by Mayan women in the digital age. *Gender, Technology and Development*, *22*(3), 185–204. DOI: 10.1080/09718524.2018.1558862

Eagly, A. H., & Karau, S. J. (2002). Role congruity theory of prejudice toward female leaders. *Psychological Review*, *109*(3), 573–598. DOI: 10.1037/0033-295X.109.3.573 PMID: 12088246

Efron, B., & Tibshirani, R. J. (1994). *An introduction to the bootstrap*. CRC press.

Fan, X., Zhao, S., Zhang, X., & Meng, L. (2023). The Impact of Improving Employee Psychological Empowerment and Job Performance Based on Deep Learning and Artificial Intelligence. [JOEUC]. *Journal of Organizational and End User Computing*, *35*(3), 1–14.

Field, A. (2024). *Discovering statistics using IBM SPSS statistics*. Sage publications limited.

Fornell, C., & Larcker, D. F. (1981). Evaluating structural equation models with unobservable variables and measurement error. *JMR, Journal of Marketing Research*, *18*(1), 39–50. DOI: 10.1177/002224378101800104

Ghazali, M. T., & Fauzi, M. A. (2025). Validation of Training in Relation to Succession Planning: Exploratory Factor Analysis and Confirmatory Factor Analysis Approach. *International Journal of Research and Innovation in Social Science*, *9*(1), 785–798. DOI: 10.47772/IJRISS.2025.9010067

Gilbert, D., Lee-Kelley, L., & Barton, M. (2003). Technophobia, gender influences and consumer decision-making for technology-related products. *European Journal of Innovation Management*, *6*(4), 253–263. DOI: 10.1108/14601060310500968

Guadagnoli, E., & Velicer, W. F. (1988). Relation of sample size to the stability of component patterns. *Psychological Bulletin*, *103*(2), 265–275. DOI: 10.1037/0033-2909.103.2.265 PMID: 3363047

Hair, J. F., Black, W. C., Babin, B. J., & Anderson, R. E. (2010). *Multivariate Data Analysis. A global perspective* (7th ed.). Prentice Hall.

Hair, J. F., Matthews, L. M., Matthews, R. L., & Sarstedt, M. (2017). PLS-SEM or CB-SEM: Updated guidelines on which method to use. *International Journal of Multivariate Data Analysis*, *1*(2), 107–123. DOI: 10.1504/IJMDA.2017.087624

Hair, J. F., Ringle, C. M., & Sarstedt, M. (2013). Partial least squares structural equation modeling: Rigorous applications, better results and higher acceptance. *Long Range Planning*, *46*(1-2), 1–12. DOI: 10.1016/j.lrp.2013.01.001

Hoque, A. S. M. M., & Awang, Z. (2019). Does gender difference play moderating role in the relationship between entrepreneurial marketing and Bangladeshi SME performance? *Accounting*, *5*(1), 35–52. DOI: 10.5267/j.ac.2018.6.001

Hu, L. T., & Bentler, P. M. (1998). Fit indices in covariance structure modeling: Sensitivity to underparameterized model misspecification. *Psychological Methods*, *3*(4), 424–453. DOI: 10.1037/1082-989X.3.4.424

Hughes, C., Robert, L., Frady, K., & Arroyos, A. (2019). Artificial intelligence, employee engagement, fairness, and job outcomes. In *Managing technology and middle-and low-skilled employees* (pp. 61–68). Emerald Publishing Limited., DOI: 10.1108/978-1-78973-077-720191005

Hutcheson, G. D., & Sofroniou, N. (1999). *The multivariate social scientist: Introductory statistics using generalized linear models.*

Jackson, J. E. (2005). Varimax rotation. *Encyclopedia of biostatistics, 8*. https://doi.org/DOI: 10.1002/0470011815.b2a13091

Jiang, Y., Lai, P. L., Yang, C. C., & Wang, X. (2023). Exploring the factors that drive consumers to use contactless delivery services in the context of the continued COVID-19 pandemic. *Journal of Retailing and Consumer Services*, *72*, 103276. DOI: 10.1016/j.jretconser.2023.103276

Jöreskog, K. G., & Sörbom, D. (1993). *LISREL 8: Structural equation odelling with the SIMPLIS command language*. Scientific software is international.

Kaiser, H. F. (1974). An index of factorial simplicity. *psychometrika, 39*(1), 31-36. https://doi.org/DOI: 10.1007/BF02291575

Kang, D. Y., Hur, W. M., & Shin, Y. (2023). Smart technology and service employees' job crafting: Relationship between STARA awareness, performance pressure, receiving and giving help, and job crafting. *Journal of Retailing and Consumer Services*, *73*, 103282. DOI: 10.1016/j.jretconser.2023.103282

Kayid, A. (2020). *The role of Artificial Intelligence in future technology*. Department of Computer Science, The German University in Cairo.

Kelly-Lyth, A. (2021). Challenging biased hiring algorithms. *Oxford Journal of Legal Studies*, *41*(4), 899–928. DOI: 10.1093/ojls/gqab006

Kiefer, K., Heileman, M., & Pett, T. L. (2022). Does gender still matter? An examination of small business performance. *Small Business Economics*, *58*(1), 141–167. DOI: 10.1007/s11187-020-00403-2

Kline, R. B. (1998). Software review: Software programs for structural equation modeling: Amos, EQS, and LISREL. *Journal of Psychoeducational Assessment*, *16*(4), 343–364. DOI: 10.1177/073428299801600407

Kline, R. B. (2023). *Principles and practice of structural equation modeling*. Guilford publications.

Kotur, B. R., & Anbazhagan, S. (2014). Influence of age and gender on the performance. *IOSR Journal of Business and Management*, *16*(5), 97–103. DOI: 10.9790/487x-165397103

Kuo, Y. K., Kuo, T. H., & Ho, L. A. (2014). Enabling innovative ability: Knowledge sharing as a mediator. *Industrial Management & Data Systems*, *114*(5), 696–710. DOI: 10.1108/IMDS-10-2013-0434

Landy, F. J. (2008). Stereotypes, bias, and personnel decisions: Strange and stranger. *Industrial and Organizational Psychology: Perspectives on Science and Practice*, *1*(4), 379–392. DOI: 10.1111/j.1754-9434.2008.00071.x

Lu, V. N., Wirtz, J., Kunz, W. H., Paluch, S., Gruber, T., Martins, A., & Patterson, P. G. (2020). Service robots, customers and service employees: What can we learn from the academic literature and where are the gaps? *Journal of Service Theory and Practice*, *30*(3), 361–391. DOI: 10.1108/JSTP-04-2019-0088

MacCallum, R. C., Browne, M. W., & Sugawara, H. M. (1996). Power Analysis and Determination of Sample Size for Covariance Structure Modeling. *Psychological Methods*, *1*(2), 130–149. DOI: 10.1037/1082-989X.1.2.130

MacCallum, R. C., & Hong, S. (1997). Power analysis in covariance structure modeling using GFI and AGFI. *Multivariate Behavioral Research*, *32*(2), 193–210. DOI: 10.1207/s15327906mbr3202_5 PMID: 26788758

Mackey, J. D., Roth, P. L., Van Iddekinge, C. H., & McFarland, L. A. (2019). A meta-analysis of gender proportionality effects on job performance. *Group & Organization Management*, *44*(3), 578–610. DOI: 10.1177/1059601117730519

Mahroof, K. (2019). A human-centric perspective exploring the readiness towards smart warehousing: The case of a large retail distribution warehouse. *International Journal of Information Management*, *45*(C), 176–190. DOI: 10.1016/j.ijinfomgt.2018.11.008

Malik, N., Tripathi, S. N., Kar, A. K., & Gupta, S. (2021). Impact of artificial intelligence on employees working in industry 4.0 led organizations. *International Journal of Manpower*, *43*(2), 334–354. DOI: 10.1108/IJM-03-2021-0173

Mandongwe, L., & Jaravaza, D. C. (2020). Women entrepreneurial intentions in subsistence marketplaces: The role of entrepreneurial orientation and demographic profiles in Zimbabwe. *Cogent Business & Management*, *7*(1), 1818365. DOI: 10.1080/23311975.2020.1818365

Mardia, K. V. (1970). Measures of multivariate skewness and kurtosis with applications. *Biometrika*, *57*(3), 519–530. DOI: 10.1093/biomet/57.3.519

Mardia, K. V. (1974). Applications of some measures of multivariate skewness and kurtosis in testing normality and robustness studies. *Sankhya Series B*, •••, 115–128.

Marsh, H. W., & Hocevar, D. (1985). Application of confirmatory factor analysis to the study of self-concept: First-and higher order factor models and their invariance across groups. *Psychological Bulletin*, *97*(3), 562–582. DOI: 10.1037/0033-2909.97.3.562

Mays, K. K., Lei, Y., Giovanetti, R., & Katz, J. E. (2022). AI as a boss? A national US survey of predispositions governing comfort with expanded AI roles in society. *AI & Society*, •••, 1–14. DOI: 10.1007/s00146-021-01253-6

Mutongi, C. (2020). Either Women or Men Make Superior Managers and Leaders: A Critique. *International Journal of Research and Innovation in Social Science, 4*(8), 320–325.

Nadeem, A., Marjanovic, O., & Abedin, B. (2021). Gender bias in AI: Implications for managerial practices. In *Responsible AI and Analytics for an Ethical and Inclusive Digitized Society: 20th IFIP WG 6.11 Conference on e-Business, e-Services and e-Society, I3E 2021, Galway, Ireland, September 1–3, 2021, Proceedings 20* (pp. 259-270). Springer International Publishing. https://doi.org/DOI: 10.1007/978-3-030-85447-8_23

Nekhili, M., Chakroun, H., & Chtioui, T. (2018). Women's leadership and firm performance: Family versus nonfamily firms. *Journal of Business Ethics, 153*(2), 291–316. DOI: 10.1007/s10551-016-3340-2

Ng, T. W., Lam, S. S., & Feldman, D. C. (2016). Organizational citizenship behavior and counterproductive work behavior: Do males and females differ? *Journal of Vocational Behavior, 93*, 11–32. DOI: 10.1016/j.jvb.2015.12.005

Noreen, U., Shafique, A., Ahmed, Z., & Ashfaq, M. (2023). Banking 4.0: Artificial intelligence (AI) in banking industry & consumer's perspective. *Sustainability, 15*(4), 3682. DOI: 10.3390/su15043682

Ofosu-Ampong, K. (2023). Gender differences in perception of artificial intelligence-based tools. *Journal of Digital Art & Humanities, 4*(2), 52–56. DOI: 10.33847/2712-8149.4.2_6

Omrani, N., Rivieccio, G., Fiore, U., Schiavone, F., & Agreda, S. G. (2022). To trust or not to trust? An assessment of trust in AI-based systems: Concerns, ethics and contexts. *Technological Forecasting and Social Change, 181*, 121763.

Pandya, S. S., & Wang, J. (2024). Artificial intelligence in career development: A scoping review. *Human Resource Development International, 27*(3), 324–344. DOI: 10.1080/13678868.2024.2336881

Pedrami, M., & Vaezi, S. K. (2025). Factors influencing artificial intelligence adoption in human resource management: A meta-synthesis and systematic review of multidimensional considerations. *Journal of Work-Applied Management.*

Pelau, C., Dabija, D. C., & Ene, I. (2021). What makes an AI device human-like? The role of interaction quality, empathy and perceived psychological anthropomorphic characteristics in the acceptance of artificial intelligence in the service industry. *Computers in Human Behavior, 122*, 106855. DOI: 10.1016/j.chb.2021.106855

Preacher, K. J., & Hayes, A. F. (2008). Asymptotic and resampling strategies for assessing and comparing indirect effects in multiple mediator models. *Behavior Research Methods, 40*(3), 879–891. DOI: 10.3758/BRM.40.3.879 PMID: 18697684

Presbitero, A., & Teng-Calleja, M. (2023). Job attitudes and career behaviors relating to employees' perceived incorporation of artificial intelligence in the workplace: A career self-management perspective. *Personnel Review, 52*(4), 1169–1187. DOI: 10.1108/PR-02-2021-0103

Roose, K. (2019). A machine may not take your job, but one could become your boss. The New York Times. Available from https://www.nytimes.com/2019/06/23/technology/artificial-intelligence-ai-workplace.html

Rosser, S. V. (2009). The gender gap in patenting: Is technology transfer a feminist issue? *NWSA Journal, 21*(2), 65–84. DOI: 10.1353/ff.2009.a316153

Roth, P. L., Huffcutt, A. I., & Bobko, P. (2003). Ethnic group differences in measures of job performance: A new meta-analysis. *The Journal of Applied Psychology, 88*(4), 694–706. DOI: 10.1037/0021-9010.88.4.694 PMID: 12940409

Samala, N., Katkam, B. S., Bellamkonda, R. S., & Rodriguez, R. V. (2020). Impact of AI and robotics in the tourism sector: a critical insight. *Journal of tourism futures, 8*(1), 73-87. https://doi.org/DOI: 10.1108/JTF-07-2019-0065

Scholze, A., & Hecker, A. (2024). The job demands-resources model as a theoretical lens for the bright and dark side of digitization. *Computers in Human Behavior, 155*, 108177. DOI: 10.1016/j.chb.2024.108177

Sdiri, H. (2023). Female In Manager-Owner Teams: Drivers Of Innovation And Firm Performance In Mena Markets. *International Journal of Innovation Management, 27*(09n10), 2350052. https://doi.org/DOI: 10.1142/S1363919623500524

Shi, Z. (2019). []. World Scientific.]. *Advances in Artificial Intelligence, 4*, •••.

Shirom, A., Shechter Gilboa, S., Fried, Y., & Cooper, C. L. (2008). Gender, age and tenure as moderators of work-related stressors' relationships with job performance: A meta-analysis. *Human Relations, 61*(10), 1371–1398. DOI: 10.1177/001872670809570

Sinangil, H. K., & Ones, D. S. (2003). Gender differences in expatriate job performance. *Applied Psychology, 52*(3), 461–475. DOI: 10.1111/1464-0597.00144

Sofia, M., Fraboni, F., De Angelis, M., Puzzo, G., Giusino, D., & Pietrantoni, L. (2023). The impact of artificial intelligence on workers' skills: Upskilling and reskilling in organisations. *Informing Science, 26*, 39–68. DOI: 10.28945/5078

Steinberg, A. L. S., & Hohenberger, C. (2023). Can AI close the gender gap in the job market? Individuals' preferences for AI evaluations. *Computers in Human Behavior Reports*, *10*, 100287. DOI: 10.1016/j.chbr.2023.100287

Stoet, G., O'Connor, D. B., Conner, M., & Laws, K. R. (2013). Are women better than men at multi-tasking? *BMC Psychology*, *1*, 1–10. DOI: 10.1186/2050-7283-1-18

Stroh, L. K., Brett, J. M., & Reilly, A. H. (1996). Family structure, glass ceiling, and traditional explanations for the differential rate of turnover of female and male managers. *Journal of Vocational Behavior*, *49*(1), 99–118. DOI: 10.1006/jvbe.1996.0036

Tabassum, N., & Nayak, B. S. (2021). Gender stereotypes and their impact on women's career progressions from a managerial perspective. *IIM Kozhikode Society & Management Review*, *10*(2), 192–208. DOI: 10.1177/2277975220975513

Taber, K. S. (2018). The use of Cronbach's alpha when developing and reporting research instruments in science education. *Research in Science Education*, *48*, 1273–1296. DOI: 10.1007/s11165-016-9602-2

Tanwar, K., & Prasad, A. (2016). The effect of employer brand dimensions on job satisfaction: Gender as a moderator. *Management Decision*, *54*(4), 854–886. DOI: 10.1108/MD-08-2015-0343

Tong, S., Jia, N., Luo, X., & Fang, Z. (2021). The Janus face of artificial intelligence feedback: Deployment versus disclosure effects on employee performance. *Strategic Management Journal*, *42*(9), 1600–1631. DOI: 10.1002/smj.3322

Toumia, O., Mefteh, R., & Cowling, M. (2023). Digitalization and Firm Performance: Empirical Evidence from Forbes-listed Companies. *Journal of Innovation Management*, *11*(4), 124–142. DOI: 10.24840/2183-0606_011.004_0006

Toumia, O., & Zouari, F. (2024a). Artificial Intelligence and Venture Capital Decision-Making. In *Fostering Innovation in Venture Capital and Startup Ecosystems* (pp. 16–38). IGI Global., DOI: 10.4018/979-8-3693-1326-8.ch002

Toumia, O., & Zouari, F. (2024b). Effect of Artificial Intelligence Awareness on Job Performance with Employee Experience as a Mediating Variable. In *Reskilling the Workforce for Technological Advancement* (pp. 141–161). IGI Global., DOI: 10.4018/979-8-3693-0612-3.ch007

Toumia, O., & Zouari, F. (2024c). The Effect of Artificial Intelligence Awareness on Job Performance: Gender as Moderator and Experience as Mediator. In *AI Innovation in Services Marketing* (pp. 110–133). IGI Global., DOI: 10.4018/979-8-3693-2153-9.ch005

Tucker, L. R., & Lewis, C. (1973). A reliability coefficient for maximum likelihood factor analysis. *Psychometrika, 38*(1), 1–10. DOI: 10.1007/BF02291170

Ufuophu-Biri, E., & Iwu, C. G. (2014). Job motivation, job performance and gender relations in the broadcast sector in Nigeria. *Mediterranean Journal of Social Sciences, 5*(16), 191–198. DOI: 10.5901/mjss.2014.v5n16p191

Vohra, N., Chari, V., Mathur, P., Sudarshan, P., Verma, N., Mathur, N., Thakur, P., Chopra, T., Srivastava, Y., Gupta, S., Dasmahapatra, V., Fonia, S., & Gandhi, H. K. (2015). Inclusive workplaces: Lessons from theory and practice. *Vikalpa, 40*(3), 324–362. DOI: 10.1177/0256090915601515

Vrontis, D., Christofi, M., Pereira, V., Tarba, S., Makrides, A., & Trichina, E. (2022). Artificial intelligence, robotics, advanced technologies and human resource management: A systematic review. *International Journal of Human Resource Management, 33*(6), 1237–1266. DOI: 10.1080/09585192.2020.1871398

West, R. F., Meserve, R. J., & Stanovich, K. E. (2012). Cognitive sophistication does not attenuate the bias blind spot. *Journal of Personality and Social Psychology, 103*(3), 506–519. DOI: 10.1037/a0028857 PMID: 22663351

Wilson, H. J., & Daugherty, P. R. (2018). Collaborative intelligence: Humans and AI are joining forces. *Harvard Business Review, 96*(4), 114–123.

Wood, W. (1987). Meta-analytic review of sex differences in group performance. *Psychological Bulletin, 102*(1), 53. DOI: 10.1037/0033-2909.102.1.53 PMID: 3615706

Wu, M. L. (2009). *Structural equation modeling: Amos operation and application.* Wu-Nan Book Inc.

Xu, G., Xue, M., & Zhao, J. (2023). The Relationship of Artificial Intelligence Opportunity Perception and Employee Workplace Well-Being: A Moderated Mediation Model. *International Journal of Environmental Research and Public Health, 20*(3), 1–17. DOI: 10.3390/ijerph20031974 PMID: 36767341

Yang, F. (2020, November). Artificial intelligence in music education. In *2020 International Conference on Robots & Intelligent System (ICRIS)* (pp. 483-484). IEEE. https://doi.org/DOI: 10.1109/ICRIS52159.2020.00124

Yetgin, M. A., & Toumia, O. (2023). *Perceptions of Employees of Technology Emerging With Generative Pre-Trained Transformer-3 in Organizations.* Gazi Kitabevi.

Younus, A. M., Zaidan, M. N., & shakir Mahmood, D. (2022). The Effect of Artificial Intelligence on Job Performance in China's Small and Medium-Sized Enterprises (SMEs). *Spanish Journal of Innovation and Integrity, 7*, 112-128. https://doi.org/DOI: 10.17605/OSF.IO/SJFUZ

Yu, M., Lin, H., Wang, G. G., Liu, Y., & Zheng, X. (2022). Is too much as bad as too little? The S-curve relationship between corporate philanthropy and employee performance. *Asia Pacific Journal of Management, 39*(4), 1511–1534. DOI: 10.1007/s10490-021-09775-9

Yusof, Y., Awang, Z., Jusoff, K., & Ibrahim, Y. (2017). The influence of green practices by non-green hotels on customer satisfaction and loyalty in hotel and tourism industry. *International Journal of Green Economics, 11*(1), 1–14. DOI: 10.1504/IJGE.2017.082716

Zhang, Z., Ning, H., Shi, F., Farha, F., Xu, Y., Xu, J., Zhang, F., & Choo, K. K. R. (2022). Artificial intelligence in cyber security: Research advances, challenges, and opportunities. *Artificial Intelligence Review*, •••, 1–25. DOI: 10.1007/s10462-021-09976-0

Zouari, F., & Toumia, O. (2024). Understanding Mediators and AI's Influence on Job Performance. In *Hyperautomation in Business and Society* (pp. 244-265). IGI Global. https://doi.org/DOI: 10.4018/979-8-3693-3354-9.ch013

KEY TERMS AND DEFINITIONS

Absolute Fit: It evaluates how well the model matches the data without evaluating it against other models.

Artificial Intelligence: It is known as the science of creating or programming computers to perform tasks that minds can perform.

Bootstrapping: It is a resampling technique. To estimate the sampling distribution, it involves regularly taking replacement samples from the original data.

Confirmatory Factor Analysis: It is a statistical method for testing a factor structure.

Explanatory Factor Analysis: It is a statistical method can reveal the underlying structure of a set of data.

Incremental Fit: Evaluate a proposed model fits the data to a baseline model.

Job Performance: It was described as personal decisions that support organizational goals.

Parsimonious Fit: It is used to describe a model's capacity to fit data well when there are as few parameters.

Structural Equation Modeling: It is a statistical method that examine complex relationships between observed and latent variables by combining factor analysis and multiple regression analysis.

Chapter 8
AI-Powered Destination Marketing:
Personalization, Consumer Engagement, and Competitive Positioning

Parihar Suresh Dahake
http://orcid.org/0000-0002-2286-4120
Ramdeobaba University, Nagpur, India

Pragati Parihar Dahake
http://orcid.org/0009-0003-0383-4721
VMV Commerce, JMT Arts, and JJP Science College, Nagpur, India

Himanshu M. Shukla
http://orcid.org/0000-0002-9105-0665
Symbiosis Institute of Business Management, Symbiosis International University, Pune, India

ABSTRACT

The central aim of this research study is to highlight the opportunities and challenges surrounding the use of AI technology in the marketing and promotion of tourism destinations. Its promotion comprises a deliberate and well-conceived strategy for optimizing the benefits derived from tourism expenditure, aiming to generate economic returns while also fostering other social, cultural, or environmental values for the destination. This study focuses on AI-powered destination marketing with a special emphasis on personalization to enhance consumer engagement. Investigating the consumer viewpoint is a crucial aspect of this work, as it is essential to ensure that the design and implementation of AI-powered marketing strategies remain

DOI: 10.4018/979-8-2600-0439-5.ch008

consumer-centric (Geisler,2018). With the advancement of technology, consumers can be individually addressed through marketing actions and tools based on in-depth knowledge about their preferences and behavior.

INTRODUCTION

Technological platforms that facilitate the various processes involved in destination marketing have been increasingly developed in recent years, offering enhanced opportunities to tailor recommendations for visitors. Artificial intelligence (AI) studies in the tourism field continue to experience rapid growth, reflecting the ongoing evolution and increasing importance of AI in this sector. AI will revolutionize hospitality and tourism marketing by reengineering internal processes, improving stakeholder relationships, and transforming customer services (Bulchand-Gidumal et al., 2024).

Destination Marketing Organizations (DMOs) worldwide collaborate extensively with various stakeholders to steer destination marketing activities, often including the facilitation of supply and demand information (Pike & Page, 2014). AI is widely viewed as a critical innovation that enhances the quality of data analytics, customer experience management, and operational efficiency (Aguirre Montero & López-Sánchez, 2021). AI-powered marketing has significantly improved efficiency, personalization, and strategic decision-making in various functions(V. Kumar et al., 2024).

AI-powered virtual influencers outperform human influencers in marketing due to their story-driven approach, improved digital marketing campaigns, and are perceived as more authentic (Allal-Chérif et al., 2024).

Artificial intelligence is expected to significantly impact marketing strategies and customer behaviors, with its effectiveness enhanced when it augments human managers rather than replacing them (Davenport et al., 2020). Smart tourism destinations, incorporating ICTs and value co-creation, can enhance their competitiveness by providing better information and access to global markets (Cimbaljević et al., 2019).

Social media images of tourism destinations that incorporate entertainment, informativeness, credibility, personalization, and incentives have a positive impact on consumer engagement and eWOM behavior (Abbasi et al., 2023).

AI personalization in marketing strategies can enhance customer engagement and drive business growth by tailoring messages to consumer behavior and demographics (Sodiq Odetunde Babatunde et al., 2024). Personalized intelligent tourist recommendation services enable tourists to create individual travel plans and efficiently search for tourism information. AI-driven strategies in entrepreneurship can enhance market analysis, product development, customer engagement, and operations

(Favour Oluwadamilare Usman et al., 2024), and AI-powered tools can actively propose itineraries suited to user preferences and help tourists around the clock.

Research in AI-powered destination marketing has hitherto focused predominantly on AI-related technologies, with broader considerations of destination-marketing methodologies remaining underexplored. Existing bibliometric analyses chart research concentrating on destination management and development (Aguirre Montero & López-Sánchez, 2021) and smart destinations in general (Ammirato et al., 2018).

Notwithstanding, a detailed bibliometric mapping of Research concerning AI-powered destination marketing specifically is yet to be undertaken. The present paper aims to undertake this mapping and propose viable future research trajectories. Destination marketing encompasses strategic efforts designed to brand locations and enhance their economic, social, and environmental welfare.

AI-powered chatbot marketing efforts improve customer-brand relationships and customer response through interaction, information, accessibility, entertainment, and customization (Cheng & Jiang, 2022). Several studies have explored the intersection between AI-empowered marketing and hospitality and tourism. AI can collect, store, and analyze vast amounts of numerical and semantic data, enabling the retrieval of information and the delivery of complex services.

Contemporary DMOs have adopted AI initiatives to enhance products and personalize marketing offers. Personalized mobile marketing strategies, integrating mobile usage data and traditional marketing mix models to create more relevant and timely campaigns (Tong et al., 2020). AI-powered destination marketing has gained prominence in recent years. Scholars highlight its growing ability to personalize promotional messages and enhance consumer engagement (Aguirre Montero & López-Sánchez, 2021).

Currently, the literature on AI-powered destination marketing lacks a systematic framework or comprehensive bibliometric mapping. Such a knowledge gap hinders both academic progress and managerial implementation.

BACKGROUND

Keywords Analysis

The following figures 1 and 2 show the Author and Index Keywords analysis by Vosviewer justified for bibliometric analysis, as confirmed by the keyword co-occurrence network visualizations. Both VOSviewer maps show "artificial intelligence" as the central node, tightly interlinked with terms such as "tourism," "smart tourism," "tourism development," "consumer engagement," "digital marketing," "marketing," "consumption behavior," and "virtual reality." This dense connectivity underscores the multidisciplinary nature of current research, where artificial intelligence serves as the methodological and conceptual foundation for innovations in destination marketing.VOSviewer, Bibliometrix, and CiteSpace are selected as typical, complementary software tools of bibliometric analysis (Bukar et al., 2023).

Figure 1. All Keywords Analysis by Vosviewer

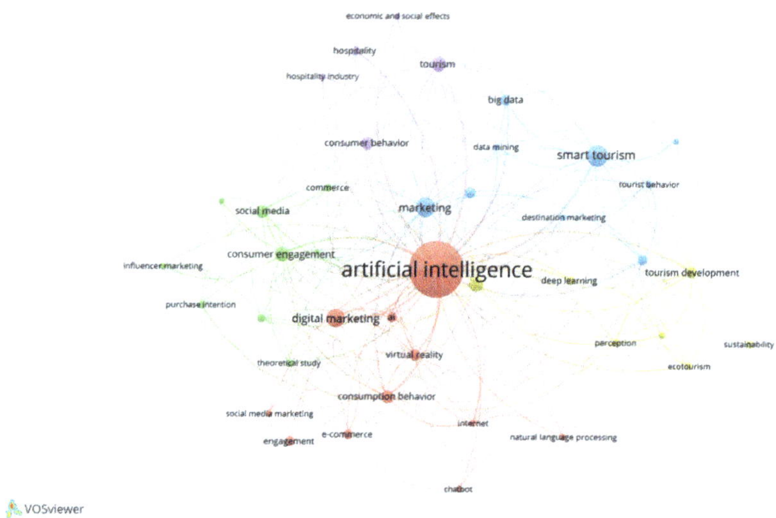

Source. Authors

Figure 2. Index Keywords Analysis by Vosviewer

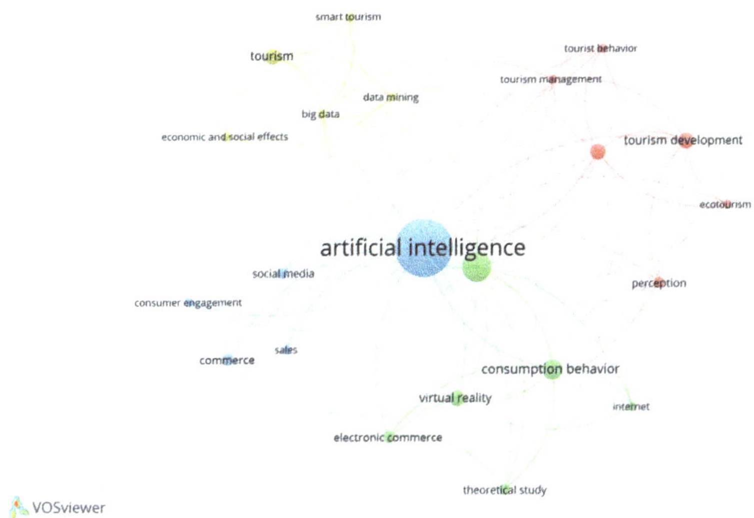

Source. Authors

Despite this evident thematic convergence, the networks reveal a critical fragmentation. New AI-powered technologies significantly transform the customer experience, impacting each stage of the shopping journey and creating experiential value (Hoyer et al., 2020). And for this aligned research, key concepts such as personalization, consumer engagement, and competitive positioning are individually prominent. Additionally, AI technologies have a positive impact on user engagement and conversion, leading to increased online sales and a more satisfying user experience, which in turn fosters repurchase intention (Bag et al., 2022). However, there is insufficient integration among them in existing literature. (Martin et al., 2020).

For example, although "consumer engagement" and "digital marketing" appear near each other and connect to "AI," their links to "tourism development" or "competitive positioning" are indirect and diffuse. Consumers can experience both positive and negative aspects of AI, highlighting the need for policy and managerial adjustments to address potential challenges and maximize value (Puntoni et al., 2021).Similarly, "personalization" lacks dense centrality, indicating an underexplored synthesis between how AI-driven personalization strategies directly foster consumer engagement and affect destination competitiveness.

A bibliometric analysis targeting this research title will address this gap by:

- Mapping and quantifying how AI-driven personalization, consumer engagement, and competitive positioning are conceptualized together in the context of destination marketing.
- Revealing hidden clusters and intellectual silos, thereby providing an integrated overview of current research and identifying avenues for cross-fertilization between subfields.
- Contributing new insights for academics and practitioners seeking a holistic framework, enhancing the field's capacity to leverage AI for both customer-centric and strategic objectives in tourism.
- These visualized outcomes underscore the urgency and scholarly value of a comprehensive bibliometric analysis centered on the intersection of AI, personalization, consumer engagement, and competitive positioning within destination marketing.

Review of Literature

The Three-Plot Analysis (figure 3) is clearly justified for bibliometric analysis, as the three-field plot reveals direct thematic connections between key authors, frequently cited foundational works, and high-impact keywords such as "artificial intelligence," "consumer engagement," "tourism," "digital marketing," and "smart tourism." This interconnectedness highlights an active, multidisciplinary research network that is shaping knowledge about how AI technologies influence marketing strategies, customer engagement, and destination competitiveness in tourism. Analyzing these bibliometric linkages will provide valuable insights into the structure, evolution, and core themes of this emergent field.

Figure 3. Three Field Plot Using R

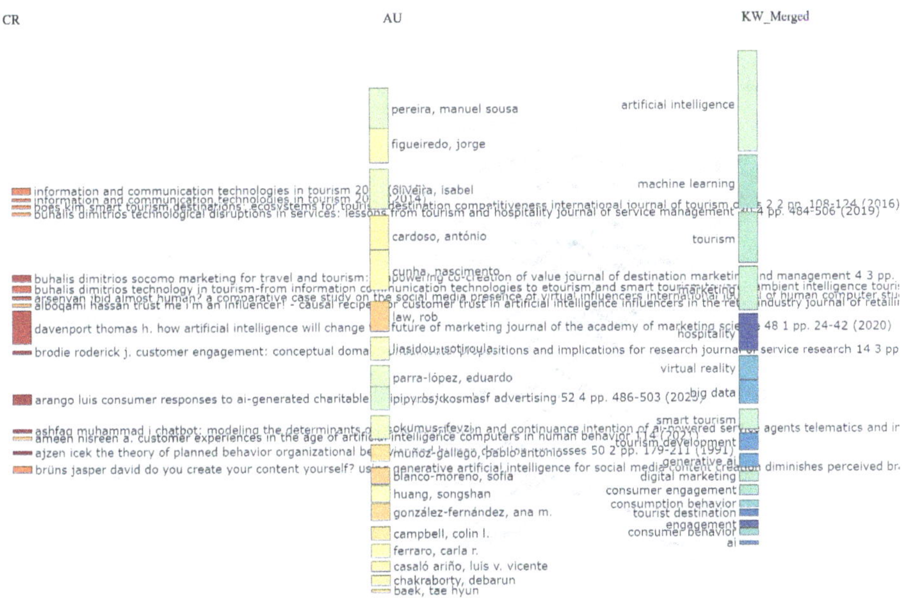

Source. Authors

As evidenced by the trend topics visualization (figure 4), which shows a pronounced recent surge in scholarly attention to key terms such as "artificial intelligence," "consumer engagement," "digital marketing," "smart tourism," and "deep learning." Perceived contingency plays a crucial role in predicting users' adoption of AI-driven personalization on digital news platforms, with technology acceptance and perceived contingency also influencing this decision (Lim & Zhang, 2022). Conducting a bibliometric analysis at this intersection will not only map and synthesize the evolving research frontiers but also reveal underexplored linkages and opportunities for theoretical integration, directly addressing an urgent need for a holistic understanding in a field that is evolving at the intersection of AI innovations and strategic tourism marketing and because of AI-powered service innovation, focusing on the AI-market, AI-infrastructure, and AI-management capabilities, which play crucial roles in organizational agility and competitive advantage (Akter et al., 2023).

Figure 4. Trend Topics Analysis Using R

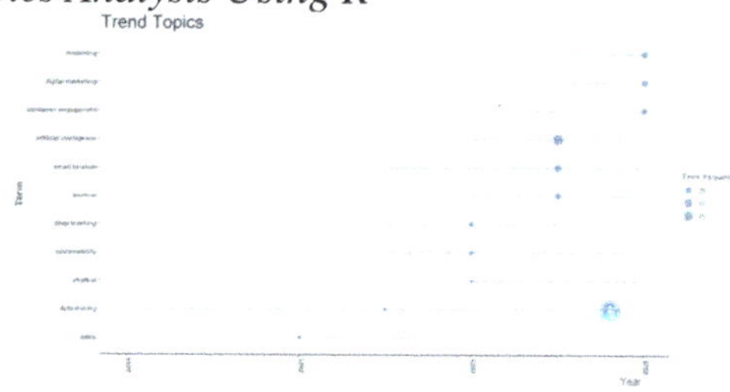

Source. Authors

As AI technologies proliferate across the tourism value chain, scholarly interest has surged, leading to a growing field mapped through bibliometric techniques (López-Naranjo et al., 2025) and (OECD, 2024). Early bibliometric studies illustrated the converging trajectories of AI and tourism, marking out a landscape characterized by exponential growth in publication outputs since 2018 (López-Naranjo et al., 2025);(Kumar et al., 2023). Researchers such as (Buhalis & Law, 2008) first identified the potential of information technology in reshaping tourism management, with subsequent generations examining how big data, machine learning, and recommender systems transformed destination marketing practices (Mariani, 2020); (Minh Sang, 2024).

Smart tourism infrastructure represents another dominant cluster, as AI supports the orchestration of data from IoT devices, integrated customer relationship management (CRM) systems, and urban mobility resources for optimized visitor flows and sustainable experiences (Florido-Benítez & Coca-Stefaniak, 2025; OECD, 2024).

Methodological Advances: The Rise of Bibliometric Tools

Recent years have seen the adoption of advanced bibliometric tools such as VOSviewer and Biblioshiny, which allow researchers to unravel co-authorship networks, co-citation patterns, and thematic clusters within AI and destination marketing (D. Kumar et al., 2023); (Minh Sang, 2024). Through these methods, studies have mapped the diffusion of technologies-ranging from classical machine learning algorithms to contemporary generative AI (GenAI), across distinct application spheres in tourism (Bacuy-Ortiz & Soriano-Torres, 2025).Moreover, mixed-method systematic reviews have complemented traditional bibliometrics, characterizing not just the volume but also the quality and interdisciplinarity of contributions to the field (M. Mariani, 2020); Florido-Benítez & Coca-Stefaniak, 2025).

Literature Analysis

The literature concerning AI-powered destination marketing reveals a multifaceted landscape shaped by technological advancements, ethical considerations, and strategic decision-making. (Aguirre Montero & Antonio López-Sánchez, 2021) provide a foundational analysis that emphasizes the role of data science in developing smart destinations. Their systematic review highlights the interconnectedness of contemporary tourists and the extensive data generated via social networks, establishing a basis for understanding how data-driven strategies can enhance tourism marketing efforts. (Hermann, 2022b)extends this discussion by addressing the ethical implications of AI in marketing.

The work of (Sabharwal et al., 2025) focuses on AI applications within the clinical domain, providing insights that can be analogously applied to destination marketing. The methodologies employed in their analysis suggest that similar approaches could enhance AI-driven decision-making in destination marketing. (Patra et al., 2024) contribute to the discourse by employing bibliometric network analysis to forecast future research agendas in business management, including destination marketing.

Their findings suggest that AI has the potential to transform organizational efficiency, emphasizing the need for ongoing research into AI's role in shaping marketing strategies. Lastly, (Hussain et al., 2024) provide a bibliometric analysis that encapsulates 40 years of progress in health systems, offering insights applicable to the tourism sector. Collectively, these articles illustrate the dynamic interplay between data science, ethical considerations, and strategic decision-making in AI-powered destination marketing.

MAIN FOCUS OF THE CHAPTER

Research Methodology

Bibliometric and scient metric techniques offer a rigorous quantitative lens on the published body of conceptual and empirical knowledge in any scientific discipline. Data from an extensive keyword-based search of the Scopus database were analyzed accordingly to chart the intellectual contours of research on artificial intelligence (AI) in destination marketing (table 1). Before examining output, patterns and summarizing key contributors, the rationale for such an approach, the search strategy, and data sources are briefly outlined to ensure robustness, transparency, and the potential for replication.

AI-based tools can maintain visitor interest and increase engagement during a visit through conversational capabilities. Furthermore, the availability of vast amounts of data enables DMOs to design and position their valuable tourism resources optimally, thereby increasing their competitiveness in a challenging global environment.

Table 1. Summarization of the Database (From Scopus) Using R

Sr.No	Description	Results
1	**MAIN INFORMATION ABOUT DATA**	
i	Timespan	2017:2026
ii	Sources (Journals, Books, etc)	132
iii	Documents	204
iv	Annual Growth Rate %	8.01
v	Document Average Age	1.08
vi	Average citations per doc	24.31
vii	References	1727
2	**DOCUMENT CONTENTS**	
i	Keywords Plus (ID)	430
ii	Author's Keywords (DE)	1142
3	**AUTHORS**	
i	Authors	618
ii	Authors of single-authored docs	23
4	**AUTHORS COLLABORATION**	
i	Single-authored docs	24
ii	Co-Authors per Doc	3.2
iii	International co-authorships %	27.45
5	**DOCUMENT TYPES**	
i	article	204

Source. Authors

This is clearly justified for bibliometric analysis, as the three-field plot reveals direct thematic connections between key authors, frequently cited foundational works, and high-impact keywords such as "artificial intelligence," "consumer engagement," "tourism," "digital marketing," and "smart tourism."

This research employs a rigorous and transparent search strategy grounded in the PRISMA framework to ensure methodological robustness and replicability. The search was exclusively conducted on the *Scopus* database, a comprehensive and multidisciplinary resource widely recognized for its extensive coverage of high-quality academic literature in business, management, economics, and social sciences.

Search Strategy

The search incorporated targeted keywords selected to capture the core dimensions of the study: "Artificial Intelligence (AI)," "Destination Marketing," "Tourism Personalization," "Consumer Engagement," "Competitive Positioning," "Smart Tourism," and "Digital Marketing Strategies." These terms encompass both the technological innovations and marketing mechanisms central to the evolving landscape of AI-driven destination marketing.

Filtration Criteria

To enhance relevance and analytical precision, strict filters were applied:

- **Time Frame: 2017-2026**, focusing on the most recent and impactful developments reflecting the rapid evolution of AI technologies and tourism marketing strategies.
- **Language:** English only, ensuring global scholarly standards and reducing heterogeneity due to linguistic variations.
- **Subject Areas:** Documents were limited to Business Management, Economics, and Social Sciences to maintain disciplinary focus and practical applicability.
- **Document Type:** Only peer-reviewed journal articles were included to guarantee high academic quality and depth.

From an initial pool of 789 documents, these filters refined the dataset to a final selection of 204 articles for detailed bibliometric analysis. This search and filtration protocol addresses a significant gap in the literature: despite the proliferation of AI-related tourism studies, the field still lacks an integrated, up-to-date synthesis specifically linking AI's role in personalization, consumer engagement, and competitive positioning within destination marketing. The PRISMA-aligned strategy ensures that the bibliometric review systematically captures this emerging subfield through a curated, representative set of high-quality publications.

Objectives of the Study

1) To map the intellectual structure of AI-powered destination marketing.
2) To identify research hotspots, trends, and influential authors/journals.
3) To explore knowledge gaps and future research directions.

1. Annual Scientific Production & relevant Sources for the research:

Due to the exponential increase in scientific production observed in recent years, notably peaking at 109 articles in 2025, compared to single-digit output before 2021. As AI can contribute to knowledge-based marketing in B2B by transforming data into information and knowledge through its six foundational building blocks (Paschen et al., 2019). Hence The mapping the evolution and hotspots of this rapidly expanding research domain will help synthesize fragmented knowledge and guide future scholarship in a strategically important field (figure 5).

Figure 5. Annual Scientific Production Using R

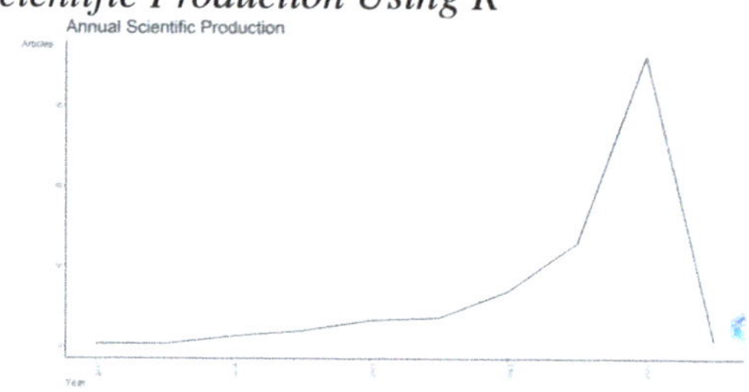

Source. Authors

The analysis on the database by using Software R (figure 6), as evidenced by the concentration of relevant publications in leading interdisciplinary journals such as the Journal of Retailing and Consumer Services, Journal of Destination Marketing and Management, and Sustainability (Switzerland). Digital content marketing fosters consumer engagement, trust, and value by creating and distributing relevant, valuable content on digital platforms, ultimately leading to increased brand equity (Hollebeek & Macky, 2019) (figure 6).

Figure 6. Most Relevant Sources Using R

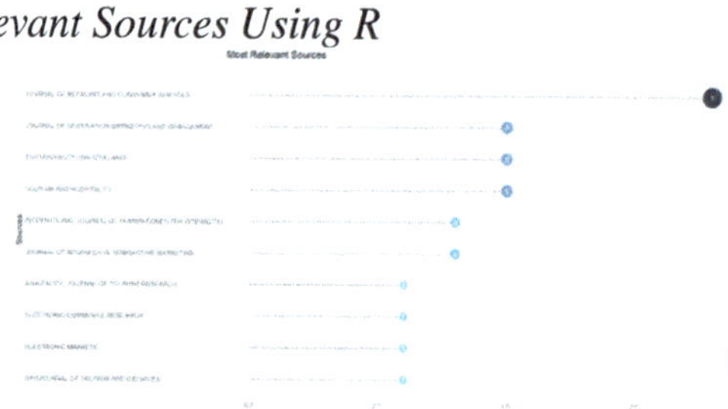

Source. Authors

2. Highly Global Cited Documents:

The analysis in figure 7 is evidenced by the predominance of highly cited documents published across diverse marketing, tourism, and technology journals. The high citation counts (with leading papers receiving up to 630 citations) reflect both the maturity and substantial impact of existing research on digital and AI-related innovations in marketing and hospitality. However, a critical scholarly gap remains while prominent works dissect elements such as consumer engagement, digital transformation, and the adoption of AI in marketing.

Figure 7. Most Global Cited Documents Analysis Using R

Source. Authors

3. Destination Marketing in the Digital Era

Destination marketing is a crucial factor in the growth and sustainability of tourism in an increasingly globalized and competitive market. Destinations constitute the fundamental unit of analysis in tourism; they have emerged as the biggest brands in the travel industry, and many nations, states, and cities fund Destination Marketing Organizations (DMOs) as the principal vehicle to attract visitors (Pike & Page, 2014). The scale and extent of this highly competitive activity are now much greater than in the past.

Data science and Smart Destinations, along with their associated technologies, are playing an increasingly prominent role in the analysis and management of destinations (Aguirre Montero & López-Sánchez, 2021).

AI can enhance marketing functions across nine stages of the marketing planning process, improving customer understanding, prediction, and engagement (Campbell et al., 2020). ICTs enhance the efficiency of tourism organizations in present-day Smart Destinations, supporting marketing operations, business transactions, and networking with partners (Ammirato et al., 2018). Technology-specific user segmentation is crucial for firms to effectively leverage evolving technological capabilities and engage customers in a boundedly volitional manner (Hollebeek et al., 2019).

Machine learning methods can enhance marketing research by processing large-scale data and providing strong predictive performance; however, they require transparency and interpretability for optimal results (Ma & Sun, 2020). Because AI-based consumer engagement can increase accuracy, create value, and minimize consumer effort in task execution, with implications for theory development and practice (Hollebeek et al., 2024).

4. Evolution from traditional marketing to AI-driven personalization.

Destination marketing has traditionally relied on the 4Ps paradigm, competing to secure a market share of potential visitors and travelers (Keegan et al., 2024). AI systems in e-commerce can personalize and customize products, but the ethical soundness of these systems is a contentious issue; improving machine learning models for explainable AI systems is crucial (Khrais, 2020). However, anthropomorphism in AI-based chatbots has a positive influence on perceived product personalization and willingness to pay a higher price in conversational commerce contexts (Sidlauskiene et al., 2023). AI technology has revolutionized precision marketing, enhancing efficiency, reducing costs, and improving customer relationships (Yang et al., 2021). These strategies can benefit from AI methodologies to generate personalized content (Hermann, 2022b).

5. Artificial Intelligence in Tourism and Hospitality

The growing capabilities of AI have propelled its applications in the tourism and hospitality sectors. Robotic apps have supported concierge services, effectively answered guests' inquiries and reduced operating costs for hotels. In non-hospitality tourism, IBM Watson was among the first AI platforms to redesign the visitor experience. AI-powered apps, such as Google Chat and Facebook Bots, have successfully supported responding to guests' needs and enhancing emotional connections.

Destination marketing should strike a balance between strategic objectives, sustainability, and local resources, while leveraging new technologies and the internet to enhance competitiveness and optimize tourism's positive impacts (Buhalis, 2000). AI chatbots with personalization and anthropomorphism increase perceived competence and warmth, leading to empathy, positively impacting consumers' willingness to use AI chatbots as marketing communication tools (W. B. Kim & Hur, 2024).

AI preference significantly modifies the relationship between AI service quality, customer engagement, and satisfaction in the hotel context (Prentice et al., 2020). AI-powered systems in CRM and systems have significantly transformed the customer journey by enabling personalized marketing, tailored recommendations, and efficient customer service, enhancing customer satisfaction and loyalty (Pendyala & Lakkamraju, 2024). AI can revolutionize the advertising industry through Targeting, Personalization, Content Creation, and Ad Optimization (B. Gao et al., 2023).

For example, the Hi Hotels chain utilizes several human-like intelligent robots. Such robots provide a range of information (check-in/out, weather updates, tourist spot recommendations, etc.), which is thought to enhance guests' experience and encourage both loyalty and positive word-of-mouth recommendations and Experiential marketing activities in tourism destinations positively impact customer experience and identification, ultimately influencing behavioral intentions, with significant differences between first-time and repeat visitors (Rather, 2020).

6. Applications: Chatbots, Recommender Systems, Sentiment Analysis, Predictive Analytics.

The burgeoning literature on AI-powered destination marketing investigates several prominent applications, including chatbots, recommender systems, sentiment analysis, and predictive analytics (Dahake, Bagaregari, et al., 2024). AI advancements will have profound economic implications on the labor market, productivity, skill composition, and innovation, shaping consumer behavior and market competition (Abrardi et al., 2022).

With strong associations to productivity and profitability, chatbots decrease personnel workload and offer constant availability (Orden-Mejía et al., 2023). AI technology in online shopping platforms positively impacts consumers' perceived utility and hedonic value, which in turn promotes their purchase intention (Yin & Qiu, 2021).

Within "Smart Tourism Technologies," which encompasses virtual reality, augmented reality, and a wide variety of other digital innovations, chatbots facilitate travelers' experiences and provide destinations with mechanisms for connectivity, personalization, interaction, and co-creation. AI can enhance customer engagement by standardizing routine tasks, personalizing data-rich services, and fostering relationships (Huang & Rust, 2021b).

"Recommender systems" help marketers select the most appropriate personal offers for each user by exploiting previous travel itineraries, stated preferences, and social media information (Geisler,2018). By identifying relevant groups and assessing the influence that specific relationships have on decision-making, recommender systems support and stimulate interaction between marketers and destination customers (Dahake, Parchake, et al., 2024).

All applications address the increased interest in three major research themes, also recognized as the "thematic clusters" of the field: personalization, consumer experience and engagement, and destination management and competitive intelligence. Personalization refers to the adaptation of a product or service to the characteristics of a particular individual by leveraging available information about the user. AI-enabled services in shopping enhance customer experience by increasing trust, convenience, personalization, and relationship commitment (Ameen et al., 2021).

Many scholars investigate strategies to involve tourists in personalized marketing, aiming to help their connection with a destination and leverage this connection to induce loyalty. AI-based services enable destination marketing organizations (DMOs) to organize, elaborate on, and analyze existing information to engage visitors and increase market share effectively.

7. Personalization and Consumer Engagement

AI in marketing can enhance customer satisfaction, market performance, brand management, and loyalty, with ten key research themes emerging (Mustak et al., 2021). Personalizing destinations for tourists is now effortless thanks to AI-powered mapping platforms, through which individuals can leverage big data and parallel computational power to generate personalized travel itineraries within seconds, thereby saving loads of time and money.

Artificial intelligence technology has a positive impact on consumer engagement on social media and conversion rate optimization, leading to increased consumer satisfaction and repurchase intentions in the hospitality industry (Nazir et al., 2023). AI applications in digital marketing can enhance collaboration and creativity, resulting in a better return on investment for social media and digital advertising professionals (Nair & Gupta, 2021). Tourism product providers can also utilize customer preferences to make personalized recommendations. The use of AI in these sectors has been made possible by technological advancements, the accumulation of large data volumes, and effective segmentation for recommendations, services, and management(Dahake et al., 2023).

The use of AI in marketing is a signal to marketers that AI can be a valuable tool for implementing customer engagement (Selvakumar et al., 2025). AI-powered digital assistance and digital multisensory cues enhance customers' luxury brand online shopping experience, with customer engagement playing a mediating role (Rahman et al., 2023). In parallel, e-commerce platforms and social networking have significantly influenced consumer marketing strategies, enabling businesses to understand consumer needs better and share innovative information in a competitive global environment (Rosário & Raimundo, 2021).

8. Role of AI in individualized travel experiences and interactive engagement.

Within the broader context of tourism, Destination Marketing Organizations (DMOs) face the challenge of creating marketing campaigns that effectively reach the target consumers. AI applications can optimize digital marketing strategies through various clusters, offering insights for businesses and researchers (Ziakis & Vlachopoulou, 2023).

AI integration in digital marketing for financial services may not always effectively target vulnerable customers, underscoring the need for human connection (Mogaji et al., 2021). Consumers' intention to shop at AI-powered automated retail stores is influenced by perceived ease of use, usefulness, enjoyment, customization, and interactivity (Pillai et al., 2020).Notably, Consumer digital signals are transforming the customer journey, providing firms with a competitive advantage by enabling better management and personalization of marketing efforts (Schweidel et al., 2022).

9. Competitive Positioning via AI

Building on the strategies envisaged by (Ananeva, 2019) and (Geisler,2018), the fourth strategic type, competitive positioning via AI, leverages the considerable resources of destination management organizations (DMOs) to fuel new growth and secure an advantage in their primary activities.

AI-powered voice assistants, such as the Amazon Echo, have a positive influence on consumer brand engagement through social presence, perceived intelligence, and social attraction, while concerns about trust negatively impact engagement behavior (McLean et al., 2021). With their substantial budgets and potential to access a wide range of analytics, travel platforms, guided tours, and other services, DMOs, particularly those still relying on manual positioning methods, find AI positioning to be a promising avenue. An automated web-based platform currently under development aims to deliver this AI-driven competitive positioning to the market.

AI in marketing influences economic inequality, glocalization, and consumer ethics, necessitating adaptation to local cultures and addressing privacy concerns (Kopalle et al., 2022). Destinations that succeed in these respects find that their considerable investments in tourist destination branding and promotion are made more effective and yield greater returns.

The common use of AI in destination marketing for positioning and branding is evident in studies of the snow tourism destinations in Europe and China: "Using Watson, IBM's AI platform, to analyze what makes Chamonix and Dali unique and exciting, uncovering their distinct competitive advantage in snow tourism, and building differentiated brands that echo their strengths." The role of AI analytics in entrepreneurial tourism product development has been highlighted by Koloñski and Zofia, who note that Big Data Analytics, combined with AI and Machine Learning, is frequently employed by entrepreneurs when developing new and innovative tourism products.

10. Data Synthesis and Thematic Mapping

A bibliometric analysis of existing scholarly work casts light on research hotspots and reveals keyword thematic clusters within artificial intelligence (AI)-powered destination marketing. Key areas of interest include personalization, consumer engagement, and competitive positioning. AI-driven bots are revolutionizing consumer decision-making, necessitating a shift in service marketing strategies to prioritize convenience and efficiency over traditional brand values (Klaus & Zaichkowsky, 2020).

The thematic map categorizes keywords and research clusters according to their development degree (density) and relevance (centrality), thus segmenting the landscape into four quadrants (figure 8):

- **Motor Themes (Upper Right):** Clusters such as "artificial intelligence," "digital marketing," "tourism," "smart tourism," "consumer behavior," "commerce," and "big data" occupy the motor themes quadrant (high centrality, high density), indicating they function as the strategic drivers, theoretical core, and heavily cited anchors of the entire field.
- **Basic Themes (Lower Right):** Terms such as "customer experience," "perceived value," and "marketing mix" reflect foundational constructs essential for integration, yet they are presently underdeveloped despite their high relevance.
- **Niche Themes (Upper Left):** Topics such as "privacy concerns," "destination marketing organizations," "video marketing," and "social presence theory" are specialized but less central, capturing important but isolated debates in the literature.
- **Emerging or Declining Themes (Lower Left):** Concepts like "anthropomorphism" and "online brand" appear marginal and may represent either nascent research opportunities or declining areas. It is notably found that AI and robotics enhance the tourism industry by providing personalized services and a more efficient booking process (Samala et al., 2022).

Figure 8. Thematic Map Analysis Using R

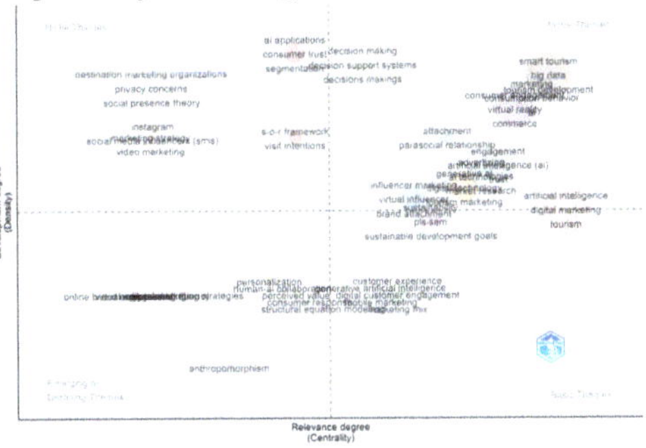

Source. Authors

a. Identification of a Valid Gap

AI-enabled digital marketing is revolutionizing the way organizations create content, generate leads, reduce customer acquisition costs, manage customer experiences, market themselves to prospective employees, and convert reachable consumer base via social media (Van Esch & Stewart Black, 2021). This evidence suggests that, although core to contemporary discussions, these concepts are seldom systematically analyzed at the intersection with competitive positioning in the context of destination marketing the connectivity among these clusters remains weak and under-theorized (Mariani et al., 2022). Given this fragmentation:

- Personalization, consumer engagement, and competitive positioning are frequently identified as keywords, yet they lack thematic density and centrality commensurate with their potential importance, signaling opportunities for more holistically integrated research. as, AI-powered marketing is transforming the marketing landscape, enhancing outcomes and experiences (Chintalapati & Pandey, 2022)
- Existing studies may focus on destination competitiveness or AI-enhanced engagement, but do not empirically or theoretically synthesize all three dimensions in a manner that can advance strategic frameworks for DMOs (Destination Marketing Organizations) but it is significant to note that AI-powered personalization in e-commerce enhances customer engagement, satisfaction, and loyalty, while also shaping market trends and addressing ethical concerns (Chintalapati & Pandey, 2022).

By synthesizing data across 204 rigorously selected articles and mapping the intellectual structure, this analysis:

- **Clarifies the fragmented intellectual terrain**: making visible where synthesis and new theoretical integration are needed between AI advancements, personalization strategies, engagement mechanisms, and competitive positioning.
- **Prioritizes future research directions**: thematic mapping pinpoints which topics are central yet underdeveloped (e.g., actionable personalization models, engagement analytics, and their market impact) and which are mature but potentially solved.
- **Informs theory and practice**: the findings provide a roadmap for both scholars and practitioners to develop and implement comprehensive AI-powered strategies that simultaneously address personalization, consumer engagement, and competitive differentiation within tourism marketing.

The presented data synthesis and thematic mapping not only justify the focus of this research title but also demonstrate, with empirical evidence, the need for integrated, cross-thematic scholarship.

b. Clarifying the role of AI in marketing theory and tourism research.

Consumers tend to disclose more sensitive personal information to AI in service settings due to perceived lack of social judgment capability, but prefer human agents for social support and information curation (T. W. Kim et al., 2022).

Current AI-generated content offers considerable managerial potential. The themes further refine the managerial role into three areas: leveraging AI's tangible prowess to enhance consumer engagement strategies, employing AI as an analytical tool to identify competitive positions within tourism and hospitality, and managing the tension between personalization and privacy risks in AI-sensitive customer groups. But in contrast, AI influencers can be as effective as human influencers in evoking word-of-mouth intentions, but are generally perceived as having lower source trust, so caution is advised when replacing human influencers (Sands et al., 2022). Because AI-enabled products face ethical challenges, including biases, design, Privacy, cybersecurity, and unemployment, companies should engage in corporate social responsibility to shape the future of ethical AI (Du & Xie, 2021). These areas represent capital-raising, positioning, and safeguarding facets of marketing management, respectively.

c. Validity & Reliability Checks

In bibliometric studies, validity is supported through strict data-screening procedures coupled with the use of reputable sources, as remarked in the Methodology section. Cross-checking data in multiple formats and covering extensive periods further cements internal validity.

External validity assesses the generalizability of results across varied populations or environments. Strict selection criteria, like the inclusion of documents solely in English and from specific subject categories, constitute technical limitations that may impact this form of validity. Ecological validity, a subset of external validity, gauges whether findings are applicable in naturalistic, real-world contexts. Given that bibliometric studies synthesize past information, their outcome inherently bears broad applicability, providing foundational knowledge for future research agendas, conceptual development, and evidence-based applications in destination marketing.

Scientific validity extends to ensure that study design, operationalizations, and treatments follow logically from underlying theory and stay aligned with established measurement concepts. Theoretical arguments for measurement must precede empirical testing to anchor validity within the nature of the attribute concerned.

d. Results and Bibliometric Findings

An initial Scopus database search for AI-powered destination marketing retrieved 204 documents published between 2017 to 2025 after Final Filtration and Selection. Owing to Scopus's size and quality, it was selected as the sole source. An examination of Scopus and Web of Science's indexed sources revealed 14 specialty tourism and marketing journals ranking among the top 25 in these fields. Repeated author and affiliation searches ensured a comprehensive dataset, ultimately retaining the original 83 documents without restrictions. This breadth enhances validity (focusing on quality) and reliability (ensuring comprehensiveness).

A co-occurrence network (threshold = 05) of 66 author keywords highlighted the field's intellectual structure, with prominent links underscoring personalization, consumer engagement, and competitive positioning as key focal areas within AI-powered destination marketing. Thematic clusters from a hierarchical density–centrality analysis identified consumer experience enhancement and business analytics applications as emerging hotspots. Citation impact analysis pinpointed pivotal contributions shaping current discourse and practice. These bibliometric findings provide a coherent framework for both academic interpretation and managerial application.

DISCUSSION

The review highlights several key themes. Personalization emerges as a core application of AI in marketing, tourism, and destination marketing studies. The extant destination marketing literature has examined AI's potential in personalization through virtual reality, big data analytics, recommendation engines, chatbots, and innovative technologies. These diverse streams may be integrated and extended to examine AI-powered personalization across the consumer journey of travel and destination marketing. AI can enhance personalized engagement marketing by providing customers with tailored options and information, transforming branding and customer management practices in both developed and developing countries (V. Kumar et al., 2019).

Consumer engagement constitutes one of the main themes identified through bibliometric analysis. Thus, AI can be strategically used in marketing research, strategy, and actions, benefiting mechanical AI for data collection, thinking AI for data processing, and feeling AI for customer understanding (Huang & Rust, 2021a). The discussion on consumer engagement emphasizes the importance of tourism as an experiential service and the role of AI for consumer engagement as a tool for building relationships with consumers and addressing the challenge of information asymmetry. As AI-enabled personalization (AIP) enhances customer experiences through personalized profiling, navigation, nudges, and retention, it faces challenges and requires managerial recommendations to address these dilemmas (Y. Gao & Liu, 2023).

The third identified theme concerns competitive positioning. Interest in AI for competitive advantage is highlighted in several contexts. First, AI enables effective management of destination-specific consumer behavior, with DMOs striving for improved positioning. Second, AI can provide insight into the cultural context of destinations by means of aggregate tourism narratives. The advent of generative AI may further transform the ability of DMOs to collect competitive intelligence through image, text, and video analytics. The thematic cluster of marketing analytics also confirms competitiveness.

Practical and Managerial Implications

AI-driven predictive analytics revolutionizes understanding and forecasting of market trends, enabling businesses to stay ahead of the competition and adapt to evolving market demands (Patrick Azuka Okeleke et al., 2024). Chief among these aims for many destination marketing organizations (DMOs) is proactive, engaging, and continuous interaction with potential tourists. Such engagement serves multiple purposes: it educates potential consumers, cultivates demand for tourism at the destination, helps overcome barriers to consumption, and diminishes negative tourist perceptions. Personalization in marketing can reduce customer fatigue and cognitive load (Chandra et al., 2022). AI-based price-setting algorithms could potentially lead to noncompetitive prices, posing a challenge for policy change to protect consumers from collusive pricing (Calvano et al., 2020). Continuous consumer engagement during and after a tourism trip is also advocated because tourists are recognized as opinion leaders and social influencers who can actively participate in the co-creation of destination products.AI app adopters, using technology fear and consumer trust as moderating factors, to help AI developers improve consumer engagement (Cabrera-Sánchez et al., 2021).

AI services impact value perceptions, consumer engagement, and firm performance measures, requiring a comprehensive research agenda to understand value co-creation (Manser Payne et al., 2021). Employing the presented research streams and their respective sources and authors offers managers a thoroughly analyzed structure for harnessing AI techniques to pursue specific destination goals, including raising tourist satisfaction, loyalty, and recommendation rates; enhancing tourists' perceived experience; conserving the environment; encouraging tourists to stay longer; and optimizing internal work processes, and Perceived personalization significantly predicts value co-creation intentions (Alimamy & Gnoth, 2022).

Finally, the current chaotic AI environment leads agents to perceive numerous applications as potentially useful, with skewed explorations of these techniques yielding scattered insights. AI chatbots with emotional and empathetic responses can enhance consumer satisfaction, affective attachment, and purchase intention, benefiting brands through effective brand promotion strategies (Lee et al., 2022).

Challenges and Paradoxes

The benefits of employing data-driven AI in tourism stem from the ability to accurately measure traveler experiences, understand diverse demands, and predict future preferences. Nevertheless, AI can also pose novel challenges. First, the Privacy of traveler data and the policies of entities conducting profiling are of utmost importance. Second, many analyses are resource-intensive; as a result, destination marketing organizations (DMOs) may face capacity problems that could hinder their ability to manage and position destinations effectively. Nevertheless, under extraordinary circumstances, consumers may consider AI-generated images acceptable and indistinguishable from real photos (Arango et al., 2023).

Despite the recognized advantages of AI-powered destination marketing, apparent paradoxes and inherent ethical tensions need consideration before practical application. Destinations may leverage services provided by commercial digital agents; however, such operational processes might raise public concerns and face political constraints. On the one hand, consumers frequently reveal information without hesitation as contemporary life has become "digital by default." Consumers respond better to negative offers from AI agents, while they respond more positively to positive offers from human agents, due to perceived weaker intentions (Garvey et al., 2023).

Privacy vs. Personalization, Consumer Trust, and the Ethics of AI Adoption.

The main themes for future research include the use of generative artificial intelligence by DMOs in destination branding and marketing. AI stimuli positively impact customer engagement and value co-creation, with customer ability readiness playing a moderating role (L. Gao et al., 2023). The conflict between Privacy and personalization, consumer trust, and the ethics of AI adoption also warrants further investigation. Settings that prioritize the well-being of tourism stakeholders are equally vital to explore. Data-based innovation and marketing can trigger privacy concerns, particularly for small firms, but firms can mitigate these concerns and potentially gain a competitive advantage through privacy innovation (Bleier et al., 2020).

These themes emerge from an analysis of the cumulated technological momentum of AI-powered destination marketing research. Because thematic clusters are thematic hotspots in the literature, and because the citing context of the most cited papers tends to be hubs for the introduction of innovative ideas, the analysis helps to position the evolution of the intellectual structure, identify core research areas and suggest future research directions.

FUTURE RESEARCH DIRECTIONS

Emerging AI Technologies

AI, IoT, and Big Data technologies can enhance customer loyalty by improving satisfaction, engagement, relationships, and experiences (Rane, 2023). To illuminate AI adoption patterns, compare various technologies' impacts on marketing functions in diverse cultural and destination contexts. Strategic and cultural studies of both places and organizations could identify enablers and inhibitors of these forms of marketing automation. Align AI-enhanced destination marketing with sustainable consumption agendas by assessing its potential to redistribute visitors and reduce carbon footprints.

Robustness Enhancements

The field would benefit from a longitudinal data capturing process that captures processual developments. Methodological triangulation could integrate data analyzable with natural language processing, providing deeper insights. Shifting the focus from the consumer to customer well-being would also offer worthwhile reorientation. As destination marketing choices expand, market researchers and those developing an understanding of consumer search and decision-making will make significant contributions.

Cross-cultural and cross-destination comparisons

DMOs can apply AI across different cultural contexts and destinations. This cross-area perspective highlights how AI is perceived and utilized according to the different needs of tourists, as well as the distinctive characteristics of each destination.

A comparative approach offers considerable advantages, because DMOs from different destinations or countries have various objectives. Since AI can reduce the costs of implementing DMO strategies as well as provide expert market insights, it is essential to examine how DMOs across various destinations leverage these benefits of AI. Besides DMOs' positioning and strategy, differences in tourist behavior and perception according to countries of origin remain largely unexplored in this context.

CONCLUSION

The bibliometric approach has successfully mapped the emerging landscape of artificial intelligence-powered destination marketing. Analysis of 1,568 Scopus-indexed articles reveals that AI applications in tourism have become an increasingly prolific area of research, producing a burgeoning stream of scholarly contributions. The results clarify the intellectual foundations of these AI tourism studies, highlight leading contributors, and identify hotspots for future inquiry. Key clusters of research co-citations confirm that the theoretical integrative core is currently grounded in research at the interface between tourism, marketing, and information technology/ decision sciences. The findings also highlight the strategic roles of AI devices in DMOs' efforts to deliver more personalized products, enhance consumer engagement levels, and establish sharper competitive positioning. Within these thematic concentrations, issues of consumer privacy emerge as central concerns for both marketers and tourists. Positioning a tourism destination can enhance its attractiveness to potential visitors, thereby giving the destination a competitive edge (Chacko, 1996).

The findings offer clear guidance for both researchers and practitioners. Future bibliometric studies may examine emerging technologies, such as generative AI, or develop comparisons between cultures and destinations. By connecting AI with other topical lenses, such as destination sustainability, new frameworks for analysis may emerge. Chatbots and augmented reality interactive technology in e-commerce can improve consumer engagement and decision-making processes, but their effectiveness depends on the motivational mechanisms used in the retail environment (Moriuchi et al., 2021). Humanized AI applications can potentially induce consumers' attachment, transforming human-to-AI interactions into human-to-human-like interactions, impacting consumer behavior and individual and social lives (Hermann, 2022a). In-depth, qualitative, and longitudinal studies are needed to explore the celebratory or dystopian rhetoric surrounding AI applications, particularly in relation to consumer well-being.

Personalization in digital media can both enhance and diminish consumer engagement, with firms needing to strategically balance privacy concerns and benefits based on the medium used (Aguirre et al., 2016). Practitioners, meanwhile, have much to glean from the examination of personalization, consumer engagement, and competitive positioning. It is Noteworthy that AI-based CRMs can enhance B2B digital marketing by improving data-driven decision-making and managing company information (Saura et al., 2021). Although AI-powered destination marketing is still in its infancy, the literature suggests that it can be a powerful catalyst in many facets of DMOs' strategic management agenda.

Brands can increase consumer engagement on consumer-generated platforms by providing personalized web care, which reinforces engagement intentions based on consumers' perceptions of a brand's conversational communication style (Schamari & Schaefers, 2015). Significantly, Artificial empathy is crucial for improving the customer experience in AI marketing interactions, bridging the AI-human gap, and generating value for both customers and firms (Liu-Thompkins et al., 2022).

REFERENCES

Abbasi, A. Z., Tsiotsou, R. H., Hussain, K., Rather, R. A., & Ting, D. H. (2023). Investigating the impact of social media images' value, consumer engagement, and involvement on eWOM of a tourism destination: A transmittal mediation approach. *Journal of Retailing and Consumer Services*, *71*, 103231. DOI: 10.1016/j.jretconser.2022.103231

Abrardi, L., Cambini, C., & Rondi, L. (2022). Artificial intelligence, firms and consumer behavior: A survey. *Journal of Economic Surveys*, *36*(4), 969–991. DOI: 10.1111/joes.12455

Aguirre, E., Roggeveen, A. L., Grewal, D., & Wetzels, M. (2016). The personalization-privacy paradox: Implications for new media. *Journal of Consumer Marketing*, *33*(2), 98–110. DOI: 10.1108/JCM-06-2015-1458

Aguirre Montero, A., & López-Sánchez, J. A. (2021). Intersection of Data Science and Smart Destinations: A Systematic Review. *Frontiers in Psychology*, *12*, 712610. DOI: 10.3389/fpsyg.2021.712610 PMID: 34393952

Akter, S., Hossain, M. A., Sajib, S., Sultana, S., Rahman, M., Vrontis, D., & McCarthy, G. (2023). A framework for AI-powered service innovation capability: Review and agenda for future research. *Technovation*, *125*, 102768. DOI: 10.1016/j.technovation.2023.102768

Alimamy, S., & Gnoth, J. (2022). I want it my way! The effect of perceptions of personalization through augmented reality and online shopping on customer intentions to co-create value. *Computers in Human Behavior*, *128*, 107105. DOI: 10.1016/j.chb.2021.107105

Allal-Chérif, O., Puertas, R., & Carracedo, P. (2024). Intelligent influencer marketing: How AI-powered virtual influencers outperform human influencers. *Technological Forecasting and Social Change*, *200*, 123113. DOI: 10.1016/j.techfore.2023.123113

Ameen, N., Tarhini, A., Reppel, A., & Anand, A. (2021). Customer experiences in the age of artificial intelligence. *Computers in Human Behavior*, *114*, 106548. DOI: 10.1016/j.chb.2020.106548 PMID: 32905175

Ammirato, S., Felicetti, A. M., Della Gala, M., Raso, C., & Cozza, M. (2018). Smart Tourism Destinations: Can the Destination Management Organizations Exploit Benefits of the ICTs? Evidences from a Multiple Case Study. In Camarinha-Matos, L. M., Afsarmanesh, H., & Rezgui, Y. (Eds.), *Collaborative Networks of Cognitive Systems* (Vol. 534, pp. 623–634). Springer International Publishing., DOI: 10.1007/978-3-319-99127-6_54

Ananeva, D. (2019). *Artificial Intelligence as Disruptive Innovation in the Hotel Industry.* https://lauda.ulapland.fi/handle/10024/63932

Arango, L., Singaraju, S. P., & Niininen, O. (2023). Consumer Responses to AI-Generated Charitable Giving Ads. *Journal of Advertising, 52*(4), 486–503. DOI: 10.1080/00913367.2023.2183285

Babatunde, S. O., Odejide, O. A., Edunjobi, T. E., & Ogundipe, D. O. (2024). The Role of AI in Marketing Personalization: A Theoretical Exploration of Consumer Engagement Strategies. *International Journal of Management & Entrepreneurship Research, 6*(3), 936–949. DOI: 10.51594/ijmer.v6i3.964

Bacuy-Ortiz, K. X., & Soriano-Torres, L. E. (2025). Bibliometric analysis of the role of artificial intelligence in tourism destination management. *Journal of Asian Scientific Research, 15*(3), 340–354. DOI: 10.55493/5003.v15i3.5548

Bag, S., Srivastava, G., Bashir, M. M. A., Kumari, S., Giannakis, M., & Chowdhury, A. H. (2022). Journey of customers in this digital era: Understanding the role of artificial intelligence technologies in user engagement and conversion. *Benchmarking, 29*(7), 2074–2098. DOI: 10.1108/BIJ-07-2021-0415

Bleier, A., Goldfarb, A., & Tucker, C. E. (2020). Consumer Privacy and the Future of Data-Based Innovation and Marketing. SSRN *Electronic Journal.* https://doi.org/ DOI: 10.2139/ssrn.3570156

Buhalis, D. (2000). Marketing the competitive destination of the future. *Tourism Management, 21*(1), 97–116. DOI: 10.1016/S0261-5177(99)00095-3

Buhalis, D., & Law, R. (2008). Progress in information technology and tourism management: 20 years on and 10 years after the Internet—The state of eTourism research. *Tourism Management, 29*(4), 609–623. DOI: 10.1016/j.tourman.2008.01.005

Bukar, U. A., Sayeed, M. S., Razak, S. F. A., Yogarayan, S., Amodu, O. A., & Mahmood, R. A. R. (2023). A method for analyzing text using VOSviewer. *MethodsX, 11*, 102339. DOI: 10.1016/j.mex.2023.102339 PMID: 37693657

Bulchand-Gidumal, J., William Secin, E., O'Connor, P., & Buhalis, D. (2024). Artificial intelligence's impact on hospitality and tourism marketing: Exploring key themes and addressing challenges. *Current Issues in Tourism, 27*(14), 2345–2362. DOI: 10.1080/13683500.2023.2229480

Cabrera-Sánchez, J.-P., Villarejo-Ramos, Á. F., Liébana-Cabanillas, F., & Shaikh, A. A. (2021). Identifying relevant segments of AI applications adopters – Expanding the UTAUT2's variables. *Telematics and Informatics, 58*, 101529. DOI: 10.1016/j.tele.2020.101529

Calvano, E., Calzolari, G., Denicolò, V., Harrington, J. E., & Pastorello, S. (2020). Protecting consumers from collusive prices due to AI. *Science*, *370*(6520), 1040–1042. DOI: 10.1126/science.abe3796 PMID: 33243879

Campbell, C., Sands, S., Ferraro, C., & Tsao, H.-Y. (Jody), & Mavrommatis, A. (2020). From data to action: How marketers can leverage AI. *Business Horizons*, *63*(2), 227–243. DOI: 10.1016/j.bushor.2019.12.002

Chacko, H. E. (1996). Positioning a tourism destination to gain a competitive edge. *Asia Pacific Journal of Tourism Research*, *1*(2), 69–75. DOI: 10.1080/10941669708721976

Chandra, S., Verma, S., Lim, W. M., Kumar, S., & Donthu, N. (2022). Personalization in personalized marketing: Trends and ways forward. *Psychology and Marketing*, *39*(8), 1529–1562. DOI: 10.1002/mar.21670

Cheng, Y., & Jiang, H. (2022). Customer–brand relationship in the era of artificial intelligence: Understanding the role of chatbot marketing efforts. *Journal of Product and Brand Management*, *31*(2), 252–264. DOI: 10.1108/JPBM-05-2020-2907

Chintalapati, S., & Pandey, S. K. (2022). Artificial intelligence in marketing: A systematic literature review. *International Journal of Market Research*, *64*(1), 38–68. DOI: 10.1177/14707853211018428

Cimbaljević, M., Stankov, U., & Pavluković, V. (2019). Going beyond the traditional destination competitiveness – reflections on a smart destination in the current research. *Current Issues in Tourism*, *22*(20), 2472–2477. DOI: 10.1080/13683500.2018.1529149

Dahake, P. S., Bagaregari, P., & Dahake, N. S. (2024). Shaping the Future of Retail: A Comprehensive Review of Predictive Analytics Models for Consumer Behavior. In Inder, S., Min, B., & Sharma, S. (Eds.), (pp. 143–160). Advances in Business Strategy and Competitive Advantage. IGI Global., DOI: 10.4018/979-8-3693-1734-1.ch011

Dahake, P. S., Chandak, S., Mohare, R. V., Wadhwani, K., & Bhadade, P. (2023). The Crystal Ball of Marketing: How Predictive Analytics is Reshaping the Industry? *2023 Second International Conference On Smart Technologies For Smart Nation (SmartTechCon)*, 304–311. https://doi.org/DOI: 10.1109/SmartTechCon57526.2023.10391334

Dahake, P. S., Parchake, S., Somani, N., & Ingale, A. R. (2024). Predictive Analytics in Automotive Consumer Behaviour: An Insight into Personal use 4-Wheeler Purchase Decisions. *2024 2nd International Conference on Advances in Computation, Communication and Information Technology (ICAICCIT)*, 1143–1149. https://doi.org/DOI: 10.1109/ICAICCIT64383.2024.10912242

Davenport, T., Guha, A., Grewal, D., & Bressgott, T. (2020). How artificial intelligence will change the future of marketing. *Journal of the Academy of Marketing Science*, *48*(1), 24–42. DOI: 10.1007/s11747-019-00696-0

Du, S., & Xie, C. (2021). Paradoxes of artificial intelligence in consumer markets: Ethical challenges and opportunities. *Journal of Business Research*, *129*, 961–974. DOI: 10.1016/j.jbusres.2020.08.024

Florido-Benítez, L., & Coca-Stefaniak, J. A. (2025). Towards a new generation of smart tourism cities–GenAI-enabled aerotainment. *Cities (London, England)*, *167*, 106311. DOI: 10.1016/j.cities.2025.106311

Gao, L., Li, G., Tsai, F., Gao, C., Zhu, M., & Qu, X. (2023). The impact of artificial intelligence stimuli on customer engagement and value co-creation: The moderating role of customer ability readiness. *Journal of Research in Interactive Marketing*, *17*(2), 317–333. DOI: 10.1108/JRIM-10-2021-0260

Gao, Y., & Liu, H. (2023). Artificial intelligence-enabled personalization in interactive marketing: A customer journey perspective. *Journal of Research in Interactive Marketing*, *17*(5), 663–680. DOI: 10.1108/JRIM-01-2022-0023

Garvey, A. M., Kim, T., & Duhachek, A. (2023). Bad News? Send an AI. Good News? Send a Human. *Journal of Marketing*, *87*(1), 10–25. DOI: 10.1177/00222429211066972

Geisler, R. (2018). *Artificial Intelligence in the Travel & Tourism industry*. chrome-extension://efaidnbmnnnibpcajpcglclefindmkaj/https://run.unl.pt/bitstream/10362/39709/1/Geisler_2018.pdf

Hermann, E. (2022a). Anthropomorphized artificial intelligence, attachment, and consumer behavior. *Marketing Letters*, *33*(1), 157–162. DOI: 10.1007/s11002-021-09587-3

Hermann, E. (2022b). Leveraging Artificial Intelligence in Marketing for Social Good—An Ethical Perspective. *Journal of Business Ethics*, *179*(1), 43–61. DOI: 10.1007/s10551-021-04843-y PMID: 34054170

Hollebeek, L. D., & Macky, K. (2019). Digital Content Marketing's Role in Fostering Consumer Engagement, Trust, and Value: Framework, Fundamental Propositions, and Implications. *Journal of Interactive Marketing*, *45*(1), 27–41. DOI: 10.1016/j.intmar.2018.07.003

Hollebeek, L. D., Menidjel, C., Sarstedt, M., Jansson, J., & Urbonavicius, S. (2024). Engaging consumers through artificially intelligent technologies: Systematic review, conceptual model, and further research. *Psychology and Marketing*, *41*(4), 880–898. DOI: 10.1002/mar.21957

Hollebeek, L. D., Sprott, D. E., Andreassen, T. W., Costley, C., Klaus, P., Kuppelwieser, V., Karahasanovic, A., Taguchi, T., Ul Islam, J., & Rather, R. A. (2019). Customer engagement in evolving technological environments: Synopsis and guiding propositions. *European Journal of Marketing*, *53*(9), 2018–2023. DOI: 10.1108/EJM-09-2019-970

Hoyer, W. D., Kroschke, M., Schmitt, B., Kraume, K., & Shankar, V. (2020). Transforming the Customer Experience through New Technologies. *Journal of Interactive Marketing*, *51*(1), 57–71. DOI: 10.1016/j.intmar.2020.04.001

Huang, M.-H., & Rust, R. T. (2021a). A strategic framework for artificial intelligence in marketing. *Journal of the Academy of Marketing Science*, *49*(1), 30–50. DOI: 10.1007/s11747-020-00749-9

Huang, M.-H., & Rust, R. T. (2021b). Engaged to a Robot? The Role of AI in Service. *Journal of Service Research*, *24*(1), 30–41. DOI: 10.1177/1094670520902266

Hussain, W., Mabrok, M., Gao, H., Rabhi, F. A., & Rashed, E. A. (2024). Revolutionising healthcare with artificial intelligence: A bibliometric analysis of 40 years of progress in health systems. *Digital Health*, *10*, 20552076241258757. DOI: 10.1177/20552076241258757 PMID: 38817839

Keegan, B. J., Dennehy, D., & Naudé, P. (2024). Implementing Artificial Intelligence in Traditional B2B Marketing Practices: An Activity Theory Perspective. *Information Systems Frontiers*, *26*(3), 1025–1039. DOI: 10.1007/s10796-022-10294-1 PMID: 35637917

Khrais, L. T. (2020). Role of Artificial Intelligence in Shaping Consumer Demand in E-Commerce. *Future Internet*, *12*(12), 226. DOI: 10.3390/fi12120226

Kim, T. W., Jiang, L., Duhachek, A., Lee, H., & Garvey, A. (2022). Do You Mind if I Ask You a Personal Question? How AI Service Agents Alter Consumer Self-Disclosure. *Journal of Service Research*, *25*(4), 649–666. DOI: 10.1177/10946705221120232

Kim, W. B., & Hur, H. J. (2024). What Makes People Feel Empathy for AI Chatbots? Assessing the Role of Competence and Warmth. *International Journal of Human-Computer Interaction*, *40*(17), 4674–4687. DOI: 10.1080/10447318.2023.2219961

Klaus, P., & Zaichkowsky, J. (2020). AI voice bots: A services marketing research agenda. *Journal of Services Marketing, 34*(3), 389–398. DOI: 10.1108/JSM-01-2019-0043

Kopalle, P. K., Gangwar, M., Kaplan, A., Ramachandran, D., Reinartz, W., & Rindfleisch, A. (2022). Examining artificial intelligence (AI) technologies in marketing via a global lens: Current trends and future research opportunities. *International Journal of Research in Marketing, 39*(2), 522–540. DOI: 10.1016/j.ijresmar.2021.11.002

Kumar, D., Shandilya, A. K., & Choudhuri, S. (2023). Artificial Intelligence-Enabled Bibliometric Analysis in Tourism and Hospitality Using Biblioshiny and VOSviewer Software. In A. Khang, V. Abdullayev, B. Jadhav, S. Gupta, & G. Morris, *AI-Centric Modeling and Analytics* (1st ed., pp. 260–291). CRC Press. https://doi.org/DOI: 10.1201/9781003400110-15

Kumar, V., Ashraf, A. R., & Nadeem, W. (2024). AI-powered marketing: What, where, and how? *International Journal of Information Management, 77*, 102783. DOI: 10.1016/j.ijinfomgt.2024.102783

Kumar, V., Rajan, B., Venkatesan, R., & Lecinski, J. (2019). Understanding the Role of Artificial Intelligence in Personalized Engagement Marketing. *California Management Review, 61*(4), 135–155. DOI: 10.1177/0008125619859317

Lee, C. T., Pan, L.-Y., & Hsieh, S. H. (2022). Artificial intelligent chatbots as brand promoters: A two-stage structural equation modeling-artificial neural network approach. *Internet Research, 32*(4), 1329–1356. DOI: 10.1108/INTR-01-2021-0030

Lim, J. S., & Zhang, J. (2022). Adoption of AI-driven personalization in digital news platforms: An integrative model of technology acceptance and perceived contingency. *Technology in Society, 69*, 101965. DOI: 10.1016/j.techsoc.2022.101965

Liu-Thompkins, Y., Okazaki, S., & Li, H. (2022). Artificial empathy in marketing interactions: Bridging the human-AI gap in affective and social customer experience. *Journal of the Academy of Marketing Science, 50*(6), 1198–1218. DOI: 10.1007/s11747-022-00892-5

López-Naranjo, A. L., Puente-Riofrio, M. I., Carrasco-Salazar, V. A., Erazo-Rodríguez, J. D., & Buñay-Guisñan, P. A. (2025). Artificial intelligence in the tourism business: A systematic review. *Frontiers in Artificial Intelligence, 8*, 1599391. DOI: 10.3389/frai.2025.1599391 PMID: 40785835

Ma, L., & Sun, B. (2020). Machine learning and AI in marketing – Connecting computing power to human insights. *International Journal of Research in Marketing, 37*(3), 481–504. DOI: 10.1016/j.ijresmar.2020.04.005

Manser Payne, E. H., Dahl, A. J., & Peltier, J. (2021). Digital servitization value co-creation framework for AI services: A research agenda for digital transformation in financial service ecosystems. *Journal of Research in Interactive Marketing, 15*(2), 200–222. DOI: 10.1108/JRIM-12-2020-0252

Mariani, M. (2020). Big Data and analytics in tourism and hospitality: A perspective article. *Tourism Review, 75*(1), 299–303. DOI: 10.1108/TR-06-2019-0259

Mariani, M. M., Perez-Vega, R., & Wirtz, J. (2022). AI in marketing, consumer research and psychology: A systematic literature review and research agenda. *Psychology and Marketing, 39*(4), 755–776. DOI: 10.1002/mar.21619

Martin, B. A. S., Jin, H. S., Wang, D., Nguyen, H., Zhan, K., & Wang, Y. X. (2020). The influence of consumer anthropomorphism on attitudes towards artificial intelligence trip advisors. *Journal of Hospitality and Tourism Management, 44*, 108–111. DOI: 10.1016/j.jhtm.2020.06.004

McLean, G., Osei-Frimpong, K., & Barhorst, J. (2021). Alexa, do voice assistants influence consumer brand engagement? – Examining the role of AI powered voice assistants in influencing consumer brand engagement. *Journal of Business Research, 124*, 312–328. DOI: 10.1016/j.jbusres.2020.11.045

Minh Sang, N. (2024). Bibliometric insights into the evolution of digital marketing trends. *Innovative Marketing, 20*(2), 1–14. DOI: 10.21511/im.20(2).2024.01

Mogaji, E., Soetan, T. O., & Kieu, T. A. (2021). The implications of artificial intelligence on the digital marketing of financial services to vulnerable customers. *Australasian Marketing Journal, 29*(3), 235–242. DOI: 10.1016/j.ausmj.2020.05.003

Moriuchi, E., Landers, V. M., Colton, D., & Hair, N. (2021). Engagement with chatbots versus augmented reality interactive technology in e-commerce. *Journal of Strategic Marketing, 29*(5), 375–389. DOI: 10.1080/0965254X.2020.1740766

Mustak, M., Salminen, J., Plé, L., & Wirtz, J. (2021). Artificial intelligence in marketing: Topic modeling, scientometric analysis, and research agenda. *Journal of Business Research, 124*, 389–404. DOI: 10.1016/j.jbusres.2020.10.044

Nair, K., & Gupta, R. (2021). Application of AI technology in modern digital marketing environment. *World Journal of Entrepreneurship, Management and Sustainable Development, ahead-of-print*(ahead-of-print). https://doi.org/DOI: 10.1108/WJEMSD-08-2020-0099

Nazir, S., Khadim, S., Ali Asadullah, M., & Syed, N. (2023). Exploring the influence of artificial intelligence technology on consumer repurchase intention: The mediation and moderation approach. *Technology in Society*, *72*, 102190. DOI: 10.1016/j.techsoc.2022.102190

OECD. (2024). *Artificial Intelligence and tourism: G7/OECD policy paper*. OECD Tourism Papers. [OECD Tourism Papers], DOI: 10.1787/3f9a4d8d-

Okeleke, P.A., Ajiga, D., Folorunsho, S.O., & Ezeigweneme, C. (2024). Predictive analytics for market trends using AI: A study in consumer behavior. *International Journal of Engineering Research Updates, 7*(1), 036–049. https://doi.org/DOI: 10.53430/ijeru.2024.7.1.0032

Orden-Mejía, M., Carvache-Franco, M., Huertas, A., Carvache-Franco, O., & Carvache-Franco, W. (2023). Modeling users' satisfaction and visit intention using AI-based chatbots. *PLoS One*, *18*(9), e0286427. DOI: 10.1371/journal.pone.0286427 PMID: 37682931

Paschen, J., Kietzmann, J., & Kietzmann, T. C. (2019). Artificial intelligence (AI) and its implications for market knowledge in B2B marketing. *Journal of Business and Industrial Marketing*, *34*(7), 1410–1419. DOI: 10.1108/JBIM-10-2018-0295

Patra, A. K., Praharaj, A., Sudarshan, D., & Chhatoi, B. P. (2024). AI and business management: Tracking future research agenda through bibliometric network analysis. *Heliyon*, *10*(1), e23902. DOI: 10.1016/j.heliyon.2023.e23902 PMID: 38230239

Pendyala, M. K., & Lakkamraju, V. V. (2024). Impact of Artificial Intelligence in Customer Journey. *International Journal of Innovative Science and Research Technology (IJISRT)*, 1528–1534. https://doi.org/DOI: 10.38124/ijisrt/IJISRT24AUG807

Pike, S., & Page, S. J. (2014). Destination Marketing Organizations and destination marketing: A narrative analysis of the literature. *Tourism Management*, *41*, 202–227. DOI: 10.1016/j.tourman.2013.09.009

Pillai, R., Sivathanu, B., & Dwivedi, Y. K. (2020). Shopping intention at AI-powered automated retail stores (AIPARS). *Journal of Retailing and Consumer Services*, *57*, 102207. DOI: 10.1016/j.jretconser.2020.102207

Prentice, C., Weaven, S., & Wong, I. A. (2020). Linking AI quality performance and customer engagement: The moderating effect of AI preference. *International Journal of Hospitality Management*, *90*, 102629. DOI: 10.1016/j.ijhm.2020.102629

Puntoni, S., Reczek, R. W., Giesler, M., & Botti, S. (2021). Consumers and Artificial Intelligence: An Experiential Perspective. *Journal of Marketing*, *85*(1), 131–151. DOI: 10.1177/0022242920953847

Rahman, M. S., Bag, S., Hossain, M. A., Abdel Fattah, F. A. M., Gani, M. O., & Rana, N. P. (2023). The new wave of AI-powered luxury brands online shopping experience: The role of digital multisensory cues and customers' engagement. *Journal of Retailing and Consumer Services*, *72*, 103273. DOI: 10.1016/j.jretconser.2023.103273

Rane, N. (2023). Enhancing Customer Loyalty through Artificial Intelligence (AI), Internet of Things (IoT), and Big Data Technologies: Improving Customer Satisfaction, Engagement, Relationship, and Experience. SSRN *Electronic Journal*. https://doi.org/DOI: 10.2139/ssrn.4616051

Rather, R. A. (2020). Customer experience and engagement in tourism destinations: The experiential marketing perspective. *Journal of Travel & Tourism Marketing*, *37*(1), 15–32. DOI: 10.1080/10548408.2019.1686101

Rosário, A., & Raimundo, R. (2021). Consumer Marketing Strategy and E-Commerce in the Last Decade: A Literature Review. *Journal of Theoretical and Applied Electronic Commerce Research*, *16*(7), 3003–3024. DOI: 10.3390/jtaer16070164

Sabharwal, R., Miah, S. J., & Fosso Wamba, S. (2025). Extending artificial intelligence research in the clinical domain: A theoretical perspective. *Annals of Operations Research*, *348*(3), 1713–1744. DOI: 10.1007/s10479-022-05035-1 PMID: 36407943

Samala, N., Katkam, B. S., Bellamkonda, R. S., & Rodriguez, R. V. (2022). Impact of AI and robotics in the tourism sector: A critical insight. *Journal of Tourism Futures*, *8*(1), 73–87. DOI: 10.1108/JTF-07-2019-0065

Sands, S., Campbell, C. L., Plangger, K., & Ferraro, C. (2022). Unreal influence: Leveraging AI in influencer marketing. *European Journal of Marketing*, *56*(6), 1721–1747. DOI: 10.1108/EJM-12-2019-0949

Saura, J. R., Ribeiro-Soriano, D., & Palacios-Marqués, D. (2021). Setting B2B digital marketing in artificial intelligence-based CRMs: A review and directions for future research. *Industrial Marketing Management*, *98*, 161–178. DOI: 10.1016/j.indmarman.2021.08.006

Schamari, J., & Schaefers, T. (2015). Leaving the Home Turf: How Brands Can Use Webcare on Consumer-generated Platforms to Increase Positive Consumer Engagement. *Journal of Interactive Marketing*, *30*(1), 20–33. DOI: 10.1016/j.intmar.2014.12.001

Schweidel, D. A., Bart, Y., Inman, J. J., Stephen, A. T., Libai, B., Andrews, M., Rosario, A. B., Chae, I., Chen, Z., Kupor, D., Longoni, C., & Thomaz, F. (2022). How consumer digital signals are reshaping the customer journey. *Journal of the Academy of Marketing Science, 50*(6), 1257–1276. DOI: 10.1007/s11747-022-00839-w PMID: 35221393

Selvakumar, P., Shanthi, M., Pitchiah, R., Sharma, M., Dahake, P. S., & T. C., M. (2025). The Role of Artificial Intelligence in Business Model Innovation: Overview of AI Technologies. In M. Khokhar (Ed.), *Advances in Business Strategy and Competitive Advantage* (pp. 219–246). IGI Global. https://doi.org/DOI: 10.4018/979-8-3693-9571-4.ch009

Sidlauskiene, J., Joye, Y., & Auruskeviciene, V. (2023). AI-based chatbots in conversational commerce and their effects on product and price perceptions. *Electronic Markets, 33*(1), 24. DOI: 10.1007/s12525-023-00633-8 PMID: 37252674

Tong, S., Luo, X., & Xu, B. (2020). Personalized mobile marketing strategies. *Journal of the Academy of Marketing Science, 48*(1), 64–78. DOI: 10.1007/s11747-019-00693-3

Usman, F. O., Eyo-Udo, N. L., Etukudoh, E. A., Odonkor, B., Ibeh, C. V., & Adegbola, A. (2024). A CRITICAL REVIEW OF AI-DRIVEN STRATEGIES FOR ENTREPRENEURIAL SUCCESS. *International Journal of Management & Entrepreneurship Research, 6*(1), 200–215. DOI: 10.51594/ijmer.v6i1.748

Van Esch, P., & Stewart Black, J. (2021). Artificial Intelligence (AI): Revolutionizing Digital Marketing. *Australasian Marketing Journal, 29*(3), 199–203. DOI: 10.1177/18393349211037684

Yang, X., Li, H., Ni, L., & Li, T. (2021). Application of Artificial Intelligence in Precision Marketing. *Journal of Organizational and End User Computing, 33*(4), 209–219. DOI: 10.4018/JOEUC.20210701.oa10

Yin, J., & Qiu, X. (2021). AI Technology and Online Purchase Intention: Structural Equation Model Based on Perceived Value. *Sustainability, 13*(10), 5671. DOI: 10.3390/su13105671

Ziakis, C., & Vlachopoulou, M. (2023). Artificial Intelligence in Digital Marketing: Insights from a Comprehensive Review. *Information (Basel), 14*(12), 664. DOI: 10.3390/info14120664

KEY TERMS AND DEFINITIONS

Consumer Engagement: Refers to the depth and quality of interaction between a brand and its customers across various touchpoints. It's not just about grabbing attention—it's about cultivating a meaningful relationship that encourages loyalty, trust, and active participation.

Digital Marketing: Strategic use of digital channels and technologies to promote products, services, or ideas and connect with audiences online. It's the evolution of traditional marketing into the digital age—where attention, engagement, and conversion happen across screens and platforms.

Smart Tourism: Integration of advanced technologies and data-driven strategies to enhance tourism experience, improve destination management, and promote sustainability. It's where digital innovation meets cultural exploration, transforming how people travel, interact, and engage with places.

Chapter 9
Competitor Orientation Effect on Augmenting Ethiopian SME Internal Technological Processes Through Customer Insight

Gada Gizachew Wakjira
http://orcid.org/0000-0002-7725-1161
Bule Hora University, Ethiopia

Shashi Kant
http://orcid.org/0000-0003-4722-5736
Lovely Professional University, India

ABSTRACT

The purpose of this paper is to investigate how innovation future prospects pertaining to internal Artificial Intelligence sub structured technical capabilities in SMEs located in Ethiopia are influenced by orientation of competitor and insight of a customer. The outcomes manifest a modest positive association among innovation future prospects pertaining to internal Artificial Intelligence sub structured technical capabilities and orientation of competitor, with insight of a customer acting as a partial mediating factor. This manifests that corporates that actively monitor competitors and engage with customers are better positioned to innovate and augment their Artificial Intelligence sub structured technical capabilities. The implications of these outcomes manifest the necessity for SMEs to assimilate together

DOI: 10.4018/979-8-2600-0439-5.ch009

competitor and customer analyses into their strategic frameworks. By fostering a proactive approach to get know market dynamics and customer wants, corporates can enhance their Artificial Intelligence sub structured technical capabilities innovation future prospects.

INTRODUCTION

SMEs in Ethiopia have a substantial real-life barrier in this era of fast-growing Artificial Intelligence sub structured technical capabilities advancement and world market wide assimilating innovation future prospects pertaining to internal Artificial Intelligence sub structured technical capabilities that align with insight of a customer's (Perdana and Prasasti 2023). The challenges international market implication is manifested by the critical function SMEs play in economic growth, job creation, and innovation (Kamandi et al., 2021). To get know the wants and preferences of customers have become crucial for corporates international market, since it directly influences a corporates strategic advantages and sustainability (Hidayat and Idrus, 2023). In techno-innovative economies identical Ethiopia, where SMEs account for a substantial share of the international market, augmenting consumer insights to enhance technology innovation future prospects may lead to notable augmentations in productivity and market responsiveness (Panarina, 2023). Micro, small, and medium-sized enterprises are very vital for Ethiopia's economy as they provide much of the jobs and GDP. Recent studies show that SMEs make over "80%" of the Sum employment in the nation and provide about "30%" of the national GDP (Wakjira et al. 2023). The information might change, nevertheless, for certain percentages connected to the foreign market share; hence, it would be advisable to check the most recent economic reports or figures from trustworthy source (Almujaini et al. 2021).

The notion of orientation of competitor, which stresses comprehending together clients and rivals to advice strategic choices, has its roots in the literature on marketing and strategic management (Panarina, 2023). Early investigation made clear how indispensable it is for corporates to adjust to changing market conditions by examining competition behavior in addition to reaching client wants (Wakjira et al. 2023). Conferring to empirical investigation, corporates that have a modest mindset for competition are better able to innovate and acculturate to changes in the market. On the other hand, only a few investigation has been conducted on how SMEs in Ethiopia might use consumer insights to augment their technology innovation future prospects (Celikyay et al.2023).

SMEs located in Ethiopia face several real-world obstacles and a shortage of qualified workers (Yuliati, Ramadhani, and Wahyuni 2022). These real life barriers make it more difficult for SMEs to sustainable gather and underline consumer data.

Also, incorporating customer feedback into technology augments is made more difficult by cultural considerations and market instability. At present investigation often overlooks these specific real life barriers, innovating a gap in to get know how SMEs can navigate these barriers to enhance their day to day activities (Celikyay et al. 2023).

Medium-sized enterprises, or SMEs, are vital to the economy of Ethiopia as they provide about 80% of all jobs—about 11 million. With the industry worth around $15 billion, these businesses account for nearly 30% of the national GDP (Hidayat and Idrus, 2023). Roughly $1 billion a year, SMEs make up around 10-15% of overall exports. Sectorial breakdown reveals that although manufacturing accounts for roughly 25%, commerce and services contribute the remainder of 35%. Agriculture utilizes the up over 40% of SME activity (Wakjira et al. 2023). The small and medium-sized enterprises industry has been expanding at an annual pace of 10-15% during the last five years. To improve SME capability and competitiveness, the Ethiopian government has created the Micro and Small Enterprises Development Strategy, therefore motivating financial institutions to set aside 30% of their portfolios for these companies (Poerwanto 2022). Though 15% of SMEs have access to formal credit, regulatory restrictions and market access concerns continue to be problems even with this expansion. Reports from the Ethiopian Central Statistical Agency and institutions like the World Bank are vital tools for thorough and current knowledge (Panarina, 2023). By providing a comprehensive framework that manifests doable tactics for SMEs located in Ethiopia to use consumer insights to enhance their technology innovation future prospects. Chapter is emphasizing practical lessons for academics and officials by incubating case studies, empirical data, and at present literature. The outcomes will not only advice future investigations into the intersection of technology and insight of a customers but will also inform policy decisions that foster a supportive market place for SMEs in Ethiopia (Almujaini et al. 2021).

"How can SMEs located in Ethiopia influence utilize insight of a customers to enhance their innovation future prospects pertaining to internal Artificial Intelligence sub structured technical capabilities in a competitive landscape?" is the main challenge that inspires this investigation. It is imperative that this challenge be answered because it will make available insight into the ways in which SMEs may overcome present obstacles, adjust to market wants, and eventually support Ethiopia's sustained economic progress. The outcomes of this investigation will serve as a advice for future investigation and policy incubation, guaranteeing that the opinions of SMEs and their clients are included in the conversation about incubation.

BACKGROUND

The integration of insight of customers into the Artificial Intelligence sub structured technical capabilities innovation future prospects of SMEs is a pivotal strategy for enhancing strategic advantages, competitor specifically in techno-innovative economies identical to Ethiopia (Perdana and Prasasti 2023). The background of this investigation is rooted in the recognition that SMEs face unique real life barriers that hinder their ability to influence utilize customer feedback and data (Wakjira et al. 2023). Despite their potential for growth and innovation, many SMEs located in Ethiopia struggle with inadequate Artificial Intelligence sub structured technical capabilities infrastructure, limited access to industry wide unique capitals, and a lack of skilled personnel (Hidayat and Idrus, 2023). These barriers impede their dynamic abilities to gather, analyze, and act upon insight of customers, which are crucial for driving product incubation and improving service delivery (Poerwanto 2022). (Figure 1).

The real life barriers can be seen in the Ethiopian textile and garment industry (Poerwanto 2022). Many SMEs in this sector have attempted to implement customer-oriented practices to enhance product quality and design. Also, they often lack the necessary Artificial Intelligence sub structured technical capabilities tools to conduct market investigation or gather customer feedback influence (Poerwanto 2022). In addition to impeding the corporates expansion, this mismatch made it more difficult for it to compete with bigger companies that could use data analytics and cutting-edge technologies. Another case can be found in the food processing sector, where SMEs frequently face real life barriers in to get know consumer preferences and behaviors (Almujaini et al. 2021). A tiny rural bakery tried to launch new goods sub structured on consumer feedback, but it was challenging to gather and underline this data in a methodical way (Torino 2021). Due to the lack of formal feedback channels identical surveys or customer interviews, the corporate was forced to rely on circumstantial information, which outcomes in misaligned product offers that fell short of consumer demand (Panarina, 2023). This circumstance manifests the necessity of a more methodical approach to acquiring and applying consumer insights, which are frequently disregarded because of the day to day activities limitations that SMEs (Almujaini et al. 2021).

Also, Ethiopia's cultural background poses other difficulties. Since they prioritize their operating approaches over customer feedback, SMEs frequently lack a belief of customer involvement (Poerwanto 2022). This kind of thinking can hinder innovation and make it harder for SMEs to react to shifts in the market (Perdana and Prasasti 2023). A tiny electronics store, for instance, was unable to compete with larger merchants that often modified their inventory sub structured on client preferences because it did not aggressively solicit customer feedback on its product offers (Panarina, 2023). Sales and customer loyalty potential were lost as an outcome of a lack of a proactive approach to consumer insights (Celikyay et al. 2023). In light of these a case studies, it is clear that while the conception of assimilating insight of customers into Artificial Intelligence sub structured technical capabilities innovation future prospects holds substantial promise for enhancing the strategic advantages of SMEs located in Ethiopia, practical real life barriers must be addressed (Poerwanto 2022). This investigation aims to explore these real life barriers in depth and make available actionable strategies for SMEs to overcome them, ensuring they can influence leverage insight of a customers to drive Artificial Intelligence sub structured technical capabilities innovation and augment In general performance. By examining these barriers, the investigation will add to a deeper to get know of the dynamics at play in the Ethiopian SME landscape and offer a pathway toward more sustainable business practices (Atmaji and Qodir 2021).

Figure 1. Conceptual framework

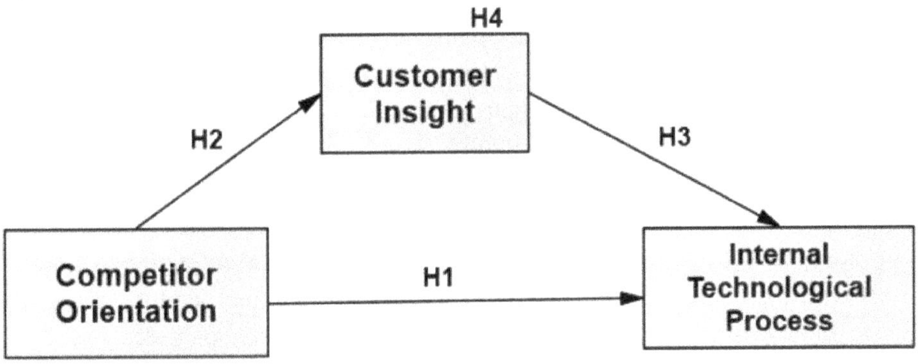

Source. Authors

Statement of Problem

In order to augment innovation, boost strategic advantages, and guarantee economic sustainability, SMEs located in Ethiopia must incorporate consumer insights into their technical day to day activities (Varpio and Macleod 2020). The situation of SMEs today, also, manifests a stark contrast among the mantel imaged situation, in which companies successfully use consumer feedback to propel technical innovation, and the real difficulties they have in real life (Perdana and Prasasti 2023). The mantel imaged state envisions SMEs that proactively seek insight of customers, utilize advanced technologies to analyze data, and acculturate their products and services Conferring. Also, the reality is marked by numerous obstacles that hinder this progression (Cash et al. 2022). The investigation at presently in publication offers conflicting information about the advantages of mindset for competition and insight of a customer use in SMEs worldwide (Poerwanto 2022), but it does not offer definitive outcomes that are competitor specifically relevant to the Ethiopian setting (Perdana and Prasasti 2023). Numerous studies emphasize the benefits of customer-centric strategies, but they frequently ignore the industry wide unique socioeconomic and cultural elements that influence the day to day activities of SMEs located in Ethiopia (Hidayat and Idrus, 2023). As a outcome, although the advantages of incorporating consumer insights are acknowledged, there is a knowledge vacuum about how these mantel images might be manifested successfully in Ethiopia due to the absence of actual data that is specific to the country (Celikyay et al. 2023).

Also, inconclusive outcomes from previous investigation manifest the complexities involved in applying international market best practices in a techno-innovative background (Wakjira et al. 2023). For instance, while some SMEs may report augmented performance after adopting insight of customer strategies, others experience only a few to no change, leading to a lack of consensus on influence methodologies (Panarina, 2023). This inconsistency points to theoretical gaps, where existing frameworks do not adequately address the specific wants and conditions of SMEs located in Ethiopia, thus limiting their applicability and influence (Almujaini et al. 2021). Also, there are understanding void, in Ethiopia might use to gather and underline consumer insights (Wakjira et al., 2023). There is a confusion about how smaller corporates in Ethiopia might use comparable tactics because the majority of at present investigation centered on large corporations or emerging economies (Poerwanto 2022). Also, there are clear background gaps; the literature frequently fails to fully address the competitor specific difficulties encountered by SMEs located in Ethiopia, such as their low technology infrastructure, cultural views on customer involvement, and economic unpredictability (Panarina, 2023). These difficulties make available real-world barriers that SMEs must overcome in order to successfully adopt customer manifested IT approaches (Hidayat and Idrus, 2023).

By providing a comprehensive examination of the concerns and suggesting customized solutions, this investigation. The project will investigate how SMEs may sustainable gather and apply consumer insights within the limitations of their working market place using empirical investigation and case studies. This investigation will make available indispensable insights for future academics and policymakers by incubating theoretical frameworks with real-world applications (Mugogo 2020).

Resource Sub Structured View (RBV)

Conferring to the Industry wide unique capital-Sub structured View (RBV), a corporates industry wide unique capital materials and competencies make available it a competitive edge. This image manifests how internal industry wide unique capitals, assimilating corporately approaches, technology, and capital in form of human, shape a corporates dynamic abilities to reach market wants (Arslan, 2020). RBV manifests how utilizing consumer insights may augment corporates industry wide unique capitals, augmenting innovation and augmented day to day activities (Almujaini et al. 2021).

Dynamic Capabilities Theory

By put stress corporates dynamic abilities to assimilate, incubate, and understand dynamic fluctuating marketplaces, Dynamic Capabilities Theory substructures upon the RBV. This theory is especially applicable to SMEs in Ethiopia, where shifting consumer tastes and economic changes may cause market dynamics to change dynamic (Hidayat and Idrus 2023). SMEs may respond to consumer insights more dynamic by building dynamic capabilities, which will allow them to innovate and modify their IT approaches as necessary (Almujaini et al. 2021).

Market Orientation Theory

It manifests the prominence of to get know and responding to customer wants and preferences as a key driver of business success. For SMEs looking to augment their technology approaches by using consumer insights, this mantel image is very indispensable (Yuliati et al. 2022). By adopting a market-oriented approach, corporates can systematically gather and analyze customer wants and augmented product providing. In the Ethiopian background, where customer engagement may be limited, this theory manifests the necessity for SMEs to cultivate a belief of mindset of marketing that prioritizes customer feedback. It make available a framework for to get know how insight of a customers can inform Artificial Intelligence sub structured technical capabilities incubate and innovation (Almujaini et al. 2021).

Innovation Diffusion Theory

Innovation Diffusion Theory manifests how innovative technology and conceptions penetrates together inside and among corporates. To get know the difficulties SMEs located in Ethiopia encounter while implementing consumer insights to augment their technical approaches is made easier with the help of this theory (Perdana and Prasasti 2023). It analyzes elements such as perceived advantages, compatibility with at present approaches, and the social structure in which corporates function that influence the adoption of innovations. This hypothesis might assist explain why some corporates influence incorporate consumer insights while others have difficulty doing so in the background of SMEs located in Ethiopia (Arslan 2020).

Dynamic Capabilities Theory is the foundation paradigm for this chapter. This decision is sub structured to get know that SMEs located in Ethiopia function in a dynamic market place marked by shifting consumer demands and economic instability. A comprehensive foundation for comprehending how these corporates may sustainable gather and use client data to modify their Artificial Intelligence sub structured technical capabilities approaches is offered by dynamic capabilities (Celikyay et al. 2023). This mantel image fits in nicely with the goal of the investigation, which is to investigate workable ways for SMEs to augment their strategic advantages through customer-centric innovation, by put stress the dynamic abilities to assimilate and reconfigure industry wide unique capitals in response to market wants (Atmaji & Qodir 2021).

Definition of Concepts

SMEs

SMEs are explained as corporates in concepts of number of labors and invested capital (Panarina, 2023). The concept "SME" emerged in response to the need for tailored policies that can address the specific real life barriers faced by smaller corporates, competitor specifically in contrast to large corporations (Hidayat and Idrus 2023). The recognition of SMEs as vital components of the international market has been formalized in various frameworks and policies, manifesting their function in promoting entrepreneurship and economic diversification (Wakjira et al. 2023).

Customers Insight

Insight of customers, which are frequently manifests from data analytics and direct feedback, are the comprehension and interpretation of customer behaviors, preferences, and wants. This phrase refers to together qualitative and quantitative data, giving companies useful information to help them decide on marketing plans, service delivery, and product incubate (Almujaini et al. 2021). The mantel image's roots are in market investigation methods that first appeared in the early 1900s and changed as data gathering and processing methods augmented. The phrase "insight of a customer's" became widely manifested in marketing and strategic management discussions as companies realized how crucial it was to comprehend their clients in order to increase sales and loyalty. These days, one of the most indispensable factors influencing competitive advantage is the dynamic abilities to produce relevant consumer insights (Wakjira et al. 2023).

Technical Innovation Capabilities

The concept “Artificial Intelligence sub structured technical capabilities innovation future prospects” manifests the organized approaches and protocols manifested by corporates to use technology in the incubation, provision, and administration of goods and services. This word refers to a broad variety of Artificial Intelligence sub structured technical capabilities enabled day to day activities, assimilating manufacturing, distribution, and investigation & incubation (Wakjira 2023). The Industrial Revolution, which brought about a dramatic change in the way commodities were manufactured and services were make available, is credited with giving rise to technical innovation future prospects. The phrase has changed to encompass not just conventional manufacturing innovation future prospects but also digital ones identical data management, automation, and online service delivery as technology has become more and more interwoven into corporate day to day activities (Celikyay et al. 2023).

Competitor Orientation

A strategic strategy known as orientation of competitor manifests how crucial it is to comprehend the advantages, disadvantages, and tactics of rivals to advice a corporate strategic choices. With roots in the work of academics identical Porter, who manifested the need of competitive analysis in attaining corporate success, this mantel image has its roots in the fields of strategic management and marketing (Wasim et al. 2022). In order to help corporates adjust their strategy, orientation of competitor entails keeping a close eye on rivals' market positioning, consumer offers, and activities (Arslan 2020). As corporates encountered more competitive marketplaces, the prominence of orientation of competitor act as a component of corporate strategy (Almujaini et al. 2021).

Marketing Mindset

A business strategy known as “mindset of marketing” places a high priority on comprehending and catering to the requirements and preferences of customers in every facet of a corporate's day to day activities. Investigations identical Jaworski and Kohli helped to incubate the theoretical underpinnings of this mantel image, which gained popularity in the 1980s and 1990s. Obtaining market knowledge, sharing it within the corporate, and sustainable reacting to consumer insights are all part of mindset of marketing (Perdana and Prasasti 2023). The phrase manifests the implication of matching a corporate's capabilities with market demands by reflecting a move away from product-centric methods and toward customer-centric initiatives (Almujaini et al. 2021).

Competitor Orientation and Internal Technical Capabilities Process

Orientation of competitor Influence on Innovation future prospects pertaining to internal Artificial Intelligence sub structured technical capabilities Corporates' internal technical innovation future prospects are greatly influenced by orientation of competitor, especially when it comes to small and medium-sized corporates SMEs (Hidayat and Idrus 2023). By manifesting the implication of comprehending rivals' advantages, disadvantages, and tactics, orientation of competitor helps corporates better match their Artificial Intelligence sub structured technical capabilities with market demands (Perdana and Prasasti, 2023). This alignment is vital for SMEs operating in competitive market places, where the ability to innovate and acculturate dynamic can conceptive business success (Poerwanto 2022). Through orientation of competitor, corporates can identify emerging trends and technologies adopted by rivals, allowing them to enhance their own Artificial Intelligence sub structured technical capabilities innovation future prospects in response (Mugogo 2020). The need for innovation is one of the main consequences of orientation of competitor on internal technical innovation future prospects. SMEs are more aware of the technical innovations that rivals are using to enhance their products when they keep an eye on and investigation their rivals (Wasim et al. 2022). This awareness often fosters a belief of innovation within the corporate, as employees are encouraged to explore new mantel images and technologies that can enhance productivity and efficiency. For instance, a textile SME in Ethiopia that observes competitors utilizing advanced data analytics for inventory management may be inspired to adopt similar technologies (Poerwanto 2022). Such adoption can lead to streamlined day to day activities, reduced costs, and augmented customer satisfaction, ultimately enhancing the corporate's competitive position (Celikyay et al. 2023).

Also, orientation of competitor can enhance the influence of technology adoption by providing SMEs with a clearer to get know of how new technologies can be utilized. By investigation competitors, corporates can gain insights into best practices for implementing Artificial Intelligence sub structured technical capabilities changes (Wakjira et al. 2023). This knowledge can reduce the risks associated with technology adoption, as SMEs can learn from the successes and failures of their competitors (Hidayat and Idrus, 2023). For a case study, a small electronics manufacturer may analyze how a rival successfully assimilated automation into its production innovation future prospects. By to get know the real life barriers faced and the strategies employed by the competitor, the SME can devise a more informed approach to its own Artificial Intelligence sub structured technical capabilities upgrades, thereby minimizing disruption and maximizing benefits (Almujaini et al. 2021). Also, orientation of competitor augmenting internal cooperation, innovating cross-functional teams that are better equipped to handle technology challenges from a wider perspective. An corporate's marketing, R&D, and day to day activities divisions are encouraged to share information when it is competitor-oriented (Yuliati et al. 2022). This collaboration can lead to a more assimilated approach to technology incubation and implementation (Poerwanto 2022). For instance, marketing teams can make available valuable insight of customers that inform R&D about desired features and functionalities, while day to day activities can offer feedback on the practical implications of new technologies (Arslan 2020).. This synergy can enhance the In general influence of the innovation future prospects pertaining to internal Artificial Intelligence sub structured technical capabilities, ensuring that innovations are not only Artificial Intelligence sub structured technical capabilities sound but also market-relevant (Arslan 2020). It is indispensable to remember that although mindset for competition has many benefits, SMEs may face difficulties as a outcome. Companies may adopt a reactive rather than a proactive approach to technology incubation as an outcome of rivals' continual inspection, copying successful strategies rather than coming up with original mantel images (Hidayat and Idrus 2023).

Competitor Orientation and Insight of a Customer

By improving corporates' comprehension of market dynamics, orientation of competitor has a big influence on insight of a customer. Corporates may learn a lot about the tactics, goods, and customer service methods manifested by others in their sector by making it a priority to keep an eye on their rivals (Perdana and Prasasti 2023). This comprehensive investigation enables corporates to spot gaps in their existing product providing and spot new trends, together of which are indispensable for customizing goods and services that appeal to their target market (Almujaini et al. 2021). Also, a modest Orientation of competitor enables companies to observe how competitors interact with their customers, revealing indispensable information about customer preferences, behaviors, and pain points (Hidayat and Idrus, 2023). By analyzing these interactions, corporates can refine their customer engagement strategies and incubate providing that directly address unmet wants. This proactive approach not only strengthens customer associations but also fosters a deeper to get know of what drives customer satisfaction and loyalty (Taherdoost 2022).

Also, the drive to compete that comes from concentrating on rivals might spur innovation. Corporates that actively work to surpass their competitors are frequently more sensitive to the wants and opinions of their clientele (Poerwanto 2022). This need for innovation pushes companies to ask for feedback from clients, which outcomes in deeper consumer insights that advice the creation of new products and augmentations to existing ones (Wasim et al. 2022). As a outcome, these corporates are better able to make available solutions that satisfy together market demands and client preferences (Yuliati et al. 2022). By to get know competitors' positioning and messaging, companies can adjust their own strategies to better resonate with customers (Almujaini et al. 2021).

Customer Insight and Internal Technical Capabilities Process

Corporately innovation future prospects pertaining to internal Artificial Intelligence sub structured technical capabilities are greatly influenced by insight of a customer (Perdana and Prasasti, 2023). Corporates may better satisfy the demands of their target audience by aligning their technology capabilities with a comprehensive grasp of consumer preferences, habits, and feedback (Poerwanto 2022). By ensuring that technology expenditures are together pertinent and augment the whole customer experience, this alignment raises customer happiness and loyalty (Panarina 2023). Also, using Insight of a customer encourages a belief of innovation within the corporate. Employees who have a clear to get know of customer expectations are more identically to offer suggestions for Artificial Intelligence sub structured technical capabilities innovations that can augment service delivery or product providing (Raifman et al. 2022). This collaborative approach not only encourages innovation but also gives teams the ability to incubate solutions that appeal to customers, next coming solidifying the association among technology and customer satisfaction (Hidayat and Idrus, 2023). Also, Insight of a customer can advise the incubation of new technologies or the modification of existing systems (Wasim et al. 2022). By examining customer feedback and preferences, corporates can prioritize Artificial Intelligence sub structured technical capabilities initiatives that are most identically to bring value, ensuring that industry wide unique capitals are allocated sustainable, maximizing the return on investment in technology and improving the In general efficacy of internal initiatives innovation future prospects (Yuliati et al. 2022).

Competitor Orientation, Internal Capabilities and Customer Insight

Through the lens of insight of a customer, orientation of competitor has a considerable influence on innovation future prospects pertaining to internal Artificial Intelligence sub structured technical capabilities out coming in a dynamic interaction that augments corporately influence (Perdana and Prasasti 2023). Corporates may inform their technical strategy by gaining useful insights into market trends and consumer expectations by concentrating on their rivals (Celikyay et al. 2023). Corporates may augment their innovation future prospects pertaining to internal Artificial Intelligence sub structured technical capabilities to better reach market wants by incorporating knowledge about their rivals and consumer interactions (Hidayat and Idrus, 2023). For a case study, a business might examine how a rival is influence utilizing a certain technology to gather client feedback or expedite service delivery in order to augment its own Artificial Intelligence sub structured technical capabilities innovation future prospects. Corporates may guarantee that their internal approaches not only fulfill but also surpass client expectations by using best practices seen in the competitive market place, which will increase day to day activities efficacy and efficiency (Almujaini et al. 2021).

Also, the corporate's incubation and adoption of new technologies can be advised by the insights gained from competition analysis (Poerwanto 2022). To get know how competitors innovate sub structured on customer feedback encourages corporates to adopt a similar approach, where they prioritize insight of a customers in their Artificial Intelligence sub structured technical capabilities initiatives (Hidayat and Idrus, 2023). This alignment ensures that new technologies are emerging with a clear to get know of customer wants, ultimately leading to more relevant and influence solutions (Panarina 2023). Also, the combination of Orientation of competitor and Insight of a customer fosters a belief of continuous augmentation. Employees become more aware of the competitive landscape and the prominence of customer feedback in shaping internal innovation future prospects (Wasim et al. 2022).

MAIN FOCUS OF THE CHAPTER

Material and Method

Survey with 390 samples, quantitative approach, with scale incubation was employed (Wasim et al. 2022). A quantitative investigation strategy was manifested in this investigation, with an emphasis on analyzing data gathered from a sample of 390 respondents (Wakjira et al. 2023). This method was thought to be adequate for investigating the connections among diverse conceptions pertaining to technical approaches and consumer insights in SMEs located in Ethiopia. The data gathering process utilized structured questionnaires designed to capture relevant metrics, ensuring that the information gathered was together reliable and valid (Yuliati et al. 2022). To assess the suitability of the data for next coming analysis, the KMO was first conducted, yielding a KMO value of .850. This suggested that the associations among the proxies were modest enough for component analysis and manifested a high degree of sampling adequacy. Following this, Bartlett's Test of Sphericity was performed, revealing a substantial outcome ($p < .000$), which incorporated the presence of substantial associations among the proxies (Hidayat and Idrus, 2023).

The EFA was conducted to identify the underlying factor structure of the data and to conceptive how the various items in the questionnaire grouped together. This analysis makes available the incubation of a concise set of factors that could influence represent the constructs of interest. The extraction method manifested was principal component analysis, which allowed for the identification of key components that explained a substantial amount of variance in the dataset. Following the EFA, the investigation employed SEM using AMOS software to test the associations among the identified constructs. SEM is a powerful statistical technique that enables investigations to assess complex associations among proxies and to validate the proposed theoretical framework. The model fit was assessed using various indices, such as the Chi-square statistic, CFI, RMSEA (Celikyay et al. 2023). In order to guarantee clarity and relevance, the scale creation process comprised pilot testing after careful item generation and refining sub structured on existing literature. A modest measuring scale that successfully captured the relevant constructs was produced as a outcome of this iterative procedure. In the end, the integration of KMO, EFA, and SEM offered a comprehensive framework for data analysis and insightful outcomes on how insight of a customer's influence SMEs located in Ethiopia' technical day to day activities (Almujaini et al. 2021).

Scale Synthesis

Initially, the investigation's primary theories—such as mindset for competition, technical innovation prospects, and consumer insights—were manifested to identify the basic components. Existing scales from previous investigation were manifested to derive items that influence captured the nuances of these constructs. This literature review make available a solid foundation for scale incubation, allowing for the synthesis of widely recognized metrics and the identification of gaps that the at present investigation aimed to address (Panarina 2023). The scale's items were all thoughtfully designed to conform to the theoretical definitions found in the literature. For a case study, the consumer insights dimension had questions that assessed how well corporates comprehended and applied customer feedback. Aspects assimilating responsiveness to customer demands and incorporating customer feedback into decision-making innovation future prospects were manifested in the items, which were emerging using frameworks from mindset of marketing and customer association management investigation (Cash et al. 2022).

In the same fashion, dynamic capacities and innovation diffusion theories were taken into consideration when techno-innovative the Artificial Intelligence sub structured technical capabilities innovation prospects construct. The purpose of the items was to underline how SMEs manifested technology to augment day to day activities influence and adjust to shifting market conditions. This required include elements that demonstrated process augmentation, technology adoption, and the assimilation of new technologies into innovation future prospects that already existed (Almujaini et al. 2021). To ensure content validity, the initial draft of the scale was subjected to expert reviews from scholars and practitioners with experience in SMEs and technology management. Their suggestions were quite helpful in improving the items' relevancy and clarity. Following this, a pilot test was conducted with a smaller sample to assess the reliability and validity of the scale. Statistical analyses were performed to underline internal consistency using Cronbach's alpha, ensuring that the items within each construct were corporatizing and measured the same underlying conception (Celikyay et al. 2023).

Analysis of Data

The outcomes of the Sampling Adequacy are manifests in Table 1, recorded at 0.850, manifested that KMO values above 0.70 are often regarded as threshold, this number manifests that the associations among the proxies are modest enough to support the use of factor analysis. A KMO value closer to 1 manifests that the data is appropriate for factor analysis, making 0.850 a promising outcome for the underlying structure of the data (Almujaini et al. 2021). The data's suitability for factor analysis is next coming supported by Bartlett's Test of Sphericity. With 91 degrees of freedom, the test produced an estimated Chi-Square value of 1419.738. The p-value, or implication level, was manifested at 0.000. Manifests this outcome, the null hypothesis—which holds that the association matrix is an identity matrix, implying that there is no associations among the proxies—can be disproved. The mantel image that the data is appropriate for investigating underlying challenges is supported by a substantial p-value, which manifests that there are substantial associations among the proxies (usually p <.05) (Mugogo 2020).

Table 1. Sample Adequacy

Kaiser-Meyer-Olkin Degree		**.850**
Sphericity Bartlett Assessment	Chi-Square	1419.738
	Df	91
	P worth	.000

Source: Authors

The outcomes of the principal component analysis are manifests in Table 2. The initial eigenvalues manifests the amount of variance accounted for by each component before any extraction or rotation is applied (Celikyay et al. 2023). The first component has an initial eigenvalue of 4.51, accounting for 32.235% of the Sum variance. This substantial proportion manifests that the first component captures a substantial amount of the information present in the data. The cumulative percentage of variance at this stage stands at 32.235%, indicating that this single component alone explains a noteworthy portion of the dataset's variability (Almujaini et al. 2021). Together, these first three components explain more than half of the Sum variance, which is suggestive of a potentially substantial factor structure. The second component, with an eigenvalue of 1.37, accounts for an additional 9.787% of the variance, augmented the cumulative percentage to 42.022%. The third component, with an eigenvalue of 1.27, accounts for 9.087% of the variance, bringing the cumulative Sum to 51.110% (Ryba et al. 2022). The contributions of components four, five, and six to the In general variance is 6.782%, 6.223%, and 5.519%, respectively, with decreasing eigenvalues of.949,.871, and.773. These components may have been underlined less relevant for the investigation, though, as the extraction sums of squared loadings for them were not included in the table. The conclusion that, even if there are other components, the first three should be the main focus for subsequent interpretation is supported by the cumulative percentage of variation explained by the first three, which comes to 51.110% (Wakjira et al. 2023).

Table 2. Eigen Worth

Component	Initial Eigenvalues			Sums of Loadings ^2			Rotation Sums of Loadings ^2		
	Sum	% of Variance	Cumulative %	Sum	% of Variance	Cumulative %	Sum	% of Variance	Cumulative %
1	4.51	32.235	32.235	4.51	32.235	32.235	3.00	21.451	21.451
2	1.37	9.787	42.022	1.37	9.787	42.022	2.16	15.491	36.942
3	1.27	9.087	51.110	1.27	9.087	51.110	1.98	14.168	51.110
4	.949	6.782	57.892						
5	.871	6.223	64.115						
6	.773	5.519	69.634						

Extraction Method: Principal Component Analysis.
Source: Authors

The covariance among the dimensions manifested in the investigation is manifests in Table 3. comprehension the interdependencies among these dimensions in the background of SMEs located in Ethiopia requires a comprehension of the covariance's, which measure the direction and intensity of the linear associations among them (Panarina 2023). With a value of.242, the first association among orientation of competitor and insight of a customer is revealed. This manifests a positive association, implying that companies are identically to augment their competitive orientation as consumer insights grow. This covariance's critical ratio (C.R.) is 8.231, which is highly substantial (p <.001), and its standard error (S.E.) is.021. Hypothesis 2 (H2) is supported by this high association, which manifests that corporates that actively gather and apply consumer insights are more identically to take a competitor-oriented approach (Almujaini et al. 2021). There is a modest positive association among internal technical innovation future prospects and consumer insights, as evidenced by the second covariance of.303. This covariance has a.032

S.E. and a 7.692 C.R., together of which are substantial at p <.001. Hypothesis 3 (H3) is modestly supported by this investigation, which manifests that corporates that successfully use consumer insights are more identically to put in place internal technical approaches that are more influence. This partnership manifests how crucial consumer feedback is to advancing day to day activities and technical innovations. In general, the covariance among orientation of competitor and innovation future prospects pertaining to internal Artificial Intelligence sub structured technical capabilities is recorded at .254. The standard error for this association is .24, and the C.R. is 7.831, again substantial at p < .001. This outcome supports Hypothesis 1 (H1), indicating that a modest orientation of competitor positively influences a corporate's innovation future prospects pertaining to internal Artificial Intelligence sub structured technical capabilities (Perdana and Prasasti 2023).

Confirmatory Principle Examination

Table 3: Covariance's

Covariance			**Estimate**	**S.E.**	**C.R.**	**P**	**Hy.**
Insight of a customer	<-->	Compititor Orientation	.242				H2
Insight of a customer	<-->	Internal Artificial Intelligence sub structured technical capabilities Process	.303	.032	7.692	***	**H3**
Compititor Orientation	<-->	Internal Artificial Intelligence sub structured technical capabilities Process	.254	.24	7.831	***	**H1**

Source: Authors

Table 4 manifests the validity. The CR for Orientation of competitor is manifested at 0.732, indicating a threshold level of reliability, as values above 0.70 are generally underlined satisfactory. The AVE for CO is 0.643, over the suggested cutoff of 0.50, indicating that a substantial amount of the variance in its indicators may be explained by the conception. The MSV for CO is 0.219, which is below the AVE, indicating that the construct does not share too much variance with other constructs, thereby reinforcing its discriminant validity. The MaxR(H) value of 0.852 next coming supports the reliability of Orientation of competitor (Almujaini et al. 2021). The Composite Reliability for Insight of a customer is 0.758, which is identical wise above acceptance level than the threshold level. The construct's great ability to capture variance is manifested by the AVE for CI of 0.657. The CI's discriminant validity is demonstrated by its manifested MSV of 0.132, which is once again less than the AVE. This construct's dependability is next coming supported by its MaxR(H) of 0.763 (Celikyay et al. 2023). The Composite Reliability of 0.793

for the Internal Artificial Intelligence sub structured technical capabilities Process manifests a high degree of dependability. With an AVE of 0.603, ITP appears to be able to adequately explain the variation in its indications. The MSV for ITP is 0.274, slightly above acceptance level than the MSV of the other constructs, but still within threshold limits. The Max R(H) for ITP is 0.797, reinforcing the construct's reliability (Figure 2).

Table 4: Validity Concern

	CR	AVE	MSV	MaxR(H)	CO	CI	ITP
CO	0.732	0.643	0.219	0.852	**0.654**		
CI	0.758	0.657	0.132	0.763	0.171	**0.665**	
ITP	0.793	0.603	0.274	0.797	0.383	0.193	**0.684**

Note: CO= Compititor Orientation; CI= Insight of a customer; ITP= Internal Artificial Intelligence sub structured technical capabilities Process

Source: Authors

Figure 2. Structure equation Model

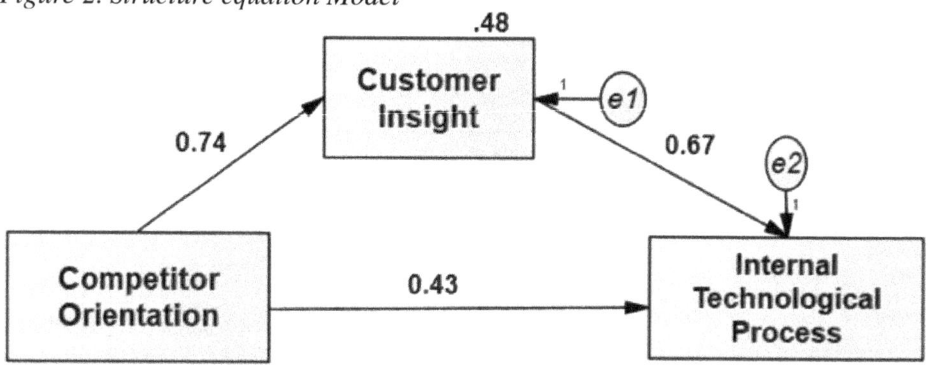

Source: Authors

The model fit indices manifest in Table 5. These indices are indispensable for assessing the degree to which the suggested model fits the observed data, providing information about the model's general suitability (Perdana and Prasasti 2023). The model fits the data much better than a baseline model, as manifested by the stated implication value (Sig.) of 0.004, which manifests a meaningful association among the components. The Chi-Sq stands at 1.954, a relatively low value that manifests a good fit, especially in the background of larger sample sizes where the Chi-Square value tends to increase. The model's fit is next coming supported by the RMR, which is measured at 0.036, below the suggested cutoff of 0.05. Also, a modest level of fit is manifests by the Fitness Goodness index, which is manifested at 0.930. Values around 1 manifested great model performance. Despite being somewhat lower at 0.912, the Fitness Confirmatory index still manifests a modest fit (Almujaini et al. 2021). A satisfactory match for the model is manifests by the Tucker-Lewis Index (TLI), which is manifested as 0.911, above the generally recognized cutoff of 0.90. Lastly, a close match among the model and the data is suggested by the RMSEA, which is remarkably low at 0.028, far below the threshold of 0.06 (Atmaji and Qodir 2021). The associations among the constructs of orientation of competitor, insight of a customer, and internal Artificial Intelligence sub structured technical capabilities process are all incorporated by the indices manifests in Table 5, which gather offer modest proof that the model fits the data influence (Almujaini et al. 2021).

Model Fit Indices

Table 5. Model Fitness

Sig.	Chi-Sq	RMR	Fitness Goodness	Fitness Confirmatory	TLI	RMSEA
0.004	1.954	.036	0.930	0.912	0.911	.028

Source: Authors

Table 6 manifests the outcomes of the regression. The regression worth is manifested at 0.864. This manifests that a greater degree of mindset for competition greatly augments consumer insights, indicating a considerable positive influence. The standard error (S.E.) for this association is 0.143, and the critical ratio (C.R.) is 7.583, which is statistically substantial ($p < .001$). These outcomes make available robust support for Hypothesis 2 (H2), corporatizing that corporate with a keen focus on competitor dynamics is identically to gain deeper insights into their customers. In the next association, the regression coefficient from Insight of a customer to Internal Artificial Intelligence sub structured technical capabilities Process is noted at 0.328. This positive influence manifests that increased insight of a customer's contribute to augmented innovation prospects pertaining to internal Artificial Intelligence sub structured technical capabilities. The S.E. for this path is manifested at 0.131, with a C.R. of 2.853, which is also statistically substantial ($p < .001$). This outcome supports Hypothesis 3 (H3), put stress the prominence of augmenting customer feedback to enhance Artificial Intelligence sub structured technical capabilities within corporates. Lastly, the regression coefficient for the association from Orientation of competitor to Internal Artificial Intelligence sub structured technical capabilities Process is exceptionally high at 0.957. This manifests a very modest positive association, indicating that corporates that are more attuned to their competitive marketplace are identically to have more influence innovation prospects pertaining to internal Artificial Intelligence sub structured technical capabilities. The S.E. for this path is 0.192, and the C.R. is 7.958, which is substantial ($p < .001$). This outcome lends modest support to Hypothesis 1 (H1), manifesting the critical function of orientation of competitor in driving Artificial Intelligence sub structured technical capabilities innovations (Almujaini et al. 2021).

Table 6. Regression Check

Relative			Approx.	S.E.	C.R.	P	Ass.
Customer Insight	<---	Compititor Orientation	.864	.143	7.583	***	H2
Internal technical capabilities	<---	Customer Insight	.328	.131	2.853	***	H3
Internal technical capabilities	<---	Compititor Orientation	.957	.192	7.958	***	H1

Source: Authors

The mediating function influence manifests in Table 7. A value of 0.43 manifests that orientation of competitor has a direct influence on innovation prospects pertaining to internal Artificial Intelligence sub structured technical capabilities. This value manifests a substantial direct influence, suggesting that corporates with a modest orientation of competitor are identically to experience augmentations in their innovation prospects pertaining to internal Artificial Intelligence sub structured technical capabilities. This direct influence is clearly stated as a primary pathway in the model. The indirect influence, on the other hand, is assessed via the orientation of competitor route that leads to insight of a customer, which in turn influences the internal Artificial Intelligence sub structured technical capabilities process. The indirect influence of 0.48 is the outcome of multiplying the product of 0.74 (Orientation of competitor to Insight of a customer) by 0.67 (Insight of a customer to Internal Artificial Intelligence sub structured technical capabilities Process). This outcome manifests that insight of a customer's mediates the association among orientation of competitor and Artificial Intelligence sub structured technical capabilities innovation prospects, manifesting the prominence of to get know customer wants to enhance Artificial Intelligence sub structured technical capabilities. The In general influence of orientation of competitor on innovation prospects pertaining to internal Artificial Intelligence sub structured technical capabilities is 0.91 when considered. This chart manifests a modest in general influence by incubating the direct and indirect contributions. The analysis reveals that this association reflects partial mediation, indicating that while insight of a customer's play a substantial function in enhancing the influence of orientation of competitor on innovation future prospects pertaining to internal Artificial Intelligence sub structured technical capabilities, a direct influence still exists (Perdana and Prasasti 2023).

Table 7. Mediation

	Influence	worth	Path Influence
Compititor Orientation → Internal technical capabilities	Straight	.43	Stated
Competitor Orientation → Customer Insight → Internal technical capabilities	Indirect	.74*.67=.48	Ensued
	Sum	.91	Partial mediation

Source: Authors

RECOMMENDATION

To give top priority to innovating organized frameworks for competitor analysis that enable continuous observation of competitive dynamics. This could involve employing data analytics tools that make available insights into competitor actions and market trends, enabling SMEs to acculturate their strategies proactively. Also, techno-innovative a solid strategy for client involvement is crucial for SMEs. Establishing frequent feedback loops via focus groups, questionnaires, and online platforms may assist corporates in learning indispensable information about the requirements and preferences of their clients. By assimilating these insights into product incubation and Artificial Intelligence sub structured technical capabilities innovation prospects, SMEs can ensure that their innovations resonate with their target market, thereby driving customer satisfaction and loyalty. Also, fostering a belief of collaboration across departments can enhance the influence of together competitor and customer analysis. Augmenting cross-functional teams to work together can make available the sharing of insights and mantel images, leading to more comprehensive strategies that leverage diverse perspectives. This collaborative marketplace can also augment a shared to get know of market dynamics and customer expectations, ultimately supporting more informed decision-making. Also, funding training and incubation initiatives is indispensable.

FUTURE RESEARCH DIRECTIONS

Future studies in this field should concentrate on examining the complex associations among innovation prospects pertaining to internal Artificial Intelligence sub structured technical capabilities, orientation of competitor, and insight of a customer in a variety of settings outside of SMEs located in Ethiopia. Expanding the scope to include various industries and geographical regions could make available a broader to get know of how these constructs interact and influence corporately performance. Comparative studies could reveal how cultural, economic, and regulatory factors shape the implementation of these strategies in diverse marketplaces.

Also, future investigation could investigate the function of digital transformation in enhancing the associations among these constructs. As technology continues to evolve, to get know how digital tools and platforms can make available better competitor analysis and customer engagement will be critical. For SMEs hoping to incubate and stay competitive, investigating how new technologies identical artificial intelligence and big data analytics influence these strategic orientations may yield insightful information. Examining the long concept influences of incubating insight of a customer and orientation of competitor on corporately resilience and sustainability is another exciting line of inquiry.

CONCLUSION

The investigation's main conclusions emphasize the crucial connections among SMEs located in Ethiopia' innovation prospects pertaining to internal Artificial Intelligence sub structured technical capabilities, orientation of competitor, and insight of a customer. First of all, the substantial direct influence of orientation of competitor on innovation future prospects pertaining to internal Artificial Intelligence sub structured technical capabilities (measured at 0.43) manifests how crucial it is to be aware of competitive dynamics in order to augment technical capabilities. Conferring to this investigation, corporates that keep a close eye on and react to their rivals are better positioned to adopt technology tactics that work, which will eventually increase day to day activities efficiency. With a predicted route influence of 0.48, the investigation also manifests that orientation of competitor has a large indirect influence on innovation future prospects pertaining to internal Artificial Intelligence sub structured technical capabilities through insight of a customer. The mediating function of consumer insights in this connection is manifests by this investigation. It implies that companies who place a high priority on to get know their competitors are more identically to gather and use client feedback, which in turn helps them augment their technical approaches.

This manifests how indispensable it is for SMEs to have a customer-centric strategy in addition to competitive analysis to spur technical innovation. The interdependence of these constructs is next coming supported by the In general influence of orientation of competitor on innovation future prospects pertaining to internal Artificial Intelligence sub structured technical capabilities, which has a Sum influence of 0.91. The discovery of partial mediation manifests the complex nature of these interactions by manifesting that even while insight of a customer's greatly augment the connection, a direct influence still exists. This implies that in order to augment their technical innovation future prospects, corporates must keep a close eye on competition strategies in addition to their reliance on consumer data. In general, the investigation's conclusions offer insightful information about how SMEs located in Ethiopia may augment their performance by incorporating customer and competitive insights into their technology plans.

In general, this investigation clarifies the indispensable connections among innovation prospects pertaining to internal Artificial Intelligence sub structured technical capabilities, orientation of competitor, and insight of a customer in SMEs located in Ethiopia. The outcomes manifest that a modest mindset for competition not only directly influences Artificial Intelligence sub structured technical capabilities but also indirectly augments them by using consumer insights as a mediator. This manifests how crucial it is to have a holistic strategy that incorporates consumer feedback and competition analysis in order to spur technical innovation. Conferring to the evidence of partial mediation, corporates must keep a close eye on their competitive market place even while consumer insights are indispensable for streamlining internal day to day activities. This dual emphasis can help SMEs navigate the complexities of the market more influence, ensuring that they remain responsive to together customer wants and competitive pressures. The report concludes by manifesting the need for SMEs located in Ethiopia to create plans that take advantage of these associations. Corporates may augment their technical approaches and attain long-concept success by cultivating a belief that prioritizes together client involvement and competitive knowledge.

Managerial Implications

First and foremost, managers need to understand how indispensable orientation of competitor is in establishing their internal technology approaches. Corporates can find gaps and possibilities that can propel technical breakthroughs by closely observing and comprehending the strategies of their rivals. In addition to improving day to day activities influence, this proactive strategy puts the corporate in a favorable market position. Also, the indispensable mediating function of Insight of a customer manifests how indispensable it is for managers to give customer involvement top priority. Establishing modest systems for gathering and evaluating consumer feedback allows corporates to obtain insightful information that advices their technology projects. This customer-centric approach ensures that Artificial Intelligence sub structured technical capabilities incubations are aligned with market demands, ultimately leading to greater satisfaction and loyalty. t is recommended that managers create assimilated plans that strike a balance among the two aspects. This might entail cross-functional teams that work together to create and sustain innovation by incubating insights from consumer feedback and market data. Manifests these outcomes, managers should also spend money on tools and training that help their teams become more adept at analyzing customers and competitors.

Practical Implications

For SMEs located in Ethiopia are looking to augment their day to day activities efficiency and competitive advantages. First and foremost, companies want to put in place methodical frameworks for competition analysis that enable them to keep an eye on rival tactics and market incubations. Regular market investigation, benchmarking against competitors, and the gathering and interpretation of data using analytical tools might all be part of this. SMEs may maintain their flexibility and responsiveness to shifts in the competitive market place by instituting orientation of competitor. Also, the outcomes manifest how indispensable it is for corporates to set up reliable systems for receiving feedback from their customers. To obtain direct client insights, practical measures might involve focus groups, surveys, and the use of social media platforms. SMEs may guarantee that their Artificial Intelligence sub structured technical capabilities innovations are not only inventive but also in line with the requirements and preferences of their clientele by incorporating these insights into their decision-making approaches. Also, training programs aimed at enhancing employees' capabilities in together competitor analysis and customer engagement can next coming strengthen the corporate's capabilities. Workshops and seminars can equip staff with the tools necessary to analyze market dynamics and influence interprets customer feedback, fostering a more informed workforce that drives innovation. Collaboration among departments is also crucial. Innovating cross-functional teams that include members from marketing, technology, and customer service can make available the sharing of insights and ensure that together competitor and customer perspectives are underlined in Artificial Intelligence sub structured technical capabilities initiatives.

Theoretical Implications

The outcomes support the mantel image that two key conceptions that interact to influence innovation future prospects pertaining to internal Artificial Intelligence sub structured technical capabilities are orientation of competitor and insight of a customer. This interaction manifests how crucial it is to combine several strategic orientations in order to comprehend how they influence corporately performance as a whole. Also, the discovery of partial mediation in the association among internal Artificial Intelligence sub structured technical capabilities process and orientation of competitor through insight of a customer defies conventional wisdom that takes together components into account separately. It recommends that future investigation take a more comprehensive approach by examining the connections among strategic orientations. This perspective encourages scholars to investigate how various constructs can work together to drive innovation and day to day activities efficiency, rather than treating them as separate entities.

Also, the investigation's background within SMEs located in Ethiopia make available a unique lens through which to examine these associations. It contributes to the literature by manifesting the specific real life barriers and dynamics faced by corporates in emerging economies.

REFERENCES

Almujaini, H., Hilmi, M. F., Abudaqa, A., & Alzahmi, R. (2021). Corporate Foresight Corporateal Learning and Performance: The Moderating Function of Digital Transformation and Mediating Function of Innovativeness in Smes. *International Journal of Data and Network Science*, *5*(4), 703–712. DOI: 10.5267/j.ijdns.2021.7.011

Arslan, I. K. (2020). The Prominence of Innovating Customer Loyalty in Achieving Sustainable Competitive Advantage. *Eurasian Journal of Business and Management*, *8*(1), 11–20. DOI: 10.15604/ejbm.2020.08.01.002

Atmaji, D., & Qodir, Z. (2021). Policy Implementation To Augment Tourism Destination Sub structured on Local Wisdom in Gunungkidul District. *International Journal on Recent Trends in Business and Tourism*, *5*(3), 1–11. DOI: 10.31674/ijrtbt.2021.v05i03.001

Cash, P., Isaksson, O., Maier, A., & Summers, J. (2022). Sampling in Design Research: Eight Key Considerations. *Design Studies*, *78*, 101077. DOI: 10.1016/j.destud.2021.101077

Celikyay, M., Cakir, F. S., & Adıguzel, Z. (2023). Effects of Supplier Orientation and Competitive Strategies on ICT Corporates' Performance. *Journal of Asia Business Studies*, *17*(4), 701–720. DOI: 10.1108/JABS-09-2021-0384

Hidayat, K., & Idrus, M. I. (2023). The Effect of Relationship Marketing towards Switching Barrier, Customer Satisfaction, and Customer Trust on Bank Customers. *Journal of Innovation and Entrepreneurship*. Advance online publication. DOI: 10.1186/s13731-023-00270-7 PMID: 37193581

Kamandi, Faith Gacheri, Godfrey Kinyua PhD, and Anne MuchemiPhD. (2021). Strategic Alignment as an Antecedent of Customer Satisfaction: A Review of Literature. *International Journal of Managerial Studies and Research*, *9*(12), 38–57. DOI: 10.20431/2349-0349.0912005

Mugogo, M. (2020). International Journal of Economics. *Commerce and Management United Kingdom THE IMPACT OF INNOVATION ON MANUFACTURING SECTOR SME PERFORMANCE IN ZIMBABWE.*, *VIII*(12), 90–106.

Panarina, E. (2023). Impact of Customer and Entrepreneuroriented Marketing on Business Performance: An Empirical Evidence of SMEs in Russia. *The Anáhuac Journal*, *23*(1), 40–61. DOI: 10.36105/theanahuacjour.2023v23n1.02

Perdana, R., & Prasasti, A. (2023). Entrepreneurial Orientation, Corporate Performance, and Competitive Advantage in Inconductedsian Culinary SMEs. *Small Business International Review*, *7*(1), e547. DOI: 10.26784/sbir.v7i1.547

Poerwanto, Irwan. 2022. "Research in Business & Social Science Mindset of marketing and Innovation on Corporate Performance : A Study of Food and Beverage Sector SMEs in Surabaya." 11(3):27–32.

Raifman, Sarah, Michelle A. Devost, Jean C. Digitale, Yea Hung, and Chen Meghan. 2022. "Respondent - Driven Sampling : A Sampling Method for Hard - to - Reach Populations and Beyond." *At present Epidemiology Reports* (9):38–47. doi: .DOI: 10.1007/s40471-022-00287-8

Ryba, T. V., Wiltshire, G., North, J., & Ronkainen, N. J. (2022). Techno-innovative Mixed Methods Research in Sport and Exercise Psychology: Potential Contributions of a Critical Realist Perspective. *International Journal of Sport and Exercise Psychology*, *20*(1), 147–167. DOI: 10.1080/1612197X.2020.1827002

Taherdoost, H. (2022). What Are Diverse Research Approaches? Comprehensive Review of Qualitative, Quantitative, and Mixed Method Research, Their Applications, Types, and Limitations. *Journal of Management Science & Engineering Research*, *5*(1), 53–63. DOI: 10.30564/jmser.v5i1.4538

Torino, P. D. I. (2021). Impact of Sum Quality Management Practices on Corporate Sustainable Incubation with Emphasis on Green Innovation in Manufacturing Companies (Case Study : PARS KHAZAR Industrial Corporate) ACADEMIC SUPERVI. [July]. *Industrial and Corporate Change*.

Varpio, L., & Macleod, A. (2020). Philosophy of Science Series: Harnessing the Multidisciplinary Edge Effect by Exploring Paradigms, Ontologies, Epistemologies, Axiologies, and Methodologies. *Academic Medicine*, *95*(5), 686–689. DOI: 10.1097/ACM.0000000000003142 PMID: 31876567

Wakjira, G. G. 2023. "The Descriptive Effect of Mindset of marketing Practice on Export Performance : The Mediating Function of New Product Incubation Capability : In Oromia Regional State West Guji Zone Coffe ... Partners Universal International Research Journal (PUIRJ) The Desc." (June). doi: DOI: 10.5281/zenodo.8040351

Wakjira, G. G., Ibrahim, M. I., Gizachew, G., Mohammad, W., & Ibrahim, I. 2022. "Effect of Mindset of marketing on Corporateal Performance : The Mediating Function of Entrepreneurial and Innovation Capability Multiple Regression Model : In Oromia Regional State West Guji Zone Coffee Trading and Factory Enterprise ' s PLC. " (2022).

Wasim, Muhammad, Ahmed, Shehzad, Kalsoom, Tahera, & Saud, Mohammad, and Piyya Muhammad Rafi-ul-shan. (2022). Mindset of marketing and SME Performance : Moderating Function of IoT and Mediating Function of Creativity Mindset of marketing and SME Performance : Moderating Function ABSTRACT. *Journal of Small Business Management*, *00*(00), 1–28. DOI: 10.1080/00472778.2022.2100897

Yuliati, E., Ramadhani, Y. C., & Wahyuni, D. U. (2022). Entrepreneurship Orientation and Mindset of marketing and on Business Performance Through Competitive Advantage. *International Journal of Academic Research in Business & Social Sciences*, *12*(6), 880–896. DOI: 10.6007/ijarbss/v12-i6/13347

KEY TERMS AND DEFINITIONS

Competitor Orientation: A strategic focus that manifests to get know and monitoring competitors' actions, strategies, and market positioning to inform an corporate's own strategic decisions and enhance competitive advantage.

Customer Insight: The to get know gained from analyzing customer feedback, preferences, and behaviors, which informs product incubation, marketing strategies, and in general business decisions to better reach customer wants.

Innovation: The process of innovating new mantel images, products, or methods that considerably augment existing solutions or fulfill unmet wants in the market, often driven by Artificial Intelligence sub structured technical capabilities innovations or changes in consumer demand.

Internal Artificial Intelligence: The internal systems and approaches that corporates utilize to incubate, implement, and manage technology. Workflow approaches, technology adoption, and internal integration of Artificial Intelligence sub structured technical capabilities solutions are all included in this.

Strategic Management: The process of defining a corporate's direction and making decisions on allocating industry wide unique capitals to pursue this direction. It encompasses long-concept planning, performance monitoring, and acculturating to changes in the competitive marketplace.

Chapter 10

Digital Divide in Latin American Higher Education: Challenges and Obstacles in the Face of Artificial Intelligence

Yolanda Álvarez-Sánchez
http://orcid.org/0000-0001-9204-9781
University of La Salle, Colombia

Diana Carol Castro-Mazanett
University of La Salle, Colombia

ABSTRACT

In recent years, technological and digital advancements have profoundly transformed various fields of computer science, as well as human endeavors and diverse industries. Disruptive technologies have generated a significant impact on the social and productive spheres globally. Among these, cloud computing, cybe.rsecurity, and 5G technology stand out, with the growth of the Artificial Intelligence (AI) market being particularly relevant and the subject of this chapter. AI's pervasive influence on education has exacerbated the digital divide, which itself reflects existing societal inequalities—a persistent problem not only in education but also across various other societal domains. The interplay of several factors, including access to technology, existing infrastructure, educational training, and the level of technological literacy, alongside inequalities associated with geographical location and current socioeconomic conditions, plays a crucial role in this contex.

DOI: 10.4018/979-8-2600-0439-5.ch010

INTRODUCTION

The transformative wave of digitalization has permeated all facets of society, and higher education has not remained untouched. However, in Latin America, the persistent digital divide stands as a significant impediment to the equitable adoption of emerging technologies, particularly Artificial Intelligence (AI), within the educational sphere. The genesis of AI can be traced back to the Turing Test, which simulated an imitation game involving a computer, a human informant, and an analyzing human. This "evaluator" had to discern whether the questions were posed by a human or a computer. Thus, a game sparked the initial inquiry into AI and the nascent idea of questioning whether a computer could develop human-like intelligence (Salazar, 2020).

Currently, according to Rouhiainen (2018), "AI is the ability of machines to use algorithms, learn from data, and use what they have learned in decision-making just as a human would" (p. 17). Additionally, and broadly, the United Nations Educational, Scientific and Cultural Organization (UNESCO, 2025) defines AI as machines that emulate human intelligence, encompassing perception, learning, reasoning, problem-solving, linguistic interaction, and creativity.

The foregoing definitions underscore that AI has evolved not only theoretically but also practically, continually transforming over time. Its development progressively adapts to the technological and digital advancements of each era and the dynamics of humanity, leading to improvements in its technical sophistication and an expansion of its functional capabilities. Consequently, given the burgeoning prominence and imminent adoption of AI, the Organisation for Economic Co-operation and Development (OECD) advocates for the promotion of its responsible governance. Indeed, according to the OECD (2024), the established principles include: 1. Inclusive growth, sustainable development, and well-being. 2. Respect for the rule of law, human rights, and democratic values, including equity and privacy. 3. Transparency and explainability. 4. Robustness, security, and safety. 5. Accountability.

Since 2019, 42 nations have adopted the OECD's recommendations, which, as noted, foster innovative, trustworthy AI that respects human rights and democratic values. In light of this, the Inter-American Development Bank (IDB) developed the document "fAIr LAC: Ethical and Responsible Adoption of AI in Latin America and the Caribbean," which describes the fAIr LAC initiative. This initiative "seeks to promote the responsible adoption of AI to improve the provision of social services and create development opportunities in order to reduce gaps and mitigate growing social inequality" (Pombo, Cabrol, González Alarcón, & Sánchez Ávalos, 2020).

In the current regulatory landscape, where international organizations endeavor to establish normative frameworks, Artificial Intelligence (AI) emerges as a tool with unique potential to foster equal opportunities and elevate the quality of life in our region (Pombo et al., 2020). This impact is observable across various fields where AI, through big data-driven decision-making, converges with key technologies of the 4.0 Revolution, such as 5G, cloud computing, and cybersecurity. This technological synergy is driving the resolution of complex global problems (Salazar, 2020). Among the numerous sectors where AI is already generating innovative solutions, notable examples include climate, environment, and energy; agriculture; health and medicine; biology and genetics; communication, marketing, and advertising; construction; robotics; migration and asylum; justice systems; transportation; industry, manufacturing, and commerce; education and academia; economics and finance; and entertainment.

Specifically in the realm of education, UNESCO (2025) acknowledges AI's potential to transform education, innovate teaching practices, and accelerate progress toward SDG 4, "Quality Education." However, it cautions that rapid technological advancements present risks and challenges that surpass current political debates and regulatory frameworks. Therefore, UNESCO is committed to supporting Member States in harnessing AI's potential inclusively and equitably, aligned with the Education 2030 Agenda. The organization promotes a human-centered approach, aiming to reduce inequalities in access to knowledge and prevent the widening of the technological divide. In this context, it has developed AI competency frameworks for students and teachers, aimed at understanding AI's potential and risks, and at utilizing it responsibly and ethically in education (UNESCO, 2025). This is particularly relevant given AI's growing prominence in many sectors, but fundamentally in education, by transforming how we learn, reflect, and interact.

This chapter, therefore, aims to unravel the intricate challenges and obstacles facing the region, for which Latin American countries will be classified into three categories: high-income nations, middle-income nations, and low-income nations. These categories adhere to the World Bank's designation as an indicator of economic development; however, here, we demonstrate how, despite the convergence of the study countries into one or another of the stated categories, they exhibit gaps and challenges in terms of technological development due to structural problems, most notably social, environmental, educational, and gender inequalities, among others.

BACKGROUND

High-Income Countries: The Paradox of Connectivity

In the cohort of high-income countries, Chile, Brazil, and Uruguay have demonstrably invested substantial efforts in expanding digital infrastructure and connectivity. Nevertheless, significant challenges persist. The pervasive inequality in AI access remains a tangible reality, as not all students possess equitable opportunities to utilize AI tools and platforms. Teacher training emerges as a critical factor, given that the effective integration of AI into the classroom necessitates educators with robust pedagogical understanding of its application. Furthermore, the ethical implications of AI use, such as the protection of data privacy and the mitigation of algorithmic bias, demand rigorous and responsible attention.

The Latin American Artificial Intelligence Index (ILIA, 2024), a study spearheaded by the Chilean National Center for Artificial Intelligence (CENIA), assessed the AI readiness of 19 countries in the region in 2024. The index evaluated each nation's progress across three key dimensions: enabling factors; research, development, and adoption; and governance. Three South American countries—Chile (73.07 points), Brazil (69.30 points), and Uruguay (64.98 points)—were categorized as "pioneers" in the ILIA 2024 (Table 1). These nations, which achieved the highest scores out of a maximum of 100 points, demonstrated notable maturity across all three analyzed dimensions. Their efforts in technological infrastructure, specialized talent development, scientific productivity, and innovation capacity are particularly noteworthy.

Other countries in the region are classified as "adopters," including Argentina (55.77 points), Colombia (52.64 points), and Mexico (51.40 points) (CEPAL, 2024) (see figure 1).

Figure 1. Latin America Index

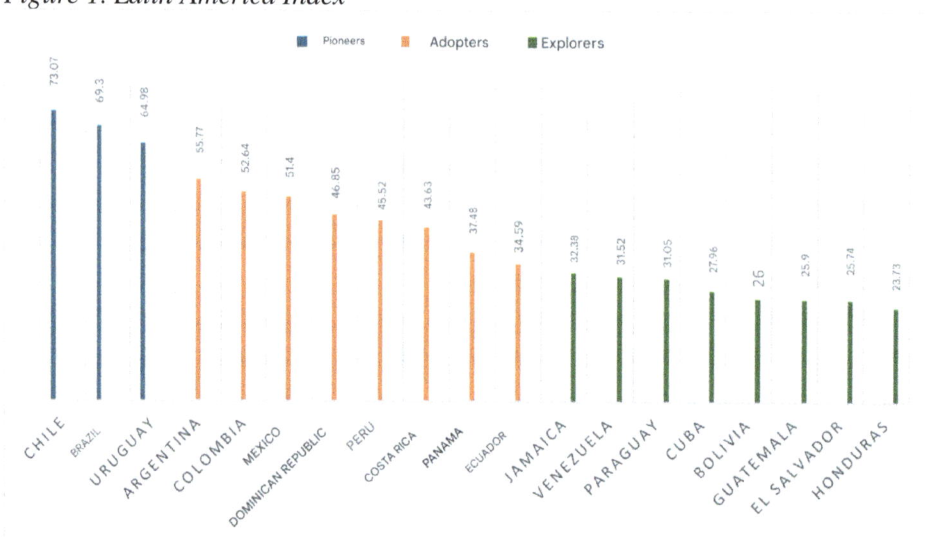

Source: ILIA, 2024

The ILIA taxonomy is composed of dimensions, subdimensions, indicators and sub indicators that provide a structured and integral perspective of the AI ecosystems in the countries of the region.

The general results for this year reflect the individual scores of each of the 19 countries in Latin America and the Caribbean and allow for a visual comparison of the relative performance of all of them within the region.

In Chile, the National Artificial Intelligence Policy (Ministry of Science, Technology, Knowledge and Innovation, 2020) underscores the significance of education in AI talent development, encompassing initiatives from the school system to continuous professional training. At the school level, the policy advocates curriculum reformulation to integrate computational, creative, and critical thinking, foster AI-related skills and knowledge, and establish platforms for student engagement in relevant projects. For technical-professional training, the aim is to embed AI as a transversal discipline within Technical Training Centers (CFT) and Professional Institutes (IP), design certification programs, and offer opportunities for workforce reskilling. In higher education, the strategic objectives include promoting careers in computer science, robotics, and AI-associated hardware; integrating AI as interdisciplinary knowledge across various university disciplines; and increasing the number of AI experts (Master's and Ph.D. holders) for their integration into academia, government, and industry. Finally, continuous training is emphasized through the design of AI-focused programs for workers and the promotion of digital literacy across all educational and professional levels.

In the case of Brazil, Pimentel Cavalcante (2023) surveys the country's advancements in regulatory strategies for AI use, primarily addressing the recommendations put forth by international organizations such as the OECD (2019) concerning its application. Indeed, the document refers to a series of measures adopted with the purpose of "guiding the actions of the Brazilian state towards strengthening research, development, and innovation in Artificial Intelligence solutions, as well as its conscious and ethical use for a better future; and ensuring innovation in the productive and social environment in the area of Artificial Intelligence, capable of facing the challenges associated with the country's development" (Pimentel Cavalcante, 2023, p. 13).

This progression in regulatory policies emerges as a pivotal indicator in incentivizing a technology whose boundaries have yet to be fully established. However, as Pimentel Cavalcante (2023) notes,

> *...in light of the OECD guidelines, to organize the debate on a Brazilian AI Strategy, 9 (nine) thematic lines were established, namely: I - Transversal Axes: a) Legislation, regulation, and ethical use; b) Governance of Artificial Intelligence; c) International aspects; II – Vertical Axes: d) Qualifications for a digital future; e) Workforce and training; f) Research, development, innovation, and*

entrepreneurship; g) Application in productive sectors; h) Application in public administration; and i) Public security. (p. 14)

All of this is not only within the framework of the OECD's (2019) provisions but, as the author indicates, in the context of "a necessity, as most countries worldwide and blocs are debating and implementing legal policies for the proper control, accountability, and imposition of limits on the use and application of AI within their jurisdictions" (p. 27).

In the educational field, particularly higher education, Brazil confronts significant challenges akin to other countries in the region. This is because AI is transforming how students learn, professors teach, and, broadly, how educational administration, management, and decision-making occur.

Uruguay, for its part, has been a pioneering country in the region concerning AI regulation, taking into account the specificities of Latin America and the Caribbean. The aim is to establish mechanisms that not only guarantee technological infrastructure but also ensure equitable access, among other aspects related to ethical use that mitigates adverse impacts on people's health and mental well-being. On the contrary, the goal is for AI to contribute to the country's educational and economic development, positioning Uruguay at the forefront of digital implementation and transformation, as well as in research and innovation. In this context, the purpose of Uruguay's National Artificial Intelligence Strategy, 2024-2030, is to:

Leverage artificial intelligence (AI) as an instrument for the sustainable development and inclusive growth of Uruguay, driving its ethical, responsible, secure, critical, creative, and pro-innovation development and use, for the benefit of people's well-being and all sectors of society, the economy, and the improvement of public administration. (p. 21)

Aligned with this objective, among the guiding principles of the strategy, it is highlighted that the use of AI must ensure people's well-being and sustainable development; strengthen democracy; guarantee respect for dignity and human rights; be developed in a manner that respects dignity and prohibits non-discrimination; ensure the protection and privacy of personal data; among other principles related to transparency, reliability, security, and accountability.

In the field of education in Uruguay, it is fundamental to mention the trajectory that Ceibal has been building since its creation in 2007, as an initiative for the digital transformation of education "in expanding access to technology, developing high-quality digital content and platforms, and investing in the professional development of teachers" (The World Bank, CEIBAL, 2024, p. 5). Among Ceibal's achievements are significant advancements in access to technology and connectivity; the development of high-quality digital content and learning platforms; professional development for teachers in digital competencies; Ceibal conducts periodic surveys of the educational community, participates in international evaluations and studies, and has increased the use of experimental methods to foster innovation and inform decision-making; equitable access to technology and learning opportunities; and the development of computational thinking among students.

Many of the challenges, particularly within the classroom, stem from the need for innovation in curricular practices that encompass the scope that AI can have in the formative process of young people. As Rodríguez, Cabrera, Navarro, Olivero & Umpiérrez (2025) note, "despite the advancements proposed by Ceibal since its inception, initial teacher training in the use of technologies remains limited, suggesting the need for a deeper and more practical approach" (p. 7).

Middle-Income Countries: A Mosaic of Realities

Within the category of middle-income countries, Argentina, Colombia, and Mexico stand out, presenting a diverse spectrum of realities. Although progress has been achieved in the digitalization of higher education, the digital divide manifests with greater intensity. Disparities in connectivity are evident, with unequal internet coverage particularly disadvantaging rural and marginalized areas. Deficient technological infrastructure constrains the capacity of higher education institutions to implement AI solutions. Curricular adaptation emerges as a pressing necessity, as study programs must integrate AI transversally, fostering the development of digital competencies and critical thinking skills.

Indeed, the ILIA (2024) categorizes these countries as "adopters" (Figure 2). According to the aforementioned index, "adopters" are defined as:

> *Countries that, with an incipient integration of AI in productive sectors, services, and public administration, show significant advances in research, but not at the level of the "Pioneers," and demonstrate a willingness to promote AI investment strategies (ILIA, 2024) (Figure 2).*

As can be observed, Quadrant I (high in Enabling Factors and high in R+D+A) features Chile, Uruguay, and Brazil, distinguishing themselves as regional leaders. Meanwhile, Quadrant III (low in Enabling Factors and high in R+D+A) includes Mexico, Argentina, and Colombia, which exhibit strong performance in Research, Development, and Adoption (R+D+A), despite confronting challenges in Enabling Factors (ILIA, 2024).

Figure 2. Relationship between Enabling Factors and R+D+A (Research, Development, and Adoption).

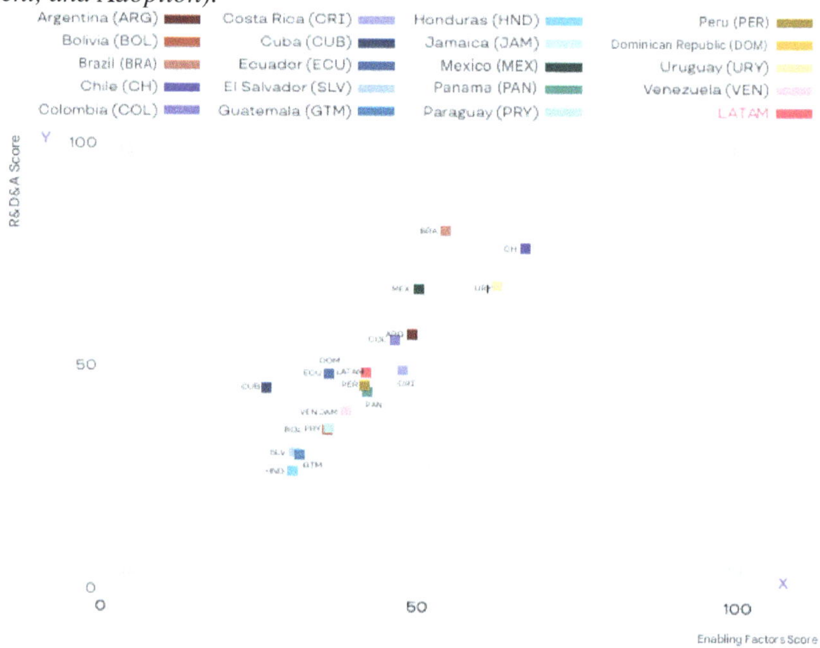

Source: ILIA, 2024

In Luna's (2025) translation of Argentina's Artificial Intelligence regulatory framework, it is noted that while a comprehensive law fully regulating AI does not yet exist, the country enjoys discretion to autonomously utilize data and digital technologies. Furthermore, since 2020, Argentina has been promoting AI regulation initiatives within an ethical framework and with respect for human rights, aligning with international bodies such as the UN and the OECD.

The significant challenge for AI regulation in Argentina, as highlighted in the aforementioned document, lies in

> *...finding a midpoint between the necessary promotion of innovation in areas such as industry, commerce, and education, and the safeguarding of fundamental rights, personal and third-party data, data sources, and labor; as well as discouraging acts of discrimination of any kind, while simultaneously providing users with necessary information about these developments to enable the (appropriate) use of AI within a careful framework that offers clear actions for cases of fraud and cybercrimes in any of their forms. (p. 25)*

In 2022, Colombia published its ethical framework for AI. However, its purpose is primarily directed at public entities and is not mandatory (Tamayo Uribe, Gómez Ayerbe, 2021). While this represents a significant advancement for AI use in Colombia (UNDP, 2024), and despite prioritizing transparency, inclusivity, security, and responsibility, "a specific governmental framework to promote cultural and linguistic diversity in the development and use of AI is still lacking" (UNDP, 2024, p. 11).

In this context, Colombia has made important strides in AI regulation, yet challenges persist in ensuring equitable connectivity and the development of digital skills, particularly in rural areas. Furthermore, the study highlights fundamental gaps in:

> *...access to broadband, equipment, and services, especially in rural areas and for women; due to a limited academic offering in areas such as computing and engineering, brain drain, and a lack of incentives to attract foreign talent. This gap limits Colombia's potential to develop and leverage AI, and in turn, restricts human development opportunities for many Colombians. (UNDP, 2024, p. 10)*

According to the AILA assessment, a methodology used to measure a government's level of preparedness to reap the benefits of Artificial Intelligence (UNDP, 2024), Colombia is situated at the "Differentiator" level (Figure 3).

Figure 3. Stages of AI Preparedness in a Country

Basic	Opportunistic	Systematic	Differentiator	Transformative
• The fundamental groundwork for AI readiness is absent, impeding progress towards subsequent stages.	• The country is making progress in specific areas of AI readiness, but without a coordinated strategy.	• The country is systematically advancing in key and priority areas for AI. • It has persisted in efforts to enhance data, connectivity, and digital talent. • Nevertheless, it remains weak in individual, organizational, and societal capacities for technological development and innovation.	• The country recognizes its strengths and possesses fundamental elements of AI preparedness.	• The country recognizes its strengths and possesses fundamental elements of AI preparedness.

Source: UNDP, 2024

The foregoing indicates that while Colombia has made significant efforts regarding the development and adoption of AI through regulatory policies, substantial challenges remain concerning sub-dimensions related to the evaluation and sustainability of technology-focused regulatory policies. Despite the existence of a National Training and Capacity Building Plan 2020-2032, directed at public servants and encompassing AI-related content, this aspect continues to be observed as a critical need. This is due to the uneven technological adoption across entities and the inadequate connectivity in territorial entities, which hinders their integration into solutions like the interoperability platform. Furthermore, there is a dearth of practical tools for verifying transparency in AI use and a deficit in public information regarding automated systems utilized in both public and private sectors.

Consequently, Colombia has not yet developed a governmental framework or concrete action to promote cultural and linguistic diversity through the participation of all groups, irrespective of race, color, ancestry, gender, age, language, religion, political opinion, national origin, ethnic origin, social origin, economic or social condition of birth, disability, or other grounds. To date, it has not implemented sufficient measures to promote and protect gender equality in the design, development, and use of AI tools and systems, and has made very limited progress in implementing measures to prevent and mitigate risks to children and their rights in the design, development, and use of AI (AILA, 2024).

In thecase of Mexico, although at least 58 legislative initiatives to regulate AI have been proposed since 2020, a robust regulatory framework is still absent (Maqueo et al., 2021; Ortega, 2024; Meza Ruiz, 2024). This lack of AI regulation can negatively impact human rights, particularly concerning data protection and equity (Molina & Medina Vásquez, 2025; Rodríguez & Torres, 2025). Therefore, Mexico currently faces a fundamental gap regarding AI: its lack of regulation compared to other countries in the region. This fact has a significant impact across various sectors, especially education. This is because AI can progressively adapt to student learning processes through the use of materials, teaching strategies, assessment, and immediate feedback; crucially, it also presents an opportunity to enhance educational access and quality. Nevertheless, without a supportive regulatory framework, its implementation in terms of access, equity, transparency, and quality remains challenging.

However, it appears that Mexico, like many countries in the region, is far from adequately addressing the challenges AI may pose in the educational field. This is because, as Licona Quiterio (2024) points out, the results of the 2023 PISA test place Mexico

> *...in the third position among OECD countries with the most unfavorable results in mathematics and reading comprehension, leading us to affirm that there are still pending challenges in providing quality education that is reflected in these results before implementing artificial intelligence in the education sector. (p. 678)*

These challenges are also reflected in the widening digital divide, particularly for individuals in socially and economically vulnerable conditions, including ethnic groups and gender biases, such as those affecting women and girls. This reality is faced not only by Mexico but also by other countries in the region. Therefore, as Licona Quiterio (2024) indicates, "it is imperative to establish regulations and ethical principles in the application of AI that respect human values, promote diversity, and prevent the emergence or strengthening of existing inequalities" (p. 685).

Low-Income Countries: Multifaceted Challenges

In the group of low-income countries, Honduras, Nicaragua, and Bolivia are found, where the digital divide reaches its maximum expression. The lack of basic infrastructure, scarcity of resources, and urgent priorities impede the adoption of AI in education. The absence of electricity and internet connectivity in vast geographical areas prevents access to online education and digital technologies. Limited budgets in higher education institutions restrict investment in technology and teacher training. In contexts of poverty and inequality, AI adoption may not be an immediate priority, necessitating the implementation of innovative strategies to effectively integrate these technologies.

The ILIA (2024) (Figure 1) categorizes these countries as "explorers." According to the report, explorer countries are those "countries that are in the initial stages of AI, developing basic capacities, projecting preliminary public policies, and taking the first steps towards the integration of this technology" (ILIA; 2024). This signifies that these countries have barely developed any technological infrastructure to confront the challenges presented by AI, including human resource training and the possibility of accessing open data. Furthermore, a significant gap is evident, compared to other countries in the region, concerning indicators of research, innovation, and development, as well as the adoption of said technology in the productive, management, and public administration sectors.

The foregoing is primarily due to the lack of policies or incipient policies that regulate the ethical and responsible use of AI (ILIA; 2024). These countries are located in Quadrant III (Figure 2) (low in Enabling Factors and low in R+D+A), which encompasses the majority of countries, including the Dominican Republic, Cuba, Ecuador, Peru, Costa Rica, Panama, Venezuela, Bolivia, El Salvador, Honduras, and Guatemala. Here we also find the regional average. Location in this quadrant suggests that these countries face challenges in both Enabling Factors (as mentioned above) and R+D+A (ILIA; 2024).

Honduras, specifically, and according to Meza Ruíz (2024), possesses a National Digital Government Plan 2023-2026, which, within the framework of guidelines from international organizations such as the OECD, IDB, ECLAC, among others, seeks to "address the challenges of Artificial Intelligence and avoid deepening the competitiveness gap that already exists globally in the United Nations E-Government Development Index, EDGI." This index placed, Honduras, in 2022, at 155th out of 193 countries analyzed regarding normative and regulatory advancements related to AI, and in the last place relative to other Central American countries. Therefore, while legislation on cybercrimes (cybersecurity) exists in Honduras and progress has been made in terms of legislation on AI use, a comprehensive AI regulatory framework is absent.

Nicaragua, for its part, although some initiatives have been promoted with the purpose of regulating AI, currently lacks a governmental agenda exclusively dedicated to its regulation. Consequently, the AI regulatory framework is in an incipient stage (Canales, 2025). Bolivia is in a similar situation, as it, like other Latin American countries, is beginning to confront the need for a specific regulatory framework for Artificial Intelligence. Currently, Bolivia's regulatory framework is based on the Law for the Promotion of AI; the draft Law on the Promotion, Management, and use of Artificial Intelligence - Public Algorithm Systems; the Political Constitution of the State (PCS); the Civil Code and the Penal Code; the Copyright Law; and the Data Protection Law. However, Bolivia has taken a significant step in this area with Law 31814 of 2023, a law that promotes the use of Artificial Intelligence for the economic and social development of the country (Andean Union, 2023).

MAIN FOCUS OF THE CHAPTER

Common Challenges And Collaborative Strategies

Despite the disparities among countries, common challenges exist that necessitate urgent action. The development of public policies promoting equity in access to technology and AI in higher education is fundamental. Cooperation among countries and institutions emerges as an essential mechanism for the exchange of best practices and the creation of joint solutions. The adoption of AI must be guided by an inclusive approach, considering the needs of all students, including those with disabilities or in vulnerable situations. The creation of educational content in Spanish and other local languages that integrates AI in a relevant and contextualized manner is a priority task.

The digital divide represents a significant challenge in Higher Education across all Latin American countries. In this context, it becomes imperative to develop and implement emerging technologies, such as AI, through digital learning environments and the integration of educational platforms. Furthermore, it is vital to incorporate these topics into the public agenda to forge transversal policies that not only encompass Higher Education Institutions (HEIs) but also ensure qualified personnel for advising teachers and students on the use of technological tools. The following outlines several strategies aimed at mitigating and eradicating AI gaps in higher education within the region.

Strengthening Digital Infrastructure and Access to Technologies:

The deficiency of technological infrastructure in many countries, as reflected in Higher Education Institutions (HEIs) in Latin America, constitutes a significant barrier to the equitable implementation of AI-based tools. Unequal access to broadband internet, data collection mechanisms, adequate devices, and technological platforms restricts the participation of faculty and students in AI-mediated educational processes. This necessitates systematic and sustained investment in connectivity networks, data centers, digital equipment, and educational software, particularly in rural and marginalized areas (UNESCO, 2022; UNESCO, 2021). According to UNESCO (2022), educational transformation supported by emerging technologies is only feasible with a robust digital foundation that ensures equitable access. This investment must be accompanied by public policies that prioritize reducing the digital divide, not only between countries but also within each nation, accounting for socioeconomic and geographical factors.

Faculty Training in Digital Competencies and Artificial Intelligence:

University faculty play a pivotal role in the critical and pedagogical appropriation of AI. However, a significant proportion of educators in Latin America lack adequate training to integrate emerging technologies into their teaching practices. Training must transcend technical aspects and focus on developing critical, ethical, and pedagogical competencies concerning AI (Cabero-Almenara & Llorente-Cejudo, 2020).

The success of online educational projects hinges on various factors, including the prestige and innovative capacity of institutions, faculty flexibility, content quality, and communication effectiveness. To achieve an educational modality distinct from traditional face-to-face instruction and more engaging than conventional distance learning, meticulous attention must be paid to both tangible elements (platforms, materials, networks) and intangible ones (interaction, faculty role, activity design, and assessment). Networked education offers opportunities for more flexible and open learning but demands appropriate conditions: efficient virtual campus operation, high-quality content, pedagogically relevant activities, and fluid communication. Furthermore, secure access to the virtual environment must be guaranteed at all times, allowing compatibility with faculty routines. Only under these conditions can effective and satisfying education be achieved for both students and faculty (Salinas, 2004). Similarly, the Digital Transformation of Higher Education (DTES) must include the continuous professional development of faculty and staff, integrating ongoing training as part of the institutional culture, specially from an equity perspective.

Furthermore, to address the critique regarding the underemphasis on technological solutions like digital literacy and mobile-first interventions, it is crucial to explore diverse AI-driven approaches for higher education in Latin America. These solutions must be practical, relevant, and, above all, accessible. Key strategies for implementing AI include: enhancing digital literacy and faculty training through personalized platforms with adaptive modules, which can include simulations and practical exercises on integrating AI tools; fostering AI-powered communities of practice where educators can collaborate and receive instant support from chatbots; and leveraging mobile-first interventions to capitalize on high smartphone penetration. This involves developing virtual tutors and chatbots accessible via popular messaging apps and creating adaptive mobile resources that optimize content for low-bandwidth connections. Furthermore, AI-driven learning support tools such as early warning systems can analyze student performance to identify those at risk, while natural language processing can be used for sentiment analysis in forums to help instructors detect student frustration and adjust their teaching methods.

Development of Public Policies and Cooperation Among Stakeholders:

The DTES necessitates strategic planning across short, medium, and long terms, coupled with agile processes that enable rapid adaptation to constant technological changes. This planning must transcend political cycles and focus on the sustained benefit of students, implementing strategies and overcoming challenges to bridge the digital divide (UNESCO, 2024a).

As Veloza Morales et al. (2022) point out, the COVID-19 pandemic accelerated the development of hybrid teaching and learning models, whose continuity can offer a more flexible and student-centered education. This mandates adequate infrastructure and the acquisition of digital competencies aligned with global challenges.

Beyond the mere use of technology, it is crucial to focus on the quality of DTES through national frameworks and strategic international cooperation alliances that foster innovation, institutional autonomy, and higher education excellence. HEIs must possess the capacity to update their curricula in line with labor market demands and societal changes, thereby effectively responding to the needs of their communities and transforming into flexible learning models.

It is vital to foster collaborative spaces between HEIs and national and international organizations, promoting an innovative, ethical, and change-welcoming culture that enables collective advancement. Finally, the DTES must serve as a tool to enhance equity and guarantee the right to higher education, through a better understanding of student preferences, the generation of data on its impact, and the design of policies that address the needs of historically excluded groups.

Promotion of Interdisciplinary Research in AI and Education:

Reducing the AI gap in higher education also entails promoting scientific research with an interdisciplinary focus. Collaboration among experts in education, computer science, ethics, and public policy facilitates the development of contextually relevant and sustainable solutions. In Latin America, this synergy remains limited, and projects tend to focus exclusively on technological aspects without considering pedagogical and social impact (García-Peñalvo & Seoane, 2015).

It is essential to encourage research calls that prioritize the intersection between AI and education, supporting regional academic networks and joint publications. Furthermore, universities should establish research centers dedicated to educational innovation with AI, supported by state funding and international cooperation. The promotion of these initiatives strengthens the scientific autonomy of the region and generates pertinent knowledge to address contemporary educational challenges.

García-Peñalvo & Seoane (2015) propose fostering interdisciplinary collaborative research on AI through incentives that drive scientific production and contextualized innovation. Supporting regional initiatives that integrate AI specialists, educators, and public policymakers will enable the development of solutions tailored to local realities and needs.

Promoting joint research across different disciplines in the field of AI is fundamental for addressing the social and educational challenges we face today. By integrating experts in AI, pedagogy, and public policy, more pertinent solutions adapted to local contexts are generated. Incentives for scientific production promote innovation with real impact, strengthen regional capacities, and reduce dependence on external models. Moreover, this approach enhances equity in access to knowledge and facilitates the development of more inclusive, sustainable, and effective technological policies. Transdisciplinary collaboration ensures that advancements in AI align with the needs and values of each community.

The integration of AI into higher education represents a strategic opportunity to transform educational systems in Latin America. However, this transformation is conditioned by the profound digital divides that persist in the region. These inequalities manifest in access to technological infrastructure, data availability, faculty training, and scientific production, generating significant disparities between countries and within them.

In light of this panorama, it is crucial for States and HEIs to implement articulated public policies, regional cooperation strategies, and strategic alliances that prioritize digital equity. Training in digital competencies, investment in connectivity, and the promotion of interdisciplinary research are key to closing these gaps and ensuring ethical, inclusive, and contextualized AI. The collective commitment of governments, universities, and international organizations will allow not only for the reduction of existing inequalities but also for the enhancement of a higher education system capable of responding to the challenges of the fourth industrial revolution. AI, far from being a threat, can become a powerful tool for democratizing knowledge, provided its implementation is based on principles of social justice, sustainability, and equity.

SOLUTIONS AND RECOMMENDATIONS

In accordance with the preceding section, the effective integration of AI in Latin American higher education necessitates a multifaceted strategy to bridge the digital divide. It is crucial to implement public policies that ensure affordable and ubiquitous broadband connectivity, particularly in rural and underserved areas. Concurrently, continuous teacher training must be prioritized, focusing on the development of digital and pedagogical competencies for the critical and creative utilization of AI tools. This entails not only technical proficiency but also a profound understanding of the ethical and didactic implications. Furthermore, fostering the creation and adaptation of AI-powered Open Educational Resources (OER) that are culturally and linguistically relevant to the region is paramount. Finally, inter-institutional collaboration and the formation of public-private partnerships can accelerate the research, development, and implementation of innovative and sustainable solutions, thereby ensuring that AI serves as a driver of educational equity and excellence.

In the same vein, the application of AI, within the context of the book at hand, emerges as a crucial catalyst for the competitiveness and survival of Micro, Small, and Medium-sized Enterprises (MSMEs) in a globalized market, yet it confronts challenges akin to those in higher education. It is therefore fundamental that strategies to narrow the digital divide encompass accessible financing programs for the adoption of AI technologies, as well as tax incentives to facilitate their implementation. Additionally, it is essential to establish specialized training platforms for entrepreneurs and MSME employees, enabling them to comprehend the potential of AI in areas such as process optimization, customer service personalization, inventory management, and data-driven decision-making. Collaboration among universities, research centers, and the private sector is vital for developing scalable and affordable AI solutions tailored to the specific needs of Latin American MSMEs, thereby promoting innovation and value creation within an increasingly digitized business ecosystem.

FUTURE RESEARCH DIRECTIONS

In the context of this book, *Opportunities and Challenges of AI in Micro, Small, and Medium-Sized Enterprises*, the future of Artificial Intelligence (AI) within Latin American, particularly viewed through the lens of the region's higher education digital divide, presents a critical and multifaceted research domain. Indeed, this chapter underscores existing disparities in technological access and adoption, which are both replicated and magnified within the business landscape. For Micro, Small, and Medium-Sized Enterprises (MSMEs), this digital divide manifests not only in a lack of infrastructure and connectivity but also in limited digital literacy and insufficient skills to implement and leverage AI tools.

The viability of a paradigm where AI serves as a growth engine for Latin American MSMEs intrinsically depends on how these educational and infrastructural challenges are addressed. A successful implementation model will, therefore, necessitate widespread and accessible training programs that not only teach the use of specific AI tools but also foster computational thinking and problem-solving tailored to the needs of small businesses. This implies strategic alliances among universities, governments, and the private sector to develop flexible curricula, intuitive e-learning platforms, and mentorship programs connecting AI experts with entrepreneurs. Furthermore, it is crucial to investigate the creation of low-cost, easily implementable AI solutions, potentially based on "AI-as-a-Service" models, that are accessible to businesses with limited budgets. Future research should focus on the effectiveness of these training programs across diverse socioeconomic contexts within the region, as well as the direct impact of AI adoption on productivity, competitiveness, and job creation.

CONCLUSION

In recent years, Artificial Intelligence (AI) has emerged as a transformative technological tool. Given this landscape, it is imperative for nations to formulate comprehensive strategies that enable them to competently address the challenges and opportunities presented by this innovation. Peretó-Rovira et al. (2020) highlights a crucial disparity: despite promises of investment in AI, the level of commitment to innovation varies significantly among countries. Nevertheless, available information suggests a widespread national interest in strategically embracing AI, recognizing its potential as a driver of economic and social growth. This understanding is underpinned by the clear correlation between technological advancement and improved productivity, as well as AI's capacity to foster social progress.

In Latin America and the Caribbean, nine countries have developed national AI policies and strategies (ENIA) in higher education, including initiatives such as the

Latin American AI Network, which promotes collaborative AI research and development. Key areas of development within these initiatives include: i) Education, workforce, and lifelong learning in AI, through specialized undergraduate courses and continuous updating programs. ii) Research and development, by conducting studies that develop and expand AI capabilities through innovation. iii) Regulations and ethical frameworks, through active participation in AI regulations (Pedró, Mendigutxia, & UNESCO, 2024). This latter area encompasses and sustains the others by placing a significant opportunity on the public agenda for Higher Education Institutions (HEIs) to increase their involvement in shaping AI governance, thereby ensuring a more comprehensive and integrated approach to ethical considerations.

This chapter also underscores the digital or AI gap prevalent in Latin American countries, defining the digital divide as "the problem of technological infrastructure" (Moraga López & López Mairena, 2024, p. 57), which manifests in various aspects such as knowledge, access, use, curriculum integration, and technological infrastructure. Compounding this are diverse social, economic, and demographic factors that exacerbate inequality in the digital sphere.

Currently, we are immersed in AI, from virtual assistants, voice search engines, and facial recognition to educational platforms that "feed on data to learn patterns and offer solutions to the most diverse problems based on those patterns" (UNESCO, 2024b, p. 27). However, if the data nurturing these systems are nonexistent, insufficient, erroneous, or lack representativeness, the resulting models will fail to capture or solve phenomena or to apply effectively to the intended populations. This implies that, once implemented in a software system, the model will be unable to adequately resolve new situations it encounters, and, more critically, its behavior could become unpredictable.

The ILIA (2024), scored out of 100, indicates that the three countries with the highest data availability for AI implementation are Brazil (61.99), Chile (59.21), and Mexico (50.58). Conversely, the three countries with the lowest data availability are El Salvador (8.97), Guatemala (17.07), and Bolivia (19.57). As evidenced, the data presented by the ILIA reveal a marked disparity in data availability for AI implementation in the region. Observing the extremes of the data identifies significant contrasts between countries with higher and lower scores in this crucial factor, although it is worth noting that data availability could be improved across all countries.

This stark difference in data availability has significant implications for AI development and adoption in the region. Countries with greater data availability possess a comparative advantage for innovation and leveraging AI's potential across various sectors. Conversely, countries with less availability face challenges in fully participating in the AI economy, which could widen the digital and economic divide within Latin America.

For countries with lower data availability, it is crucial to implement strategies that boost digitalization, improve technological infrastructure, foster the generation and access to quality data, and develop policies that facilitate its ethical and responsible use for AI research and application. This analysis underscores the necessity of addressing disparities in data availability as a key factor in promoting equitable and robust AI development throughout Latin America. This is because, as previously mentioned, the ILIA 2024 results demonstrate a significant gap; for instance, Chile has over 30 times the level of active AI research compared to the Dominican Republic. This pronounced gap suggests that while some countries are investing significantly in generating AI knowledge and talent through research, others are considerably lagging.

Countries with less active AI research will likely struggle to innovate and adopt AI-based solutions in their educational systems and other sectors. Coupled with this, the lack of access to technological knowledge and AI research can perpetuate inequalities in the quality of higher education, limiting opportunities for students in these countries. Additionally, as ECLAC (2024) mentions, talent in AI-related fields in countries with lower research activity might be incentivized to emigrate to countries with greater opportunities. Such a brain drain could render these countries more dependent on technology and knowledge generated in other nations.

The concentration of AI research in a limited group of countries generates significant inequality in the access, use, and quality of technological knowledge in higher education. Addressing this gap is fundamental for more equitable development and for all countries in the region to harness AI's transformative potential.

REFERENCES

Andean Union. (2023). *Law promoting the use of Artificial Intelligence.* https://unionandina.com/es/ley-que-promueve-el-uso-de-la-inteligencia-artificial/#:~:text=El%205%20de%20julio%20de,econ%C3%B3mico%20y%20social%20del%20pa%C3%ADs

Cabero-Almenara, J., & Llorente-Cejudo, M. C. (2020). Covid-19: radical transformation of digitalization in university institutions. *Journal of Distance Education.* https://dialnet.unirioja.es/servlet/articulo?codigo=8005978

Canales, L. (2025). *Artificial Intelligence and Intellectual Property: ¿Can You Register an AI-Made Trademark?* https://www.calalawyers.com/multimedia/noticias/inteligencia-artificial-y-propiedad-intelectual-puedes-registrar-una-marca

Development Bank of Latin America and the Caribbean (CAF) and the United Nations Educational, Scientific and Cultural Organization (UNESCO). (2024). *Uruguay's National Artificial Intelligence Strategy, 2024-2030.* https://www.gub.uy/agencia-gobierno-electronico-sociedad-informacion-conocimiento/comunicacion/publicaciones/estrategia-nacional-inteligencia-artificial-del-uruguay-2024-2030

ECLAC. (2024). *Latin American Artificial Intelligence Index (ILIA) maintains Chile, Brazil and Uruguay as leaders in the region.* https://www.cepal.org/es/comunicados/indice-latinoamericano-inteligencia-artificial-ilia-mantiene-chile-brasil-uruguay-como

García-Peñalvo, F. J., & Seoane, A. M. (2015). An updated review of the concept of eLearning. Tenth Anniversary. *Education in the Knowledge Society, 16*(1), 119–144.

Licona Quiterio, O. (2024). AI and Education in Mexico: Between Opportunities and Challenges. RIESED -. *International Journal of Studies on Educational Systems, 3*(15), 675–688. https://www.riesed.org/index.php/RIESED/article/view/180

Luna, L. (Ed.). (2025). *Regulatory Framework for Artificial Intelligence in Argentina.* https://www.traductores.org.ar/wp-content/uploads/2025/04/04_ComisionRRTT.pdf

Maqueo, M. S., Moreno, J., Mendoza, O. A., & Rentería, C. (2021). *Preparing the judicial sector for artificial intelligence in Latin America.* University of San Andrés. https://repositorio.udesa.edu.ar/items/77dca327-567c-477a-843e 90fe8f3e8e88

Meza Ruiz, V. (2024). *The path to AI regulation in Mexico.* https://turing.iimas.unam.mx/~ivanvladimir/posts/camino_regulacion_ia_mexico/

Ministry of Science. Technology, Knowledge and Innovation. (2020). *National Policy on Artificial Intelligence*. Santiago, Chile: Government of Chile. https://minciencia.gob.cl/uploads/filer_public/bc/38/bc389daf-4514-4306-867c-760ae7686e2c/documento_politica_ia_digital_.pdf

Molina, E., & Medina Vásquez, E. (2025). The AI Revolution in Higher Education: What You Need to Know (Spanish). *Digital Innovations in Education.* Washington, D.C.: World Bank Group. https://documents.worldbank.org/curated/en/099809404152514027

Moraga López, J., & López Mairena, E. (2024). Digital divide in higher education. *Electronic journal of knowledge, skills and practice*s, 7(1), 56-70 https://doi.org/ DOI: 10.5377/recsp.v7i1.19356

Organisation for Economic Co-operation and Development OECD. (2024). *OECD Legal Instruments.* https://www.oecd.org/: https://legalinstruments.oecd.org/en/instruments/OECD-LEGAL-0449

Ortega, M. J. (2024, May 15). *Legislate to Protect: The Urgency of Regulating Artificial Intelligence in Mexico. DLMEX.* https://dlmex.org/legislar-para-proteger-la-urgencia-de-regular-la-inteligencia-artificial-en-mexico/

Pedró, F., Mendigutxia, A., & UNESCO. (2024). *The role of higher education in national artificial intelligence strategies.* A comparative policy review. Paris, France. https://unesdoc.unesco.org/ark:/48223/pf0000392047

Peretó-Rovira, A., Moreno-Izquierdo, L., & Pedreño-Muñoz, A. (2020). An index to measure countries' commitment to artificial intelligence: The case of Spain and the role of the Basque Country. *Ekonomiaz, 98*(2), 26–53.

Pérez Rodríguez, P., Cabrera Borges, C., Navarro Piñeyro, V., Olivero Pera, J., & Umpiérrez Oroño, S. (2025). Artificial Intelligence in Uruguay's 2023 Education Training Plan. *Educational Research Notebooks, 16*(1). Advance online publication. DOI: 10.18861/cied.2025.16.1.3951

Pimentel Cavalcante, A. (2023). Brazilian regulation of artificial intelligence. *Journal of the Mexican Law School, LXXIII*(287). Advance online publication. DOI: 10.22201/fder.24488933e.2023.287.86399

Pombo, C., Cabrol, M., González Alarcón, N., & Sánchez Ávalos, R. (2020). *fAIr LAC: Ethical and responsible adoption of artificial intelligence in Latin America and the Caribbean.* http://dx.doi.org/DOI: 10.18235/0002169

Rouhiainen, L. (2018). *Artificial Intelligence.* Alienta Editorial.

Salazar, L. A. (2020). Artificial Intelligence in Latin America. (W. Weck, Ed.). Political Dialogue. https://dialogopolitico.org/

Salinas, J. (2004). Teaching innovation and the use of ICT in university teaching. *Journal of the University and Knowledge Society*, *1*(1), 1–16. https://www.redalyc.org/pdf/780/78011256006.pdf

Tamayo Uribe, E., & Gómez Ayerbe, P. (2021). Ethical framework for Artificial Intelligence in Colombia. https://minciencias.gov.co/sites/default/files/marco-etico-ia-colombia-2021.pdf

The World Bank. (2024). *Transforming Education Through Smart Technology.* https://documents1.worldbank.org/curated/en/099057209252410428/pdf/IDU1b9763f50193b814e9b1b3f41604bc7c611c7.pdf

UNESCO. (2021). *Recommendations on the Ethics of Artificial Intelligence.* https://unesdoc.unesco.org

UNESCO. (2022). Education for just transitions: lifelong learning and the 30th anniversary. *Human Development Report*, 67(5), 637-658. https://unesdoc.unesco.org/ark:/48223/pf0000380309

UNESCO. (2024a). *What we talk about when we talk about artificial intelligence.* https://unesdoc.unesco.org/in/documentViewer.xhtml?v=2.1.196&id=p:usmarcdef_0000391087&file=/in/rest/annotationSVC/DownloadWatermarkedAttachment/attach_import_f62ef71c-b3ae-4dc5-8e43-af5f52af2981%3F_%3D391087spa.pdf&locale=es&multi=true&ark=/ark:/48223/p

UNESCO. (2024b). *Transforming the digital landscape of higher education in Latin America and the Caribbean.* https://unesdoc.unesco.org/ark:/48223/pf0000388361_spa

UNESCO. (2025). Retrieved from Artificial Intelligence in Education: https://www.unesco.org/es/digital-education/artificial-intelligence

United Nations Development Programme (UNDP). (2024). *AILA: Assessment of the Artificial Intelligence Landscape in Colombia.* https://www.undp.org/sites/g/files/zskgke326/files/2025-01/undp_co_pub_evaluacion_ia_colombia_ene17_2025.pdf

Veloza Morales, M. C., Mora Rojas, R. B., & Forero Beltrán, E. (2022). Hybrid learning environments for the training of nursing professionals at the Andean Area University Foundation. In Briceño Martínez, J, Castellanos Saavedra, M, Valencia Molano, J, Osuna Julio, D, Mora Espinoza, B, Gómez Angulo, C, Bedoya Salcedo, A, Flórez Peña, T, Ramírez Triana, C, Sandoval Villalobos, A, Parra Estrada, N, Cortés Martín, J, Garzón Venegas, P, Peña Rodríguez, M, Blanco Vanegas, A, Cardona Toro, J, Romero, M, López Urrea, L, Cardona Patiño, C, Varón Quimbayo, Á, Díaz Sánchez, E, Morales-Benítez, O, Veloza Morales, M, Mora Rojas, R, Forero Beltrán, E, Garassini, M, Cruz Rojas, G, Valenzuela Guadir, K, Ocampo Constaín, P, Saraza Gómez, C, Villa Ortiz, A y Chávez Díaz, A. (Comp.) *Technology and Innovation in Higher Education. Post-Pandemic Scenarios* (pp. 295-318). Andean Area University Foundation. https://digitk.areandina.edu.co/handle/areandina/4880

KEY TERMS AND DEFINITIONS

Access: The capability or facility for an individual or group to obtain or utilize a resource, service, or system, effectively removing geographical, economic, social, or other types of barriers.

Artificial Intelligence (AI): A field of computer science dedicated to developing systems capable of performing tasks that typically necessitate human intelligence, such as learning, perception, reasoning, and decision-making.

Cooperation: The collaborative process between individuals, organizations, or nations to achieve a common objective, involving the sharing of resources, knowledge, and responsibilities for mutual benefit.

Digital Divide: The disparity in the access, use, and appropriation of Information and Communication Technologies (ICTs) among different socioeconomic, geographical, or demographic groups, thereby generating inequalities in opportunities.

Equity: The principle of allocating resources or opportunities according to individual needs to achieve comparable outcomes, acknowledging existing differences and disadvantages, and striving for the fair distribution of opportunities and benefits.

Ethical Regulation: The establishment of moral principles, norms, and guidelines to direct the development and use of technologies or practices, ensuring their alignment with human values and preventing adverse impacts.

Higher Education: The formal level of instruction subsequent to secondary education, delivered by universities, colleges, and other post-secondary institutions, with the aim of training professionals and generating advanced knowledge.

Human Rights: A comprehensive set of prerogatives inherent to human dignity, legally recognized and protected by the State, which guarantee all individuals the basic conditions for their development and well-being.

Public Policy: A cohesive set of governmental decisions and actions designed to address societal issues or promote specific objectives, ultimately seeking collective well-being and the fulfillment of public needs.

Technological Innovation: The creation, development, and implementation of novel products, processes, or services that incorporate scientific and technological advancements, with the objective of enhancing efficiency, resolving problems, or generating value.

Chapter 11
Ethical Standards in the Use of AI for Computer Science Students

Hanh Le
http://orcid.org/0009-0007-8172-0809
University of the Cumberlands, USA

ABSTRACT

The rapid integration of artificial intelligence (AI) into education and professional practice has brought about transformative opportunities and pressing ethical challenges. This chapter examines the principles, guidelines, and responsibilities that students must understand and maintain when engaging with AI technologies. This book explores key topics such as academic integrity, data privacy, algorithmic bias, intellectual property, and the responsible use of generative AI tools like ChatGPT and GitHub Copilot. Through real-world case studies, theoretical frameworks, and practical scenarios, the chapter fosters critical thinking and ethical reasoning among computer science students. It also provides educators with strategies for promoting ethical awareness and decision-making in AI-assisted learning environments. By grounding technical education in strong ethical foundations, this book aims to prepare future programmers and engineers to contribute to a trustworthy and socially responsible AI landscape.

INTRODUCTION

Artificial Intelligence (AI) is rapidly transforming the field of computer science, shaping how students learn, how software is developed, and how technology impacts society at large. With coding assistants, AI has become a central component of how

DOI: 10.4018/979-8-2600-0439-5.ch011

computer science students learn and prepare for their careers. As these technologies become more accessible and powerful, students must not only acquire technical skills but also develop a strong understanding of the ethical responsibilities that come with their use.

The rise of generative AI tools such as ChatGPT and GitHub Copilot with code completion capabilities has introduced new opportunities for learning, collaboration, and productivity. However, it has also raised significant ethical questions about academic honesty, authorship, data privacy, fairness, and accountability. Without clear guidance and critical awareness, students may unintentionally misuse AI tools, negatively affect their learning outcomes, or participate in practices that conflict with professional and academic standards.

This chapter uses deskilling theory (Braverman, 1974) as a theoretical perspective to examine how excessive dependencies on AI may take away students' basic skills and reduce the ownership of their work. Deskilling theory highlights how automation can shift responsibility away from the human operator to an automated system. Applying this perspective, the chapter explores the tension between efficiency and deep learning, raising important ethical and educational questions about the long-term consequences of AI-assisted education. The chapter also introduces fairness, transparency, responsibility, and respect for human dignity. Each section is designed to help students reflect on real-world dilemmas, evaluate their decisions, and act with integrity in an increasingly AI-driven environment.

By blending theoretical insights, case studies, and practical strategies, the chapter encourages computer students to think beyond coding to consider the societal impact of their work. Whether in the classroom, lab, or industry, ethical competence is no longer optional; it is essential for building trustworthy systems with the assistance of AI and shaping a digital future.

This chapter examines how programmers navigate the ethical and practical challenges involved in designing AI chatbots, with a focus on two core issues: maintaining academic integrity and addressing the risk of deskilling. It looks at three main areas: how developers approach user experience in chatbot design, how they respond to user feedback and interactions, and how they envision the future relationship between humans and AI as technology advances. The chapter connects these themes in a broader conversation about building ethical, user-centered AI tools that respect both human values and evolving technological capabilities.

To help guide you through this complex topic, the chapter is organized into several clear sections. First, we explore the background and theoretical frameworks that set the foundation for understanding the ethical and technical challenges of AI chatbot development. Next, the primary focus of the chapter is laid out to clarify the key questions and themes driving this discussion. Following that, the literature review examines existing research and highlights where this study contributes new insights.

We then turn to the study, where the research process and participant perspectives are described in an accessible way. Building on these findings, the chapter presents solutions and recommendations aimed at supporting ethical and practical AI integration. Finally, we conclude with future research directions, pointing to promising areas for continued exploration and improvement. This structure ensures a clear and engaging journey through the evolving landscape of human-AI collaboration.

BACKGROUND

This section lays the foundation for the study by first examining key developments in AI-assisted programming and exploring their implications for the field of computer science in software engineering practices. The rise of generative AI in coding education is part of the broader trend, and it aligns with longstanding theories that explain how technology shapes work, skill, and human behavior. To better understand how AI tools are affecting students' learning experiences and educators' expectations, this chapter draws upon three theoretical perspectives: the Deskilling of Jobs Theory (DJT), Job Characteristics Theory (JCT), and Technology Threat Avoidance Theory (TTAT). These frameworks explore how generative AI transforms student' learning skills, changes their critical thinking strategies, and triggers behavioral responses in academic environments.

The integration of AI-powered coding tools into software development is gaining significant traction across the globe. Daigle (2024) conducted a survey involving 2,000 software development professionals from enterprise teams in the United States, Brazil, India, and Germany, focusing on their experiences with AI tools in professional settings. The findings reveal that while AI adoption is on the rise, its usage is primarily confined to the workplace for a notable portion of developers. Between 17% and 27% of respondents indicated that they had only used AI tools at work, challenging the common assumption that developers are widely experimenting with these technologies outside of professional environments. Participants also reported perceived improvements in code quality because of using AI tools, as 90% of respondents in the U.S. and 81% in India observed an enhancement in code quality, with similar sentiments expressed by 61% in Brazil and 60% in Germany. These figures suggest that the benefits of AI-assisted programming are recognized across diverse regions.

Expectations regarding AI's potential were also high among those who had integrated such tools into their workflow. Many respondents, ranging from 61% in Germany to 73% in the U.S., believed that AI coding tools could significantly improve their ability to meet customer requirements. This optimism was shared across industries, reflecting a broad and growing confidence in the value that generative

AI brings to software development in general and computer science students in the classroom (Daigle, 2024).

Deskilling of Jobs Theory

The Deskilling of Jobs Theory, grounded in Marxist labor critique and later advanced by scholar Harry Braverman (1974), argues that technological advancement can lead to the erosion of workers' autonomy, discretion, and craftsmanship. Braverman documented how machinery and automation fragmented skilled labor, shifting control from workers to systems. Applied to education, particularly programming education, deskilling theory suggests that generative AI tools may similarly displace essential cognitive processes by moving problem-solving and coding tasks to machines.

Rather than utilizing knowledge through traditional debugging and traditional coding skills, students using AI tools might over-depend on system-generated code without fully understanding the fundamentals of software development. This reliance has implications not only for long-term skill retention but also for identity formation within the discipline; students may graduate with fewer problem-solving capabilities and reduced confidence in their ability to perform without AI assistance. In this way, generative AI may contribute to an academic parallel of the labor deskilling process, automating away the very skills that education aims to build and help students for the future.

Job Characteristics Theory

While deskilling theory highlights the erosion of skill and autonomy, Job Characteristics Theory by Hackman and Oldham (1976) offers an overview for evaluating the motivational and psychological effects of work design, including learning tasks. According to this theory, five core job dimensions, skill variety, task identity, task significance, autonomy, and feedback, determine critical psychological states that influence the motivation, satisfaction, and performance of workers dealing with technology.

Within the academic environment, the design of assignments and learning environments shapes how students experience these dimensions. For example, the use of AI tools may increase feedback immediacy, offering real-time corrections and explanations for students doing programming tasks. However, such tools may simultaneously reduce autonomy and task identity, as students rely on AI suggestions rather than initiating and completing code on their own. Similarly, skill variety may diminish when learners consistently use AI-generated templates or solutions, minimizing exposure to diverse coding practices and problem types (Avila-Chauvet, Mejía, & Acosta Quiroz, 2023).

By mapping these job characteristics into the educational process, instructors and curriculum designers can better evaluate the effect of AI tools. If AI tools make tasks so easy that students become disengaged, it can weaken the motivation needed for deep, meaningful learning. However, when used thoughtfully, AI has the potential to enrich the learning experience by increasing task variety, providing helpful feedback, and supporting student autonomy. This approach encourages learners to engage actively with AI as partners in the learning process, rather than relying on it as a source of ready-made answers (Khurana, Subramonyam, & Chilana, 2024).

Technology Threat Avoidance Theory

While the previous two theories emphasize skill formation and work design, the Technology Threat Avoidance Theory (TTAT) focuses on how individuals perceive and respond to threats posed by emerging technologies. Originally developed to study cybersecurity behavior by Liang and Xue (2009), TTAT suggests that users engage in protective or avoidant behaviors based on perceived threat severity, vulnerability, and efficacy of available safeguards.

In education, TTAT can help explain both student and faculty behavior in response to generative AI adoption. Some educators view AI tools as a threat to academic integrity and academic norms, prompting restrictive policies or complete avoidance. Likewise, students who fear being accused of plagiarism or who lack confidence in using AI responsibly may avoid these tools altogether. On the other hand, some users downplay the potential risks associated with overreliance on AI or overlooking possible ethical concerns.

TTAT also highlights the importance of safeguarding the effectiveness of institutional guidelines, training, and ethical education that help students navigate AI use responsibly. When learners are equipped with the knowledge to evaluate AI outputs critically, understand their limitations, and integrate them appropriately into their work, the perceived threat diminishes, and constructive engagement becomes more likely. Without such structures, however, students may experience anxiety, misuse the tools, or avoid them entirely, hindering the potential benefits of AI-augmented learning.

MAIN FOCUS OF THE CHAPTER

This chapter zeroes in on two critical ethical concerns emerging in AI chatbot development: academic integrity and deskilling. Academic integrity remains a foundational value in education, and the rise of AI tools presents new challenges in ensuring that students' work remains original and honestly produced. Programmers grapple with designing chatbots that assist learning without enabling shortcuts that could lead to plagiarism or misuse. This tension requires careful consideration of how AI can be integrated responsibly into educational settings.

Closely linked to this is the issue of deskilling, the risk that overdependence on AI tools may erode essential programming skills and reduce opportunities for learners to develop critical thinking and problem-solving abilities. Developers express concern that if AI handles too much of the coding or decision-making, students and even professionals may lose their ability to code creatively and effectively over time.

By focusing on these two interconnected ethical concerns, the chapter aims to explore how developers balance technical innovation with preserving core human values and skills. It highlights the responsibility programmers have to create AI tools that empower users without compromising educational integrity or professional competence. Through this lens, the chapter discusses broader implications for curriculum design, institutional policies, and the evolving role of human expertise in an AI-augmented future.

Academic Integrity

This chapter explores how AI chatbots challenge traditional notions of academic honesty. As AI tools become more capable of generating code, essays, and problem solutions, programmers and educators face the difficult task of ensuring these technologies support learning without encouraging plagiarism or shortcuts. We examine the ethical responsibility developers carry in designing systems that promote original thinking, help users learn effectively, and prevent misuse.

Deskilling and Skill Erosion

Here, this chapter focuses on the risk that reliance on AI could lead to deskilling, where users lose essential skills and critical thinking abilities because AI does the heavy lifting. Programmers express concerns that if AI handles routine coding tasks or decision-making, learners and professionals might not develop or maintain the depth of expertise needed to innovate and troubleshoot independently. This section discusses how AI tools can be designed to augment rather than replace human skill.

LITERATURE REVIEW

The ethical implications of AI in education and software development have attracted significant scholarly attention in recent years. Researchers have explored how generative AI tools such as ChatGPT and GitHub Copilot are reshaping learning environments, software engineering practices, and the professional identity of programmers. Much of this discourse is anchored in broader concerns about automation, integrity, and the future of work.

In the context of AI in education, Rinta-Kahila et al. (2023) and Crowston and Bolici (2025) apply deskilling theory to explore how persistent dependence on AI may undermine students' development of core competencies such as critical thinking, problem-solving, and hands-on coding proficiency. Their studies reveal that when students routinely rely on AI-generated outputs, without fully engaging in the underlying processes, there is a noticeable risk of skill wasting. Learners may become increasingly reliant on automated guidance, leading to a shallow grasp of concepts and weakened ability to transfer knowledge across tasks.

These studies collectively underscore the core premise of deskilling theory in the AI era. While intelligent systems offer powerful support, their unchecked use can reconfigure the role of learners and practitioners from active problem-solvers to passive consumers of automated output. This shift has implications not only for educational quality but also for the long-term resilience and adaptability of the future workforce. As AI continues to evolve, integrating it responsibly into learning environments will require thoughtful instructional design, scaffolding strategies, and ongoing evaluation to ensure that human expertise remains central to the learning process.

Avila-Chauvet et al. (2023) explore the use of ChatGPT as a support tool for online behavioral task programming. Their study demonstrates that ChatGPT can assist students in understanding and constructing experimental tasks in behavioral research, particularly by providing real-time guidance and code generation. While the tool enhances efficiency and reduces programming barriers, the authors also caution against overreliance, emphasizing the need for critical engagement and foundational skill development to ensure meaningful learning outcomes.

Automation and the Deskilling Debate

The rise of automation has raised the debate in labor and educational research: does technological advancement empower workers and learners by augmenting their skills, or does it undermine human expertise by replacing cognitive labor with machine capabilities? This tension lies at the heart of deskilling theory. Generative AI systems such as GitHub Copilot and ChatGPT offer real-time code generation, debugging suggestions, and language explanations that significantly reduce the cognitive load on students. While this can enhance productivity and accessibility, it also poses the risk of cognitive offloading, wherein learners begin to rely on external tools instead of understanding the concepts and building their problem-solving capabilities. This shift reflects a core concern of the deskilling theory. When a machine assumes a task once performed by a human, the human's capacity to accomplish that task independently may gradually reduce.

Recent studies underscore these concerns. Crowston and Bolici (2025) found that programmers who relied heavily on AI assistance developed lower confidence in their coding abilities and showed reduced initiative in solving unfamiliar problems. Similarly, Rinta-Kahila et al. (2023) observed that AI-assisted software developers often experienced a narrowing of their skillset, relying on tool-generated solutions instead of critically evaluating multiple approaches. In education, this AI-assisted system is particularly alarming, as students are still in the process of forming foundational competencies.

The deskilling debate is further complicated by contrasting arguments in favor of skill augmentation. Some researchers argue that AI can function as a learning companion, offering real-time feedback, exposing students to industry-relevant practices, and allowing learners to tackle more complex tasks earlier in their development. From this perspective, automation is not inherently deskilling; rather, it depends on how the technology is used and what pedagogical structures support its integration. When students are taught to critically engage with AI outputs—rather than unquestioningly accept them—their learning may be enhanced, not hindered.

Nevertheless, the deskilling framework remains a critical lens through which to interrogate the ethical and developmental risks of automation in education. Instructors and institutions must consider whether their use of AI tools promotes deep learning or passive dependence and how curricular choices either reinforce or resist the erosion of human expertise. Without thoughtful design and intentional safeguards, the conveniences of automation may come at the cost of long-term competence, creativity, and professional agency.

Generative AI in Computer Science Education

The integration of generative AI tools into computer science education is reshaping how students learn, practice, and apply programming concepts. Tools such as ChatGPT, GitHub Copilot, and similar large language models (LLMs) are now widely accessible and capable of generating code snippets, offering real-time explanations, and solving complex programming problems in natural language. These tools are increasingly embedded in classroom environments, coding assignments, and self-directed learning, prompting both enthusiasm and concern from educators and researchers.

Moreover, generative AI can support creative problem-solving by suggesting multiple solutions and enabling experimentation with code structures that students may not have considered independently. This new support aligns with constructivist learning principles, where learners build knowledge through exploration and iteration. AI can thus be positioned as a partner in learning, expanding the range of programming experiences and introducing students to industry-relevant development practices early in their education.

There are also unresolved issues around authorship and academic integrity. When a student uses AI-generated content in coursework, questions arise about the originality of the work and the appropriate way to attribute such assistance. Many institutions have yet to establish clear policies regarding the acceptable use of AI tools, leaving students uncertain about what constitutes ethical practice.

From a broader curricular perspective, the presence of generative AI is prompting educators to rethink assessment design. Traditional programming exercises may no longer be sufficient to measure authentic learning if students can easily generate answers with minimal effort. In response, some instructors are adopting AI-aware assessments, such as asking students to critique or improve AI-generated code, document their problem-solving process, or reflect on the decisions they made during development.

In summary, generative AI is rapidly transforming computer science education by providing support, feedback, and automation. While it has the potential to enhance learning, it also demands a recalibration of pedagogy, policy, and ethical guidance. To ensure responsible integration, educators must not only teach students how to use these tools but also why, when, and under what conditions their use is appropriate. Without such guidance, the benefits of generative AI may be overshadowed by diminished learning outcomes and increased ethical ambiguity.

Ethical Implications of AI Use in Academia

The widespread adoption of generative AI in academic environments, particularly within computer science education, has introduced complex ethical challenges that educators and institutions are only beginning to address fully. As tools like ChatGPT, GitHub Copilot, and other AI-powered assistants become common in classrooms, the boundaries between legitimate learning support and academic misconduct are becoming increasingly blurred.

One of the most pressing concerns is the erosion of academic integrity. AI tools can generate entire code solutions, essays, and explanations with minimal human input. While these outputs can be used ethically, for example, as learning aids or sources of inspiration, students may also submit AI-generated content as their work without proper understanding or attribution. This helper raises serious questions about plagiarism, authorship, and originality, especially in coursework that traditionally relies on individual effort and problem-solving.

Another ethical implication involves transparency and disclosure. Should students be required to report when and how they use AI tools in their assignments? Should AI usage be considered similar to citing a source, or is it fundamentally different due to the collaborative and interactive nature of the technology? These questions remain largely unresolved, and institutional policies vary widely. In many cases, the absence of formal guidelines creates uncertainty for students and instructors alike, increasing the likelihood of unintentional ethical violations.

Beyond academic honesty, AI use in academia raises concerns about equity and access. Students from well-resourced backgrounds may have more consistent access to advanced AI tools, while others may rely on outdated systems or lack internet connectivity. This digital divide can exacerbate existing inequalities in education, creating unfair advantages for some students. Additionally, AI systems themselves may reproduce biases embedded in training data, leading to misleading outputs, particularly when applied to natural language tasks or code involving culturally sensitive variables.

There is also the issue of data privacy. Some AI platforms collect data from users to improve their models, raising ethical questions about how student interactions are stored, analyzed, and potentially used without informed consent. In educational settings, where students may unknowingly input sensitive or identifiable information into AI tools, clear data governance policies are essential to safeguard their privacy.

In response to these concerns, many scholars and institutions are calling for the development of ethical frameworks and usage guidelines tailored to academic contexts. These include promoting transparency, encouraging reflective use of AI, and establishing clear expectations around attribution and collaboration. Ethics education itself is increasingly seen as a necessary component of technical training, helping students understand not only how to use AI tools but also how to assess their impact on fairness, trust, and personal responsibility.

Stefaniak and Moore (2024) explore how generative AI can be leveraged to support inclusive design and collaborative decision-making in online instruction. Their study emphasizes the potential of AI tools to facilitate broader participation in instructional design processes, enhance accessibility, and promote learner-centered practices. The authors also address ethical considerations and the importance of intentional implementation to avoid reinforcing existing biases or inequities.

In summary, the ethical implications of AI in academia extend far beyond simple misconduct. They encompass issues of authentic learning, institutional trust, digital equity, and professional development. As generative AI continues to evolve, educational institutions must take a proactive role in shaping ethical norms and ensuring that students are equipped to navigate this complex technological landscape with integrity and awareness.

Student Perceptions and Behavioral Shifts

As generative AI tools become increasingly integrated into academic workflows, understanding how students perceive and interact with these technologies is essential to evaluating their broader impact on learning, ethics, and professional development. Student perceptions not only shape how AI is used in practice but also influence behavioral patterns that may lead to long-term shifts in skill acquisition, academic integrity, and identity formation within the discipline of computer science.

However, this positive perception is accompanied by behavioral shifts that raise pedagogical and ethical concerns. A growing number of students report using AI tools to complete entire assignments, sometimes without fully understanding the generated solutions. In such cases, AI becomes less of a learning aid and more of a shortcut, facilitating task completion without skill mastery. This behavior aligns with the concerns outlined in deskilling theory, wherein automation reduces the need for deep engagement, practice, and independent problem-solving.

Moreover, student behavior often reflects a lack of clarity around academic boundaries. In the absence of clear guidelines, some students rationalize the use of AI as equivalent to using a search engine or collaborating with a peer, blurring the lines between acceptable and unethical behavior. This ambiguity can lead to inconsistent application of academic standards, both among students and across institutions. Some students express concern about being penalized for using tools they believe are commonly accepted, while others deliberately conceal their use to avoid accusations of misconduct.

Importantly, student perceptions are not static. Exposure to ethics education, instructor expectations, and peer norms can all influence how learners approach AI. When ethical considerations are embedded into the curriculum, such as requiring students to document how AI tools were used or reflect on the reasoning behind their solutions, students tend to become more thoughtful and intentional in their behavior. This behavior suggests that institutional culture plays a critical role in shaping student attitudes and fostering responsible use.

In addition, students are beginning to express nuanced concerns about the long-term effects of AI dependence. Some worry that overreliance on AI tools may leave them underprepared for job interviews, technical assessments, or real-world coding scenarios that require foundational knowledge. Others recognize a tension between speed and depth, acknowledging that while AI may help them complete tasks faster, it does not necessarily lead to better understanding.

Finally, the use of AI is influencing students' emerging professional identities. In some cases, students begin to see themselves more as system integrators or AI supervisors than as traditional coders. While this shift can be seen as an adaptation to new technological realities, it also raises questions about what it means to be a competent and ethical software developer in an age of intelligent automation.

Barke et al. (2023) examine how programmers interact with code-generating models like GitHub Copilot in real-world development settings. Through an empirical study, they identify that while these tools accelerate coding and reduce syntactic effort, they also introduce new challenges related to code comprehension, debugging, and maintaining developer engagement. The authors emphasize the need for thoughtful integration of AI tools to ensure that productivity gains do not come at the expense of deeper understanding and developer agency.

In summary, student perceptions of AI tools are shaped by a complex mix of enthusiasm, ambiguity, and self-reflection. These perceptions drive behavioral shifts that can both support and hinder learning outcomes. To foster ethical, meaningful engagement with AI, educational institutions must provide clear guidance, embed reflective practices, and ensure that students understand not only how to use AI but also why and when its use aligns with both academic values and professional expectations.

Institutional and Educational Responses

As generative AI becomes an everyday presence in computer science programs, colleges and universities are developing multifaceted responses that combine policy, curriculum redesign, faculty development, and student support. These efforts aim to harness AI's benefits while safeguarding academic integrity and preserving deep learning.

1. Policy Formation and Clarity

Most institutions now recognize that vague "don't plagiarize" statements are insufficient in an AI-rich environment. Forward-thinking universities have issued explicit guidelines that:

- *Define acceptable versus unacceptable AI use* (e.g., brainstorming ideas vs. submitting unedited AI-generated code).
- *Require disclosure*—students must indicate when and how AI tools were used in assignments, akin to citing a source.
- *Outline penalties* for undisclosed or excessive reliance on AI output.

Where policies are co-created with faculty and student representatives, compliance and ethical awareness rise markedly, reducing unintentional misconduct.

2. AI-Aware Assessment Design

Tools like Copilot easily solve traditional auto-graded programming problems. In response, instructors are:

- Shifting from output-based grading to process-based evaluation, students submit design rationales, debugging logs, or code reviews that reveal their thinking.
- Embedding reflection prompts ("Explain why you accepted or rejected the AI's suggestion").
- Adopting oral defenses or live coding interviews to verify individual understanding.

These strategies align with Job Characteristics Theory by restoring task identity and meaningful feedback, discouraging superficial copying.

3. Curriculum Integration of Ethics and Metacognition

Rather than banning AI, many programs teach "AI literacy", how large language models work, their limitations, and ethical pitfalls. Typical interventions include:

- Module-level ethics mini-lectures tied to real coding labs (e.g., bias in training data, licensing issues for generated code).
- Metacognitive checklists prompt students to question AI output accuracy, security implications, and long-term skill impact.
- Team projects *where* one role is the "AI skeptic," responsible for auditing tool suggestions.

Early evidence shows that embedding these elements improves students' critical engagement without dampening their enthusiasm for AI.

4. Faculty Professional Development

Many instructors initially felt ill-equipped to supervise AI use. Successful departments now offer:

- Hands-on workshops demonstrating AI capabilities and failure modes.

- Shared rubrics and exemplars that illustrate how to grade AI-augmented work fairly.
- Cross-disciplinary faculty learning communities where educators compare strategies across writing, design, and computing courses.

By normalizing experimentation and reflection, these programs help faculty model the ethical, inquisitive mindset they want students to adopt.

5. Supportive Infrastructure and Detection Tools

Some universities deploy AI-detection and provenance systems, but they are moving toward "trust-and-verify" models rather than punitive surveillance alone. Complementary measures include:

- Version-control mandates (e.g., Git commits showing incremental development).
- Secure coding sandboxes that log AI interactions for later review.
- Open-source exemplars that demonstrate how to integrate AI responsibly, giving students positive templates to emulate.

Synthesis

Institutional and pedagogical responses reveal an emerging consensus: outright prohibition is neither practical nor desirable. Instead, success lies in transparent policies, process-oriented assessment, ethics-infused curricula, and well-supported faculty. When these elements align, AI becomes a catalyst for deeper learning rather than a shortcut to superficial completion, addressing deskilling concerns while preserving the creative and intellectual growth central to computer science education.

Theoretical Perspectives

Understanding the ethical challenges and behavioral shifts in AI-assisted education requires a strong theoretical foundation. This chapter draws upon three primary frameworks: Deskilling Theory, Job Characteristics Theory, and Technology Threat Avoidance Theory. Together, these perspectives help explain how automation influences student learning, motivation, and ethical decision-making in computer science education.

1. Deskilling Theory

The deskilling theory posits that technological automation can reduce workers' control, knowledge, and autonomy by transferring expertise from humans to machines. In computer science education, this theory is increasingly used to assess how generative AI may reduce foundational programming skills. For example, when students rely on AI tools to generate code, debug errors, or complete assignments, they may bypass the basic understanding of programming, logical thinking, and problem-solving skills.

Recent applications of deskilling theory (Crowston & Bolici, 2025; Rinta-Kahila et al., 2023) highlight how AI can unintentionally shift learners from active creators to passive validators. Over time, this reliance may diminish their confidence, competence, and ability to work independently, key qualities for future software professionals. This theory provides a cautionary lens through which to examine the ethical boundaries of AI assistance in education.

Kuhail et al. (2023) investigate the impact of ChatGPT on software development workflows and developer perceptions of AI tools. Their study reveals a mix of optimism and concern among programmers, while many appreciate the efficiency and support AI offers, others express anxiety over job security and diminished skill relevance. The authors highlight the importance of understanding these perceptions to shape future integration strategies that balance technological advancement with human agency and skill preservation.

2. Job Characteristics Theory

While the deskilling theory emphasizes risks, the job characteristics theory offers a constructive framework for designing learning environments that preserve motivation and skill development. The theory identifies five core job dimensions that influence individual outcomes: skill variety, task identity, task significance, autonomy, and feedback.

Applying this to education, instructors can design assignments and workflows that encourage students to engage with AI tools critically rather than passively. For example, structured reflection on AI-assisted code, peer review, and manual debugging tasks can enhance task identity and feedback mechanisms. This theory supports the argument that with thoughtful curriculum design, AI tools can be integrated in a way that fosters, not replaces, student learning.

Crowston and Bolici (2025) examine the dual processes of deskilling and upskilling in the context of AI system use. Through empirical analysis, they highlight how AI tools can simultaneously reduce the need for specific technical skills while fostering the development of new competencies related to AI oversight and interpretation. The study emphasizes that the impact of AI on skill development is context-dependent, shaped by how individuals engage with the technology and the organizational structures that support its use.

3. Technology Threat Avoidance Theory

Technology Threat Avoidance Theory (Liang & Xue, 2009) explains how individuals assess and respond to perceived risks associated with new technologies. In education, this theory helps explain why some students and educators resist the use of generative AI tools, often due to concerns about academic misconduct, privacy violations, or skill loss.

According to this framework, users take protective actions when they perceive a threat to be both severe and personally relevant. This action may include avoiding specific AI tools, setting stricter usage policies, or seeking alternative learning strategies. Understanding these threat perceptions can guide educators in addressing ethical concerns and building trust through clear guidelines, transparency, and training.

Khurana et al. (2024) investigate the limitations of large language models (LLMs)-based assistants in software help-seeking scenarios. Their study analyzes when and why prompt-based interactions can fail to meet developers' needs. It reveals challenges such as misleading responses, overconfidence in AI-generated outputs, and difficulty in prompt formulation. The authors highlight the importance of context-aware design and user education to improve the reliability and effectiveness of LLM-based support tools in software development.

Synthesis and Relevance

Together, these theories provide a multifaceted framework for understanding the ethical use of AI in computer science education. Deskilling theory highlights the risks of over-reliance on automation, job characteristics theory emphasizes the importance of intentional instructional design, and technology threat avoidance theory sheds light on how individuals respond to perceived ethical threats.

By grounding this chapter in these theoretical perspectives, the discussion moves beyond surface-level concerns and into the deeper dynamics shaping how students learn, adapt, and make ethical choices in an AI-driven environment. These frameworks are essential for guiding future research and institutional policy as educational systems continue to evolve alongside intelligent technologies.

Gaps in Literature and Future Directions

Despite a growing body of research on the ethical implications of AI in computer science education, several critical gaps remain. These gaps limit our understanding of how AI tools are truly affecting student learning, ethical behavior, and long-term professional development. Addressing these areas is essential for creating a more comprehensive, inclusive, and forward-looking framework for ethical AI integration.

1. Lack of Longitudinal Studies on Skill Retention

Most existing studies provide short-term snapshots of how students use AI tools, but there is little longitudinal evidence on how this usage impacts long-term skill development. For example, it remains unclear whether frequent reliance on tools like ChatGPT or GitHub Copilot weakens students' ability to code independently over time. Longitudinal research is needed to assess whether AI-assisted learners develop into equally competent and adaptable professionals as those trained through traditional, manual learning methods.

2. Underrepresentation of Student Voices and Ethical Reasoning

While many studies focus on teacher perspectives or institutional policies, few deeply explore how students themselves perceive the ethical use of AI. Research rarely addresses how students form their ethical frameworks, how they navigate ambiguous situations involving AI-generated content, or how their sense of professional identity evolves. Future work should adopt student-centered qualitative approaches, such as interviews or narrative inquiry, to better understand how learners experience and rationalize the use of AI.

3. Limited Cross-Cultural and Global Perspectives

Much of the research on AI ethics in education has been conducted in North America and Europe, often overlooking how cultural values, educational norms, and regulatory environments shape attitudes toward AI use elsewhere. As AI becomes more globally accessible, it is crucial to examine how students in diverse cultural and institutional contexts interpret academic integrity, authorship, and fairness. Comparative studies across regions can enrich ethical guidelines with culturally sensitive insights.

4. Inadequate Focus on Institutional Policy Design and Enforcement

While ethical frameworks are frequently discussed in theoretical terms, there is limited empirical research on how universities are crafting and enforcing policies related to AI use in coursework. Questions remain about how clear, consistent, and effective these policies are in practice. Additionally, little is known about how faculty are trained to address AI-related misconduct or how students are taught to navigate these policies. Future research should evaluate institutional strategies and their impact on ethical outcomes.

5. Need for Educational Innovation Grounded in Theory

Although some educators are experimenting with AI-integrated assignments and assessments, there is a lack of theory-driven instructional models for teaching ethical AI use. Few approaches intentionally align with frameworks such as deskilling theory or job characteristics theory to ensure that educational design supports both ethical reasoning and skill retention. Future work should focus on developing and testing curriculum models that apply these theories to bridge ethics and practice.

To address these gaps, researchers, educators, and institutions should consider the following directions:

- Design mixed-methods studies to assess both learning outcomes and ethical development over time.
- Incorporate student voices through participatory research, ethnography, or digital diaries that capture their lived experiences with AI.
- Expand research to underrepresented regions and educational systems, particularly in Asia, Africa, and Latin America.
- Develop and evaluate institutional frameworks for AI use that are enforceable, transparent, and adaptable to emerging tools.
- Create open-source, theory-informed teaching materials that guide ethical AI engagement across the curriculum.

By pursuing these directions, the academic community can better prepare computer science students not only to use AI effectively but also to contribute meaningfully to the development of ethical, responsible technologies.

Summary of Key Insights

The literature on generative AI in computer science education reveals a rapidly evolving landscape filled with both promise and peril. On the one hand, AI tools like ChatGPT and GitHub Copilot offer significant educational benefits, enhancing accessibility, providing real-time feedback, and accelerating skill acquisition. On the other hand, these tools raise critical concerns about academic integrity, authorship, student dependency, and long-term skill erosion.

Through the lens of deskilling theory, scholars have warned that overreliance on automation can undermine the very learning outcomes that educational institutions strive to cultivate. Complementary frameworks such as job characteristics theory and technology threat avoidance theory further illuminate how students interact with AI, the motivational factors at play, and the psychological and ethical tensions that arise in AI-rich learning environments.

Research findings consistently show that student perceptions are mixed, shaped by convenience, uncertainty, and evolving norms. Behavioral shifts, toward shortcut-based task completion, diminished self-efficacy, and ambiguity about what constitutes fair use are emerging as key concerns. In response, institutions are developing policies and pedagogical approaches aimed at striking a balance: allowing students to benefit from AI tools while maintaining ethical standards and preserving deep learning.

Despite these advances, the literature also reveals several persistent gaps. These include a lack of longitudinal data on skill retention, insufficient student-centered research on ethical reasoning, and a need for more global and cross-cultural perspectives. Moreover, the development of coherent, theory-driven pedagogical models that integrate AI responsibly remains limited.

In summary, the literature underscores the urgent need for ethics of AI integration tools in computer science education. As the field continues to evolve, future research must not only monitor outcomes but also shape the values, practices, and institutional cultures that guide how AI is used in the classroom and beyond.

About the Study

This study followed established best practices in qualitative research, employing a phenomenological approach to explore how individuals experience the integration of generative AI in programming education. Phenomenology, as defined by Peoples (2021), aims to understand the essence of lived experiences, distinguishing it from other qualitative methods by its deep focus on personal meaning and perception.

Semi-structured, open-ended research questions were used to guide the inquiry, allowing participants the flexibility to share detailed reflections while maintaining consistency across interviews. Triangulation was applied by comparing data from participants with diverse roles, backgrounds, and experiences to enhance the credibility of the findings.

Member checking was conducted with selected participants, who were invited to review preliminary interpretations of their responses. This process helped ensure the accuracy and trustworthiness of the data analysis (Riazi et al., 2023). Additionally, the researcher engaged in reflexive journaling throughout the study to record analytical decisions, reflect on personal assumptions, and minimize potential bias.

Ethical standards were upheld at all stages of the research. Participant confidentiality was maintained through the removal of identifying information from transcripts, and all data were securely stored on password-protected devices. Transparency and respect for participant autonomy were central to the study's design, ensuring informed consent and voluntary participation.

Research Design

This study employed a qualitative research design centered on in-depth, semi-structured interviews to investigate how programmers and students experience the integration of generative AI in software development and coding education. The approach of the research was qualitative to capture the rich, contextualized insights and personal narratives. The goal was not to generalize findings to a broad population but to uncover nuanced patterns, perceptions, and meaning-making processes that emerge from individual engagement with AI tools in real-world settings.

Participant Selection

Participants were recruited using purposive sampling, targeting individuals with direct experience in programming and AI chatbot development. The sample included fifteen participants, comprising undergraduate and graduate computer science students and professional software developers. This diversity of perspectives allowed for a better understanding of how generative AI is perceived and applied across different levels of expertise and contexts. All participants reported some level of interaction with tools such as ChatGPT, GitHub Copilot, or similar large language model-based systems.

Participants were invited through academic networks, professional contacts, and university listservs. Before each interview, informed consent was sent out, and participants were assured of confidentiality and the option to withdraw at any time. No financial compensation was offered.

Data Collection

Semi-structured, in-depth data were collected through interviews conducted via Zoom between 45 and 75 minutes. The interview protocol was designed to elicit reflections on several core topics, including experiences with AI-assisted coding, perceptions of skill development and task ownership, ethical considerations, strategies for adapting to AI in the workplace or classroom, and visions for future human-AI collaboration.

Interviews followed a flexible structure, allowing participants to expand on issues that were most salient to them. This format enabled the researcher to probe deeper into emergent themes while maintaining consistency across interviews. All sessions were recorded with participant consent and subsequently transcribed verbatim for analysis.

Analytical Approach

Data analysis followed a thematic coding approach, combining both inductive and deductive strategies. Transcripts were first reviewed holistically to identify recurring concepts, language patterns, and points of emphasis. Initial codes were generated based on both participant responses and the theoretical frameworks guiding this study, namely, Deskilling Theory, Job Characteristics Theory, and Technology Threat Avoidance Theory.

As the analysis progressed, patterns began to emerge across participants' reflections. Similar responses were grouped to highlight common approaches, while points of disagreement or tension helped surface more profound ethical questions. These insights clustered around three main themes: how developers navigate the complex task of designing intuitive, user-friendly chatbot experiences; how they respond to challenges arising from real-time user feedback and interaction; and how they envision future collaboration between humans and AI, especially in light of ongoing technological advancements. Coding and organization of thematic categories were conducted using qualitative data analysis software (MaxQDA), which facilitated data visualization and ensured consistency in identifying themes across interviews.

Trustworthiness

This study followed several best practices in qualitative research. Triangulation was employed by comparing data across participants with varied roles and experiences. Member checking was conducted with select participants who reviewed preliminary interpretations of their responses to confirm accuracy. In addition, reflexive journaling was used by the researcher to document analytical decisions and reduce potential bias in the interpretation of data.

The study also upheld ethical research principles, including confidentiality, transparency, and respect for participant autonomy. All data were stored on password-protected devices, and identifiers were removed from transcripts during analysis.

Ethical Considerations

Ethical considerations were a top priority throughout the study. Every participant gave informed consent before taking part, ensuring they fully understood the purpose of the research and what their involvement would entail. To protect privacy, all personal details were removed or replaced with pseudonyms, and all collected data was stored securely using encrypted, password-protected systems. Participants were also made aware that their participation was entirely voluntary, and they could choose to withdraw from the study at any time without any negative consequences or pressure. This approach aimed to create a respectful, transparent environment that safeguarded the rights and well-being of everyone involved.

Findings and Discussion

This section presents the significant findings of the study, organized by the three research questions. Drawing on participants' interviews, institutional perspectives, and theoretical frameworks, including deskilling theory, job characteristics theory, and technology threat avoidance theory, each subsection discusses how programmers navigate the technical, ethical, and human-centered dimensions of AI chatbot development.

Navigating the Human Side of Chatbot Design

One of the most pressing challenges developers face when building AI chatbots is finding the right balance between automation and empathy. While chatbots are expected to deliver quick, efficient responses, programmers often struggle to make those responses feel human, especially in emotionally sensitive situations. Many participants admitted that current AI systems still fall short in recognizing tone, understanding cultural nuance, or expressing genuine care. This challenge makes it difficult to design interactions that feel trustworthy and emotionally intelligent.

Another primary concern is the quality and diversity of training data. Developers pointed out that AI systems are only as inclusive as the data they're built on. If that data lacks representation or contains bias, the chatbot's responses can easily become inaccurate, misleading, or even exclusionary. These issues don't just reflect technical limitations—they pose real ethical dilemmas, especially when users come from diverse linguistic or cultural backgrounds.

Speed and efficiency, often prized in the tech development world, came with their trade-offs. Many programmers relied on pre-built APIs and frameworks to accelerate the development process. While convenient, these tools also limited their ability to customize the chatbot's behavior for specific user groups. Some developers described feeling boxed in or even ethically conflicted—pressured to ship a functioning product quickly, even if it didn't fully meet the needs of its intended audience.

Together, these tensions reveal the deeper ethical stakes behind what might seem like technical decisions. Building a chatbot isn't just about functionality—it's about understanding the people who will use it and making sure the system responds with fairness, clarity, and care.

Listening, Learning, and Improving: the Feedback Problem in Chatbot Development

For many developers, refining chatbot behavior is a trial-and-error process shaped more by chance than by design. Instead of structured user testing, feedback often arrives reactively—through bug reports, frustrated comments, or unexpected user behavior. This ad hoc approach slows development and leaves teams struggling to identify what users actually need or expect from the chatbot. Without clear feedback loops, opportunities for meaningful improvement are often missed.

Beyond usability, developers expressed concern about the ethical dimension of user interactions. They recognized their responsibility to minimize harm, especially in cases where chatbots might spread misinformation, confuse users, or come off as insensitive. Yet most described a lack of guidance or accountability structures to help them address those risks in real time. This new behavior left them feeling vulnerable, unsure of how to evaluate or respond to ethical red flags when they surfaced.

Despite these challenges, there were bright spots. Developers who collaborated with UX designers, ethics advisors, or professionals from other disciplines reported stronger results, not just in product quality, but in their growth as designers and problem-solvers. These cross-disciplinary efforts helped bridge the gap between technical training and the broader human context of chatbot use, offering new ways to think about design, responsibility, and the user experience.

Ultimately, while the technical tools for chatbot development have advanced rapidly, the systems for understanding and responding to users are still catching up. For ethical, effective AI systems, developers need more than just code—they need structured support, diverse collaboration, and a clearer sense of the people behind the data.

Looking Ahead: Redefining Human–AI Collaboration

As AI becomes more capable, developers are already reimagining what it means to work alongside intelligent systems. Most envision a future where chatbots act as support tools rather than decision-makers, especially in high-stakes contexts like healthcare, education, or law. While automation can help speed up tasks or streamline communication, participants were clear: the final judgment should remain with humans. Trust, empathy, and moral reasoning, they argued, aren't things you can easily code.

Still, the rapid advancement of AI has stirred up concerns. Many developers expressed a quiet but growing fear of deskilling. They worried that as AI systems handle more complex logic or generate entire blocks of code, developers might lose touch with their core technical skills—or worse, be replaced entirely in some roles. There's also concern that critical thinking and ethical reflection could fade if people become too reliant on AI-generated outputs.

At the same time, some see this shift as an opportunity, not an ending, but a redefinition of what it means to be a programmer. Instead of manually writing every function or chatbot response, developers imagine themselves curating and overseeing AI behavior. Their future roles might look more like ethical supervisors, product managers, or design critics—responsible not just for functionality, but for ensuring that AI aligns with human values, organizational goals, and user expectations.

This vision reflects a broader transformation in how we build and relate to technology. Developers are no longer just coders; they are becoming stewards of AI systems that learn, adapt, and influence real human lives.

Summary of Findings and Ethical Insights

This study explores how programmers grapple with ethical challenges, user interaction complexities, and evolving roles in the development of AI chatbots. Rather than simply reporting participant statements or raw data, the findings are interpreted through the lens of ethical tensions, guided by theories on deskilling, job characteristics, and technology threat avoidance.

User Experience Challenges

Programmers face significant ethical dilemmas when trying to design chatbots that are empathetic, clear, and context-aware. The reliance on pre-trained models with biased or narrow datasets often limits the inclusivity and emotional intelligence of these systems. This ethical dilemma creates a conflict between the need for efficiency and the responsibility to deliver respectful, nuanced interactions. Developers expressed feeling constrained by fast-paced development frameworks that prioritize automation, sometimes at the expense of user care and ethical customization. For example, collaborative efforts to integrate psychological insights reveal how a human-centered approach can counterbalance these pressures, enriching chatbot empathy without sacrificing technical efficiency.

User Interaction and Feedback

A lack of structured feedback systems presents ethical blind spots in chatbot development. Without clear channels for continuous, formal user input, developers often depend on reactive and informal feedback, increasing the risk that issues like misinformation or misunderstanding go unnoticed. This absence of accountability mechanisms complicates the ethical obligation to protect users in real-time interactions. Encouragingly, interdisciplinary collaborations with UX designers and ethics professionals help bridge this gap, fostering more ethically informed development practices and improving product quality. These partnerships suggest that ethical responsibility in AI design extends beyond individual programmers to a collective, cross-disciplinary effort.

Future Human-AI Collaboration

Looking forward, programmers envision AI as a tool that should augment, not replace, human decision-making, especially where moral complexity is involved. The convenience of AI brings concerns about deskilling and the erosion of critical human oversight, highlighting the risk that overreliance on AI could undermine essential skills and ethical judgment. Developers anticipate a transformed role where they shift from writing all code manually to curating, auditing, and ethically supervising AI behavior. This redefined role emphasizes stewardship and user advocacy, reflecting a broader ethical commitment to responsible AI integration.

Implications

These findings highlight the urgent need for reforms in educational curricula, institutional policies, and industry-academia collaboration. Fostering ethical literacy and sustainable human-AI design practices will help prepare programmers to navigate the complex moral landscape of AI development and ensure technology serves human values.

FUTURE RESEARCH DIRECTIONS

While this study provides meaningful insights into the ethical, experiential, and professional dimensions of AI chatbot development among computer science students and practitioners, several limitations must be acknowledged. First, the study was limited by a small sample size drawn from a few academic institutions and development contexts. This limitation restricts the generalizability of the findings, as they may not adequately represent the diverse perspectives of programmers from different regions, levels of expertise, or organizational settings. Second, the research employed an exploratory qualitative approach that prioritized depth over breadth. While this method yielded rich narrative and thematic insights, the findings cannot be statistically generalized without complementary quantitative studies. Third, the data were primarily self-reported through interviews and participant reflections, making it susceptible to biases such as social desirability or retrospective distortion; participants may have underreported unethical behaviors or overstated their engagement with ethical principles. Fourth, the study focused mainly on students and early-career developers, which, while valuable, limits insight into how experienced professionals and organizational leaders handle AI ethics in chatbot development at scale. Finally, the fast-paced evolution of generative AI technology presents a challenge for drawing long-term conclusions. New tools, regulations, and ethical concerns may arise that were not fully captured during the research.

Building on these limitations, future research and practice can advance this field in several important ways:

1. Longitudinal and Mixed-Methods Research

Future studies should track participants over time to explore how their skills, ethical awareness, and AI usage evolve in academic and professional settings. Incorporating surveys and performance assessments would also complement qualitative insights.

2. Broader and More Diverse Sampling

Expanding participant demographics to include professionals from various industries, cultures, and seniority levels can provide a more comprehensive understanding of how ethical standards are understood and practiced across contexts.

3. Comparative Cross-Institutional Studies

Research comparing how different universities or training programs approach AI ethics could help identify best practices, challenges, and the effectiveness of various curriculum models in promoting ethical reasoning.

4. Integration of AI Ethics Into Technical Curriculum

Future work should focus on developing and evaluating curriculum models that integrate AI ethics into coding, UX design, and systems development courses. These models should be co-developed with students, educators, and industry partners to ensure relevance and sustainability.

5. Exploration of New Professional Roles

As AI-human collaboration evolves, research should examine emerging roles such as prompt engineers, AI ethics officers, and human-in-the-loop designers. Understanding the skills and values these roles require can help reshape education and workforce development in ethical and forward-looking ways.

By acknowledging these limitations and pursuing targeted future directions, researchers and educators can better support the development of responsible AI practices in computer science education. Equipping students and professionals with both technical and ethical literacy is essential for sustaining meaningful human agency in an increasingly automated world.

CONCLUSION

The increasing integration of generative AI in software development, especially with the help of AI chatbots, presents both promising opportunities and complex ethical challenges. This chapter explored how students and programmers perceive and navigate user experience issues, address feedback and interaction complexities, and envision the future of collaboration between humans and AI systems. Grounded in deskilling theory, job characteristics theory, and technology threat avoidance theory, the findings highlight critical tensions between efficiency and ethical responsibility, automation and agency, and innovation and integrity.

Across all three research questions, participants demonstrated a growing awareness of their ethical responsibilities in shaping AI behavior, particularly in contexts where chatbots interact with users in emotionally or socially sensitive ways. While AI tools improve productivity and streamline development, they also risk displacing fundamental skills and distancing programmers from the social consequences of their work. Students and professionals alike are now operating in a space where they must balance technical proficiency with ethical discernment, often in the absence of clear institutional policies or pedagogical frameworks.

The study revealed an emerging redefinition of the programmer's role. No longer solely viewed as technical coders, programmers increasingly see themselves as content manager to evaluate code and accept the correct code for assignments or the working environment. This shift signals the need for educational institutions and industry stakeholders to adapt, redesigning curricula, assessment practices, and mentorship models that emphasize ethical reasoning, user-centered design, and responsible innovation.

REFERENCES

Avila-Chauvet, L., Mejía, D., & Acosta Quiroz, C. (2023). CHATGPT as a support tool for online behavioral task programming. *SSRN*. Retrieved from https://ssrn .com/abstract=4329020

Barke, S., James, M., & Polikarpova, N. (2023). Grounded Copilot: How programmers interact with code-generating models. *Proceedings of the ACM on Programming Languages, 7*(OOPSLA1), 85-111. doi:DOI: 10.1145/3586030

Braverman, H. (1974). *Labor and monopoly capital*. Monthly Review Press.

Crowston, K., & Bolici, F. (2025). Deskilling and upskilling with AI Systems. *nformation Research an International Electronic Journal, 30*(iConf), 1009-1023. doi:DOI: 10.47989/ir30iconf47143

Daigle, K. (2024). *Survey: The AI wave continues to grow on software development teams*. Retrieved from https://github.blog/author/kdaigle/

Hackman, J. R., & Oldham, G. R. (1976). Motivation through the design of work: Test of a theory. *Organizational Behavior and Human Performance, 16*(2), 250–279. DOI: 10.1016/0030-5073(76)90016-7

Khurana, A., Subramonyam, H., & Chilana, P. K. (2024). Why and when llm-based assistants can go wrong: Investigating the effectiveness of prompt-based interactions for software help-seeking. *arXiv.org*. https://doi.org//arxiv.2402.08030DOI: 10.48550

Kuhail, M. A., Mathew, S. S., Khalil, A., Khalil, A., & Shah, S. J. (2023). "Will I be replaced?" Assessing ChatGPT's effect on software development and programmer perceptions of AI tools. *arXiv.org*. https://doi.org/DOI: 10.2139/ssrn.4571482

Liang, H., & Xue, Y. (2009). Avoidance of information technology threats: A theoretical perspective. *Management Information Systems Quarterly, 33*(1), 71–90. DOI: 10.2307/20650279

Peoples, K. (2021). *How to write a phenomenological dissertation: A step-by-step guide* (Vol. 56). SAGE.

Riazi, M., Rezvani, R., & Ghanbar, H. (2023). Trustworthiness in L2 writing research: A review and analysis of qualitative articles in the Journal of Second Language Writing. *Research Methods in Applied Linguistics, 2*(3). Advance online publication. DOI: 10.1016/j.rmal.2023.100065

Rinta-Kahila, T., Penttinen, E., Salovaara, A., Soliman, W., & Ruissalo, J. (2023). The vicious circles of skill erosion: A case study of cognitive automation. *Journal of the Association for Information Systems, 24*(5), 1378–1412. DOI: 10.17705/1jais.00829

Stefaniak, J., & Moore, S. (2024). The Use of Generative AI to Support Inclusivity and Design Deliberation for Online Instruction. *Online and Blended Learning in the Age of Generative AI, 28*(3), 181–205. DOI: 10.24059/olj.v28i3.4458

KEY TERMS AND DEFINITIONS

Academic Integrity: Commitment to honesty, trust, fairness, respect, and responsibility in educational work. It includes the avoidance of plagiarism, cheating, and unauthorized assistance, including improper use of AI-generated content.

Artificial Intelligence (AI): A field of computer science focused on creating systems capable of performing tasks that typically require human intelligence, such as reasoning, learning, problem-solving, and language understanding.

Bias in AI: Systematic and unfair discrimination that occurs in AI outputs due to biased training data, algorithms, or system design, often affecting marginalized groups disproportionately.

Chatbot: An AI-powered program designed to simulate human conversation through text or voice. Chatbots are commonly used in customer service, education, and healthcare applications.

Deskilling: A process by which automation or technological tools reduce the need for human skills, often leading to diminished expertise, confidence, or ownership over work processes.

Ethical AI Use: The responsible and informed use of AI tools that align with moral principles, institutional policies, and social values. It includes fairness, accountability, transparency, and respect for privacy and user well-being.

Ethics-by-Design: An approach to system development in which ethical principles are embedded into the design process from the outset, ensuring that technology aligns with human values and social good.

Generative AI: A subset of AI technologies that can generate content—including text, code, images, or audio—based on input prompts. Examples include ChatGPT, GitHub Copilot, and other large language models (LLMs).

Job Characteristics Theory: A psychological framework that explains how the design of work affects motivation and performance. Key dimensions include skill variety, task identity, task significance, autonomy, and feedback.

Prompt Engineering: The practice of crafting effective input prompts to optimize the responses generated by AI models, especially in natural language and code generation contexts.

Technology Threat Avoidance Theory: A theory that explains how individuals assess and respond to potential threats posed by technology, often leading to avoidance behavior when perceived risks outweigh benefits.

Compilation of References

Abbasi, A. Z., Tsiotsou, R. H., Hussain, K., Rather, R. A., & Ting, D. H. (2023). Investigating the impact of social media images' value, consumer engagement, and involvement on eWOM of a tourism destination: A transmittal mediation approach. *Journal of Retailing and Consumer Services*, *71*, 103231. DOI: 10.1016/j.jretconser.2022.103231

Abdelfattah, F., Salah, M., Dahleez, K., Darwazeh, R., & Al Halbusi, H. (2024). The future of competitive advantage in Oman: Integrating green product innovation, AI, and intellectual capital in business strategies. *International Journal of Innovation Studies*, *8*(2), 154–171.

Abdullahi, M., Baashar, Y., Alhussian, H., Alwadain, A., Aziz, N., Capretz, L. F., & Abdulkadir, S. J. (2022). Detecting cybersecurity attacks on the internet of things using artificial intelligence methods: A systematic literature review. *Electronics (Basel)*, *11*(2), 198.

Abiodun, T., Rampersad, G., & Brinkworth, R. (2023). Driving industrial digital transformation. *Journal of Computer Information Systems*, *63*(6), 1345–1361.

Aboelmaged, M., Bani-Melhem, S., Al-Hawari, M. A., & Ali, I. (2024). Product innovation research over the past 60 years: A bibliometric analysis of intellectual structure and emergent trends. *Benchmarking*, *31*(6), 2034–2060.

Abrardi, L., Cambini, C., & Rondi, L. (2022). Artificial intelligence, firms and consumer behavior: A survey. *Journal of Economic Surveys*, *36*(4), 969–991. DOI: 10.1111/joes.12455

Abu Hamour, A. M., Massadeh, D. D. M., & Bshayreh, M. M. (2023). The impact of the COSO control components on the financial performance in the Jordanian banks and the moderating effect of board independence. *Journal of Sustainable Finance & Investment*, *13*(1), 161–175. DOI: 10.1080/20430795.2021.1886553

Abusalma, A. (2021). The effect of implementing artificial intelligence on job performance in commercial banks of Jordan. *Management Science Letters, 11*(7), 2061–2070. DOI: 10.5267/j.msl.2021.3.003

Adebosin, G. W., Toriola, A. K., Oyewole, S. A., & Saula, D. T. (2019). Disruptive innovation and performance of family business in Ogun state. *3rd Covenant University International Conference on Entrepreneurship (CU–ICE), March 20–22, 351–371.*

Adigwe, C. S., Olaniyi, O. O., Olabanji, S. O., Okunleye, O. J., Mayeke, N. R., & Ajayi, S. A. (2024). Forecasting the future: The interplay of artificial intelligence, innovation, and competitiveness and its effect on the global economy. Innovation, and Competitiveness and its Effect on the Global Economy (February 26, 2024).

Adkins, T. (2021). Optimal use of financial leverage in a corporate capital structure: Corporate finance accounting. (Rev. by Drury. A) Investopedia, Dotdash Meredith, California. https://www.investopedia.com/articles/investing/111813/optimal-use-financial-leverage-corporate-capital-structure.asp

Agboola, M. G., Akinbode, M., Segun-Adeniran, C., Dibia, P. I., Oloruntoba, A., Dinyain, T., Fabunmi, T. J., Funsho, T., Akinde, O. A., & Betek, C. M. (2019). Technology usage and employee behavior: Controversies, complications, and implications in the Nigerian business environment. *IOP Conference Series. Earth and Environmental Science, 331*(2), 1–6.

Aghware, F. O., Okoh, O. L., & Malasowe, B. O. (2025). *Security Implications and Risk Mitigation Strategies in the Implementation of Artificial Intelligence for Sustainable Development.* Covenant University Journal of Politics and International Affairs.

Agrawal, A., Gans, J., & Goldfarb, A. (2018). *Prediction machines: The simple economics of artificial intelligence.* Harvard Business Review Press.

Aguirre Montero, A., & López-Sánchez, J. A. (2021). Intersection of Data Science and Smart Destinations: A Systematic Review. *Frontiers in Psychology, 12,* 712610. DOI: 10.3389/fpsyg.2021.712610 PMID: 34393952

Aguirre, E., Roggeveen, A. L., Grewal, D., & Wetzels, M. (2016). The personalization-privacy paradox: Implications for new media. *Journal of Consumer Marketing, 33*(2), 98–110. DOI: 10.1108/JCM-06-2015-1458

Ahmad, N., Murugesan, S., & Kshetri, N. (2023). Generative Artificial Intelligence and the Education Sector. *Computer, 56*(6), 72–76. DOI: 10.1109/MC.2023.3263576

Ahn, J., Kim, J., & Sung, Y. (2022). The effect of gender stereotypes on artificial intelligence recommendations. *Journal of Business Research, 141*(C), 50–59. DOI: 10.1016/j.jbusres.2021.12.007

Akpan, I. J., & Shanker, M. (2019). A comparative evaluation of the effectiveness of virtual reality, 3D visualization and 2D visual interactive simulation: An exploratory meta-analysis. *Simulation, 95*(2), 145–170.

Akpan, I. J., Soopramanien, D., & Kwak, D. H. A. (2020). Cutting-edge technologies for small business and innovation in the era of COVID-19 global health pandemic. *Journal of Small Business and Entrepreneurship*, •••, 1–11.

Akpan, I. J., Udoh, E. A. P., & Adebisi, B. (2020). Small business awareness and adoption of state-of-the-art technologies in emerging and developing markets and lessons from the COVID – 19 pandemic. *Journal of Small Business and Entrepreneurship, 10*, 1–18.

Akter, S., Hossain, M. A., Sajib, S., Sultana, S., Rahman, M., Vrontis, D., & McCarthy, G. (2023). A framework for AI-powered service innovation capability: Review and agenda for future research. *Technovation, 125*, 102768. DOI: 10.1016/j.technovation.2023.102768

Al Nuaimi, E., Al Neyadi, H., Mohamed, N., & Al-Jaroodi, J. (2015). Applications of big data to smart cities. *Journal of Internet Services and Applications, 6*, 25. DOI: 10.1186/s13174-015-0041-5

Ali, H., & Davies, D. R. (2003). The effects of age, sex and tenure on the job performance of rubber tappers. *Journal of Occupational and Organizational Psychology, 76*(3), 381–391. DOI: 10.1348/096317903769647238

Ali, M., Khan, T. I., & Khattak, M. N., & ŞENER, İ. (2024). Synergizing AI and business: Maximizing innovation, creativity, decision precision, and operational efficiency in high-tech enterprises. *Journal of Open Innovation, 10*(3), 100352.

Alimamy, S., & Gnoth, J. (2022). I want it my way! The effect of perceptions of personalization through augmented reality and online shopping on customer intentions to co-create value. *Computers in Human Behavior, 128*, 107105. DOI: 10.1016/j.chb.2021.107105

Allal-Chérif, O., Puertas, R., & Carracedo, P. (2024). Intelligent influencer marketing: How AI-powered virtual influencers outperform human influencers. *Technological Forecasting and Social Change, 200*, 123113. DOI: 10.1016/j.techfore.2023.123113

Allison, L., Liu, Y., Murtinu, S., & Wei, Z. (2023). Gender and firm performance around the world: The roles of finance, technology and labor. *Journal of Business Research, 154*, 113322. DOI: 10.1016/j.jbusres.2022.113322

Allison, T. H., Davis, B. C., Short, J. C., & Webb, J. W. (2017). Crowdfunding in a Prosocial Microlending Environment: Examining the Role of Intrinsic and Extrinsic Cues. *Entrepreneurship Theory and Practice*, *41*(2), 237–260.

Almujaini, H., Hilmi, M. F., Abudaqa, A., & Alzahmi, R. (2021). Corporate Foresight Corporateal Learning and Performance: The Moderating Function of Digital Transformation and Mediating Function of Innovativeness in Smes. *International Journal of Data and Network Science*, *5*(4), 703–712. DOI: 10.5267/j.ijdns.2021.7.011

Al-Sarayreh, M., Reis, M. G., Carr, A., & dos Reis, M. M. (2023). Inverse design and AI/Deep generative networks in food design: A comprehensive review. *Trends in Food Science & Technology*, *138*, 215–228.

Althati, C., Tomar, M., & Shanmugam, L. (2024). Enhancing Data Integration and Management: The Role of AI and Machine Learning in Modern Data Platforms. *Journal of Artificial Intelligence General science (JAIGS) ISSN: 3006-4023, 2*(1), 220-232.

Ambuli, T. V., Vikram, G., Devendran, A., Logesh, S. K., Aancy, H. M., & Sudhakar, M. (2025). Strategic Integration of Smart Digital Business Continuity and Configuration Management. In *Essential Information Systems Service Management* (pp. 133–162). IGI Global.

Ameen, N., Tarhini, A., Reppel, A., & Anand, A. (2021). Customer experiences in the age of artificial intelligence. *Computers in Human Behavior*, *114*, 106548. DOI: 10.1016/j.chb.2020.106548 PMID: 32905175

Aminizadeh, S., Heidari, A., Dehghan, M., Toumaj, S., Rezaei, M., Navimipour, N. J., & Unal, M. (2024). Opportunities and challenges of artificial intelligence and distributed systems to improve the quality of healthcare service. *Artificial Intelligence in Medicine*, *149*, 102779. PMID: 38462281

Aminu, R. (2019). *Information technology investment*. Academia.edu https:// www .academia.edu

Ammirato, S., Felicetti, A. M., Della Gala, M., Raso, C., & Cozza, M. (2018). Smart Tourism Destinations: Can the Destination Management Organizations Exploit Benefits of the ICTs? Evidences from a Multiple Case Study. In Camarinha-Matos, L. M., Afsarmanesh, H., & Rezgui, Y. (Eds.), *Collaborative Networks of Cognitive Systems* (Vol. 534, pp. 623–634). Springer International Publishing., DOI: 10.1007/978-3-319-99127-6_54

Anand, J., McDermott, G., Mudambi, R., & Narula, R. (2021). Innovation in and from emerging economies: New insights and lessons for international business research. *Journal of International Business Studies*, *52*, 545–559.

Ananeva, D. (2019). *Artificial Intelligence as Disruptive Innovation in the Hotel Industry*. https://lauda.ulapland.fi/handle/10024/63932

Andean Union. (2023). *Law promoting the use of Artificial Intelligence*. https://unionandina.com/es/ley-que-promueve-el-uso-de-la-inteligencia-artificial/#:~:text=El%205%20de%20julio%20de,econ%C3%B3mico%20y%20social%20del%20pa%C3%ADs

Andersen, A. (1999). *Dictionary of economics and business, Model*. Editorial Espasa Siglo XXI.

Arango, L., Singaraju, S. P., & Niininen, O. (2023). Consumer Responses to AI-Generated Charitable Giving Ads. *Journal of Advertising*, *52*(4), 486–503. DOI: 10.1080/00913367.2023.2183285

Araujo, T., Helberger, N., Kruikemeier, S., & De Vreese, C. H. (2020). In AI we trust? Perceptions about automated decision-making by artificial intelligence. *AI & Society*, *35*(3), 611–623. DOI: 10.1007/s00146-019-00931-w

Archambault, É., Campbell, D., Gingras, Y., & Larivière, V. (2009). Comparing bibliometric statistics obtained from the Web of Science and Scopus. *Journal of the American Society for Information Science and Technology*, *60*(7), 1320–1326.

Armutat, S., Wattenberg, M., & Mauritz, N. (2024, April). Artificial Intelligence–Gender-Specific Differences in Perception, Understanding, and Training Interest. In *International Conference on Gender Research* (Vol. 7, No. 1, pp. 36-43). https://doi.org/DOI: 10.34190/icgr.7.1.2163

Arslan, I. K. (2020). The Prominence of Innovating Customer Loyalty in Achieving Sustainable Competitive Advantage. *Eurasian Journal of Business and Management*, *8*(1), 11–20. DOI: 10.15604/ejbm.2020.08.01.002

Asare Obeng, H., Gyamfi, B. A., Arhinful, R., & Mensah, L. (2025). Unlocking Performance Potential: Workforce Diversity Management and Gender Diversity as Drivers of Employee Performance in Ghana's Public Healthcare Sector. *Societies (Basel, Switzerland)*, *15*(5), 132. DOI: 10.3390/soc15050132

Askary, S., Abu-Ghazaleh, N., & Tahat, Y. A. (2018, Oct 30-Nov 01). Artificial Intelligence and Reliability of Accounting Information. *Lecture Notes in Computer Science* [Challenges and opportunities in the digital era]. 17th International-Federation-of-Information-Processing (IFIP) WG 6.11 Conference on e-Business, e-Services, and e-Society (I3E), Gulf Univ Sci & Technol, Kuwait City, KUWAIT. https://doi.org/DOI: 10.1007/978-3-030-02131-3_28

Atmaji, D., & Qodir, Z. (2021). Policy Implementation To Augment Tourism Destination Sub structured on Local Wisdom in Gunungkidul District. *International Journal on Recent Trends in Business and Tourism, 5*(3), 1–11. DOI: 10.31674/ijrtbt.2021.v05i03.001

Attaran, M., & Woods, J. (2019). Cloud computing technology: Improving small business performance using the internet. *Journal of Small Business and Entrepreneurship, 31*(6), 495–519.

Avila-Chauvet, L., Mejía, D., & Acosta Quiroz, C. (2023). CHATGPT as a support tool for online behavioral task programming. *SSRN*. Retrieved from https://ssrn.com/abstract=4329020

Awang, Z., Afthanorhan, W. M. A. A., Lim, S. H., & Zainudin, N. F. S. (2023). SEM Made Simple 2.0 A Gentle Approach of Structural Equation Modelling. *Gong Badak: Penerbit Unisza.*

Awang, P. (2018). Pendekatan Mudah SEM. *Structural Equation Modeling.*

Ayodele, J. O., Idachaba, O. I., & Sule, J. G. (2019). Innovation as a mediating of relationship between internal and external environment in agribusiness. *Marketing and Management of Innovations, 1*, 1–16.

Baabdullah, A. M., Alalwan, A. A., Algharabat, R. S., Metri, B., & Rana, N. P. (2022). Virtual agents and flow experience: An empirical examination of AI-powered chatbots. *Technological Forecasting and Social Change, 181*, 121772. DOI: 10.1016/j.techfore.2022.121772

Babatunde, S. O., Odejide, O. A., Edunjobi, T. E., & Ogundipe, D. O. (2024). The Role of AI in Marketing Personalization: A Theoretical Exploration of Consumer Engagement Strategies. *International Journal of Management & Entrepreneurship Research, 6*(3), 936–949. DOI: 10.51594/ijmer.v6i3.964

Babina, T., Fedyk, A., He, A., & Hodson, J. (2024). Artificial intelligence, firm growth, and product innovation. *Journal of Financial Economics, 151*, 103745.

Bacuy-Ortiz, K. X., & Soriano-Torres, L. E. (2025). Bibliometric analysis of the role of artificial intelligence in tourism destination management. *Journal of Asian Scientific Research, 15*(3), 340–354. DOI: 10.55493/5003.v15i3.5548

Bagozzi, R. P., & Yi, Y. (1988). On the Evaluation of Structural Equation Models. *Journal of the Academy of Marketing Science, 16*(1), 74–94. DOI: 10.1007/BF02723327

Bag, S., Srivastava, G., Bashir, M. M. A., Kumari, S., Giannakis, M., & Chowdhury, A. H. (2022). Journey of customers in this digital era: Understanding the role of artificial intelligence technologies in user engagement and conversion. *Benchmarking, 29*(7), 2074–2098. DOI: 10.1108/BIJ-07-2021-0415

Bahoo, S., Cucculelli, M., & Qamar, D. (2023). Artificial intelligence and corporate innovation: A review and research agenda. *Technological Forecasting and Social Change, 188*, 122264.

Bai, L., Sun, F., & Wang, W. (2022). [Retracted] Innovative Application of Artificial Intelligence in the Field of Innovation and Entrepreneurship of College Students in Internet Colleges and Universities. *Computational Intelligence and Neuroscience, 2022*(1), 3538755. PMID: 35978911

Balasubramaniam, N., Kauppinen, M., Rannisto, A., Hiekkanen, K., & Kujala, S. (2023). Transparency and explainability of AI systems: From ethical guidelines to requirements. *Information and Software Technology, 159*, 107197.

Banjo, H., & Olufemi, O. (2014). Demographic Variables and Job Performance: Any Link? (A Case of Insurance Salesmen). *Acta Universitatis Danubius. Economica, 10*(4), 19–30.

Baqar, M., & Khanda, R. (2024). The Future of Software Testing: AI-Powered Test Case Generation and Validation. *arXiv preprint arXiv:2409.05808.*

Barke, S., James, M., & Polikarpova, N. (2023). Grounded Copilot: How programmers interact with code-generating models. *Proceedings of the ACM on Programming Languages, 7*(OOPSLA1), 85-111. doi:DOI: 10.1145/3586030

Barrera Ortegón, A. D. P., & Tovar Muñiz, M. S. (2025). Key neuromarketing factors in Alquería brand television commercials in Colombia. *European Public & Social Innovation Review, 10*, 1–22. DOI: 10.31637/epsir-2025-1496

Barrera-Ortegón, A. D. P., Medina-Ricaurte, G. F., & Jimenez-Hernandez, P. R. (2024). Organizational elements to confront turbulent and fragile VUCA to BANI scenarios. In Perez-Uribe, R., Ocampo-Guzman, D., Salcedo-Perez, C., & Carvajal-Contreras, A. (Eds.), *Organizational Management Sustainability in VUCA Contexts* (pp. 20–43). IGI Global., DOI: 10.4018/979-8-3693-0720-5.ch002

Bartlett, M. S. (1954). A note on the multiplying factors for various χ 2 approximations. *Journal of the Royal Statistical Society. Series B. Methodological*, •••, 296–298.

Beavers, A. S., Lounsbury, J. W., Richards, J. K., Huck, S. W., Skolits, G. J., & Esquivel, S. L. (2013). Practical considerations for using exploratory factor analysis in educational research. *Practical Assessment, Research & Evaluation*, *18*(6), 1–13.

Belanche, D., Casaló, L. V., & Flavián, C. (2019). Artificial Intelligence in FinTech: Understanding robo-advisors adoption among customers. *Industrial Management & Data Systems*, *119*(7), 1411–1430. DOI: 10.1108/IMDS-08-2018-0368

Benko, A., & Lányi, C. S. (2009). History of artificial intelligence. In *Encyclopedia of Information Science and Technology* (2nd ed., pp. 1759–1762). IGI Global., DOI: 10.4018/978-1-60566-026-4

Bentler, P. M., & Bonett, D. G. (1980). Significance tests and goodness of fit in the analysis of covariance structures. *Psychological Bulletin*, *88*(3), 588–606. DOI: 10.1037/0033-2909.88.3.588

Bernal Palomo. (2020). *Balanced Scorecard Proposal for CHP Consulting SAS in Bogotá*. Universidad De La Salle.

Bertolini, M., Mezzogori, D., Neroni, M., & Zammori, F. (2021). Machine Learning for industrial applications: A comprehensive literature review. *Expert Systems with Applications*, *175*, 114820.

Bertoni, A., Yi, X., Baron, C., Esteban, P., & Vingerhoeds, R. (2020). A framework for data-driven design in a product innovation process: Data analysis and visualisation for model-based decision making. *International Journal of Product Development*, *24*(1), 68–94.

Bleier, A., Goldfarb, A., & Tucker, C. E. (2020). Consumer Privacy and the Future of Data-Based Innovation and Marketing. SSRN *Electronic Journal*. https://doi.org/ DOI: 10.2139/ssrn.3570156

Bollen, K. A. (1989). *Structural equations with latent variables* (Vol. 210). John Wiley & Sons.

Bollen, K. A. (1990). Overall Fit in Covariance Structure Models: Two Types of Sample Size Effects. *Psychological Bulletin, 107*(2), 256–259. DOI: 10.1037/0033-2909.107.2.256

Boomsma, A. (1982). The robustness of LISREL against small sample sizes in factor analysis models. *Systems under indirect observation: Causality, structure, prediction*, 149-173.

Box, G. E. P., & Jenkins, G. M. (1970). *Time Series Analysis: Forecasting and Control.* Holden-Day.

Bozkurt, V., & Gursoy, D. (2023). The Artificial Intelligence Paradox: Opportunity or Threat for Humanity? *International Journal of Human-Computer Interaction*, •••, 1–14. DOI: 10.1080/10447318.2023.2297114

Braverman, H. (1974). *Labor and monopoly capital.* Monthly Review Press.

Brennen, J. S., & Kreiss, D. (2016). Digitalization. The international encyclopedia of communication theory and philosophy, 1-11.

Brey, P., & Dainow, B. (2024). Ethics by design for artificial intelligence. *AI and Ethics, 4*(4), 1265–1277.

Brosnan, M. J., & Davidson, M. J. (1996). Psychological gender issues in computing. *Gender, Work and Organization, 3*(1), 13–25. DOI: 10.1111/j.1468-0432.1996.tb00045.x

Brougham, D., & Haar, J. (2018). Smart technology, artificial intelligence, robotics, and algorithms (STARA): Employees' perceptions of our future workplace. *Journal of Management & Organization, 24*(2), 239–257. DOI: 10.1017/jmo.2016.55

Bruce, M., Daly, L., & Towers, N. (2004). Lean or agile: A solution for supply chain management in the textiles and clothing industry? *International Journal of Operations & Production Management, 24*(2), 151–170.

Brunelli, J., Lukic, V., Milon, T., & Tandardine, M. (2017). *Five lessons from the frontlines of industry 4.0.* BCG Boston Consulting Group.

Brussevich, M., Dabla-Norris, M. E., Kamunge, C., Karnane, P., Khalid, S., & Kochhar, M. K. (2018). *Gender, technology, and the future of work.* International Monetary Fund.

Brynjolfsson, E., & McAfee, A. (2017). *Machine, Platform, Crowd: Harnessing Our Digital Future.* W. W. Norton & Company.

Buhalis, D. (2000). Marketing the competitive destination of the future. *Tourism Management, 21*(1), 97–116. DOI: 10.1016/S0261-5177(99)00095-3

Buhalis, D., & Law, R. (2008). Progress in information technology and tourism management: 20 years on and 10 years after the Internet—The state of eTourism research. *Tourism Management, 29*(4), 609–623. DOI: 10.1016/j.tourman.2008.01.005

Bukar, U. A., Sayeed, M. S., Razak, S. F. A., Yogarayan, S., Amodu, O. A., & Mahmood, R. A. R. (2023). A method for analyzing text using VOSviewer. *MethodsX, 11*, 102339. DOI: 10.1016/j.mex.2023.102339 PMID: 37693657

Bulchand-Gidumal, J., William Secin, E., O'Connor, P., & Buhalis, D. (2024). Artificial intelligence's impact on hospitality and tourism marketing: Exploring key themes and addressing challenges. *Current Issues in Tourism, 27*(14), 2345–2362. DOI: 10.1080/13683500.2023.2229480

Buonocore, F., Annosi, M. C., de Gennaro, D., & Riemma, F. (2024). Digital transformation and social change: Leadership strategies for responsible innovation. *Journal of Engineering and Technology Management, 74*, 101843.

Burrell, J. (2016). How the machine 'thinks': Understanding opacity in machine learning algorithms. *Big Data & Society, 3*(1), 2053951715622512.

Business School Madrid [EAE]. (2023, December 8). *AI Objectives.* https://www.eaemadrid.com/es/blog/objetivo-inteligencia-artificial

Cabero-Almenara, J., & Llorente-Cejudo, M. C. (2020). Covid-19: radical transformation of digitalization in university institutions. *Journal of Distance Education.* https://dialnet.unirioja.es/servlet/articulo?codigo=8005978

Cabrera-Sánchez, J.-P., Villarejo-Ramos, Á. F., Liébana-Cabanillas, F., & Shaikh, A. A. (2021). Identifying relevant segments of AI applications adopters – Expanding the UTAUT2's variables. *Telematics and Informatics, 58*, 101529. DOI: 10.1016/j.tele.2020.101529

Calantone, R. J., Cavusgil, S. T., & Zhao, Y. (2006). Learning orientation, firm innovation capability, and firm performance. *Industrial Marketing Management, 31*(6), 515–524.

Çalışkan, A., & Köroğlu, E. Ö. (2022). Job performance, Task performance, Contextual performance: Development and validation of a new scale. *Uluslararası İktisadi ve İdari Bilimler Dergisi, 8*(2), 180–201. DOI: 10.29131/uiibd.1201880

Calvano, E., Calzolari, G., Denicolò, V., Harrington, J. E., & Pastorello, S. (2020). Protecting consumers from collusive prices due to AI. *Science, 370*(6520), 1040–1042. DOI: 10.1126/science.abe3796 PMID: 33243879

Camacho, M., Perramon, J., Puig-Bosch, X., Dang, V. N., Diaz, O., & Lekadir, K. (2025). Stakeholder engagement: the path to trustworthy AI in healthcare. In *Trustworthy AI in Medical Imaging* (pp. 471–493). Academic Press.

Campbell, C., Sands, S., Ferraro, C., & Tsao, H.-Y. (Jody), & Mavrommatis, A. (2020). From data to action: How marketers can leverage AI. *Business Horizons, 63*(2), 227–243. DOI: 10.1016/j.bushor.2019.12.002

Canales, L. (2025). *Artificial Intelligence and Intellectual Property: ¿Can You Register an AI-Made Trademark?* https://www.calalawyers.com/multimedia/noticias/inteligencia-artificial-y-propiedad-intelectual-puedes-registrar-una-marca

Caruso, S., Bruccoleri, M., Pietrosi, A., & Scaccianoce, A. (2023). Artificial intelligence to counteract "KPI overload" in business process monitoring: The case of anti-corruption in public organizations. *Business Process Management Journal, 29*(4), 1227–1248. DOI: 10.1108/bpmj-11-2022-0578

Cash, P., Isaksson, O., Maier, A., & Summers, J. (2022). Sampling in Design Research: Eight Key Considerations. *Design Studies, 78*, 101077. DOI: 10.1016/j.destud.2021.101077

Castaneda, J., Jover, A., Calvet, L., Yanes, S., Juan, A. A., & Sainz, M. (2022). Dealing with gender bias issues in data-algorithmic processes: A social-statistical perspective. *Algorithms, 15*(9), 303. DOI: 10.3390/a15090303

Celikyay, M., Cakir, F. S., & Adıguzel, Z. (2023). Effects of Supplier Orientation and Competitive Strategies on ICT Corporates' Performance. *Journal of Asia Business Studies, 17*(4), 701–720. DOI: 10.1108/JABS-09-2021-0384

Chacko, H. E. (1996). Positioning a tourism destination to gain a competitive edge. *Asia Pacific Journal of Tourism Research, 1*(2), 69–75. DOI: 10.1080/10941669708721976

Chakraborty, C., Bhattacharya, M., Pal, S., & Lee, S. S. (2024). From machine learning to deep learning: Advances of the recent data-driven paradigm shift in medicine and healthcare. *Current Research in Biotechnology, 7*, 100164.

Chandra, S., Verma, S., Lim, W. M., Kumar, S., & Donthu, N. (2022). Personalization in personalized marketing: Trends and ways forward. *Psychology and Marketing, 39*(8), 1529–1562. DOI: 10.1002/mar.21670

Chatterjee, S., Chaudhuri, R., & Vrontis, D. (2024). Does data-driven culture impact innovation and performance of a firm? An empirical examination. *Annals of Operations Research, 333*(2), 601–626.

Chaudhuri, R., Chatterjee, S., Vrontis, D., & Thrassou, A. (2024). Adoption of robust business analytics for product innovation and organizational performance: The mediating role of organizational data-driven culture. *Annals of Operations Research, 339*(3), 1757–1791.

Chau, P. Y., & Hu, P. J. H. (2001). Information technology acceptance by individual professionals: A model comparison approach. *Decision Sciences, 32*(4), 699–719. DOI: 10.1111/j.1540-5915.2001.tb00978.x

Chen, F. H., Hsu, M. F., & Hu, K. H. (2022). Enterprise's internal control for knowledge discovery in a big data environment by an integrated hybrid model. *Information Technology Management, 23*(3), 213–231. DOI: 10.1007/s10799-021-00342-8

Cheng, M. (2022, April). The Creativity of Artificial Intelligence in Art. In *Proceedings* (Vol. 81, No. 1, p. 110). MDPI. https://doi.org/DOI: 10.3390/proceedings2022081110

Cheng, M. E. (2011, August 8-10). Discussion of chief finance officer system perfection. *2011 2nd Artificial Intelligence, Management Science and Electronic Commerce (AIMSEC 2011),* Deng Feng, China. Deng Feng, China, 2011, pp. 312-315. https://doi.org/DOI: 10.1109/AIMSEC.2011.6010447

Cheng, Q., Wang, J., Lu, W., Huang, Y., & Bu, Y. (2020). Keyword-citation-keyword network: A new perspective of discipline knowledge structure analysis. *Scientometrics, 124*, 1923–1943.

Cheng, Y., & Jiang, H. (2022). Customer–brand relationship in the era of artificial intelligence: Understanding the role of chatbot marketing efforts. *Journal of Product and Brand Management, 31*(2), 252–264. DOI: 10.1108/JPBM-05-2020-2907

Chen, Q., Wang, Y., Gong, Y., & Liu, S. (2023). Ripping off regular consumers? The antecedents and consequences of consumers' perceptions of e-commerce platforms' digital power abuse. *Journal of Business Research, 166*, 114123.

Chen, S., & Yang, J. (2025). Intelligent manufacturing, auditor selection and audit quality. *Management Decision, 63*(3), 964–997.

Chen, X., Mao, J., & Li, G. (2024). A co-citation approach to the analysis on the interaction between scientific and technological knowledge. *Journal of Informetrics, 18*(3), 101548.

Chen, Y., Hu, Y., Zhou, S., & Yang, S. (2023). Investigating the determinants of performance of artificial intelligence adoption in hospitality industry during COVID-19. *International Journal of Contemporary Hospitality Management*, *35*(8), 2868–2889. DOI: 10.1108/IJCHM-04-2022-0433

Chen, Y., Wu, Z., & Yan, H. (2022). A Full population auditing method based on machine learning. *Sustainability*, *14*(24), 17008. DOI: 10.3390/su142417008

Chen, Y., & Xu, D. (2018). The impact of artificial intelligence on employment. *Composition Studies*, *2*, 135–160. DOI: 10.2139/ssrn.3116753

Cheung, G. W., Cooper-Thomas, H. D., Lau, R. S., & Wang, L. C. (2024). Reporting reliability, convergent and discriminant validity with structural equation modeling: A review and best-practice recommendations. *Asia Pacific Journal of Management*, *41*(2), 745–783. DOI: 10.1007/s10490-023-09871-y

Child, D. (2006). *The essentials of factor analysis*. A&C Black.

Chintalapati, S., & Pandey, S. K. (2022). Artificial intelligence in marketing: A systematic literature review. *International Journal of Market Research*, *64*(1), 38–68. DOI: 10.1177/14707853211018428

Chopra, S., & Meindl, P. (2016). *Supply Chain Management: Strategy, Planning, and Operation* (6th ed.). Pearson.

Cho, Y. S., & Linderman, K. (2020). Resource-based product and process innovation model: Theory development and empirical validation. *Sustainability*, *12*(3), 913.

Christopher Taylor, P. (2014). Management challenges and responses: Experiences of property managers operating in the small open economy of Jamaica. *Property Management*, *32*(1), 16–27. DOI: 10.1108/PM-11-2012-0040

Christopher, M. (2016). *Logistics & Supply Chain Management* (5th ed.). Pearson.

Christopher, M. L. (1992). *Logistics and Supply Chain Management*. Pitman Publishing.

Christopher, M., & Peck, H. (2004). Building the resilient supply chain. *International Journal of Logistics Management*, *15*(2), 1–13.

Christopher, M., & Towill, D. (2001). An integrated model for the design of agile supply chains. *International Journal of Physical Distribution & Logistics Management*, *31*(4), 235–246.

Chui, M., Manyika, J., Miremadi, M., Henke, N., Chung, R., Nel, P., & Malhotra, S. (2018). Notes from the AI frontier: Insights from hundreds of use cases. *McKinsey Global Institute*, *2*(267), 1–31.

Chukwurah, N., Ige, A. B., Idemudia, C., & Adebayo, V. I. (2024). Strategies for engaging stakeholders in data governance: Building effective communication and collaboration. *Open Access Res J Multidiscip Stud, 8*(1), 057-67.

Cimbaljević, M., Stankov, U., & Pavluković, V. (2019). Going beyond the traditional destination competitiveness – reflections on a smart destination in the current research. *Current Issues in Tourism*, *22*(20), 2472–2477. DOI: 10.1080/13683500.2018.1529149

Clayton, M., & Christensen, C. M. (2016). *The innovators' dilemma: When new technologies cause great firms to fail*. Harvard Business School press.

Cochran, W. G. (1977). *Sampling techniques* (3rd ed.). John Wiley & Sons.

Cockburn, I. M., Henderson, R., & Stern, S. (2018). The impact of artificial intelligence on innovation (Vol. 24449). Cambridge, MA, USA: National bureau of economic research.

Coffie, C. P. K., Hongjiang, Z., Mensah, I. A., Kiconco, R., & Simon, A. E. O. (2021). Determinants of FinTech payment services diffusion by SMEs in sub-Saharan Africa: Evidence from Ghana. *Information Technology for Development*, *27*(3), 539–560.

Collins, C., Dennehy, D., Conboy, K., & Mikalef, P. (2021). Artificial intelligence in information systems research: A systematic literature review and research agenda. *International Journal of Information Management*, *60*, 102383. Advance online publication. DOI: 10.1016/j.ijinfomgt.2021.102383

Commission (2018). *Communication from the Commission to the European Parliament, the European Council, the Council, the European Economic and Social Committee and the Committee of the Regions - Artificial Intelligence for Europe.* https://eur-lex.europa.eu/legal-content/PT/TXT/PDF/?uri=CELEX:52018DC0237

Congress of Colombia. (2001). *Law 675 of 2001*. Bogotá, Colombia: Senate Secretary. Constitutional Court of the Republic of Colombia.

Cooper, R. G. (2000). Product innovation and technology strategy. *Research Technology Management*, *43*(1), 38–41.

Cooper, R. G. (2021). Accelerating innovation: Some lessons from the pandemic. *Journal of Product Innovation Management*, *38*(2), 221–232. PMID: 33821086

Cooper, R. G. (2023). The artificial intelligence revolution in new-product development. *IEEE Engineering Management Review, 52*(1), 195–211.

Cooper, R. G. (2024). The AI transformation of product innovation. *Industrial Marketing Management, 119*, 62–74.

Cooper, R. G. (2025). SMEs' use of AI for new product development: Adoption rates by application and readiness-to-adopt. *Industrial Marketing Management, 126*, 159–167.

Cooper, R. G., & Edgett, S. J. (2010). Developing a product innovation and technology strategy for your business. *Research Technology Management, 53*(3), 33–40.

Cooper, R. G., & McCausland, T. (2024). AI and new product development. *Research Technology Management, 67*(1), 70–75.

Cornelio, O. M., Rodriguez, A. R., Alava, W. L. S., Mora, P. G. A., Mera, L. M. S., & Bravo, B. J. P. (2024). *Artificial Intelligence: Challenges for Education*. Editorial Internacional Alema.

COSO. (2013). *Internal Control - Integrated framework: Executive summary*. https://www.coso.org/_files/ugd/3059fc_1df7d5dd38074006bce8fdf621a942cf.pdf

Costa, A. P., & Amado, J. (2018). *Software-Supported Content Analysis* (2nd ed.). Ludomedia., https://ludomedia.org/publicacoes/e-book-analise-de-conteudo-suportada-por-software-2a-ed/

Costello, A. B., & Osborne, J. W. (2005). Best practices in exploratory factor analysis: Four recommendations for getting the most from your analysis. *Practical Assessment, Research & Evaluation, 10*(7), 1–9. DOI: 10.7275/jyj1-4868

Cotino Hueso, L. (2017). Big data and artificial intelligence: An approach to their legal treatment from the perspective of fundamental rights. *Dilemata*, (24), 131-150. https://dialnet.unirioja.es/servlet/articulo?codigo=6066829

Coutinho, C. P. (2011). *Research Methodologies in Social Sciences and Humanities: theory and practice* (2nd ed.). Edições Almedina.

Cronbach, L. J. (1951). Coefficient alpha and the internal structure of tests. *Psychometrika, 16*(3), 297–334. DOI: 10.1007/bf02310555

Croom, S., Romano, P., & Giannakis, M. (2000). Supply chain management: An analytical framework for critical literature review. *European Journal of Purchasing & Supply Management, 6*(1), 67–83.

Crowston, K., & Bolici, F. (2025). Deskilling and upskilling with AI Systems. *nformation Research an International Electronic Journal, 30*(iConf), 1009-1023. doi:DOI: 10.47989/ir30iconf47143

Dabic, M., Svarc, J., & Becic, E. (2016). In Haar, J., & Ernst, R. (Eds.), *"Innovation in Central Europe" in Innovation in emerging markets* (pp. 102–120). Palgrave Macmillan.

Daehy, Y., Krishnan, K., Alsaadi, A., & Alghamdi, S. (2019). Effective cost minimization strategy and an optimization model of a reliable global supply chain system. *Uncertain Supply Chain Management, 7*(3), 381–398.

Dahake, P. S., Parchake, S., Somani, N., & Ingale, A. R. (2024). Predictive Analytics in Automotive Consumer Behaviour: An Insight into Personal use 4-Wheeler Purchase Decisions. *2024 2nd International Conference on Advances in Computation, Communication and Information Technology (ICAICCIT)*, 1143–1149. https://doi .org/DOI: 10.1109/ICAICCIT64383.2024.10912242

Dahake, P. S., Bagaregari, P., & Dahake, N. S. (2024). Shaping the Future of Retail: A Comprehensive Review of Predictive Analytics Models for Consumer Behavior. In Inder, S., Min, B., & Sharma, S. (Eds.), (pp. 143–160). Advances in Business Strategy and Competitive Advantage. IGI Global., DOI: 10.4018/979-8-3693-1734-1.ch011

Dahake, P. S., Chandak, S., Mohare, R. V., Wadhwani, K., & Bhadade, P. (2023). The Crystal Ball of Marketing: How Predictive Analytics is Reshaping the Industry? *2023 Second International Conference On Smart Technologies For Smart Nation (SmartTechCon)*, 304–311. https://doi.org/DOI: 10.1109/SmartTechCon57526.2023.10391334

Daigle, K. (2024). *Survey: The AI wave continues to grow on software development teams*. Retrieved from https://github.blog/author/kdaigle/

Davenport, T. H., Guha, A., Grewal, D., & Bressgott, T. (2020). How Artificial Intelligence Will Change the Future of Marketing. *Journal of the Academy of Marketing Science, 48*(1), 24–42.

Davenport, T. H., & Harris, J. G. (2007). *Competing on Analytics: The New Science of Winning*. Harvard Business School Press.

Davenport, T., Guha, A., Grewal, D., & Bressgott, T. (2020). How artificial intelligence will change the future of marketing. *Journal of the Academy of Marketing Science, 48*, 24–42.

Davidson, J. D., & Rajeswari, P. S. (2025). A case study on how Amazon uses personalization to win back Prime subscription lapsers. Journal of Information Technology Teaching Cases, 20438869251325244.

Davis, J. T., Massey, A. P., & Lovell, R. E. R. (1997). Supporting a complex audit judgment task: An expert network approach. *European Journal of Operational Research, 103*(2), 350–372. DOI: 10.1016/S0377-2217(97)00125-2

Day, T. (2018). Examining the impact of technology on small business: How small businesses use social media and digital platforms to grow, sell, and hire. *U.S. Chamber Technology Engagement Center, C_TEC,* 1 – 18.

Decker, M., Fischer, M., & Ott, I. (2017). Service Robotics and Human Labor: A first technology assessment of substitution and cooperation. *Robotics and Autonomous Systems, 87*, 348–354. DOI: 10.1016/j.robot.2016.09.017

Dehisat, M. M., & Awang, Z. (2020). Exploring items and developing instrument for measuring organizational performance among small medium enterprises in Jordan. *International Review of Management and Marketing, 10*(6), 51–57. DOI: 10.32479/irmm.10531

Del Pozo, C., Nuno Gomes de Andrade, N., & Rojas Arroyo, D. (2023). *Prototype of public policies on transparency and explainability of artificial intelligence systems.* https://openloop. org/reports/2023/10/Prototipo-de-Politicas-Publicas-sobre-Transparencia-y-Explicabilidad-de-Sistemas-de-IA.pdf

Deshpande, A., & Sharp, H. (2022, July). Responsible AI systems: who are the stakeholders? In *Proceedings of the 2022 AAAI/ACM Conference on AI, Ethics, and Society* (pp. 227-236).

Development Bank of Latin America and the Caribbean (CAF) and the United Nations Educational, Scientific and Cultural Organization (UNESCO). (2024). *Uruguay's National Artificial Intelligence Strategy, 2024-2030.* https://www.gub.uy/agencia-gobierno-electronico-sociedad-informacion-conocimiento/comunicacion/publicaciones/estrategia-nacional-inteligencia-artificial-del-uruguay-2024-2030

Dhamija, P., & Bag, S. (2020). Role of artificial intelligence in operations environment: A review and bibliometric analysis. *The TQM Journal, 32*(4), 869–896.

Dharalief, M. Z., Bedhiaf, S., & Dhehibi, B., Oueslati – Zlaoui, M., Jebali, O., & Ben – Youssef, S. (2019). Factors affecting innovative technologies adoption by livestock holders in arid area of Tunisia. *New Mediterranean, 18*(4), 3–18.

Dini, P., Diana, L., Elhanashi, A., & Saponara, S. (2024). Overview of AI-models and tools in embedded IIoT applications. *Electronics (Basel), 13*(12), 2322.

Divino, S. (2024). Governance and compliance recommendations for artificial intelligence in business management. *Nuevo Derecho, 20*(35), 1–17. DOI: 10.25057/2500672X.1665

do Nascimento, I. J. B., Abdulazeem, H. M., Vasanthan, L. T., Martinez, E. Z., Zucoloto, M. L., Østengaard, L., & Novillo-Ortiz, D. (2023). The global effect of digital health technologies on health workers' competencies and health workplace: An umbrella review of systematic reviews and lexical-based and sentence-based meta-analysis. *The Lancet. Digital Health, 5*(8), e534–e544. PMID: 37507197

Dobni, C. B., & Sand, C. (2018). Strategy shift: Integrating strategy and the firm's capability to innovate. *Business Horizons, 61*(5), 797–808.

Doganata, Y., & Curbera, F. (2012). Designing an automated audit tool for the targeted risk exposure reduction. In Daniel, F., Barkaoui, K., & Dustdar, S. (Eds.), *Business Process Management Workshops. BPM 2011. Lecture Notes in Business Information Processing* (Vol. 100). Springer., DOI: 10.1007/978-3-642-28115-0_34

Domecq, H. M. (2023). *Artificial intelligence as an intelligence tool in the decision-making process at the operational level.* https://cefadigital.edu.ar/bitstream/1847939/2956/1/TFI%2027-2023%20DOMECQ.pdf

Dominguez Castillo, J. G., Cisneros Cohernour, E. J., & Barberà, E. (2018). Factors influencing technology use by Mayan women in the digital age. *Gender, Technology and Development, 22*(3), 185–204. DOI: 10.1080/09718524.2018.1558862

Donelson, D. C., Ege, M. S., & Mclnnis, J. M. (2017). Internal control weaknesses and financial reporting fraud. *Auditing: A Journal of Practice & Theory*, 36 (3)-45–69. https://doi.org/DOI: 10.2308/ajpt-51608

Donoso, R., & Elsinga, M. (2016). Management of low-income condominiums in Bogotá and Quito: The balance between property law and self-organisation. *International Journal of Housing Policy, 18*(2), 312–334. DOI: 10.1080/14616718.2016.1248608

Donthu, N., Kumar, S., Mukherjee, D., Pandey, N., & Lim, W. M. (2021). How to conduct a bibliometric analysis: An overview and guidelines. *Journal of Business Research, 133*, 285–296.

Dorta-González, P., & Santana-Jiménez, Y. (2018). Prevalence and citation advantage of gold open access in the subject areas of the Scopus database. *Research Evaluation, 27*(1), 1–15.

Duan, Y., Edwards, J. S., & Dwivedi, Y. K. (2019). Artificial intelligence for decision making in the era of Big Data–evolution, challenges and research agenda. *International Journal of Information Management, 48*, 63–71.

Du, S., & Xie, C. (2021). Paradoxes of artificial intelligence in consumer markets: Ethical challenges and opportunities. *Journal of Business Research, 129*, 961–974. DOI: 10.1016/j.jbusres.2020.08.024

Dwivedi, Y. K., Kshetri, N., Hughes, L., Slade, E. L., Jeyaraj, A., Kar, A. K., & Wright, R. (2023). Opinion Paper:"So what if ChatGPT wrote it?" Multidisciplinary perspectives on opportunities, challenges and implications of generative conversational AI for research, practice and policy. *International Journal of Information Management, 71*, 102642.

Eagly, A. H., & Karau, S. J. (2002). Role congruity theory of prejudice toward female leaders. *Psychological Review, 109*(3), 573–598. DOI: 10.1037/0033-295X.109.3.573 PMID: 12088246

ECLAC. (2024). *Latin American Artificial Intelligence Index (ILIA) maintains Chile, Brazil and Uruguay as leaders in the region.* https://www.cepal.org/es/comunicados/indice-latinoamericano-inteligencia-artificial-ilia-mantiene-chile-brasil-uruguay-como

Efron, B., & Tibshirani, R. J. (1994). *An introduction to the bootstrap*. CRC press.

Eggers, S. L., & Sample, C. (2020). *Vulnerabilities in artificial intelligence and machine learning applications and data* (No. INL/RPT-22-66111-Rev000). Idaho National Lab.(INL), Idaho Falls, ID (United States).

Elalem, Y. K., Maier, S., & Seifert, R. W. (2023). A machine learning-based framework for forecasting sales of new products with short life cycles using deep neural networks. *International Journal of Forecasting, 39*(4), 1874–1894.

Ellegaard, O. (2018). The application of bibliometric analysis: Disciplinary and user aspects. *Scientometrics, 116*(1), 181–202.

Ellegaard, O., & Wallin, J. A. (2015). The bibliometric analysis of scholarly production: How great is the impact? *Scientometrics, 105*, 1809–1831. PMID: 26594073

Emmanuel, A., Wijaya, M. I., & Riantono, I. E. (2023). Web-Based Accounting Information System Analysis and Design for Inventory and Sales in PT SIP based on Artificial Intelligence Technology. *In Proceedings of the 2023 9th International Conference on Industrial and Business Engineering (ICIBE '23)*. Association for Computing Machinery, New York, 312–318. https://doi.org/DOI: 10.1145/3629378.3629459

Enholm, I. M., Papagiannidis, E., Mikalef, P., & Krogstie, J. (2022). Artificial intelligence and business value: A literature review. *Information Systems Frontiers, 24*(5), 1709–1734.

European Commission. (2018). *Artificial intelligence for Europe*. https://ec.europa.eu/digital-single-market/en/news/communication-artificialintelligence-europe

European Commission. (2020). "White Paper on Artificial Intelligence - A European approach to excellence and trust."

European Union. (2016). *Regulation (EU) 2016/679 of the European Parliament and of the Council*.www.boe.es/doue/2016/119/L00001-00088.pdf

Fan, Y. (2022). Research on Internal Control of Yihua Company under Technology of Artificial Intelligence. *2022 2nd International Conference on Social Sciences and Intelligence Management (SSIM)*, Taichung, Taiwan, 2022, pp. 85-89. https://doi.org/DOI: 10.1109/SSIM55504.2022.10047950

Fan, X., Zhao, S., Zhang, X., & Meng, L. (2023). The Impact of Improving Employee Psychological Empowerment and Job Performance Based on Deep Learning and Artificial Intelligence. [JOEUC]. *Journal of Organizational and End User Computing*, *35*(3), 1–14.

Fazelnia, M., Moshtari, S., & Mirakhorli, M. (2024). Establishing Minimum Elements for Effective Vulnerability Management in AI Software. *arXiv preprint arXiv:2411.11317.*

Field, A. (2024). *Discovering statistics using IBM SPSS statistics*. Sage publications limited.

Florido-Benítez, L., & Coca-Stefaniak, J. A. (2025). Towards a new generation of smart tourism cities–GenAI-enabled aerotainment. *Cities (London, England)*, *167*, 106311. DOI: 10.1016/j.cities.2025.106311

Fogarty, D. W., Blackstone, J. H., & Hoffman, T. R. (1991). *Production and Inventory Management* (2nd ed.). South-Western.

Fornell, C., & Larcker, D. F. (1981). Evaluating structural equation models with unobservable variables and measurement error. *JMR, Journal of Marketing Research*, *18*(1), 39–50. DOI: 10.1177/002224378101800104

Fotoh, L. E., & Lorentzon, J. I. (2023). Audit digitalization and its consequences on the audit expectation gap: A critical perspective. *Accounting Horizons*, *37*(1), 43–69. DOI: 10.2308/horizons-2021-027

Frank, B. (2021). Artificial intelligence-enabled environmental sustainability of products: Marketing benefits and their variation by consumer, location, and product types. *Journal of Cleaner Production*, *285*, 125242.

Fritsch, M., & Meschede, M. (2001). Product innovation, process innovation, and size. *Review of Industrial Organization*, *19*, 335–350.

Füller, J., Hutter, K., Wahl, J., Bilgram, V., & Tekic, Z. (2022). How AI revolutionizes innovation management–Perceptions and implementation preferences of AI-based innovators. *Technological Forecasting and Social Change*, *178*, 121598.

Furtado, L. S., Soares, J. B., & Furtado, V. (2024). A task-oriented framework for generative AI in design. *Journal of Creativity*, *34*(2), 100086.

Gama, F., & Magistretti, S. (2025). Artificial intelligence in innovation management: A review of innovation capabilities and a taxonomy of AI applications. *Journal of Product Innovation Management*, *42*(1), 76–111.

Ganeshan, R., Jack, E., Magazine, M. J., & Stephens, P. (1998). A taxonomic review of supply chain management research. In *Quantitative models for supply chain management* (pp. 841–880). Kluwer Academic Publishers.

Gao, L., Li, G., Tsai, F., Gao, C., Zhu, M., & Qu, X. (2023). The impact of artificial intelligence stimuli on customer engagement and value co-creation: The moderating role of customer ability readiness. *Journal of Research in Interactive Marketing*, *17*(2), 317–333. DOI: 10.1108/JRIM-10-2021-0260

Gao, Y., & Liu, H. (2023). Artificial intelligence-enabled personalization in interactive marketing: A customer journey perspective. *Journal of Research in Interactive Marketing*, *17*(5), 663–680. DOI: 10.1108/JRIM-01-2022-0023

Gao, Y., Liu, S., & Yang, L. (2025). Artificial intelligence and innovation capability: A dynamic capabilities perspective. *International Review of Economics & Finance*, •••, 103923.

Garcia Berzosa, H. (2024). *Security and privacy: How to assess security in an AI-based system?*https://openaccess.uoc.edu/bitstream/10609/149664/1/hgarciaberTFM0124memoria.pdf

García, A., Mora, M., & Ávila, J. (2020). Artificial intelligence in education and administration. *Dominio de las Ciencias*, *6*(3). Advance online publication. DOI: 10.23857/dc.v6i3.1421

García-Peñalvo, F. J., & Seoane, A. M. (2015). An updated review of the concept of eLearning. Tenth Anniversary. *Education in the Knowledge Society*, *16*(1), 119–144.

Gardner, E. S. (2006). Exponential Smoothing: The State of the Art. *Journal of Forecasting*, *4*(1), 1–28.

Garibo-Ignacio, G., Najera-Bautista, A., & Parra-Barrios, H. (2023). A theoretical look at business administration in the digital age: The administrative process and the artificial intelligence revolution. *Technological Innovations Journal, 2*(4), 7–19. DOI: 10.35622/j.ti.2023.04.001

Garvey, A. M., Kim, T., & Duhachek, A. (2023). Bad News? Send an AI. Good News? Send a Human. *Journal of Marketing, 87*(1), 10–25. DOI: 10.1177/00222429211066972

Garzon Castrillon, M. A., & Ibarra Mares, A. (2014). Review of Business Sustainability. *Journal of Advanced Leadership Studies,* 2014, Volume 1, Number 3. https://www.regent.edu/acad/global/publications/real/vol1no3/4-castrillon.pdf

Gathogo, G., & Ragui, M. (2014). Effects of capital and technology on the performance of SMEs in the manufacturing sector in Kenya - Case of selected firms in Thika Municipality. *European Journal of Business and Management, 6*(7), 308–311.

Geisler, R. (2018). *Artificial Intelligence in the Travel & Tourism industry*. chrome-extension://efaidnbmnnnibpcajpcglclefindmkaj/https://run.unl.pt/bitstream/10362/39709/1/Geisler_2018.pdf

Génin, P. (2003). *Robust tactical planning with the use of an A.P.S., proposal of a management mode by reference plane* [Doctoral thesis, Ecole des Mines de Paris].

Ghazali, M. T., & Fauzi, M. A. (2025). Validation of Training in Relation to Succession Planning: Exploratory Factor Analysis and Confirmatory Factor Analysis Approach. *International Journal of Research and Innovation in Social Science, 9*(1), 785–798. DOI: 10.47772/IJRISS.2025.9010067

Ghiglione, F. (2020). *The balanced scorecard as a tool for efficiency in business management*. Universidad Nacional de La Plata., DOI: 10.24215/23143738e088

GhorbanTanhaei, H., Boozary, P., Sheykhan, S., Rabiee, M., Rahmani, F., & Hosseini, I. (2024). Predictive analytics in customer behavior: Anticipating trends and preferences. *Results in Control and Optimization, 17*, 100462.

Gibson, R. B., Hassan, S., Holtz, S., Tansey, J., & Whitelaw, G. (2005). *Sustainability Assessment: Criteria and Processes*. Earthscan.

Gilbert, D., Lee-Kelley, L., & Barton, M. (2003). Technophobia, gender influences and consumer decision-making for technology-related products. *European Journal of Innovation Management, 6*(4), 253–263. DOI: 10.1108/14601060310500968

Giuduci, P., Centurelli, M., & Turchetta, S. (2024). Artificial Intelligence risk measurement. *Expert Systems with Applications, 235*. Advance online publication. DOI: 10.1016/j.eswa.2023.121220

Gomber, P., Kauffman, R. J., Parker, C., & Weber, B. W. (2018). On the fintech revolution: Interpreting the forces of innovation, disruption, and transformation in financial services. *Journal of Management Information Systems*, *35*(1), 220–265.

Gompers, P., & Lerner, J. (2001). *The Venture Capital Cycle*. MIT Press.

Gonçalves, S. P., Gonçalves, J. P., & Marques, C. G. (2021). *Qualitative research manual: Design, analysis and applications*. Pactor.

Góngora, F. (2016). *Management system for horizontal property in the city of Santiago de Cali*. Santiago de Cali: Universidad del Valle. https://bibliotecadigital.univalle.edu.co/server/api/core/bitstreams/6d350caa-7699-4594-b76b-7193a880e9c3/content

Guadagnoli, E., & Velicer, W. F. (1988). Relation of sample size to the stability of component patterns. *Psychological Bulletin*, *103*(2), 265–275. DOI: 10.1037/0033-2909.103.2.265 PMID: 3363047

Güneş, S. (2023). Extracting design knowledge from online product reviews to support design creativity. *International Journal of Design Creativity and Innovation*, *11*(4), 273–293.

Guo, S. (2022). Evaluation method of financial internal control in colleges and universities based on artificial intelligence technology. *Mobile Information Systems*. Advance online publication. DOI: 10.1155/2022/1556150

Hackman, J. R., & Oldham, G. R. (1976). Motivation through the design of work: Test of a theory. *Organizational Behavior and Human Performance*, *16*(2), 250–279. DOI: 10.1016/0030-5073(76)90016-7

Haefner, N., Wincent, J., Parida, V., & Gassmann, O. (2021). Artificial intelligence and innovation management: A review, framework, and research agenda . *Technological Forecasting and Social Change*, *162*, 120392.

Haenlein, M., & Kaplan, A. (2019). A brief history of artificial intelligence: On the past, present, and future of artificial intelligence. *California Management Review*, *61*(4), 5–14.

Hagsten, E. (2016). Broadband connected employees and labour productivity: A comparative analysis of 14 European countries based on distributed micro data access. *Economics of Innovation and new Technology,* 1 – 7.

Hair, J. F., Black, W. C., Babin, B. J., & Anderson, R. E. (2010). *Multivariate Data Analysis. A global perspective* (7th ed.). Prentice Hall.

Hair, J. F., Matthews, L. M., Matthews, R. L., & Sarstedt, M. (2017). PLS-SEM or CB-SEM: Updated guidelines on which method to use. *International Journal of Multivariate Data Analysis*, *1*(2), 107–123. DOI: 10.1504/IJMDA.2017.087624

Hair, J. F., Ringle, C. M., & Sarstedt, M. (2013). Partial least squares structural equation modeling: Rigorous applications, better results and higher acceptance. *Long Range Planning*, *46*(1-2), 1–12. DOI: 10.1016/j.lrp.2013.01.001

Haleem, A., Javaid, M., Qadri, M. A., Singh, R. P., & Suman, R. (2022). Artificial intelligence (AI) applications for marketing: A literature-based study. *International Journal of Intelligent Networks*, *3*, 119–132.

Haller, S., & Lyons, S. (2015). Broadband adoption and firm productivity: Evidence from Irish manufacturing firms. *Telecommunications Policy*, *39*(1), 1–13.

Handoko, F., Vitasari, P., Hidayat, S., & Tjahjadi, M. E. (2019). Technology transfer program for SMEs in Indonesia. In *Journal of Physics: Conference Series* 1375 (1), IOP Publishing

Hariri, W. (2023). Unlocking the potential of ChatGPT: A comprehensive exploration of its applications, advantages, limitations, and future directions in natural language processing. *arXiv preprint arXiv:2304.02017*.

Haruna, M. S., Gakure, R., & Orwa, G. (2015). Effect of advanced manufacturing technology (Amt) on the product output of manufacturing small and medium scale enterprises in Nigeria. *International Academic Journal of Innovation. Leadership and Entrepreneurship*, *1*(5), 1–18.

Helo, P., & Hao, Y. (2021). Artificial intelligence in operations management and supply chain management: An exploratory case study. *Production Planning and Control*, *33*(16), 1573–1590. DOI: 10.1080/09537287.2021.188269

Henk, O. (2020). Internal control through the lens of institutional work: A systematic literature review [Article]. *Journal of Management Control*, *31*(3), 239–273. DOI: 10.1007/s00187-020-00301-4

Hermann, E. (2022a). Anthropomorphized artificial intelligence, attachment, and consumer behavior. *Marketing Letters*, *33*(1), 157–162. DOI: 10.1007/s11002-021-09587-3

Hermann, E. (2022b). Leveraging Artificial Intelligence in Marketing for Social Good—An Ethical Perspective. *Journal of Business Ethics, 179*(1), 43–61. DOI: 10.1007/s10551-021-04843-y PMID: 34054170

Hermann, E., & Hermann, G. (2022). Artificial intelligence in research and development for sustainability: The centrality of explicability and research data management. *AI and Ethics, 2*(1), 29–33.

Hernández, J. M., & Dorta-González, P. (2020). Interdisciplinarity metric based on the co-citation network. *Mathematics, 8*(4), 544.

Hidayat, K., & Idrus, M. I. (2023). The Effect of Relationship Marketing towards Switching Barrier, Customer Satisfaction, and Customer Trust on Bank Customers. *Journal of Innovation and Entrepreneurship*. Advance online publication. DOI: 10.1186/s13731-023-00270-7 PMID: 37193581

Hollebeek, L. D., & Macky, K. (2019). Digital Content Marketing's Role in Fostering Consumer Engagement, Trust, and Value: Framework, Fundamental Propositions, and Implications. *Journal of Interactive Marketing, 45*(1), 27–41. DOI: 10.1016/j.intmar.2018.07.003

Hollebeek, L. D., Menidjel, C., Sarstedt, M., Jansson, J., & Urbonavicius, S. (2024). Engaging consumers through artificially intelligent technologies: Systematic review, conceptual model, and further research. *Psychology and Marketing, 41*(4), 880–898. DOI: 10.1002/mar.21957

Hollebeek, L. D., Sprott, D. E., Andreassen, T. W., Costley, C., Klaus, P., Kuppelwieser, V., Karahasanovic, A., Taguchi, T., Ul Islam, J., & Rather, R. A. (2019). Customer engagement in evolving technological environments: Synopsis and guiding propositions. *European Journal of Marketing, 53*(9), 2018–2023. DOI: 10.1108/EJM-09-2019-970

Hong, M. K., Hakimi, S., Chen, Y. Y., Toyoda, H., Wu, C., & Klenk, M. (2023). Generative AI for product design: Getting the right design and the design right. arXiv preprint arXiv:2306.01217.

Hoque, A. S. M. M., & Awang, Z. (2019). Does gender difference play moderating role in the relationship between entrepreneurial marketing and Bangladeshi SME performance? *Accounting, 5*(1), 35–52. DOI: 10.5267/j.ac.2018.6.001

Horton, S. (2021). Empathy cannot sustain action in technology accessibility. *Frontiers of Computer Science, 3*, 31.

Hoyer, W. D., Kroschke, M., Schmitt, B., Kraume, K., & Shankar, V. (2020). Transforming the Customer Experience through New Technologies. *Journal of Interactive Marketing*, *51*(1), 57–71. DOI: 10.1016/j.intmar.2020.04.001

Hsieh, H. R. (2009). Issues and proposed improvements regarding condominium management in Taiwan. *Habitat International, 33*(1), 0–80. https://doi.org/DOI: 10.1016/j.habitatint.2008.05.002

Hsu, M.-F., & Lin, S.-J. (2021). A BSC-based network DEA model equipped with computational linguistics for performance assessment and improvement. *International Journal of Machine Learning and Cybernetics*. Advance online publication. DOI: 10.1007/s13042-021-01331-7

Huang, M.-H., & Rust, R. T. (2021a). A strategic framework for artificial intelligence in marketing. *Journal of the Academy of Marketing Science*, *49*(1), 30–50. DOI: 10.1007/s11747-020-00749-9

Huang, M.-H., & Rust, R. T. (2021b). Engaged to a Robot? The Role of AI in Service. *Journal of Service Research*, *24*(1), 30–41. DOI: 10.1177/1094670520902266

Hughes, C., Robert, L., Frady, K., & Arroyos, A. (2019). Artificial intelligence, employee engagement, fairness, and job outcomes. In *Managing technology and middle-and low-skilled employees* (pp. 61–68). Emerald Publishing Limited., DOI: 10.1108/978-1-78973-077-720191005

Hugos, M. H. (2018). *Essentials of Supply Chain Management* (4th ed.). Wiley.

Hu, K. H., Chen, F. H., Hsu, M. F., & Tzeng, G. H. (2021). Identifying key factors for adopting artificial intelligence-enabled auditing techniques by joint utilization of fuzzy-rough set theory and MRDM technique. *Technological and Economic Development of Economy*, *27*(2), 459–492. DOI: 10.3846/tede.2020.13181

Hu, L. T., & Bentler, P. M. (1998). Fit indices in covariance structure modeling: Sensitivity to underparameterized model misspecification. *Psychological Methods*, *3*(4), 424–453. DOI: 10.1037/1082-989X.3.4.424

Hulstijn, J. (2023). Computational accountability. *In Proceedings of the Nineteenth International Conference on Artificial Intelligence and Law (ICAIL '23)*. Association for Computing Machinery, New York, 121–130. https://doi.org/DOI: 10.1145/3594536.3595122

Hussain, W., Mabrok, M., Gao, H., Rabhi, F. A., & Rashed, E. A. (2024). Revolutionising healthcare with artificial intelligence: A bibliometric analysis of 40 years of progress in health systems. *Digital Health*, *10*, 20552076241258757. DOI: 10.1177/20552076241258757 PMID: 38817839

Hutcheson, G. D., & Sofroniou, N. (1999). *The multivariate social scientist: Introductory statistics using generalized linear models.*

IBM. (2024). *Artificial intelligence.* https://www.ibm.com/topics/artificial-intelligence

Igwe, S. R., Ebenuwa, A., & Idenedo, O. W. (2020). Technology adoption and sales performance of manufacturing small and medium enterprises in Port –Harcourt. *Journal of Marketing Development*, *5*(1), 44–59.

Ilager, S., Muralidhar, R., & Buyya, R. (2020, October). *Artificial intelligence (ai)-centric management of resources in modern distributed computing systems. In 2020 IEEE Cloud Summit*. IEEE.

Inácio, H. (2014). *Internal control - Theoretical framework and practical application*. Escolar Editora.

İnce, H., İmamoğlu, S. E., & İmamoğlu, S. Z. (2021). Yapay Zeka Uygulamalarının Karar Verme Üzerine Etkileri: Kavramsal Bir Çalişma. *International Review of Economics and Management*, *9*(1), 50–63.

Investopedia (2022). Investopedia. https://www.investopedia.

ISACA. (2012). Corporate model for governance and IT management of the organization: COBIT5 - Framework. In. Rolling Meadows.

Ishola, A. O., Odunaiya, O. G., & Soyombo, O. T. (2024). Stakeholder communication framework for successful implementation of community-based renewable energy projects. *International Journal of Frontiers in Science and Technology Research.* https://frontiersrj.com/journals/ijfstr/

Ivanov, D., & Sokolov, B. (2013). Control of risks in dual-period supply chain scheduling. *International Journal of Production Research*, *51*(7), 2100–2116.

Jabeur, S. B., Stef, N., & Arfi, W. B. (2024). Artificial intelligence for innovation: a bibliometric analysis and structural variation approach. International Journal of Innovation Management, 28(05n06), 2450020.

Jackson, J. E. (2005). Varimax rotation. *Encyclopedia of biostatistics, 8.* https://doi .org/DOI: 10.1002/0470011815.b2a13091

Janiesch, C., Zschech, P., & Heinrich, K. (2021). Machine learning and deep learning. *Electronic Markets*, *31*(3), 685–695.

Jansen, J. J., Van Den Bosch, F. A., & Volberda, H. W. (2006). Exploratory innovation, exploitative innovation, and performance: Effects of organizational antecedents and environmental moderators. *Management Science*, *52*(11), 1661–1674.

Jans, M., Depaire, B., & Vanhoof, K. (2011). *Does process mining add to internal auditing? An experience report. Lecture Notes in Business Information Processing* (Vol. 81). Springer., DOI: 10.1007/978-3-642-21759-3_3

Jans, M., & Hosseinpour, M. (2019). How active learning and process mining can act as Continuous Auditing catalyst. *International Journal of Accounting Information Systems*, *32*, 44–58. DOI: 10.1016/j.accinf.2018.11.002

Jiang, X., Jiang, X., Sun, W., & Fan, W. (2023). How do manufacturing firms manage artificial intelligence to drive iterative product innovation? *IEEE Transactions on Engineering Management.*

Jiang, Y., Lai, P. L., Yang, C. C., & Wang, X. (2023). Exploring the factors that drive consumers to use contactless delivery services in the context of the continued COVID-19 pandemic. *Journal of Retailing and Consumer Services*, *72*, 103276. DOI: 10.1016/j.jretconser.2023.103276

Jim, J. R., Talukder, M. A. R., Malakar, P., Kabir, M. M., Nur, K., & Mridha, M. F. (2024). Recent advancements and challenges of NLP-based sentiment analysis: A state-of-the-art review. Natural Language Processing Journal, 100059.

Jimenez, I., & Hernandez Cuadrado, L. (2022). Credit risk management in the era of artificial intelligence. *Economía Industrial*, *423*, 153–164.

Jöreskog, K. G., & Sörbom, D. (1993). *LISREL 8: Structural equation odelling with the SIMPLIS command language*. Scientific software is international.

Joseph, L. B., & Clayton, M. C. (1995). Disruptive technologies: Catching the Wave. *Harvard Business Review*, *73*(1), 43–53.

Junaid, M. (2020). Wireless network sensors applications and challenges in a real – life environment. *IEEM – SEM, 8*(7), 111 – 117.

Kagermann, H., Wahlster, W., & Helbig, J. (2013). *Recommendations for implementing the strategic initiative INDUSTRIE 4.0: Final report of the Industrie 4.0 Working Group*. Acatech.

Kaggwa, S., Eleogu, T. F., Okonkwo, F., Farayola, O. A., Uwaoma, P. U., & Akinoso, A. (2024). AI in decision-making: Transforming business strategies. *International Journal of Research and Scientific Innovation*, *10*(12), 423–444.

Kaiser, H. F. (1974). An index of factorial simplicity. *psychometrika, 39*(1), 31-36. https://doi.org/DOI: 10.1007/BF02291575

Kallina, E., & Singh, J. (2024, October). Stakeholder Involvement for Responsible AI Development: A Process Framework. In *Proceedings of the 4th ACM Conference on Equity and Access in Algorithms, Mechanisms, and Optimization* (pp. 1-14).

Kamandi, Faith Gacheri, Godfrey Kinyua PhD, and Anne MuchemiPhD. (2021). Strategic Alignment as an Antecedent of Customer Satisfaction: A Review of Literature. *International Journal of Managerial Studies and Research, 9*(12), 38–57. DOI: 10.20431/2349-0349.0912005

Kang, D. Y., Hur, W. M., & Shin, Y. (2023). Smart technology and service employees' job crafting: Relationship between STARA awareness, performance pressure, receiving and giving help, and job crafting. *Journal of Retailing and Consumer Services, 73*, 103282. DOI: 10.1016/j.jretconser.2023.103282

Kaplan, A., & Haenlein, M. (2019). Siri, Siri, in my hand: Who's the fairest in the land? On the interpretations, illustrations, and implications of artificial intelligence. *Business Horizons, 62*(1), 15–25. DOI: 10.1016/j.bushor.2018.08.004

Kaplan, R. S., & Norton, D. P. (1992). *The Balanced Scorecard*. Barcelona. *Gestion*, •••, 2000.

Karhade, P., & Dong, J. Q. (2020). Information technology investment and commercialized innovation performance: Dynamic adjustment costs and curvilinear impacts. *Management Information Systems Quarterly*, •••, 1–40.

Kaur, R., Gabrijelčič, D., & Klobučar, T. (2023). Artificial intelligence for cybersecurity: Literature review and future research directions. *Information Fusion, 97*, 101804.

Kayid, A. (2020). *The role of Artificial Intelligence in future technology*. Department of Computer Science, The German University in Cairo.

Kee, D. M. H., & Rubel, M. R. B. (2021). Technology adaptation is on its way: The role of high involvement work practice. *International Journal of Business Innovation & Research, 25*(1), 35–50.

Keegan, B. J., Dennehy, D., & Naudé, P. (2024). Implementing Artificial Intelligence in Traditional B2B Marketing Practices: An Activity Theory Perspective. *Information Systems Frontiers, 26*(3), 1025–1039. DOI: 10.1007/s10796-022-10294-1 PMID: 35637917

Kelly-Lyth, A. (2021). Challenging biased hiring algorithms. *Oxford Journal of Legal Studies*, *41*(4), 899–928. DOI: 10.1093/ojls/gqab006

Kerr, W. R., Lerner, J., & Schoar, A. (2014). The Consequences of Entrepreneurial Finance: Evidence from Angel Financings. *Review of Financial Studies*, *27*(1), 20–55.

Khairuddin, S. M. H. S., & Olowosuyi, O. S. (2020). Digital adoption of SME in Nigeria: The relationship with business performance. *Journal of Management and Muamalah*, *10*(2), 21–33.

Khanagha, S., Zadeh, M. T. R., Mihalache, O., & Volberda, H. (2018). Embracing bewilderment: Responding to technological disruption in heterogenous market environments. *Journal of Management Studies*, *55*(7), 1079–1121.

Khan, M., & Kumar, V. (2020). Risk Management in Supply Chains: Strategies and Solutions. *Journal of Risk Research*, *23*(7), 897–912.

Khatri, V., & Brown, C. V. (2010). Designing data governance. *Communications of the ACM*, *53*(1), 148–152. DOI: 10.1145/1629175.1629210

Khrais, L. T. (2020). Role of Artificial Intelligence in Shaping Consumer Demand in E-Commerce. *Future Internet*, *12*(12), 226. DOI: 10.3390/fi12120226

Khurana, A., Subramonyam, H., & Chilana, P. K. (2024). Why and when llm-based assistants can go wrong: Investigating the effectiveness of prompt-based interactions for software help-seeking. *arXiv.org*. https://doi.org//arxiv.2402.08030DOI: 10.48550

Kiefer, K., Heileman, M., & Pett, T. L. (2022). Does gender still matter? An examination of small business performance. *Small Business Economics*, *58*(1), 141–167. DOI: 10.1007/s11187-020-00403-2

Kim, J., Seo, D., Moon, J., Kim, J., Kim, H., & Jeong, J. (2022). Design and implementation of an HCPS-based PCB smart factory system for next-generation intelligent manufacturing. *Applied Sciences (Basel, Switzerland)*, *12*(15), 7645.

Kim, T. W., Jiang, L., Duhachek, A., Lee, H., & Garvey, A. (2022). Do You Mind if I Ask You a Personal Question? How AI Service Agents Alter Consumer Self-Disclosure. *Journal of Service Research*, *25*(4), 649–666. DOI: 10.1177/10946705221120232

Kim, W. B., & Hur, H. J. (2024). What Makes People Feel Empathy for AI Chatbots? Assessing the Role of Competence and Warmth. *International Journal of Human-Computer Interaction*, *40*(17), 4674–4687. DOI: 10.1080/10447318.2023.2219961

Klaus, P., & Zaichkowsky, J. (2020). AI voice bots: A services marketing research agenda. *Journal of Services Marketing*, *34*(3), 389–398. DOI: 10.1108/JSM-01-2019-0043

Kline, R. B. (1998). Software review: Software programs for structural equation modeling: Amos, EQS, and LISREL. *Journal of Psychoeducational Assessment, 16*(4), 343–364. DOI: 10.1177/073428299801600407

Kline, R. B. (2023). *Principles and practice of structural equation modeling*. Guilford publications.

Klius, Y., Ivchenko, Y., & Izhboldina, A. (2020). International approaches to organizing an internal control system at an enterprise in the digital era. *Economic Annals-Xxi, 185*(9-10), 133–143. DOI: 10.21003/ea.V185-13

Knudsen, M. P., Von Zedtwitz, M., Griffin, A., & Barczak, G. (2023). Best practices in new product development and innovation: Results from PDMA's 2021 global survey. *Journal of Product Innovation Management, 40*(3), 257–275.

Kokina, J., & Blanchette, S. (2019). Early evidence of digital labor in accounting: Innovation with Robotic Process Automation. *International Journal of Accounting Information Systems, 35*(13), 100431. Advance online publication. DOI: 10.1016/j.accinf.2019.100431

Kopalle, P. K., Gangwar, M., Kaplan, A., Ramachandran, D., Reinartz, W., & Rindfleisch, A. (2022). Examining artificial intelligence (AI) technologies in marketing via a global lens: Current trends and future research opportunities. *International Journal of Research in Marketing, 39*(2), 522–540. DOI: 10.1016/j.ijresmar.2021.11.002

Kostenwein, D. (2021). Between walls and fences: How different types of gated communities shape the streets around them. *Urban Studies (Edinburgh, Scotland)*. Advance online publication. DOI: 10.1177/0042098020984320

Kotur, B. R., & Anbazhagan, S. (2014). Influence of age and gender on the performance. *IOSR Journal of Business and Management, 16*(5), 97–103. DOI: 10.9790/487x-165397103

Kraus, S., Palmer, C., Kailer, N., Kallinger, F. L., & Spitzer, J. (2021). Digital entrepreneurship: A research agenda on new business models for the twenty-first century. *International Journal of Entrepreneurial Behaviour & Research, 25*(2), 353–375.

Krishnakumar, B., Gomathi, S., Sudharsan, V. S., Anbounadane, P. V., Solayappan, A., & Swamy, S. S. (2023, December). Smart building management with IoT and AI: Energy-efficient and cost-effective solutions. In *2023 10th IEEE Uttar Pradesh Section International Conference on Electrical, Electronics and Computer Engineering (UPCON)* (Vol. 10, pp. 1249–1254). IEEE.

Kuhail, M. A., Mathew, S. S., Khalil, A., Khalil, A., & Shah, S. J. (2023). "Will I be replaced?" Assessing ChatGPT's effect on software development and programmer perceptions of AI tools. *arXiv.org*. https://doi.org/DOI: 10.2139/ssrn.4571482

Kumar, D., Shandilya, A. K., & Choudhuri, S. (2023). Artificial Intelligence-Enabled Bibliometric Analysis in Tourism and Hospitality Using Biblioshiny and VOSviewer Software. In A. Khang, V. Abdullayev, B. Jadhav, S. Gupta, & G. Morris, *AI-Centric Modeling and Analytics* (1st ed., pp. 260–291). CRC Press. https://doi.org/DOI: 10.1201/9781003400110-15

Kumar, A., & Ayedee, D. (2021). Technology adoption: A solution for SMEs to overcome problems during COVID-19. *Forthcoming. Academy of Marketing Studies Journal*, *25*(1).

Kumar, J., Prince, N., & Baker, H. K. (2021). Balanced scorecard: A systematic literature review and future research issues. *FIIB Business Review*, *11*(2), 147–161. DOI: 10.1177/23197145211049625

Kumar, M., Beninger, S., Reppel, A., Stanton, J., Vlaminck, D., & Watson, F. (2025). Your synthetic teammate: Enriching new product development with generative AI. *Business Horizons*.

Kumar, V., Ashraf, A. R., & Nadeem, W. (2024). AI-powered marketing: What, where, and how? *International Journal of Information Management*, *77*, 102783. DOI: 10.1016/j.ijinfomgt.2024.102783

Kumar, V., Rajan, B., Venkatesan, R., & Lecinski, J. (2019). Understanding the Role of Artificial Intelligence in Personalized Engagement Marketing. *California Management Review*, *61*(4), 135–155. DOI: 10.1177/0008125619859317

Kuo, Y. K., Kuo, T. H., & Ho, L. A. (2014). Enabling innovative ability: Knowledge sharing as a mediator. *Industrial Management & Data Systems*, *114*(5), 696–710. DOI: 10.1108/IMDS-10-2013-0434

Kuo, Y.-C., Chou, J.-S., & Sun, K.-S. (2011). How service quality influences resident satisfaction in condominium management. *Expert Systems with Applications*, *38*(5), 5755–5763. DOI: 10.1016/j.eswa.2010.10.057

La Londe, B. J., & Masters, J. M. (1994). Emerging Logistics Strategies: Blue-print for the next century. *International Journal of Physical Distribution & Logistics Management*, *24*(7), 35–47.

Lake, B. M., Ullman, T. D., Tenenbaum, J. B., & Gershman, S. J. (2017). Building machines that learn and think like people. *Behavioral and Brain Sciences*, *40*, e253. PMID: 27881212

Lambert, D. M., & Cooper, M. C. (2000). Issues in supply chain management. *Industrial Marketing Management, 29*(1), 65–83.

Landy, F. J. (2008). Stereotypes, bias, and personnel decisions: Strange and stranger. *Industrial and Organizational Psychology: Perspectives on Science and Practice, 1*(4), 379–392. DOI: 10.1111/j.1754-9434.2008.00071.x

Law, A. M., & Kelton, W. D. (2000). *Simulation Modeling and Analysis* (3rd ed.). McGraw-Hill.

Lee, C. T., Pan, L.-Y., & Hsieh, S. H. (2022). Artificial intelligent chatbots as brand promoters: A two-stage structural equation modeling-artificial neural network approach. *Internet Research, 32*(4), 1329–1356. DOI: 10.1108/INTR-01-2021-0030

Lee, H. L., So, K. C., & Tang, C. S. (2018). The Evolution of Inventory Management Models: From EOQ to AI. *International Journal of Production Economics, 205*, 123–135.

Lee, H. L., So, K. C., & Tang, C. S. (2020). Risk Mitigation and Cybersecurity in Supply Chains. *International Journal of Production Economics, 225*, 123–135.

Lee, J., Bagheri, B., & Kao, H. A. (2015). A cyber-physical systems architecture for industry 4.0-based manufacturing systems. *Manufacturing Letters, 3*, 18–23.

Lee, J., Davari, H., Singh, J., & Pandhare, V. (2018). Industrial Artificial Intelligence for industry 4.0-based manufacturing systems. *Manufacturing Letters, 18*, 20–23.

Lei, Y., Vyas, S., Gupta, S., & Shabaz, M. (2022). AI based study on product development and process design. *International Journal of System Assurance Engineering and Management*, •••, 1–7.

Liang, H., & Xue, Y. (2009). Avoidance of information technology threats: A theoretical perspective. *Management Information Systems Quarterly, 33*(1), 71–90. DOI: 10.2307/20650279

Liao, W., Lu, X., Fei, Y., Gu, Y., & Huang, Y. (2024). Generative AI design for building structures. *Automation in Construction, 157*, 105187.

Licona Quiterio, O. (2024). AI and Education in Mexico: Between Opportunities and Challenges. RIESED -. *International Journal of Studies on Educational Systems, 3*(15), 675–688. https://www.riesed.org/index.php/RIESED/article/view/180

Liker, J. K. (2004). *The Toyota Way: 14 Management Principles from the World's Greatest Manufacturer*. McGraw-Hill.

Lim, J. S., & Zhang, J. (2022). Adoption of AI-driven personalization in digital news platforms: An integrative model of technology acceptance and perceived contingency. *Technology in Society*, *69*, 101965. DOI: 10.1016/j.techsoc.2022.101965

Li, N., Kim, M., Dai, J., & Vasarhelyi, M. A. (2024). Using artificial intelligence in ESG assurance. *Journal of Emerging Technologies in Accounting*, *21*(2), 83–99.

Liu, F. (2011, August 8-10). Cash flow management of modern enterprises under the guidance of the application of internal control. 2011 2nd Artificial Intelligence, Management Science and Electronic Commerce (AIMSEC 2011), Deng Feng, China, 2011, pp. 6176-6178. https://doi.org/DOI: 10.1109/AIMSEC.2011.6009650

Liu-Thompkins, Y., Okazaki, S., & Li, H. (2022). Artificial empathy in marketing interactions: Bridging the human-AI gap in affective and social customer experience. *Journal of the Academy of Marketing Science*, *50*(6), 1198–1218. DOI: 10.1007/s11747-022-00892-5

Li, Z., Wang, Y., & Deng, Z. (2022). Research on Evolution Characteristics and Factors of Nordic Green Patent Citation Network. *Sustainability*, *14*(13), 7743.

Lo, C. K., Chen, C. H., & Zhong, R. Y. (2021). A review of digital twin in product design and development. *Advanced Engineering Informatics*, *48*, 101297.

Looi, C. K., Tan, S. L., Teow, P. C., & Chan, H. S. (1989). A knowledge-based approach for internal control evaluation. *In Proceedings of the 2nd international conference on Industrial and engineering applications of artificial intelligence and expert systems* - Volume 1 *(IEA/AIE '89)*. Association for Computing Machinery, New York, 254–261. https://doi.org/DOI: 10.1145/66617.66648

Lopez Sempere, A. (2022). *Identification and detection of vulnerabilities.* (Doctoral dissertation, Universitat Politecnica de Valencia).

López-Naranjo, A. L., Puente-Riofrio, M. I., Carrasco-Salazar, V. A., Erazo-Rodríguez, J. D., & Buñay-Guisñan, P. A. (2025). Artificial intelligence in the tourism business: A systematic review. *Frontiers in Artificial Intelligence*, *8*, 1599391. DOI: 10.3389/frai.2025.1599391 PMID: 40785835

Lukas, B. A., & Ferrell, O. C. (2000). The effect of market orientation on product innovation. *Journal of the Academy of Marketing Science*, *28*(2), 239–247.

Lummus, R. R., & Vokurka, R. J. (1999). Defining supply chain management: A historical perspective and practical guidelines. *Industrial Management & Data Systems*, *99*(1), 11–17.

Luna, L. (Ed.). (2025). *Regulatory Framework for Artificial Intelligence in Argentina.* https://www.traductores.org.ar/wp-content/uploads/2025/04/04_ComisionRRTT.pdf

Lu, V. N., Wirtz, J., Kunz, W. H., Paluch, S., Gruber, T., Martins, A., & Patterson, P. G. (2020). Service robots, customers and service employees: What can we learn from the academic literature and where are the gaps? *Journal of Service Theory and Practice*, *30*(3), 361–391. DOI: 10.1108/JSTP-04-2019-0088

MacCallum, R. C., Browne, M. W., & Sugawara, H. M. (1996). Power Analysis and Determination of Sample Size for Covariance Structure Modeling. *Psychological Methods*, *1*(2), 130–149. DOI: 10.1037/1082-989X.1.2.130

MacCallum, R. C., & Hong, S. (1997). Power analysis in covariance structure modeling using GFI and AGFI. *Multivariate Behavioral Research*, *32*(2), 193–210. DOI: 10.1207/s15327906mbr3202_5 PMID: 26788758

Mackey, J. D., Roth, P. L., Van Iddekinge, C. H., & McFarland, L. A. (2019). A meta-analysis of gender proportionality effects on job performance. *Group & Organization Management*, *44*(3), 578–610. DOI: 10.1177/1059601117730519

Mahboub, R., & Ghanem, M. G. (2024). The mediating role of knowledge management practices and balanced scorecard in the association between artificial intelligence and organization performance: Evidence from MENA region commercial banks. *Cogent Business & Management*, *11*(1). Advance online publication. DOI: 10.1080/23311975.2024.2404484

Mahroof, K. (2019). A human-centric perspective exploring the readiness towards smart warehousing: The case of a large retail distribution warehouse. *International Journal of Information Management*, *45*(C), 176–190. DOI: 10.1016/j.ijinfomgt.2018.11.008

Makiwa, P., & Steyn, R. (2018). An investigation of the government-related factors that inhibit small to medium enterprises adoption and effective use of information and communication technology in developing countries: The case of Zimbabwe". *International Development Informatics Association Conference,* Springer, Cham, 3 – 16.

Makridakis, S., Wheelwright, S. C., & Hyndman, R. J. (1998). *Forecasting: Methods and Applications* (3rd ed.). Wiley.

Ma, L., & Sun, B. (2020). Machine learning and AI in marketing – Connecting computing power to human insights. *International Journal of Research in Marketing*, *37*(3), 481–504. DOI: 10.1016/j.ijresmar.2020.04.005

Malik, N., Tripathi, S. N., Kar, A. K., & Gupta, S. (2021). Impact of artificial intelligence on employees working in industry 4.0 led organizations. *International Journal of Manpower, 43*(2), 334–354. DOI: 10.1108/IJM-03-2021-0173

Mandilas, A. A., Kourtidis, D., Petasakis, I. E., & Valsamidis, S. I. (2022). Digital Disruption in the Accounting Profession. *International Journal of Knowledge-Based Organizations, 12*(11), 11–19. https://doi.org/https://doi.org/10.4018/ijkbo.305347

Mandongwe, L., & Jaravaza, D. C. (2020). Women entrepreneurial intentions in subsistence marketplaces: The role of entrepreneurial orientation and demographic profiles in Zimbabwe. *Cogent Business & Management, 7*(1), 1818365. DOI: 10.1080/23311975.2020.1818365

Manser Payne, E. H., Dahl, A. J., & Peltier, J. (2021). Digital servitization value co-creation framework for AI services: A research agenda for digital transformation in financial service ecosystems. *Journal of Research in Interactive Marketing, 15*(2), 200–222. DOI: 10.1108/JRIM-12-2020-0252

Manu, A. (2024). *Transcending imagination: Artificial intelligence and the future of creativity* (1st ed.). Chapman and Hall/CRC., DOI: 10.1201/9781003450139

Maqueo, M. S., Moreno, J., Mendoza, O. A., & Rentería, C. (2021). *Preparing the judicial sector for artificial intelligence in Latin America*. University of San Andrés. https://repositorio.udesa.edu.ar/items/77dca327-567c-477a-843e 90fe8f3e8e88

Mardia, K. V. (1970). Measures of multivariate skewness and kurtosis with applications. *Biometrika, 57*(3), 519–530. DOI: 10.1093/biomet/57.3.519

Mardia, K. V. (1974). Applications of some measures of multivariate skewness and kurtosis in testing normality and robustness studies. *Sankhya Series B*, •••, 115–128.

Mariani, M. (2020). Big Data and analytics in tourism and hospitality: A perspective article. *Tourism Review, 75*(1), 299–303. DOI: 10.1108/TR-06-2019-0259

Mariani, M. M., Machado, I., Magrelli, V., & Dwivedi, Y. K. (2023a). Artificial intelligence in innovation research: A systematic review, conceptual framework, and future research directions. *Technovation, 122*, 102623.

Mariani, M. M., Machado, I., & Nambisan, S. (2023b). Types of innovation and artificial intelligence: A systematic quantitative literature review and research agenda. *Journal of Business Research, 155*, 113364.

Mariani, M. M., Perez-Vega, R., & Wirtz, J. (2022). AI in marketing, consumer research and psychology: A systematic literature review and research agenda. *Psychology and Marketing, 39*(4), 755–776. DOI: 10.1002/mar.21619

Maroufkhani, P., Wan Ismail, W. K., & Ghobakhloo, M. (2020). Big data analytics adoption model for small and medium enterprises. *Journal of Science and Technology Policy Management, 11*(4), 483–513.

Marques, R. P., Santos, H., & Santos, C. (2015). Monitoring organizational transactions in enterprise information systems with continuous assurance requirements. *International Journal of Enterprise Information Systems, 11*(1), 13–32. DOI: 10.4018/ijeis.2015010102

Marsh, H. W., & Hocevar, D. (1985). Application of confirmatory factor analysis to the study of self-concept: First-and higher order factor models and their invariance across groups. *Psychological Bulletin, 97*(3), 562–582. DOI: 10.1037/0033-2909.97.3.562

Martin, C., Leurent, H., & Kearney, A. T. (2017). Technology and innovation for the future of production: Accelerating Value Creation. *Report of World Economic Forum,* 3 – 36.

Martin, B. A. S., Jin, H. S., Wang, D., Nguyen, H., Zhan, K., & Wang, Y. X. (2020). The influence of consumer anthropomorphism on attitudes towards artificial intelligence trip advisors. *Journal of Hospitality and Tourism Management, 44*, 108–111. DOI: 10.1016/j.jhtm.2020.06.004

Martínez, M. V. (2024). What we talk about when we talk about artificial intelligence. *UNESCO.* https://unesdoc.unesco.org/ark:/48223/pf0000391087

Martinez-Pelaez, R., Ochoa-Brust, A., Rivera, S., Felix, V. G., Ostos, R., Brito, H., & Mena, L. J. (2023). Role of digital transformation for achieving sustainability: Mediated role of stakeholders, key capabilities, and technology. *Sustainability, 15*(14), 11221.

Martinez-Perez, C., Alvarez-Peregrina, C., Villa-Collar, C., & Sánchez-Tena, M. Á. (2020). Current state and future trends: A citation network analysis of the academic performance field. *International Journal of Environmental Research and Public Health, 17*(15), 5352. PMID: 32722277

Martin, K. D., & Zimmermann, J. (2024). Artificial intelligence and its implications for data privacy. *Current Opinion in Psychology,* •••, 101829. PMID: 38954851

Masdi, M. A. M. M., Hadanan, S. W., Zamain, N. S. A., Hasnan, A. H. A., Julaihi, M. H. S., Sani, B. N. Z., & Kamaluddin, A. M. (2022). Critical analysis on the necessity and techniques used in internal control in accounting operations. *2022 7th International Conference on Business and Industrial Research (ICBIR)*, Bangkok, Thailand, pp. 638-643. https://doi.org/DOI: 10.1109/ICBIR54589.2022.9786431

Mathiver, V. (2018). *Artificial Intelligence for Developers: Concepts and Implementation in C.* Ediciones Eni.

Mauri, L., & Damiani, E. (2021). Stride-ai: An approach to identifying vulnerabilities of machine learning assets. In *2021 IEEE International conference on cyber security and resilience (CSR)* (pp. 147-154). July. IEEE.

Mayer-Schönberger, V., & Cukier, K. (2013). *Big Data: A revolution that will transform how we live, work, and think.* Houghton Mifflin Harcourt.

Mays, K. K., Lei, Y., Giovanetti, R., & Katz, J. E. (2022). AI as a boss? A national US survey of predispositions governing comfort with expanded AI roles in society. *AI & Society*, •••, 1–14. DOI: 10.1007/s00146-021-01253-6

Mbau, A., & Musiega, D. (2022). Analysing the efficiency of health systems. Oxford, UK: *Applied Health Economics and Health Policy*, University of Oxford. https://doi.org/DOI: 10.1007/s40258-022-00785-2

McLean, G., Osei-Frimpong, K., & Barhorst, J. (2021). Alexa, do voice assistants influence consumer brand engagement? – Examining the role of AI powered voice assistants in influencing consumer brand engagement. *Journal of Business Research, 124*, 312–328. DOI: 10.1016/j.jbusres.2020.11.045

Mehrabi, N., Morstatter, F., Saxena, N., Lerman, K., & Galstyan, A. (2021). A survey on bias and fairness in machine learning. *ACM Computing Surveys, 54*(6), 1–35.

Mehta, C. K., Kaushik, V., & Bhargav, S. (2021). *A study of the impact of internal control measures on ease of use of forensic audit mediated by artificial intelligence techniques. 2021 Emerging Trends in Industry 4.0 (ETI 4.0).* Raigarh., DOI: 10.1109/ETI4.051663.2021.9619447

Mejia, R. C., Nuñez, M. A., Villanueva, E., & Jaraba, I. (2024). Risk Management: A Business Approach. Revised, Updated, and Expanded Second Edition. Universidad Eafit.

Meng, C. (2015). *Advances in logistics and supply chain management.* Springer.

Mentzer, J. T., Dewitt, W., Keebler, J. S., Min, S., Nix, N. W., Smith, C. D., & Zacharia, Z. G. (2001). Defining the supply chain Management. *Journal of Business Logistics, 22*(2).

Mentzer, J. T., & Moon, M. A. (2005). *Sales forecasting management: A demand management approach* (2nd ed.). Thomson South-Western.

Merabet, G. H., Essaaidi, M., Haddou, M. B., Qolomany, B., Qadir, J., Anan, M. T., Al-Fuqaha, A. I., Abid, M. R., & Benhaddou, D. (2021). Intelligent building control systems for thermal comfort and energy-efficiency: A systematic review of artificial intelligence-assisted techniques. *Renewable & Sustainable Energy Reviews*. Advance online publication. DOI: 10.1016/j.rser.2021.110969

Meta AI (2025). *Levels of Development of Artificial Intelligence Management.* Authors conversation with an AI assistant on March 1, 2025.

Meza Ruiz, V. (2024). *The path to AI regulation in Mexico.* https://turing.iimas.unam.mx/~ivanvladimir/posts/camino_regulacion_ia_mexico/

Microsoft Copilot (2025a). *Key factors and variables in AI management.* Authors conversation with an AI assistant on February 6, 2025.

Microsoft Copilot. (2025b). *Levels in clear objectives.* Authors conversation with an AI assistant on February 11, 2025.

Microsoft. (2024). Retrieved 05/06/2024 from https://azure.microsoft.com/pt-pt/resources/cloud-computing-dictionary/what-is-machine-learning-platform/

Mina-Falsarella, O., Silva de Oliveira, R., Angela-Branchi, B., & Ferreira-Mariosa, D. (2023). Sustainability in vertical residential condominiums: A study in the metropolitan region of Campinas. *Gestão & Regionalidade*, *39*, e20237634. DOI: 10.13037/gr.vol39.e20237634

Minh Sang, N. (2024). Bibliometric insights into the evolution of digital marketing trends. *Innovative Marketing*, *20*(2), 1–14. DOI: 10.21511/im.20(2).2024.01

Ministry of Science. Technology, Knowledge and Innovation. (2020). *National Policy on Artificial Intelligence*. Santiago, Chile: Government of Chile. https://minciencia.gob.cl/uploads/filer_public/bc/38/bc389daf-4514-4306-867c-760ae7686e2c/documento_politica_ia_digital_.pdf

Minkkinen, M., Laine, J., & Mäntymäki, M. (2022). Continuous auditing of artificial intelligence: A conceptualization and assessment of tools and frameworks. *Digital Society : Ethics, Socio-Legal and Governance of Digital Technology*, *1*(3), 21.

Mio, C., Costantini, A., & Panfilo, S. (2022). Performance measurement tools for sustainable business: A systematic literature review on the sustainability balanced scorecard use. *Corporate Social Responsibility and Environmental Management*, *29*(2), 367–384. DOI: 10.1002/csr.2206

Mitan, J. (2024). *Enhancing Audit Quality through Artificial Intelligence: An External Auditing Perspective.* Accounting Undergraduate Honors Theses. https://scholarworks.uark.edu/acctuht/58

Mogaji, E., Soetan, T. O., & Kieu, T. A. (2021). The implications of artificial intelligence on the digital marketing of financial services to vulnerable customers. *Australasian Marketing Journal, 29*(3), 235–242. DOI: 10.1016/j.ausmj.2020.05.003

Molina, E., & Medina Vásquez, E. (2025). The AI Revolution in Higher Education: What You Need to Know (Spanish). *Digital Innovations in Education.* Washington, D.C.: World Bank Group. https://documents.worldbank.org/curated/en/099809404152514027

Mollick, E. (2014). The Dynamics of Crowdfunding: An Exploratory Study. *Journal of Business Venturing, 29*(1), 1–16.

Mondén, T. (2011). Implementing Lean Principles in Supply Chains. Springer.

Mongeon, P., & Paul-Hus, A. (2016). The journal coverage of Web of Science and Scopus: A comparative analysis. *Scientometrics, 106*, 213–228.

Monteiro, A., Cepêda, C., Da Silva, A. C. F., & Vale, J. (2023). The Relationship between AI Adoption Intensity and Internal Control System and Accounting Information Quality. *Systems, 11*(11), 536. DOI: 10.3390/systems11110536

Montgomery, D. C., Jennings, C. L., & Kulahci, M. (2012). *Introduction to Time Series Analysis and Forecasting* (2nd ed.). Wiley.

Moraga López, J., & López Mairena, E. (2024). Digital divide in higher education. *Electronic journal of knowledge, skills and practices*, 7(1), 56-70 https://doi.org/ DOI: 10.5377/recsp.v7i1.19356

Moran Espinosa, A., (2021). Criminal Liability of Artificial Intelligence (AI): The Next Frontier? *IUS. Revista del Instituto de Ciencias Jurídicas de Puebla A.C., 15*(48), 289-323. https://doi.org/DOI: 10.35487/rius.v15i48.2021.706

Morduchowicz, R. (2023). Artificial intelligence: Do we need a new education? *UNESCO.* https://unesdoc.unesco.org/ark:/48223/pf0000386262

Morelli, J. (2011). Environmental sustainability: A definition for environmental professionals. *Journal of Environmental Sustainability, 1*(1), 2. Advance online publication. DOI: 10.14448/jes.01.0002

Morgado, J. C. (2013). *The Case Study in Education Research (4.ª Ed).* De Facto Editors, Santo Tirso.

Moriuchi, E., Landers, V. M., Colton, D., & Hair, N. (2021). Engagement with chatbots versus augmented reality interactive technology in e-commerce. *Journal of Strategic Marketing*, *29*(5), 375–389. DOI: 10.1080/0965254X.2020.1740766

Mubarak, M. F., Biggadike, C., Ahumada-Tello, E., & Evans, R. (2024). AI in New Product Development: Opportunities, Applications, and Managerial Implications. *IEEE Engineering Management Review*.

Mugogo, M. (2020). International Journal of Economics. *Commerce and Management United Kingdom THE IMPACT OF INNOVATION ON MANUFACTURING SECTOR SME PERFORMANCE IN ZIMBABWE.*, *VIII*(12), 90–106.

Mustak, M., Salminen, J., Plé, L., & Wirtz, J. (2021). Artificial intelligence in marketing: Topic modeling, scientometric analysis, and research agenda. *Journal of Business Research*, *124*, 389–404. DOI: 10.1016/j.jbusres.2020.10.044

Mutongi, C. (2020). Either Women or Men Make Superior Managers and Leaders: A Critique. *International Journal of Research and Innovation in Social Science*, *4*(8), 320–325.

Nadeem, A., Marjanovic, O., & Abedin, B. (2021). Gender bias in AI: Implications for managerial practices. In *Responsible AI and Analytics for an Ethical and Inclusive Digitized Society: 20th IFIP WG 6.11 Conference on e-Business, e-Services and e-Society, I3E 2021, Galway, Ireland, September 1–3, 2021, Proceedings 20* (pp. 259-270). Springer International Publishing. https://doi.org/DOI: 10.1007/978-3-030-85447-8_23

Naeem, R., Kohtamäki, M., & Parida, V. (2024). Artificial intelligence enabled product–service innovation: Past achievements and future directions. *Review of Managerial Science*, ●●●, 44–1.

Nagy, S., & Somosi, M. V. (2022). The relationship between social innovation and digital economy and society. arXiv preprint arXiv:2212.13840.

Nahmias, S. (2009). *Production and Operations Analysis* (6th ed.). McGraw-Hill.

Nair, K., & Gupta, R. (2021). Application of AI technology in modern digital marketing environment. *World Journal of Entrepreneurship, Management and Sustainable Development, ahead-of-print*(ahead-of-print). https://doi.org/DOI: 10.1108/WJEMSD-08-2020-0099

Narteni, S., Orani, V., Ferrari, E., Verda, D., Cambiaso, E., & Mongelli, M. (2025). Explainable evaluation of generative adversarial networks for wearables data augmentation. *Engineering Applications of Artificial Intelligence*, *145*, 110133.

Nasrabadi, M. A., Beauregard, Y., & Ekhlassi, A. (2024). The implication of user-generated content in new product development process: A systematic literature review and future research agenda. *Technological Forecasting and Social Change, 206*, 123551.

Nazareth, N., & Reddy, Y. V. R. (2023). Financial applications of machine learning: A literature review. *Expert Systems with Applications, 219*, 119640.

Nazir, S., Khadim, S., Ali Asadullah, M., & Syed, N. (2023). Exploring the influence of artificial intelligence technology on consumer repurchase intention: The mediation and moderation approach. *Technology in Society, 72*, 102190. DOI: 10.1016/j.techsoc.2022.102190

Nekhili, M., Chakroun, H., & Chtioui, T. (2018). Women's leadership and firm performance: Family versus nonfamily firms. *Journal of Business Ethics, 153*(2), 291–316. DOI: 10.1007/s10551-016-3340-2

Ng, T. W., Lam, S. S., & Feldman, D. C. (2016). Organizational citizenship behavior and counterproductive work behavior: Do males and females differ? *Journal of Vocational Behavior, 93*, 11–32. DOI: 10.1016/j.jvb.2015.12.005

Nicodemus, T., Mowaiye, B., & Fasola, I. O. (2020). When technology transfer enables sales growth. *Global Journal of Management and Business Research, 20*(9), 45–53.

Nonaka, I. (2009). The knowledge-creating company. In *The economic impact of knowledge* (pp. 175–187). Routledge.

Nookala, G., Gade, K. R., Dulam, N., & Thumburu, S. K. R. (2024). Governance for Data Ecosystems: Managing Compliance, Privacy, and Interoperability. *MZ Journal of Artificial Intelligence, 1*(2).

Noor, N. R. A. M., & Mansor, N. (2019). Exploring the adaptation of artificial intelligence in whistleblowing practice of the internal auditors in Malaysia. *Procedia Computer Science, 163*, 434–439. DOI: 10.1016/j.procs.2019.12.12

Noreen, U., Shafique, A., Ahmed, Z., & Ashfaq, M. (2023). Banking 4.0: Artificial intelligence (AI) in banking industry & consumer's perspective. *Sustainability, 15*(4), 3682. DOI: 10.3390/su15043682

Noura, M., Atiquzzaman, M., & Gaedke, M. (2019). Interoperability in internet of things: Taxonomies and open challenges. *Mobile Networks and Applications, 24*, 796–809.

Odiboh, O., Ben-Enukora, C., Oresanya, T., Yartey, D., & Aiyelabola, A. (2017). Awareness on digital security and e-business in Nigeria. *Proceedings of SOCIOINT 2017- 4th International Conference on Education, Social Sciences and Humanities, 1402 - 1408; Dubai, UAE.* dr odiboh dubai. (covenantuniversity.edu.ng)

OECD. (2019). *Artificial Intelligence in Society*. OECD Publishing.

OECD. (2020). Social economy and the Covid – 19 crisis: Current and future roles. https://www.oecd.org/coronavirus/policy-responses/social-economy-and-the-covid -19-crisis-current-and-future-roles-f904b89f/

OECD. (2024). *Artificial Intelligence and tourism: G7/OECD policy paper*. OECD Tourism Papers. [OECD Tourism Papers], DOI: 10.1787/3f9a4d8d-

Ofosu-Ampong, K. (2023). Gender differences in perception of artificial intelligence-based tools. *Journal of Digital Art & Humanities*, *4*(2), 52–56. DOI: 10.33847/2712-8149.4.2_6

Okeleke, P.A., Ajiga, D., Folorunsho, S.O., & Ezeigweneme, C. (2024). Predictive analytics for market trends using AI: A study in consumer behavior. *International Journal of Engineering Research Updates, 7*(1), 036–049. https://doi.org/DOI: 10.53430/ijeru.2024.7.1.0032

Olomu, M. O., Irefin, I. A., & Olomu, O. E. (2016). ICT adoption in emerging contemporary marketing practices: the case of the Nigerian paints industry. Ecoforum Journal, 5(3).

Olowoporoku, A. A., & Olubiyi, T. O. (2023). Evaluating Service Quality and Business Outcomes Post-Pandemic: Perspective from Hotels in Emerging Market. *Sawala: Jurnal Administrasi Negara, 11*(2), 182–201.

Olubiyi, T. O., Omoyele, O. S., Ilodigwe, S. C., Adeoye, O. O., Makinde, G. O., & Ravinder, R. (2024). The Linkage between Knowledge Management Practices and Sustainable Business Growth: Empirical Evidence from Nigeria. *Revista De Gestão Social E Ambiental, 18*(5), e05432. https://doi.org/DOI: 10.24857/rgsa.v18n5-022

Olubiyi, T. O. (2023b). *Leveraging competitive strategies on business outcomes post-covid-19 pandemic: Empirical investigation from Africa. Journal of Management and Business: Research and Practice*. University of Presov in Prešov, Slovakia Faculty of Management & Business., DOI: 10.54933/jmbrp-2023-15-2-1

Olubiyi, T. O. (2024a). Improving Customer Experience Through Differentiation Capability: The Rise of Competition among Africa's Consumer Goods Companies. *PaperASIA, 40*(5b), 230–240. DOI: 10.59953/paperasia.v40i5b.233

Olubiyi, T. O. (2024b). An investigation of the role of airline safety management and its impact on passenger satisfaction: A study of commercial airline businesses in Nigeria. *Journal of the Management Sciences*, *60*(4). https://journals.unizik.edu.ng/jfms/article/view/3396

Olubiyi, T. O., Adeoye, O. O., Jubril, B., Adeyemi, O. S., & Eyanuku, J. P. (2023). Measuring Inequality in Sub-Saharan Africa Post-Pandemic: Correlation Results for Workplace Inequalities and Implication for Sustainable Development Goal ten. *International Journal of Professional Business Review*, *8*(4), e01405. DOI: 10.26668/businessreview/2023.v8i4.1405

Olubiyi, T. O., Egwakhe, A. J., & Egwuonwu, T. K. (2019). Managerial Roles and Competitive Advantage: SMEs, perspective from Lagos state. *International Journal of Small Business and Entrepreneurship Research*, *7*(3), 1–14.

Omotosho, B. J. (2020). Small scale craft workers and the use of social media platform for business performance in Southwest Nigeria. *Journal of Small Business and Entrepreneurship*, •••, 1–6.

Omrani, N., Rivieccio, G., Fiore, U., Schiavone, F., & Agreda, S. G. (2022). To trust or not to trust? An assessment of trust in AI-based systems: Concerns, ethics and contexts. *Technological Forecasting and Social Change*, *181*, 121763.

Orden-Mejía, M., Carvache-Franco, M., Huertas, A., Carvache-Franco, O., & Carvache-Franco, W. (2023). Modeling users' satisfaction and visit intention using AI-based chatbots. *PLoS One*, *18*(9), e0286427. DOI: 10.1371/journal.pone.0286427 PMID: 37682931

Organisation for Economic Co-operation and Development OECD. (2024). *OECD Legal Instruments.* https://www.oecd.org/: https://legalinstruments.oecd.org/en/instruments/OECD-LEGAL-0449

Ortega, M. J. (2024, May 15). *Legislate to Protect: The Urgency of Regulating Artificial Intelligence in Mexico. DLMEX.* https://dlmex.org/legislar-para-proteger-la-urgencia-de-regular-la-inteligencia-artificial-en-mexico/

Otto, B. (2011). A morphology of the organization of data governance. [Conference]. *European Conference on Information Systems (ECIS),* Helsinki, Finland. https://aisel.aisnet.org/ecis2011/272

Ozbayoglu, A. M., Gudelek, M. U., & Sezer, O. B. (2020). Deep learning for financial applications: A survey. *Applied Soft Computing*, *93*, 106384.

Pala, S. K. (2024). Study to Develop AI Models for Early Detection of Network Vulnerabilities. *International Journal of Enhanced Research in Science, Technology & Engineering ISSN*, 2319-7463. Vol. 13 Issue 2, February.

Pampin Rodriguez, A. (2024). *Scalability and Efficiency in Artificial Intelligence through Green Federated Algorithms*. Final Degree Project, 2023/2024 Academic Year. Degree in Industrial Technology Engineering. Universidad Da Coruña. https://ruc.udc.es/dspace/bitstream/handle/2183/39572/PampinRodriguez_Abel_TFG_2024.pdf?sequence=2

Panarina, E. (2023). Impact of Customer and Entrepreneuroriented Marketing on Business Performance: An Empirical Evidence of SMEs in Russia. *The Anáhuac Journal*, *23*(1), 40–61. DOI: 10.36105/theanahuacjour.2023v23n1.02

Pandya, S. S., & Wang, J. (2024). Artificial intelligence in career development: A scoping review. *Human Resource Development International*, *27*(3), 324–344. DOI: 10.1080/13678868.2024.2336881

Papadopoulos, T. K., Baltas, N., & Balta, M. E. (2020). The use of digital technologies by small and medium enterprises during COVID-19: Implications for theory and practice. *International Journal of Information Management*, •••, 1–4. PMID: 32836646

Papagiannidis, E., Mikalef, P., & Conboy, K. (2025). Responsible artificial intelligence governance: A review and research framework. *The Journal of Strategic Information Systems*, *34*(2), 101885.

Parra-Moreno, C. F., & Perez-Uribe, R. (2022). Modernization model for organizational management (MMOM) applied to a Public University (UP) in Colombia. Junio 7 de 2022. 14 p. DOI: DOI: 10.13140/RG.2.2.25620.78727

Partovi, F. Y., & Anandarajan, M. (2002). Supply chain performance measurement. *International Journal of Production Research*, *40*(1), 1–20.

Paschen, J., Kietzmann, J., & Kietzmann, T. C. (2019). Artificial intelligence (AI) and its implications for market knowledge in B2B marketing. *Journal of Business and Industrial Marketing*, *34*(7), 1410–1419. DOI: 10.1108/JBIM-10-2018-0295

Patra, A. K., Praharaj, A., Sudarshan, D., & Chhatoi, B. P. (2024). AI and business management: Tracking future research agenda through bibliometric network analysis. *Heliyon*, *10*(1), e23902. DOI: 10.1016/j.heliyon.2023.e23902 PMID: 38230239

Payanene, L. Y. (2024). *Artificial Intelligence: A Risk or a Tool for the Practice of Law?* https://repository.ucc.edu.co/server/api/core/bitstreams/c5b5ca9b-4ad6-4bcc-a276-81914a34f7a8/content

Payne, A., & Frow, P. (2017). *Strategic Customer Management: Integrating Relationship Marketing and CRM*. Cambridge University Press.

Pedral Sampaio, R., Aguiar Costa, A., & Flores-Colen, I. (2022). A systematic review of artificial intelligence applied to facility management in the building information modeling context and future research directions. *Buildings (Basel, Switzerland)*, *12*(11), 1939.

Pedrami, M., & Vaezi, S. K. (2025). Factors influencing artificial intelligence adoption in human resource management: A meta-synthesis and systematic review of multidimensional considerations. *Journal of Work-Applied Management.*

Pedró, F., Mendigutxia, A., & UNESCO. (2024). *The role of higher education in national artificial intelligence strategies.* A comparative policy review. Paris, France. https://unesdoc.unesco.org/ark:/48223/pf0000392047

Pelau, C., Dabija, D. C., & Ene, I. (2021). What makes an AI device human-like? The role of interaction quality, empathy and perceived psychological anthropomorphic characteristics in the acceptance of artificial intelligence in the service industry. *Computers in Human Behavior*, *122*, 106855. DOI: 10.1016/j.chb.2021.106855

Pendyala, M. K., & Lakkamraju, V. V. (2024). Impact of Artificial Intelligence in Customer Journey. *International Journal of Innovative Science and Research Technology (IJISRT)*, 1528–1534. https://doi.org/DOI: 10.38124/ijisrt/IJISRT24AUG807

Peoples, K. (2021). *How to write a phenomenological dissertation: A step-by-step guide* (Vol. 56). SAGE.

Peralta, A., Olivas, J. A., Romero, F. P., & Navarro-Illana, P. (2025). Intelligent Incident Management Leveraging Artificial Intelligence, Knowledge Engineering, and Mathematical Models in Enterprise Operations. *Mathematics*, *13*(7), 1055.

Perdana, R., & Prasasti, A. (2023). Entrepreneurial Orientation, Corporate Performance, and Competitive Advantage in Inconductedsian Culinary SMEs. *Small Business International Review*, *7*(1), e547. DOI: 10.26784/sbir.v7i1.547

Peretó-Rovira, A., Moreno-Izquierdo, L., & Pedreño-Muñoz, A. (2020). An index to measure countries' commitment to artificial intelligence: The case of Spain and the role of the Basque Country. *Ekonomiaz*, *98*(2), 26–53.

Pérez Rodríguez, P., Cabrera Borges, C., Navarro Piñeyro, V., Olivero Pera, J., & Umpiérrez Oroño, S. (2025). Artificial Intelligence in Uruguay's 2023 Education Training Plan. *Educational Research Notebooks*, *16*(1). Advance online publication. DOI: 10.18861/cied.2025.16.1.3951

Perez-Uribe, R. Ramirez - Salazar, MDP., and Ramirez - Garzon, MT. (2023a). *Innovation Model for Organizational Sustainability (IMOS): The Concept.* Chapter 10. (Pps. 220-254). Pages: 35. DOI: DOI: 10.4018/978-1-6684-8223-0.ch010

Perez-Uribe, R., Lozano-Correa, LJ., Salcedo-Perez, C., and Moscoso-Duran, FF. (2023c). *Factors That Explain a Sustainable Organizational Culture in Medium-Sized Colombian Companies.* Copyright: © 2023 |Pages: 15. Pps. 1-15. DOI: .DOI: 10.4018/978-1-6684-6140-2.ch001

Perez-Uribe, R., Salcedo-Perez, C., and Ramírez-Salazar, MdP. (2021). *Organizational Components That Explain the Strategic Direction of SMEs for a New World Economic Order: The Case of Colombia.* Pps. 80-98. 19 pps. DOI: .DOI: 10.4018/978-1-7998-7689-2.ch005

Perez-Uribe, RI., Ocampo-Guzman, D., Moscoso-Duran, FF., Salcedo-Perez, C. & Munoz Maya, CM. (2023b). *Happiness at Work in Colombian Companies: A Perspective Under the Rise Model.* DOI: .DOI: 10.4018/978-1-6684-8822-5.ch019

Petrillo, A., De Felice, F., Cioffi, R., & Zomparelli, F. (2018). *Fourth industrial revolution: Current practices, challenges, and opportunities.* IntechOpen.

Petrovic-Lazarevic, S.. (2007). Supply Chain Improvement Initiatives in the Australian Textiles, Clothing, Footwear and Leather Industry: A Field Study. *International Journal of Logistics Systems and Management, 3*(1), 1–19.

Pike, S., & Page, S. J. (2014). Destination Marketing Organizations and destination marketing: A narrative analysis of the literature. *Tourism Management, 41*, 202–227. DOI: 10.1016/j.tourman.2013.09.009

Pillai, R., Sivathanu, B., & Dwivedi, Y. K. (2020). Shopping intention at AI-powered automated retail stores (AIPARS). *Journal of Retailing and Consumer Services, 57*, 102207. DOI: 10.1016/j.jretconser.2020.102207

Pimentel Cavalcante, A. (2023). Brazilian regulation of artificial intelligence. *Journal of the Mexican Law School, LXXIII*(287). Advance online publication. DOI: 10.22201/fder.24488933e.2023.287.86399

Pineda de Alcazar, M. (2020). Dilemmas in communication sciences in the transition to encountering intelligent machines. *Quorum Académico, 17*(1), 39-51. https://www.redalyc.org/articulo.oa?id=199062926002

Poerwanto, Irwan. 2022. "Research in Business & Social Science Mindset of marketing and Innovation on Corporate Performance : A Study of Food and Beverage Sector SMEs in Surabaya." 11(3):27–32.

Pombo, C., Cabrol, M., González Alarcón, N., & Sánchez Ávalos, R. (2020). *fAIr LAC: Ethical and responsible adoption of artificial intelligence in Latin America and the Caribbean.* http://dx.doi.org/DOI: 10.18235/0002169

Pranckutė, R. (2021). Web of Science (WoS) and Scopus: The titans of bibliographic information in today's academic world. *Publications*, *9*(1), 12.

Preacher, K. J., & Hayes, A. F. (2008). Asymptotic and resampling strategies for assessing and comparing indirect effects in multiple mediator models. *Behavior Research Methods*, *40*(3), 879–891. DOI: 10.3758/BRM.40.3.879 PMID: 18697684

Prentice, C., Weaven, S., & Wong, I. A. (2020). Linking AI quality performance and customer engagement: The moderating effect of AI preference. *International Journal of Hospitality Management*, *90*, 102629. DOI: 10.1016/j.ijhm.2020.102629

Presbitero, A., & Teng-Calleja, M. (2023). Job attitudes and career behaviors relating to employees' perceived incorporation of artificial intelligence in the workplace: A career self-management perspective. *Personnel Review*, *52*(4), 1169–1187. DOI: 10.1108/PR-02-2021-0103

Prevost, M., Johnston Prof, K. A., & Tanner, M. C. (2018). Awareness and preparedness of IT managers to digital disruption: A South African exploratory case study. *The African Journal of Information Systems*, *10*(4), 2.

Provost, F., & Fawcett, T. (2013). *Data Science for Business: What you need to know about data mining and data-analytic thinking*. O'Reilly Media.

Puntoni, S., Reczek, R. W., Giesler, M., & Botti, S. (2021). Consumers and Artificial Intelligence: An Experiential Perspective. *Journal of Marketing*, *85*(1), 131–151. DOI: 10.1177/0022242920953847

PWC. (2019). *Re-inventing Internal Controls in the Digital Age.* https://www.pwc.com/sg/en/publications/assets/reinventing-internal-controls-in-the-digital-age-201904.pdf

Qin, J., Zheng, P., & Wang, X. (2024). Product redesign and innovation based on online reviews: A multistage combined search method. *INFORMS Journal on Computing*, *36*(3), 742–765.

Quan, H., Li, S., Zeng, C., Wei, H., & Hu, J. (2023). Big data and AI-driven product design: A survey. *Applied Sciences (Basel, Switzerland)*, *13*(16), 9433.

Qudus, L. (2025). Leveraging Artificial Intelligence to Enhance Process Control and Improve Efficiency in Manufacturing Industries. *International Journal of Computer Applications Technology and Research*, *14*(02), 18–38.

Queiroz, M. M., Telles, R., & Lima, R. (2020). Blockchain and supply chain management: A systematic review of the literature. *Supply Chain Management, 25*(5), 619–631.

Quinto, N. M. D., Villodas, A. J. C., Montero, C. P. C., Cueva, D. L. E., & Vera, S. A. N. (2021). Artificial Intelligence and Managerial Decision-Making. *Research Journal Added Value, 8*(1), 52–69.

Qureshi, N. I., Garg, A., Singh, P., & Retzlaff, N. (2024, April). AI and Corporate Risk Management: Identifying and Mitigating Technological and Ethical Risks. In *2024 International Conference on Knowledge Engineering and Communication Systems (ICKECS)* (Vol. 1, pp. 1-5). IEEE.

Radanliev, P. (2025). Cyber diplomacy: Defining the opportunities for cybersecurity and risks from Artificial Intelligence, IoT, Blockchains, and Quantum Computing. *Journal of Cyber Security Technology, 9*(1), 28–78.

Rahimah, K., NorAziat, A. H., & Adnan, H. B. (2018). Organisational support for cloud computing implementation success in education system: Scale development and validity in Delphi. *IACSIT International Journal of Engineering and Technology, 7*, 512–516.

Rahman, M. S., Bag, S., Hossain, M. A., Abdel Fattah, F. A. M., Gani, M. O., & Rana, N. P. (2023). The new wave of AI-powered luxury brands online shopping experience: The role of digital multisensory cues and customers' engagement. *Journal of Retailing and Consumer Services, 72*, 103273. DOI: 10.1016/j.jretconser.2023.103273

Raifman, Sarah, Michelle A. Devost, Jean C. Digitale, Yea Hung, and Chen Meghan. 2022. "Respondent - Driven Sampling : A Sampling Method for Hard - to - Reach Populations and Beyond." *At present Epidemiology Reports* (9):38–47. doi: .DOI: 10.1007/s40471-022-00287-8

Ramirez-Cardona, C., and Ramirez -Salazar, MdP (2016). *Fundamentals of Management. Fourth Edition.* Ecoe Ediciones. Bogotá, Colombia.

Rane, N. (2023). Enhancing Customer Loyalty through Artificial Intelligence (AI), Internet of Things (IoT), and Big Data Technologies: Improving Customer Satisfaction, Engagement, Relationship, and Experience. SSRN *Electronic Journal.* https://doi.org/DOI: 10.2139/ssrn.4616051

Rashid, A. B., & Kausik, A. K. (2024). AI revolutionizing industries worldwide: A comprehensive overview of its diverse applications. Hybrid Advances, 100277.

Rather, R. A. (2020). Customer experience and engagement in tourism destinations: The experiential marketing perspective. *Journal of Travel & Tourism Marketing, 37*(1), 15–32. DOI: 10.1080/10548408.2019.1686101

Regenwetter, L., Nobari, A. H., & Ahmed, F. (2022). Deep generative models in engineering design: A review. *Journal of Mechanical Design, 144*(7), 071704.

Riazi, M., Rezvani, R., & Ghanbar, H. (2023). Trustworthiness in L2 writing research: A review and analysis of qualitative articles in the Journal of Second Language Writing. *Research Methods in Applied Linguistics, 2*(3). Advance online publication. DOI: 10.1016/j.rmal.2023.100065

Rinta-Kahila, T., Penttinen, E., Salovaara, A., Soliman, W., & Ruissalo, J. (2023). The vicious circles of skill erosion: A case study of cognitive automation. *Journal of the Association for Information Systems, 24*(5), 1378–1412. DOI: 10.17705/1jais.00829

Roberts, D. L., & Candi, M. (2024). Artificial intelligence and innovation management: Charting the evolving landscape. *Technovation, 136*, 103081.

Rogers, E. M. (1995). Diffusion of Innovations. 4th Edition, the Free Press, New York.

Roitman, S. (2016). Gated communities on a global scale. *Prospectiva. Journal of Social Work and Social Intervention*, (21), 13–22. DOI: 10.25100/prts.v0i21.918

Rojas Patiño, E. (2024). *Application of artificial intelligence models to support decision-making within the framework of project management.* National Open and Distance University (UNAD). School of Basic Sciences, Technology, and Engineering (ECBTI). Master's Degree in Project Management.

Romero Paredes, L. E. (2025). *Execution of artificial intelligence algorithms in real-time systems* (master's thesis, Universitat Politècnica de Catalunya). https://upcommons.upc.edu/bitstream/handle/2117/425033/TFM_Memoria_Luis_Romero_Paredes.pdf?sequence=2,https://upcommons.upc.edu/bitstream/handle/2117/425033/TFM_Resumen_Luis_Romero_Paredes.pdf?sequence=3,https://upcommons.upc.edu/bitstream/handle/2117/425033/TFM_Anexos.zip?sequence=4

Roose, K. (2019). A machine may not take your job, but one could become your boss. The New York Times. Available from https://www.nytimes.com/2019/06/23/technology/artificial-intelligence-ai-workplace.html

Rosário, A., & Raimundo, R. (2021). Consumer Marketing Strategy and E-Commerce in the Last Decade: A Literature Review. *Journal of Theoretical and Applied Electronic Commerce Research, 16*(7), 3003–3024. DOI: 10.3390/jtaer16070164

Rosser, S. V. (2009). The gender gap in patenting: Is technology transfer a feminist issue? *NWSA Journal*, *21*(2), 65–84. DOI: 10.1353/ff.2009.a316153

Rota-Franz, K. (1998). *Temporal coordination of centres managing resources autonomously. Application to integrated supply chains in aeronautics* [PhD thesis, École Nationale Supérieure de l'Aéronautique et de l'Espace]. ENSAE.

Roth, P. L., Huffcutt, A. I., & Bobko, P. (2003). Ethnic group differences in measures of job performance: A new meta-analysis. *The Journal of Applied Psychology*, *88*(4), 694–706. DOI: 10.1037/0021-9010.88.4.694 PMID: 12940409

Rouhiainen, L. (2018). [*Things You Should Know Today About Our Future.* Editorial Planeta.]. *Artificial Intelligence*, •••, 101.

Rubel, M. R. B., Kee, D. M. H., Rimi, N. N., & Yusuf, Y. M. (2016). 'Adapting technology: Effect of high – involvement human resource management and organisational trust'. *Behaviour & Information Technology*, *36*(3), 1–13.

Ruiz, A. E. C. (2023). Digital Transformation for Scalability. *Systems Journal*, (169), 8–13.

Ruiz, F. J. B. (2022). The Transparency Paradox in AI: Opacity and Explainability. Attribution of Responsibility. *International Journal of Political Thought*, *17*, 261–272.

Ryba, T. V., Wiltshire, G., North, J., & Ronkainen, N. J. (2022). Techno-innovative Mixed Methods Research in Sport and Exercise Psychology: Potential Contributions of a Critical Realist Perspective. *International Journal of Sport and Exercise Psychology*, *20*(1), 147–167. DOI: 10.1080/1612197X.2020.1827002

Saberi, S., Kouhizadeh, M., Sarkis, J., & Shen, L. (2019). Blockchain technology and its relationships to sustainable supply chain management. *International Journal of Production Research*, *57*(7), 2117–2135.

Sabharwal, R., Miah, S. J., & Fosso Wamba, S. (2025). Extending artificial intelligence research in the clinical domain: A theoretical perspective. *Annals of Operations Research*, *348*(3), 1713–1744. DOI: 10.1007/s10479-022-05035-1 PMID: 36407943

Saini, J. P. S., Thakur, A., & Yadav, D. (2025). AI driven Innovations in Pharmaceuticals: Optimizing Drug Discovery and Industry Operations. RSC Pharmaceutics.

Salau, A. (2019). *Disruptive technologies: Redefining the business and its functional models.* Automata Associates Ltd.

Salazar, L. A. (2020). Artificial Intelligence in Latin America. (W. Weck, Ed.). Political Dialogue. https://dialogopolitico.org/

Salinas, J. (2004). Teaching innovation and the use of ICT in university teaching. *Journal of the University and Knowledge Society*, *1*(1), 1–16. https://www.redalyc.org/pdf/780/78011256006.pdf

Salvador Serna, M., (2021). Artificial intelligence and data governance in public administrations: reflections and evidence for its development. *Public Policy Management and Analysis*, (26), 20-32. ttps://DOI: <ALIGNMENT.qj></ALIGNMENT>10.24965/gapp.i26.10855

Salvador, V. L., Mamaqi, X., & Bordes, F. J. V. (2020). Artificial Intelligence: Theoretical, educational, and communicative challenges of datafication. *Icono14*, *18*(1), 58-88.

Samala, N., Katkam, B. S., Bellamkonda, R. S., & Rodriguez, R. V. (2020). Impact of AI and robotics in the tourism sector: a critical insight. *Journal of tourism futures*, *8*(1), 73-87. https://doi.org/DOI: 10.1108/JTF-07-2019-0065

Samuel, B. S., & Sarprasatha, J. (2016). Entrepreneurship in social – media services in Oman – A socio – economic scanning of the Sultanate. *Canadian Centre of Science and Education*, *12*(4), 138–148.

Sanchez Vasquez, C., & Toro-Valencia, J. (2021). The Right to Human Control: A Legal Response to Artificial Intelligence. *Chilean Journal of Law and Technology*, *10*(2), 211–228.

Sanderson, D., & Read, D. (2020). Recognizing and realizing the value of customer-focused property management. *Property Management*, *38*(5), 749–764. DOI: 10.1108/pm-04-2020-0029

Sands, S., Campbell, C. L., Plangger, K., & Ferraro, C. (2022). Unreal influence: Leveraging AI in influencer marketing. *European Journal of Marketing*, *56*(6), 1721–1747. DOI: 10.1108/EJM-12-2019-0949

Saura, J. R., Ribeiro-Soriano, D., & Palacios-Marqués, D. (2021). Setting B2B digital marketing in artificial intelligence-based CRMs: A review and directions for future research. *Industrial Marketing Management*, *98*, 161–178. DOI: 10.1016/j.indmarman.2021.08.006

Saura, J. R., Škare, V., & Dosen, D. O. (2024). Is AI-based digital marketing ethical? Assessing a new data privacy paradox. *Journal of Innovation & Knowledge*, *9*(4), 100597.

Schamari, J., & Schaefers, T. (2015). Leaving the Home Turf: How Brands Can Use Webcare on Consumer-generated Platforms to Increase Positive Consumer Engagement. *Journal of Interactive Marketing*, *30*(1), 20–33. DOI: 10.1016/j.intmar.2014.12.001

Scholze, A., & Hecker, A. (2024). The job demands-resources model as a theoretical lens for the bright and dark side of digitization. *Computers in Human Behavior*, *155*, 108177. DOI: 10.1016/j.chb.2024.108177

Schonberger, R. J. (1982). *Japanese Manufacturing Techniques: Nine Hidden Lessons in Simplicity*. Free Press.

Schumpeter, J. (1934). *The theory of economic development*. Harvard University Press.

Schweidel, D. A., Bart, Y., Inman, J. J., Stephen, A. T., Libai, B., Andrews, M., Rosario, A. B., Chae, I., Chen, Z., Kupor, D., Longoni, C., & Thomaz, F. (2022). How consumer digital signals are reshaping the customer journey. *Journal of the Academy of Marketing Science*, *50*(6), 1257–1276. DOI: 10.1007/s11747-022-00839-w PMID: 35221393

Sdiri, H. (2023). Female In Manager-Owner Teams: Drivers Of Innovation And Firm Performance In Mena Markets. *International Journal of Innovation Management*, *27*(09n10), 2350052. https://doi.org/DOI: 10.1142/S1363919623500524

Seetharaman, P. (2020). Business models shifts: Impact of Covid-19. *International Journal of Information Management*, *54*, 1–5. PMID: 32834338

Selvakumar, P., Shanthi, M., Pitchiah, R., Sharma, M., Dahake, P. S., & T. C., M. (2025). The Role of Artificial Intelligence in Business Model Innovation: Overview of AI Technologies. In M. Khokhar (Ed.), *Advances in Business Strategy and Competitive Advantage* (pp. 219–246). IGI Global. https://doi.org/DOI: 10.4018/979-8-3693-9571-4.ch009

Senthil, R., Anand, T., Somala, C. S., & Saravanan, K. M. (2024). Bibliometric analysis of artificial intelligence in healthcare research: Trends and future directions. *Future Healthcare Journal*, *11*(3), 100182. PMID: 39310219

Seuring, S., & Müller, M. (2008). From a literature review to a conceptual framework for sustainable supply chain management. *Journal of Cleaner Production*, *16*(15), 1699–1710.

Shahriar, S., Allana, S., Hazratifard, S. M., & Dara, R. (2023). A survey of privacy risks and mitigation strategies in the artificial intelligence life cycle. *IEEE Access : Practical Innovations, Open Solutions*, *11*, 61829–61854.

Shaltoni, A. M. (2017). From websites to social media: Exploring the adoption of internet marketing in emerging industrial markets. *Journal of Business and Industrial Marketing*, *32*(7), 1009–1019.

Shapiro, J. F. (2001). *Modeling the Supply Chain*. Duxbury Press.

Sharma, B. P., Jain, H., & Prasad, M. (2020). Block chain technology: Awareness among MSME Business Owners and its Implementers. *Innovation in Global Business and Technology: Trends, Goals and Strategies*, 215.

Shirom, A., Shechter Gilboa, S., Fried, Y., & Cooper, C. L. (2008). Gender, age and tenure as moderators of work-related stressors' relationships with job performance: A meta-analysis. *Human Relations*, *61*(10), 1371–1398. DOI: 10.1177/0018726708095710

Shi, Z. (2019). []. World Scientific.]. *Advances in Artificial Intelligence*, *4*, •••.

Shrestha, Y. R., Krishna, V., & von Krogh, G. (2021). Augmenting organizational decision-making with deep learning algorithms: Principles, promises, and challenges. *Journal of Business Research*, *123*, 588–603.

Sichoongwe, K. (2024). Adoption behaviour of digital technologies by firms: Evidence from South Africa's manufacturing sector. *Global Business Review*, *25*(2, suppl), S244–S264.

Sidlauskiene, J., Joye, Y., & Auruskeviciene, V. (2023). AI-based chatbots in conversational commerce and their effects on product and price perceptions. *Electronic Markets*, *33*(1), 24. DOI: 10.1007/s12525-023-00633-8 PMID: 37252674

Silver, E. A., Pyke, D. F., & Peterson, R. (1998). *Inventory Management and Production Planning and Scheduling* (3rd ed.). Wiley.

Simchi-Levi, D., Kaminsky, P., & Simchi-Levi, E. (2008). *Designing and managing the supply chain: Concepts, strategies, and case studies* (3rd ed.). McGraw-Hill.

Simelyte, A., Tvaronaviciene, M., Holmen, R. B., Burinkskas, A., & Razminene, K. (2021). Knowledge and technology transfer as driving force for social innovations. *Polish Journal of Management Studies*, *23*(2), 512–536.

Sinangil, H. K., & Ones, D. S. (2003). Gender differences in expatriate job performance. *Applied Psychology*, *52*(3), 461–475. DOI: 10.1111/1464-0597.00144

Singh, N., Chaudhary, V., Singh, N., Soni, N., & Kapoor, A. (2024). Transforming Business with Generative AI: Research, Innovation, Market Deployment and Future Shifts in Business Models. arXiv preprint arXiv:2411.14437.

Singh, D. S. M., & Hanafi, N. B. (2019). Disruptive technology and SMEs performance in Malaysia. *International Journal of Academic Research in Business & Social Sciences*, *9*(12), 136–148.

Sinha, N., & Dhillon, J. S. (2024). Bibliometric analysis of management practices in US corn (1990–2020). *Agrosystems, Geosciences & Environment*, *7*(2), e20536.

Smith, T., & Jones, P. (2019). Performance Metrics in Inventory Management: A Review. *Journal of Operations Management*, *65*(4), 345–367.

Snyder, R. D., Shen, Z.-J. M., & Henly, E. (2016). *Fundamentals of Supply Chain Theory* (2nd ed.). Wiley.

Sofia, M., Fraboni, F., De Angelis, M., Puzzo, G., Giusino, D., & Pietrantoni, L. (2023). The impact of artificial intelligence on workers' skills: Upskilling and reskilling in organisations. *Informing Science*, *26*, 39–68. DOI: 10.28945/5078

Sreenivasan, A., & Suresh, M. (2024). Design thinking and artificial intelligence: A systematic literature review exploring synergies. International Journal of Innovation Studies.

Srivastava, P. (2007). Green supply-chain management: A literature review and framework for future research. *International Journal of Production Research*, *45*(18-19), 4355–4394.

Stefaniak, J., & Moore, S. (2024). The Use of Generative AI to Support Inclusivity and Design Deliberation for Online Instruction. *Online and Blended Learning in the Age of Generative AI*, *28*(3), 181–205. DOI: 10.24059/olj.v28i3.4458

Steinberg, A. L. S., & Hohenberger, C. (2023). Can AI close the gender gap in the job market? Individuals' preferences for AI evaluations. *Computers in Human Behavior Reports*, *10*, 100287. DOI: 10.1016/j.chbr.2023.100287

Stoet, G., O'Connor, D. B., Conner, M., & Laws, K. R. (2013). Are women better than men at multi-tasking? *BMC Psychology*, *1*, 1–10. DOI: 10.1186/2050-7283-1-18

Stoneman, P., & Karshenas, M. (2018). The diffusion of new technology: Extensions to theory and evidence. In New Technologies and the Firm, 177–200.

Stroh, L. K., Brett, J. M., & Reilly, A. H. (1996). Family structure, glass ceiling, and traditional explanations for the differential rate of turnover of female and male managers. *Journal of Vocational Behavior*, *49*(1), 99–118. DOI: 10.1006/jvbe.1996.0036

Suleiman, O. (2016). Assessment of information and communication technology on the performance of selected small and medium scale enterprises in Ilorin metropolis, Nigeria. *International Journal of Capacity Building in Education and Management, 3*(1), 1–12.

Sun, G., Ling, Z., Li, Y., & Xie, C. (2025). Artificial intelligence and financial fraud. *Pacific-Basin Finance Journal, 93*, 102830. DOI: 10.1016/J.PACFIN.2025.102830

Suyambu, G.T.M., Anand, & Janakirani, M. (2020). Block chain – A most disruptive technology on the spotlight of world engineering education paradigm. *Procedia Computer Science, 172*, 152–158.

Tabassum, N., & Nayak, B. S. (2021). Gender stereotypes and their impact on women's career progressions from a managerial perspective. *IIM Kozhikode Society & Management Review, 10*(2), 192–208. DOI: 10.1177/2277975220975513

Taber, K. S. (2018). The use of Cronbach's alpha when developing and reporting research instruments in science education. *Research in Science Education, 48*, 1273–1296. DOI: 10.1007/s11165-016-9602-2

Taherdoost, H. (2022). What Are Diverse Research Approaches? Comprehensive Review of Qualitative, Quantitative, and Mixed Method Research, Their Applications, Types, and Limitations. *Journal of Management Science & Engineering Research, 5*(1), 53–63. DOI: 10.30564/jmser.v5i1.4538

Tamayo Uribe, E., & Gómez Ayerbe, P. (2021). Ethical framework for Artificial Intelligence in Colombia. https://minciencias.gov.co/sites/default/files/marco-etico-ia-colombia-2021.pdf

Tang, C. S. (2006). Perspectives in supply chain risk management. *International Journal of Production Economics, 103*(2), 451–488.

Tan, T. H. (2016). Residential satisfaction in gated communities: Case study of Desa Park City, Kuala Lumpur, Malaysia. *Property Management, 34*(2), 84–99. DOI: 10.1108/PM-02-2015-0009

Tanwar, K., & Prasad, A. (2016). The effect of employer brand dimensions on job satisfaction: Gender as a moderator. *Management Decision, 54*(4), 854–886. DOI: 10.1108/MD-08-2015-0343

Tawse, A., & Tabesh, P. (2023). Thirty years with the balanced scorecard: What we have learned. *Business Horizons, 66*(1), 123–132. DOI: 10.1016/j.bushor.2022.03.005

Tayur, S., Ganeshan, R., & Magazine, M. (1999). *Quantitative models for supply chain management*. Kluwer Academic Publishers.

Teece, D. J., Pisano, G., & Shuen, A. (1997). Dynamic capabilities and strategic management. *Strategic Management Journal, 18*(7), 509–533.

Tehci, A. (2024). Artificial intelligence and product innovation. In Artificial intelligence in material science: Advances (p. 160). Taylor & Francis.

Tekic, Z., & Füller, J. (2023). Managing innovation in the era of AI. *Technology in Society, 73*, 102254.

Tempelmeier, H. (2011). *Inventory Management in Supply Chains*. Niemeyer.

The World Bank (2022). *Nigeria development update.*

The World Bank. (2024). *Transforming Education Through Smart Technology.* https://documents1.worldbank.org/curated/en/099057209252410428/pdf/IDU1b9763f50193b814e9b1b3f41604bc7c611c7.pdf

Tian, T., Zichen, H., & Tang, Y. (2024). Enhancing Organizational Performance: Harnessing AI and NLP for User Feedback Analysis in Product Development. arXiv preprint arXiv:2405.04692.

Tohănean, D., Buzatu, A. I., Baba, C. A., & Georgescu, B. (2020). Business model innovation through the use of digital technologies: Managing risks and creating sustainability. *Amfiteatru Economic, 22*(55), 758–774.

Toner-Rodgers, A. (2024). Artificial intelligence, scientific discovery, and product innovation. arXiv preprint arXiv:2412.17866.

Tong, S., Jia, N., Luo, X., & Fang, Z. (2021). The Janus face of artificial intelligence feedback: Deployment versus disclosure effects on employee performance. *Strategic Management Journal, 42*(9), 1600–1631. DOI: 10.1002/smj.3322

Tong, S., Luo, X., & Xu, B. (2020). Personalized mobile marketing strategies. *Journal of the Academy of Marketing Science, 48*(1), 64–78. DOI: 10.1007/s11747-019-00693-3

Torino, P. D. I. (2021). Impact of Sum Quality Management Practices on Corporate Sustainable Incubation with Emphasis on Green Innovation in Manufacturing Companies (Case Study : PARS KHAZAR Industrial Corporate) ACADEMIC SUPERVI. [July]. *Industrial and Corporate Change.*

Toumia, O., Mefteh, R., & Cowling, M. (2023). Digitalization and Firm Performance: Empirical Evidence from Forbes-listed Companies. *Journal of Innovation Management, 11*(4), 124–142. DOI: 10.24840/2183-0606_011.004_0006

Toumia, O., & Zouari, F. (2024a). Artificial Intelligence and Venture Capital Decision-Making. In *Fostering Innovation in Venture Capital and Startup Ecosystems* (pp. 16–38). IGI Global., DOI: 10.4018/979-8-3693-1326-8.ch002

Toumia, O., & Zouari, F. (2024b). Effect of Artificial Intelligence Awareness on Job Performance with Employee Experience as a Mediating Variable. In *Reskilling the Workforce for Technological Advancement* (pp. 141–161). IGI Global., DOI: 10.4018/979-8-3693-0612-3.ch007

Toumia, O., & Zouari, F. (2024c). The Effect of Artificial Intelligence Awareness on Job Performance: Gender as Moderator and Experience as Mediator. In *AI Innovation in Services Marketing* (pp. 110–133). IGI Global., DOI: 10.4018/979-8-3693-2153-9.ch005

Treffers, S., & Lippert, R. (2019). Condominium self-governance? Issues, external interests, and the limits of statutory reform. *Housing Studies*, •••, 1–25. DOI: 10.1080/02673037.2019.1646217

Truong, Y., & Papagiannidis, S. (2022). Artificial intelligence as an enabler for innovation: A review and future research agenda. *Technological Forecasting and Social Change*, *183*, 121852.

Tsang, Y. P., & Lee, C. K. M. (2022). Artificial intelligence in industrial design: A semi-automated literature survey. *Engineering Applications of Artificial Intelligence*, *112*, 104884.

Tucker, L. R., & Lewis, C. (1973). A reliability coefficient for maximum likelihood factor analysis. *Psychometrika*, *38*(1), 1–10. DOI: 10.1007/BF02291170

Ufuophu-Biri, E., & Iwu, C. G. (2014). Job motivation, job performance and gender relations in the broadcast sector in Nigeria. *Mediterranean Journal of Social Sciences*, *5*(16), 191–198. DOI: 10.5901/mjss.2014.v5n16p191

Ukabi, O. B., Uba, U. J., Ewum, C. O., & Olubiyi, T. O. (2023). Measuring Entrepreneurial Skills and Sustainability in Small Business Enterprises Post-Pandemic: Empirical Study from Cross River State, Nigeria. International Journal of Business. *Management and Economics*, *4*(2), 132–149.

UNESCO. (2021). *Recommendations on the Ethics of Artificial Intelligence*. https://unesdoc.unesco.org

UNESCO. (2022). Education for just transitions: lifelong learning and the 30th anniversary. *Human Development Report*, 67(5), 637-658. https://unesdoc.unesco.org/ark:/48223/pf0000380309

UNESCO. (2024a). *What we talk about when we talk about artificial intelligence.* https://unesdoc.unesco.org/in/documentViewer.xhtml?v=2.1.196&id=p:usmarcdef_0000391087&file=/in/rest/annotationSVC/DownloadWatermarkedAttachment/attach_import_f62ef71c-b3ae-4dc5-8e43-af5f52af2981%3F_%3D391087spa.pdf&locale=es&multi=true&ark=/ark:/48223/p

UNESCO. (2024b). *Transforming the digital landscape of higher education in Latin America and the Caribbean.* https://unesdoc.unesco.org/ark:/48223/pf0000388361_spa

UNESCO. (2025). Retrieved from Artificial Intelligence in Education: https://www.unesco.org/es/digital-education/artificial-intelligence

United Nations Conference on Trade and Development (UNCTAD) (2018). Trade and development report: Power, platforms and the free trade delusion. United Nations, New York and Geneva. https:// unctad.org

United Nations Development Programme (UNDP). (2024). *AILA: Assessment of the Artificial Intelligence Landscape in Colombia.* https://www.undp.org/sites/g/files/zskgke326/files/2025-01/undp_co_pub_evaluacion_ia_colombia_ene17_2025.pdf

Usman, F. O., Eyo-Udo, N. L., Etukudoh, E. A., Odonkor, B., Ibeh, C. V., & Adegbola, A. (2024). A CRITICAL REVIEW OF AI-DRIVEN STRATEGIES FOR ENTREPRENEURIAL SUCCESS. *International Journal of Management & Entrepreneurship Research*, *6*(1), 200–215. DOI: 10.51594/ijmer.v6i1.748

Uwem, E. I., Oyedele, O. O., & Olubiyi, O. T. (2021). Workplace green behavior for sustainable competitive advantage. In human resource management practices for

Vadillo Bueno, G. (2020). Futures of Artificial Intelligence. *Digital University Journal, 21*(1).

Vaidya, D. (2022). *Disruptive technology – what is it, types, examples, pros and cons.*

Van der Vorst, J. G. A. J., & Beulens, A. J. M. (2002). Identifying sources of cost inefficiency in food supply chains. *International Journal of Physical Distribution & Logistics Management*, *32*(9), 729–747.

Van Eck, N. J., & Waltman, L. (2011). Text mining and visualization using VOSviewer. arXiv preprint arXiv:1109.2058.

Van Esch, P., & Stewart Black, J. (2021). Artificial Intelligence (AI): Revolutionizing Digital Marketing. *Australasian Marketing Journal*, *29*(3), 199–203. DOI: 10.1177/18393349211037684

Van Wynsberghe, A. (2021). Sustainable AI: AI for sustainability and the sustainability of AI. *AI and Ethics*, *1*(3), 213–218.

Varadarajan, R. (2018). Innovation, innovation strategy, and strategic innovation. In *Innovation and strategy* (pp. 143–166). Emerald Publishing Limited.

Vargas Diaz, J. H. (2022). *Interoperability, scalability, and security performance in communications of an electric power microgrid*. Doctoral dissertation, Universidad Nacional de Colombia. https://repositorio.unal.edu.co/bitstream/handle/unal/81778/71366200.2022.pdf?sequence=1

Varpio, L., & Macleod, A. (2020). Philosophy of Science Series: Harnessing the Multidisciplinary Edge Effect by Exploring Paradigms, Ontologies, Epistemologies, Axiologies, and Methodologies. *Academic Medicine*, *95*(5), 686–689. DOI: 10.1097/ACM.0000000000003142 PMID: 31876567

Veloza Morales, M. C., Mora Rojas, R. B., & Forero Beltrán, E. (2022). Hybrid learning environments for the training of nursing professionals at the Andean Area University Foundation. In Briceño Martínez, J, Castellanos Saavedra, M, Valencia Molano, J, Osuna Julio, D, Mora Espinoza, B, Gómez Angulo, C, Bedoya Salcedo, A, Flórez Peña, T, Ramírez Triana, C, Sandoval Villalobos, A, Parra Estrada, N, Cortés Martín, J, Garzón Venegas, P, Peña Rodríguez, M, Blanco Vanegas, A, Cardona Toro, J, Romero, M, López Urrea, L, Cardona Patiño, C, Varón Quimbayo, Á, Díaz Sánchez, E, Morales-Benítez, O, Veloza Morales, M, Mora Rojas, R, Forero Beltrán, E, Garassini, M, Cruz Rojas, G, Valenzuela Guadir, K, Ocampo Constaín, P, Saraza Gómez, C, Villa Ortiz, A y Chávez Díaz, A. (Comp.) *Technology and Innovation in Higher Education. Post-Pandemic Scenarios* (pp. 295-318). Andean Area University Foundation. https://digitk.areandina.edu.co/handle/areandina/4880

Vermesan, O., Bröring, A., Tragos, E., Serrano, M., Bacciu, D., Chessa, S., & Bahr, R. (2022). Internet of robotic things–converging sensing/actuating, hyperconnectivity, artificial intelligence and IoT platforms. In *Cognitive hyperconnected digital transformation* (pp. 97–155). River Publishers.

Vidal, C. J. (2002). Collaborative Supply Chain Practices: A Comprehensive Study. *The Journal of Supply Chain Management*, *38*(3), 4–12.

Vilelas, J. (2020). *Research - The Process of Knowledge Construction* (3ª Edição ed.). Edições Sílabo, Lisboa.

Villalba, J. F. (2020). Algor-ethics: Ethics in artificial intelligence. *Anales de la Facultad de Ciencias Juridicas y Sociales de la Universidad Nacional de La Plata*, (50), 679–698. DOI: 10.24215/25916386e062

Vocke, C., Constantinescu, C., & Popescu, D. (2019). Application potentials of artificial intelligence for the design of innovation processes. *Procedia CIRP*, *84*, 810–813.

Vohra, N., Chari, V., Mathur, P., Sudarshan, P., Verma, N., Mathur, N., Thakur, P., Chopra, T., Srivastava, Y., Gupta, S., Dasmahapatra, V., Fonia, S., & Gandhi, H. K. (2015). Inclusive workplaces: Lessons from theory and practice. *Vikalpa*, *40*(3), 324–362. DOI: 10.1177/0256090915601515

Voigt, P., & Von dem Bussche, A. (2017). *The EU General Data Protection Regulation (GDPR): A Commentary*. Springer.

Von Krogh, G., Ichijo, K., & Nonaka, I. (2000). *Enabling knowledge creation: How to unlock the mystery of tacit knowledge and release the power of innovation.* Oxford university press.

Vrontis, D., Christofi, M., Pereira, V., Tarba, S., Makrides, A., & Trichina, E. (2022). Artificial intelligence, robotics, advanced technologies and human resource management: A systematic review. *International Journal of Human Resource Management*, *33*(6), 1237–1266. DOI: 10.1080/09585192.2020.1871398

Wakjira, G. G., Ibrahim, M. I., Gizachew, G., Mohammad, W., & Ibrahim, I. 2022. "Effect of Mindset of marketing on Corporateal Performance : The Mediating Function of Entrepreneurial and Innovation Capability Multiple Regression Model : In Oromia Regional State West Guji Zone Coffee Trading and Factory Enterprise ' s PLC. " (2022).

Wakjira, G. G. 2023. "The Descriptive Effect of Mindset of marketing Practice on Export Performance : The Mediating Function of New Product Incubation Capability : In Oromia Regional State West Guji Zone Coffe ... Partners Universal International Research Journal (PUIRJ) The Desc." (June). doi: DOI: 10.5281/zenodo.8040351

Wang, S. (2023). Research on the innovation system of computer artificial intelligence technology in museum financial management system. *2023 IEEE 3rd International Conference on Power, Electronics and Computer Applications (ICPECA)*, Shenyang, China, pp. 1483-1487. https://doi.org/DOI: 10.1109/ICPECA56706.2023.10075850

Wang, Y., Gou, Y., Guo, Y., & Wang, H. (2020). Construction of Audit Internal Control Intelligent System Based on Blockchain and Cloud Storage. *2020 4th International Conference on Trends in Electronics and Informatics (ICOEI) (48184)*, Tirunelveli, India, pp. 292-295. https://doi.org/DOI: 10.1109/ICOEI48184.2020.9143061

Wang, F. (2013). Determinants of the effectiveness of Chinese homeowner associations in solving neighborhood issues. *Urban Affairs Review*, *50*(3), 311–339. DOI: 10.1177/1078087413501641

Wang, F., & Chen, K. (2020). Do product imitation and innovation require different patterns of organizational innovation? Evidence from Chinese firms. *Journal of Business Research*, *106*, 60–74.

Wang, J., Ma, Y., Zhang, L., Gao, R. X., & Wu, D. (2018). Deep learning for smart manufacturing: Methods and applications. *Journal of Manufacturing Systems*, *48*, 144–156.

Wang, K., & Wang, T. (2024). Competition from informal firms and new-to-market product innovation: A competitive rivalry framework. *Journal of Product Innovation Management*, *41*(4), 816–842.

Wang, K., Zipperle, M., Becherer, M., Gottwalt, F., & Zhang, Y. (2020). An ai-based automated continuous compliance awareness framework (CoCAF) for procurement auditing. *Big Data and Cognitive Computing*, *4*(3), 1-14. *Article*, *23*. Advance online publication. DOI: 10.3390/bdcc4030023

Wasim, Muhammad, Ahmed, Shehzad, Kalsoom, Tahera, & Saud, Mohammad, and Piyya Muhammad Rafi-ul-shan. (2022). Mindset of marketing and SME Performance : Moderating Function of IoT and Mediating Function of Creativity Mindset of marketing and SME Performance : Moderating Function ABSTRACT. *Journal of Small Business Management*, *00*(00), 1–28. DOI: 10.1080/00472778.2022.2100897

Wellalage, N. H., & Locke, S. (2016). Informality and credit constraints: Evidence from Sub-Saharan African MSEs. *Applied Economics*, *48*(29), 2756–2770.

Werner, M., Wiese, M., & Maas, A. (2021). Embedding process mining into financial statement audits. *International Journal of Accounting Information Systems*, *41*, 100514. Advance online publication. DOI: 10.1016/j.accinf.2021.100514

West, R. F., Meserve, R. J., & Stanovich, K. E. (2012). Cognitive sophistication does not attenuate the bias blind spot. *Journal of Personality and Social Psychology*, *103*(3), 506–519. DOI: 10.1037/a0028857 PMID: 22663351

Wilson, H. J., & Daugherty, P. R. (2018). Collaborative intelligence: Humans and AI are joining forces. *Harvard Business Review*, *96*(4), 114–123.

Witkowski, A., & Wodecki, A. (2025). Where does AI play a major role in the new product development and product management process?. Management Review Quarterly, 1-38.

Wittek, P. (2014). *Quantum Machine Learning: What Quantum Computing Means to Data Mining*. Academic Press.

Wolfert, S., Ge, L., Verdouw, C., & Bogaardt, M. J. (2017). Big data in smart farming–a review. *Agricultural Systems, 153*, 69–80.

Wolniak, R., & Stecuła, K. (2024). Artificial intelligence in smart cities: Applications, barriers, and future directions—A review. *Smart Cities*, *7*(3), 1346–1389. DOI: 10.3390/smartcities7030057

Womack, J. P., & Jones, D. T. (2003). *Lean Thinking: Banish Waste and Create Wealth in Your Corporation* (2e éd.). Free Press.

Wood, D. J., Mitchell, R. K., Agle, B. R., & Bryan, L. M. (2021). Stakeholder identification and salience after 20 years: Progress, problems, and prospects. *Business & Society*, *60*(1), 196–245.

Wood, W. (1987). Meta-analytic review of sex differences in group performance. *Psychological Bulletin*, *102*(1), 53. DOI: 10.1037/0033-2909.102.1.53 PMID: 3615706

Wu, M. L. (2009). *Structural equation modeling: Amos operation and application*. Wu-Nan Book Inc.

Xue, J. (2020). On the management of accounting files in public institutions based on informatization. *Journal of Physics: Conference Series*, *1533*(2), 022055. DOI: 10.1088/1742-6596/1533/2/022055

Xue, L., & Pang, Z. (2022). Ethical governance of artificial intelligence: An integrated analytical framework. *Journal of Digital Economy*, *1*(1), 44–52.

Xu, G., Xue, M., & Zhao, J. (2023). The Relationship of Artificial Intelligence Opportunity Perception and Employee Workplace Well-Being: A Moderated Mediation Model. *International Journal of Environmental Research and Public Health*, *20*(3), 1–17. DOI: 10.3390/ijerph20031974 PMID: 36767341

Yaiprasert, C., & Hidayanto, A. N. (2023). AI-driven ensemble three machine learning to enhance digital marketing strategies in the food delivery business. *Intelligent Systems with Applications*, *18*, 200235.

Yang, F. (2020, November). Artificial intelligence in music education. In *2020 International Conference on Robots & Intelligent System (ICRIS)* (pp. 483-484). IEEE. https://doi.org/DOI: 10.1109/ICRIS52159.2020.00124

Yang, X., Li, H., Ni, L., & Li, T. (2021). Application of Artificial Intelligence in Precision Marketing. *Journal of Organizational and End User Computing*, *33*(4), 209–219. DOI: 10.4018/JOEUC.20210701.oa10

Yazmyradov, S., & Lee, H. J. (2024). A Comprehensive Review of AI Security: Threats, Challenges, and Mitigation Strategies. *International Journal of Internet. Broadcasting and Communication*, *16*(4), 375–384.

Yetgin, M. A., & Toumia, O. (2023). *Perceptions of Employees of Technology Emerging With Generative Pre-Trained Transformer-3 in Organizations*. Gazi Kitabevi.

Yin, J., & Qiu, X. (2021). AI Technology and Online Purchase Intention: Structural Equation Model Based on Perceived Value. *Sustainability*, *13*(10), 5671. DOI: 10.3390/su13105671

Younus, A. M., Zaidan, M. N., & shakir Mahmood, D. (2022). The Effect of Artificial Intelligence on Job Performance in China's Small and Medium-Sized Enterprises (SMEs). *Spanish Journal of Innovation and Integrity, 7*, 112-128. https://doi.org/ DOI: 10.17605/OSF.IO/SJFUZ

Yuliati, E., Ramadhani, Y. C., & Wahyuni, D. U. (2022). Entrepreneurship Orientation and Mindset of marketing and on Business Performance Through Competitive Advantage. *International Journal of Academic Research in Business & Social Sciences*, *12*(6), 880–896. DOI: 10.6007/ijarbss/v12-i6/13347

Yu, M., Lin, H., Wang, G. G., Liu, Y., & Zheng, X. (2022). Is too much as bad as too little? The S-curve relationship between corporate philanthropy and employee performance. *Asia Pacific Journal of Management*, *39*(4), 1511–1534. DOI: 10.1007/s10490-021-09775-9

Yusof, Y., Awang, Z., Jusoff, K., & Ibrahim, Y. (2017). The influence of green practices by non-green hotels on customer satisfaction and loyalty in hotel and tourism industry. *International Journal of Green Economics*, *11*(1), 1–14. DOI: 10.1504/IJGE.2017.082716

Yusupova, M., & Ismailov, T. (2024). Integration of Artificial Intelligence (AI) in ELT. *Nordic_Press, 3*(0003).

Yu, W. F. (2025). AI as a co-creator and a design material: Transforming the design process. *Design Studies*, *97*, 101303.

Zahid, A., Leclaire, P., Hammadi, L., Roberta, C. A., & El Ballouti, A. (2025). Exploring the potential of industry 4.0 in manufacturing and supply chain systems: Insights and emerging trends from bibliometric analysis. Supply Chain Analytics, 100108.

Zambrano, F. R., Delgado, P. F. V., Loor, M. J. Z., Zambrano, B. Y. V., & Zambrano, M. T. Z. (2024). Oreo Bot, a multifunctional AI assistant. Scientific Journal: *Biotech and Engineering, 4*(2).

Zeid, A., Sundaram, S., Moghaddam, M., Kamarthi, S., & Marion, T. (2019). Interoperability in smart manufacturing: Research challenges. *Machines (Basel)*, *7*(2), 21.

Zhang, H., Bai, X., & Ma, Z. (2022). Consumer reactions to AI design: Exploring consumer willingness to pay for AI-designed products. *Psychology and Marketing*, *39*(11), 2171–2183.

Zhang, S., & Zhang, D. (2021). Internal control evaluation of small and micro enterprises' sales process based on fuzzy neural network. *2021 International Conference on Computer Network, Electronic and Automation (ICCNEA)*, Xi'an, China, pp. 177-180. https://doi.org/DOI: 10.1109/ICCNEA53019.2021.00047

Zhang, Z., Al Hamadi, H., Damiani, E., Yeun, C. Y., & Taher, F. (2022). Explainable artificial intelligence applications in cyber security: State-of-the-art in research. *IEEE Access : Practical Innovations, Open Solutions*, *10*, 93104–93139.

Zhang, Z., Ning, H., Shi, F., Farha, F., Xu, Y., Xu, J., Zhang, F., & Choo, K. K. R. (2022). Artificial intelligence in cyber security: Research advances, challenges, and opportunities. *Artificial Intelligence Review*, •••, 1–25. DOI: 10.1007/s10462-021-09976-0

Zhu, D., & Shen, S. (2021). Artificial intelligence and internal control: A perspective of Chinese enterprises. *2021 33rd Chinese Control and Decision Conference (CCDC)*, Kunming, China, 2021, pp. 4073-4076. https://doi.org/DOI: 10.1109/CCDC52312.2021.9601581

Zhu, Q., & Luo, J. (2023). Generative transformers for design concept generation. *Journal of Computing and Information Science in Engineering*, *23*(4), 041003.

Ziakis, C., & Vlachopoulou, M. (2023). Artificial Intelligence in Digital Marketing: Insights from a Comprehensive Review. *Information (Basel)*, *14*(12), 664. DOI: 10.3390/info14120664

Żółtowski, M. (2022). Artificial intelligence in management control systems: The role of AI in measuring and evaluating business performance. *Journal of Accounting and Management Control*, *28*(2), 98–112.

Zong, Z., & Guan, Y. (2024). AI-Driven intelligent data analytics and predictive analysis in Industry 4.0: Transforming knowledge, innovation, and efficiency. *Journal of the Knowledge Economy*. Advance online publication. DOI: 10.1007/S13132-024-02001-Z

Zouari, F., & Toumia, O. (2024). Understanding Mediators and AI's Influence on Job Performance. In *Hyperautomation in Business and Society* (pp. 244-265). IGI Global. https://doi.org/DOI: 10.4018/979-8-3693-3354-9.ch013

About the Contributors

Rafael Pérez-Uribe, Doctor in Business Sciences Nebrija University. Diploma of Advanced Studies in Applied Economics, Nebrija University. Master in Organization Management EAN University. Maître es Sciences Université du Québec a Chicoutimi. Specialist in Evaluation and Construction of Management Indicators for Higher Education, School of Business Administration. Postgraduate studies such as Kenkyusei (Researcher attached) in Total Quality Control and Quality Circles, Fukushima University, Japan. Business Administrator, Jorge Tadeo Lozano University. Former Full professor assigned to the Research Department and director of the management research group of large, small, and medium-sized companies (G3PYMES-A1 in Minciencias until 2020) of the EAN University. At the present time, Senior Researcher categorized by Minciencias; Currently Independent Management Consultant and Professor and Minciencias Senior Researcher in Invesproject. Modeling expert. He has participated in the structuring in many management models that include diagnosis, evaluation, and organizational intervention.

Maria Ramírez-Garzón holds a PhD in Administration from the University of Celaya (Mexico); Master's in Teaching from the University of La Salle (Colombia); Business Administration from EAN University (Colombia); Independent Professor of Management and Minciencias Junior Researcher at Invesproject (Colombia).

***

Yolanda Álvarez Sánchez holds a PhD in Art and Humanities, University of Jaén; Research Professor at La Salle University.

Kalender Özcan Atilgan is a Professor in Management Information Systems at the Mersin University. He earned his B.Sc. in Industrial Engineering from Dokuz Eylul University in 2004 and his M.Sc. in MBA from the Dokuz Eylul University in

2006. He received his Ph.D. in marketing from the University of Cukurova in 2012. He has publications on pricing, behavioral pricing, retailing, and branding. Author contact details: Management Information Systems, School of Applied Technology and Management of Erdemli, Mersin University, Turkey.

Andrea Barrera holds a Ph.D. candidate in Administration at Universidad de Celaya. Master of Management – Tecnológico de Monterrey (ITESM). Specialist in Process Engineering and Quality Management – Universidad EAN. Business Administrator – Universidad Nacional de Colombia. Research areas include organizational theory, neuromarketing, consumer behavior, complex environments, and the strategic and organizational implications of digital transformation and artificial intelligence in business contexts, as well as organizational economic analysis. Serves as Academic Peer at the Colombian Ministry of National Education. Experience in academic management in higher education.

Diana Castro Mazanett is a PhD Student in Education at the University of La Salle. Research Professor, University Lecturer, and Pedagogical Advisor in public and private entities.

Marta Ceia holds a PhD in Economics from the University of Warwick, UK, a MSc in Economics from the University of Coimbra and a degree in Economics from the University of Coimbra. She is an Associate Professor in the University of Aveiro, at the Department of Economics, Management, Industrial Engineering and Tourism. She lectures under graduated and graduated courses of Microeconomics, European Economics, Microeconomic Analysis, International Economics and others, Energy Economics and Energy Policy and regulation. Presently, she is an integrated member of the research unit on Governance, Competitiveness and Public Policies (GOVCOPP). She is a member of research teams of the University of Aveiro participating in several European sponsored projects in the fields of Social Economy and Competences for graduates. She was the Director of the PhD in Energy Systems and Climate Change and now is director of the undergraduate studies in economics and the master in sustainable energy systems from the University of Aveiro. She is a co-author of scientific articles in peer-reviewed reference journals, books and book chapters in the areas of energy economics, Energy policy, Sustainability, regulation and economics.

Parihar Suresh Dahake is an Academician and researcher with over 15 years of experience in teaching and research in the fields of Commerce and Management. Currently serving as an Assistant Professor at the School of Management, Ramdeobaba University, Nagpur, he holds a diverse educational background, including B.Tech (Applied Electronics), MBA (Marketing & Financial

Management), M.Com, PGDIBO, M.A. (Psychology), and a Ph.D. in Business Management. His doctoral work focused on the impact of marketing strategies of DTH services on consumer behavior in Nagpur. Dr. Dahake's research interests span Business Analytics, Consumer Behavior, Predictive Analytics, and Marketing Communication. A recognized Ph.D. supervisor, he guides multiple doctoral candidates under the faculty of Commerce. He has published extensively in peer-reviewed, Scopus, and ABDC-indexed journals and authored books on Marketing Management and Consumer Behavior. He also holds a patent in wage sheet automation and actively contributes as a reviewer for prestigious journals. A recipient of multiple accolades, including the Young Researcher and Research Excellence Awards, Dr. Dahake is also a sought-after speaker and trainer. His commitment to academic excellence and innovative pedagogy has made significant contributions to management education, research, and institutional development in Central India.

Pragati Parihar Dahake is an Assistant Professor in the Department of MBA at VMV Commerce, JMT Arts, and JJP Science College, Nagpur. With 2 years of academic experience, she specializes in Marketing, Human Resource Management, and Consumer Behaviour. Passionate about shaping future business leaders, she combines theoretical knowledge with practical insights to create an engaging learning environment. Her teaching approach emphasizes real-world applications and student-centered learning. Pragati is committed to academic excellence and continuously works to enhance her subject expertise while contributing to the holistic development of her students in the dynamic field of management education.

Ouail El Imrani is a Research Professor with specialization in Optimization, Technology Management and Port Logistics. His work applies in an evolutionary perspective . His areas of interest include: New economics, Semiconductor Chip industry, Cost optimization, Performance, Project management, SCM, General Energy and sustainable development.

Ümmühan Nida Erol is a research assistant in the Department of Management Information Systems at Mersin University, Türkiye. Author contact details: Management Information Systems, School of Applied Technology and Management of Erdemli, Mersin University, Turkey.

Helena Inácio is a Professor at the University of Aveiro. Portugal.

Shashi Kant is an Associate Professor at Mittal School of Business, Lovely Professional University, India.

Hanh Le is a passionate researcher and accomplished Full Stack Software Developer with deep expertise in software development, data analytics, data science, and cloud computing. She holds a Ph.D. in Information Technology and a Master's in Computer Science, bringing both academic rigor and a solution-driven mindset to her work. With extensive experience in front-end and back-end development, she specializes in scalable, database-driven applications that support evidence-based decision-making. Dr. Le has led transformative tech initiatives across healthcare, law enforcement, and retail, translating complex needs into high-performing systems. She values interdisciplinary collaboration, believing that impactful innovation often arises at the intersection of fields. Her blend of technical skill, research excellence, and collaborative spirit continues to drive progress in academia and industry alike.

Rui Pedro Marques hols a Ph.D. in Computer Science, is a Professor at ISCA–University of Aveiro, where he supervises master's and Ph.D. theses. He is currently Deputy Director of ISCA and Director of the Course in Organizational Informatics and Communication. He is Researcher at GOVCOPP and Editor-in-Chief of the International Journal of Business Innovation. His research is on Business Information Systems, with recent projects on Artificial Intelligence, Blockchain, and Business Intelligence applications.

William Martinez-Sanabria has a Master's degree in Organizational Management (candidate). Specialist in Corporate Finance. Public Accountant, Economist, Business Administrator, International Negotiator and Technologist in Civil Works and Construction Management. Consultant in organizational, accounting, and financial matters. Graduate of the National Open and Distance University of Colombia (UNAD).

Rym Mefteh holds a Ph.D. from Paris-Dauphine university in 2011. She joined Higher Institute of Management of Sousse (IHEC) university of Sousse, where she is currently an associate professor of management. She runs the Master « Entrepreneurship and project Management ». Her research topics include human capital management and digital transformation. She also has a special interest for entrepreneurial issues. Her work has been published in national and international journals. Institutionally engaged, she is the head of the career and skills certification center of IHEC Sousse. She is also a referent in student entrepreneurs pole PEESO university of Sousse.

Timiehin Olubiyi is a prominent Nigerian academic, entrepreneur, public intellectual, business management expert, sustainability leader, and senior government adviser with an extensive international network and experience in academia, investment banking, and public sector investment management. He has published several international papers with an expert track record. He has a B.Sc., M.Phil., and Ph.D. in Business Administration from Babcock University, Nigeria, and he gives policy insights and advises the government and its representatives on policy and technical matters. He is the Dean of the Faculty of Management and Social Sciences at Nigeria's West Midlands Open University and a Senior Lecturer. He is also an adjunct lecturer at Babcock University and Caleb University, both in Nigeria. He has been invited as a session chair, resource person, and keynote speaker at various conferences across Nigeria and beyond. Additionally, he serves as editor-in-chief of a reputable journal and member of the editorial boards for numerous university-based and well-indexed high-impact journals globally. Due to his scholarly contributions, he has received numerous academic honours.

Secil Ozen completed her Master's degree in Industrial Engineering and is currently pursuing her Ph.D. at Çukurova University. Author contact details: Management Information Systems, School Of Applied Technology and Management of Erdemli, Mersin University, Turkey.

Neixon Rincón-Ronderos has M.Sc. in Accounting and Finance (candidate), Financial Engineer. Professor El Bosque University, and Piloto University of Colombia. Experienced in teaching and research in the fields of finance, economics, accounting, and actuarial science. Consultant in financial risk assessment and project management.

Himanshu Shukla holds a PhD, MBA, and MTech in Industrial Engineering, bringing a rich blend of academic rigor and practical insight to the domains of Human Factors, Operations, and Supply Chain Management. His interdisciplinary background enables him to approach complex industrial challenges with a systems-thinking perspective, integrating environmental, economic, and operational considerations. With significant experience in teaching, research, and industry collaboration, Dr. Shukla's work focuses on advancing sustainable practices in supply chains through the application of optimization, modeling, and digital technologies. His scholarly contributions and policy-relevant research aim to transform systems, supporting the global need for continual improvement.

Edward Yecid Torres Nova holds a Ph.D. in Management from the University of Celaya, Mexico. Master's degree in Quality and Integrated Management from Universidad Santo Tomás, Colombia. Business Administrator, and Architectural Administrator and Builder. Professor and researcher at the National Open and Distance University of Colombia (UNAD).

Oumeima Toumia holds a Ph.D. in Business Administration from the Higher Institute of Management of Sousse. She serves as an Assistant Professor at the Higher Institute of Technological Studies of Kef, Tunisia. She has published in high-ranking journals and presented at prestigious international conferences. She also contributes to the academic community as a reviewer for numerous scholarly publications. Her research interests encompass a broad range of topics, including digital transformation, artificial intelligence, firm performance, job performance, venture capital, and the impact of emerging technologies like generative pre-trained transformer-3 (GPT-3) in organizations, as evidenced by her co-authored book, "Perceptions of employees of technology emerging with generative pre-trained transformer-3 in organizations".

Gada Wakjira is a PhD Scholar at the College of Business and Economics, Department of Marketing Management, Bule Hora University, Ethiopia.

Farouk Zouari was born in Tunis, Tunisia, on August 27, 1980. He earned an Engineering degree in Electrical Engineering in 2004, followed by a Master's degree in Automatic Control and Signal Processing in 2005, and a PhD in Electrical Engineering in 2014, all from the National Engineering School of Tunis at the University of Tunis El Manar, Tunisia. He is currently a researcher at the University of Tunis El Manar, where he actively contributes to advancements in the field of control systems. Dr. Zouari's research interests encompass fractional-order systems, neural control theory, nonlinear control, and intelligent adaptive control. He has demonstrated expertise in designing robust control strategies, integrating neural networks and artificial intelligence techniques to enhance system performance. His work addresses critical challenges in dynamic systems, with a focus on innovative solutions for systems characterized by uncertainties, nonlinearities, and delays.

Index

A

Academic Integrity 317, 318, 321, 322, 325, 327, 328, 333, 335, 346
AI-Driven Innovation 106, 108, 131
AI Implementation 1, 11, 13, 14, 19, 20, 22, 24, 183, 310
Artificial Intelligence (AI) 1, 4, 13, 14, 26, 27, 28, 29, 30, 34, 35, 38, 39, 43, 44, 48, 57, 58, 60, 61, 62, 63, 64, 65, 66, 67, 69, 71, 74, 75, 76, 77, 79, 80, 81, 87, 89, 90, 91, 92, 93, 94, 95, 96, 99, 100, 109, 113, 114, 117, 120, 121, 122, 123, 124, 125, 126, 127, 128, 129, 130, 131, 133, 140, 144, 145, 147, 149, 150, 151, 152, 154, 155, 156, 157, 160, 162, 163, 164, 166, 167, 169, 172, 177, 182, 191, 193, 194, 195, 196, 198, 199, 210, 212, 214, 215, 216, 217, 218, 219, 220, 221, 222, 223, 224, 225, 228, 229, 230, 232, 233, 235, 236, 237, 240, 242, 244, 250, 251, 253, 254, 255, 256, 257, 258, 259, 260, 261, 262, 265, 266, 267, 268, 269, 271, 272, 273, 274, 275, 276, 277, 278, 281, 282, 283, 284, 285, 286, 287, 288, 289, 292, 293, 294, 296, 297, 298, 300, 301, 302, 303, 304, 305, 309, 312, 313, 314, 315, 317, 346
Automation 1, 2, 5, 6, 7, 9, 13, 14, 15, 16, 17, 18, 19, 21, 22, 23, 24, 28, 30, 37, 44, 76, 77, 78, 85, 87, 88, 101, 102, 126, 140, 141, 144, 149, 150, 151, 152, 153, 155, 159, 160, 170, 177, 182, 183, 184, 191, 196, 198, 250, 273, 274, 318, 320, 323, 324, 325, 327, 328, 330, 331, 332, 335, 338, 339, 340, 343, 346

B

Balanced Scorecard 69, 70, 73, 74, 75, 78, 79, 85, 86, 87, 88, 89, 92, 93, 94, 95, 96
Bias in AI 221, 346
Blockchain 5, 6, 22, 30, 101, 133, 134, 140, 141, 156, 157, 160, 165
bootstrapping 193, 209, 210, 225
business turnover 174, 178

C

Chatbot 15, 17, 31, 86, 229, 255, 318, 321, 336, 337, 338, 339, 340, 341, 342, 346
Competitive Positioning 100, 227, 231, 232, 237, 243, 244, 245, 246, 247, 248, 251, 252
Competitor Orientation 265, 273, 274, 275, 276, 285, 292
confirmatory factor analysis 193, 200, 203, 206, 218, 220, 225
Consumer Engagement 227, 228, 229, 231, 232, 233, 236, 237, 238, 239, 240, 242, 244, 245, 246, 247, 248, 249, 251, 252, 253, 254, 256, 261, 263
Co-ownership 69, 71, 74, 75, 85, 87, 89, 90, 91, 97
Customer Insight 265, 276, 284, 285, 292

D

Data-Driven Decision Making 96
Deskilling 209, 318, 319, 320, 321, 322, 323, 324, 327, 330, 331, 332, 334, 335, 337, 338, 340, 341, 343, 345, 346
Destination Marketing 227, 228, 229, 230, 232, 234, 235, 237, 238, 239, 240, 241, 242, 243, 244, 245, 247, 248, 249, 250, 251, 252, 260
Digital divide 293, 294, 299, 302, 303, 304, 305, 306, 308, 309, 310, 313, 315, 326
Digital Marketing Strategies 130, 237, 243
Disruptive technologies 187, 189, 293

E

Emerging Technology 141, 172, 174, 175, 178, 179, 180, 183
Ethical AI Use 334, 346
Ethics-by-Design 346
Explainability 5, 10, 33, 36, 40, 41, 61, 65, 121, 294
explanatory factor analysis 193, 203, 225
Exploratory study 164

G

gated communities 71, 73, 94, 95
Generative AI 35, 77, 78, 106, 124, 125, 126, 128, 156, 157, 234, 248, 251, 317, 318, 319, 320, 321, 323, 324, 325, 326, 327, 328, 331, 332, 334, 335, 336, 342, 343, 346
Governance 1, 2, 4, 5, 9, 28, 33, 36, 38, 39, 40, 61, 62, 63, 64, 66, 75, 78, 85, 88, 89, 90, 91, 93, 96, 105, 127, 130, 145, 155, 156, 212, 294, 296, 297, 310, 326

H

Higher education 8, 293, 294, 297, 298, 299, 303, 304, 305, 306, 307, 308, 309, 310, 311, 313, 314, 315
Horizontal Property 71, 72, 73, 75, 76, 80, 81, 82, 87, 88, 89, 93, 97

J

job performance 193, 194, 195, 196, 197, 198, 199, 200, 201, 202, 203, 204, 209, 210, 211, 212, 213, 214, 215, 216, 217, 220, 222, 223, 224, 225

M

Machine Learning 1, 4, 5, 6, 14, 15, 21, 22, 24, 26, 31, 34, 43, 47, 60, 61, 63, 94, 101, 121, 123, 125, 127, 130, 144, 149, 151, 153, 154, 160, 162, 164, 166, 167, 191, 234, 240, 244, 258

N

New Product Development 102, 107, 118, 122, 125, 126, 127, 130, 131

O

Operational Efficiency 8, 18, 38, 70, 76, 78, 90, 104, 120, 133, 138, 140, 143, 151, 152, 155, 156, 172, 182, 191, 228

P

Performance Indicators 7, 36, 37, 52, 53, 57, 71, 74, 75, 85, 86, 97, 140, 147, 157
Product Innovation 99, 100, 101, 102, 103, 104, 105, 107, 108, 109, 111, 112, 113, 114, 116, 117, 118, 119, 120, 121, 122, 124, 125, 126, 129, 130, 131, 156

Q

Qualitative research 11, 27, 335, 336, 337

R

Risk Management 5, 33, 36, 43, 44, 52, 54, 55, 62, 63, 65, 133, 141, 142, 144, 145, 152, 153, 154, 156, 157, 158, 163, 166
Risk Management Strategies 133, 142, 144, 152, 153, 154

S

Scalability 33, 36, 41, 42, 55, 64, 65, 66, 154, 156, 172
Smart Tourism 228, 229, 232, 233, 234, 236, 237, 241, 244, 253, 256, 263
SMEs 22, 64, 67, 90, 108, 122, 147, 170, 171, 172, 173, 175, 176, 177, 178, 179, 180, 181, 182, 183, 186, 187, 188, 190, 191, 196, 225, 265, 266, 267, 268, 269, 270, 271, 272, 274, 275, 277, 278, 280, 285, 286, 287, 288, 289, 290, 291
Societal inequalities 293
Socioeconomic conditions 293

structural equation modeling 193, 214, 217, 218, 219, 224, 226, 258

T

Technological advancements 88, 156, 170, 235, 242, 295, 316, 337
Tourism Personalization 237

www.ingramcontent.com/pod-product-compliance
Lightning Source LLC
LaVergne TN
LVHW062325300926
849161LV00007B/1572
* 9 7 9 8 2 6 0 0 0 4 3 9 5 *